AAA
BRITAIN
TravelBook™

Published by AAA Publishing, 1000 AAA
Drive, Heathrow, Florida 32746

Text © AAA Publishing 1997
All rights reserved
Reprinted with amendments 1999
Maps © The Automobile Association 1997

Cover Design: Mike McCrary
AAA Cover Photo Research: Diane Norden,
   Patricia Nasser

The *AAA Britain TravelBook* was created
and produced for AAA Publishing by AA
Publishing, Basingstoke, England.

Front cover
Main photo: Queen's Guard, Buckingham
Palace, London, England
VCG/FPG
Insert: Young girl, Wales
© Travelpix/FPG
Spine
Beefeater, London, England
© Bachmann

ISBN 1-56251-326-5

Cataloging-in-Publication Data is on file with
the Library of Congress.

Color separation by Daylight Colour Art
PTE Ltd., Singapore

Typesetting by Anton Graphics Ltd.,
Andover, England

Printed and bound at G. Canale &
C., Turin, Italy

CONTENTS

SYMBOLS AND ABBREVIATIONS
How to use the star rating
★★★ **do not miss**
★★ **highly recommended**
★ **worth seeing**
Map references
20B4 – the first number refers to the page and the following letter and number to the grid square on the map
Abbreviations
The following abbreviations have been used:
EH – English Heritage; NT – National Trust; NTS – National Trust Scotland. See page 283 for further details about these organizations.

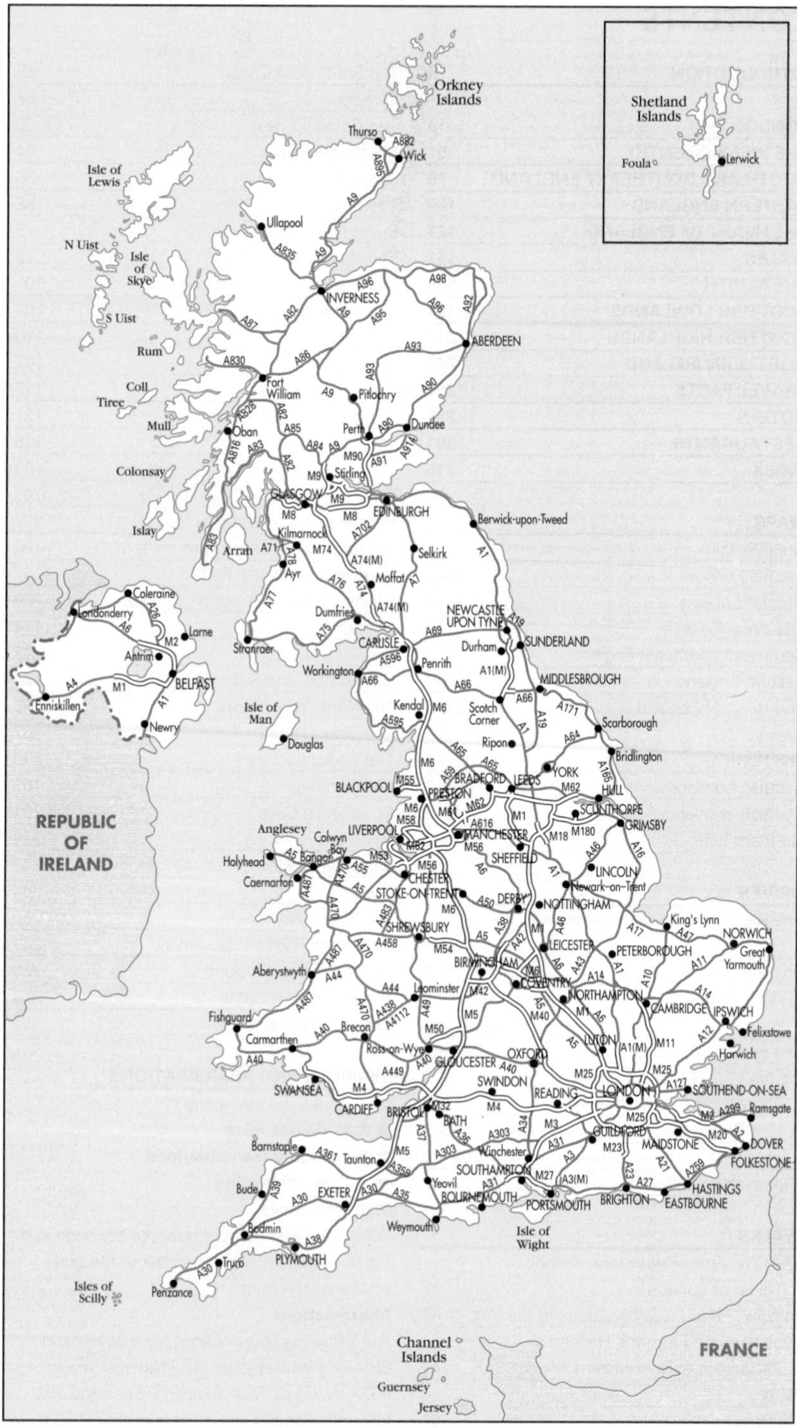
Orkney Islands
Shetland Islands
Foula
Lerwick
Thurso
A882
Wick
A895
A9
Isle of Lewis
Ullapool
A835
N Uist
Isle of Skye
S Uist
INVERNESS
A96
A98
A92
A82
A87
A95
ABERDEEN
A93
Rum
A830
Fort William
A86
Pitlochry
A90
Coll
Tiree
A828
Mull
Oban
A85
Perth
Dundee
A816
A83
A84
M90
A91
A914
Colonsay
Stirling
M9
GLASGOW
M8
EDINBURGH
Berwick-upon-Tweed
Islay
Arran
A702
A71
Kilmarnock
M74
A78
Ayr
A74(M)
Selkirk
A1
Coleraine
Moffat
A7
A26
Londonderry
A6
A76
A77
Dumfries
A74(M)
NEWCASTLE UPON TYNE
A19
Larne
M2
Antrim
Stranraer
A75
CARLISLE
A69
SUNDERLAND
A596
Penrith
Durham
A1(M)
A4
M1
BELFAST
Workington
A66
MIDDLESBROUGH
Enniskillen
A7
Isle of Man
Kendal
M6
Scotch Corner
A171
Newry
A595
Scarborough
Douglas
Ripon
A64
Bridlington
A65
A59
YORK
A165
M55
BRADFORD
LEEDS
BLACKPOOL
PRESTON
M62
HULL
REPUBLIC OF IRELAND
M61
M1
SCUNTHORPE
M58
A616
M180
GRIMSBY
Anglesey
LIVERPOOL
MANCHESTER
M18
Colwyn Bay
M56
SHEFFIELD
A46
A16
Holyhead
A5
Bangor
A55
M53
LINCOLN
Caernarfon
A487
A470
CHESTER
Newark-on-Trent
STOKE-ON-TRENT
A50
DERBY
NOTTINGHAM
A483
SHREWSBURY
King's Lynn
A47
NORWICH
A17
A458
M54
LEICESTER
Great Yarmouth
Aberystwyth
A44
BIRMINGHAM
PETERBOROUGH
A11
A43
A14
A10
COVENTRY
Leominster
M42
NORTHAMPTON
A438
A4112
A49
M5
M40
CAMBRIDGE
IPSWICH
Fishguard
A40
Brecon
M50
Felixstowe
Carmarthen
Ross-on-Wye
LUTON
A1(M)
M11
A12
Harwich
GLOUCESTER
OXFORD
A449
M25
SWINDON
A127
SWANSEA
M4
READING
LONDON
SOUTHEND-ON-SEA
CARDIFF
BRISTOL
M32
BATH
M25
A299
Ramsgate
A37
A36
A303
A34
M3
GUILDFORD
MAIDSTONE
M20
Barnstaple
A361
Taunton
A358
Winchester
A31
M23
DOVER
FOLKESTONE
SOUTHAMPTON
M27
A3(M)
A21
A259
A23
A27
HASTINGS
Bude
A39
EXETER
A30
A35
Yeovil
BOURNEMOUTH
PORTSMOUTH
BRIGHTON
EASTBOURNE
Weymouth
Isle of Wight
Bodmin
A38
PLYMOUTH
Truro
Isles of Scilly
Penzance
Channel Islands
Guernsey
Jersey
FRANCE

England, its monarchy, regal ceremonies and triumphant history, remains Shakespeare's "precious stone set in the silver sea." So much is familiar about England – Morris dancers, thatched cottages, cricket – that Wales, with its lush valleys, sheep-laden hills and medieval castles almost pales from view. Scotland also, bristles yonder, a semi-wilderness of tartan, drams of whiskey, misty glens and the legendary Loch Ness monster.

Wherever you go there beckons royal palaces and pageantry, scores of fine country houses filled with precious antiques, and historic cities focused around soaring Gothic cathedrals. You can make pilgrimages to dozens of evocative literary and artistic shrines; nowhere, for example, is Shakespeare performed better than in his birthplace of Stratford-upon-Avon. Popular culture, meanwhile, is summoned up in the form of Liverpool's Beatles, shopping by London's fashion stores and Harrods, dining out for tea at the Ritz. Such are the halcyon images of Britain promoted around the world.

Happily, for many tourists there is a core of reality in all these visions. Yet England is also a land of scenic mountains, as well as great urban sprawls and congested roads; Scotland has two of the country's most absorbing cities; Wales offers superb

introductions to a lost industrial heritage; Northern Ireland's soft landscapes confound the violence seen on TV news reports. Fringe theater, backstreet markets and French bistros may fill your cultural, shopping and culinary diet. While cherishing its uniquely rich and long history, Britain is not a backward-looking, old-fashioned nation. On

the contrary, it's making a determined effort to come to terms with the post-industrial age, with being a lesser player on the world's stage after having been a leader for so long, with being part of a rapidly unifying Europe, and with having an ever-diversifying multicultural society.

Morris dancers (above) in Oxford and beautiful Derwent Water (opposite) in the Lake District are two of England's charms

CULTURE

In many respects, Britain doesn't have a single national culture. This isn't surprising when you consider that Britain (or more correctly, Great Britain) came into being through the union between England and what were, at the time, the totally separate countries of Wales (in 1536) and Scotland (in 1707). Added to these is Northern Ireland: Great Britain and Northern Ireland make up the United Kingdom.

Each to their own

Each nationality has its stereotypes, but none of these are really of any value, except perhaps that of the Englishman. English people do, as a rule, seem zealously polite, saying "please" and "thank you" and queuing (lining up) at every opportunity: "an Englishman, even if he is alone, forms an orderly queue of one," a saying goes. They are emotionally restrained ("the English have an extraordinary ability for flying into a great calm," according to another quip), and do often live up to their reputation for being excessively reserved (best observed on a silent commuter train!). Perhaps the one common trait of British, as opposed to English, people is a sense of irony and self-deprecation: foreigners can find it hard to understand how the British can be so rude about their own country, taking it to the limit on TV comedies.

Nationalist sentiment runs strong for the Scots, Welsh and Northern Irish: woe betide the person who calls any one of them English! By contrast, the English, unsubjugated since the Norman conquest in 1066, show a pervasive indifference to their English nationhood: some might call it a quiet self-assurance, others arrogance. Whatever the case, anyone running up the Union Jack (the national flag) in their front garden might be suspected of being a member of the fascist British National Party.

A culturally divided Britain is reinforced by the fact that the various parts of the union have their own national sports teams (rugby and soccer matches between the countries are fought with bitter rivalry), as well as their own newspapers. Scotland has its own education and legal system, while Wales (and to a lesser extent Scotland) even has its own language.

Insanity at the Scottish Highland Games!

CULTURE 7

Scotland celebrates its Highland Games, Hogmanay on New Year's Eve, and the poet Robert Burns' birthday with haggis (a Scottish dish made from sheep's offal) and whiskey suppers. Wales has the music, poetry and drama competitions of its Eisteddfodau. Northern Ireland's Orangemen march to the sound of the drum to commemorate William of Orange's victory at the Battle of the Boyne.

Festivals

Yet the countries of the union do share some festivals, like Guy Fawkes' Night on November 5 when fireworks are set off all round the country (see p.23), and odd traditions like April Fool's Day on April 1 when people perform all sorts of pranks on each other: even the BBC once broadcast a seemingly serious documentary about spaghetti growing on trees. England, typically, doesn't have any national festivals of its own. It makes up for this in some wonderfully quirky local events, such as Cornwall's Furry Dance in Helston and 'Obby 'Oss in Padstow (see p.72), cheese rolling in Brockworth, Gloucester, and Shrovetide Football in places like Ashbourne, Derbyshire.

Class systems

England's cultural diversity is often simplified into the notion of a land of two cultures, separated by a north/south divide. Simplistically, the south is construed as being soft and middle class, the north hardier and working class.

All over the country, you come across marked regional accents, from "Scouse" in Liverpool to "Geordie" in Newcastle and "Cockney" in London; the latter is known for its rhyming slang, for example, "trouble and strife" for wife. "It is impossible for an Englishman to open his mouth without making some other Englishman despise him," wrote George Bernard Shaw. Shaw's play, *Pygmalion*, demonstrated the hindrance a regional accent could be if you wished to get on in the world.

Even today, despite there being far more social mobility than a mere 20 years ago, the English class system still infects the whole country. Most would agree, however, that matters have improved enormously since 1941, when George Orwell said, "England is the most class-ridden country under the sun; it is a land of snobbery and privilege, ruled largely by the old and silly."

English people's antennae are so sensitive about class distinctions that they can pigeonhole people according to what clothes they wear, where they go on vacation, what TV programs they watch or what newspapers they read.

Certain aspects of everyday British life do bind everyone together, crossing class and geographical boundaries. First there is the TV. With only five terrestrial channels everyone watches the same programs, although satellite and cable TV are available and

becoming increasingly popular. Newsreaders and sports broadcasters are household names, while home-grown soaps like *EastEnders*, set in the East End of London, and *Brookside*, set in Liverpool, can give fairly realistic portrayals of life in Britain.

Sporting distinctions

Match of the Day is a TV institution: even if they've never actually been to a game, many males (and increasingly more females) throughout Britain support a football (soccer) team, football being the national winter sport. Towns in the north also focus on the professional game of rugby league and, elsewhere in the country, on rugby union, at its best in the annual rousing games of the Five Nations Championship between England, Wales, Scotland, the Republic of Ireland and France.

In summer, the focus turns to Wimbledon for the tennis championships and cricket, particularly for "test" matches against Australia or the West Indies.

Most people place a small bet on the Grand National in April, the world's most famous and grueling steeplechase, which has been run at Aintree, near Liverpool, since 1839. Lots of people also bet on the score of football matches by entering the Pools for million-pound prizes, or risk a pound or two each week on the National Lottery, begun at the end of 1994. The odds against winning are high, but the jackpot can be as much as £18 million.

Eating and drinking

Perhaps the homogenous side of Britain's culture best manifests itself in the pub – called "the local" if it's a regular haunt – and all that goes with it: pints of bitter (beer), darts, and the publican's shouts of "last orders" and "time please" (signaling last orders for drinks). Socializing at home often takes place over a cup of tea, or "a cuppa," which isn't just drunk at 4 p.m., but in vast quantities throughout the day! In tourist areas you're rarely far from a tea shop, where you can enjoy home-baked scones and jam. The traditional British fried breakfast is a feature primarily found in bed-and-breakfasts and hotels, while fish and chips wrapped in paper no longer has the monopoly on takeout meals, thanks to fast-food burger, pizza and Chinese establishments. The national dish of England is certainly roast beef and Yorkshire pudding, served for Sunday lunch. Every region of Britain has local specialties, such as haggis in Scotland, made from minced sheep's heart, liver and lungs boiled together in a bag made from the sheep's stomach.

Many nations together

Now integrated with varying degrees of success into this social fabric are another 2½ million people bringing different cultures, cuisines and customs. In the 1950s, huge numbers came to Britain, particularly from the Indian subcontinent and the Caribbean, settling in the big cities such as London, Birmingham and Leeds.

MONARCHY

Britain is a constitutional monarchy, which means that the head of state is the Queen. In theory, the Queen can call and disband Parliament whenever she wishes, but in practice she doesn't. Her parliamentary role is now virtually entirely ritualistic, giving royal assent to laws passed by Parliament, and opening and closing its sessions.

The royal family

Of course, the royal family also plays a much broader role in British society; it's believed that they might be the single biggest allure for foreign visitors coming to Britain. Not only are there several superlative royal palaces to visit, but also lavishly colorful royal ceremonies to watch, such as Trooping the Colour (see p.22). However, polls show that the British public are becoming increasingly sceptical about the role of the royal family in late 20th-century Britain, though the majority of people are still in favor of its existence. Royalists argue that the monarchy provides a certain adhesive to the whole country's framework, and provides a sense of permanence, a link between past and present.

Generally, the Queen is held in high regard for her dedication to public service. She also improved her standing after a fire at Windsor Castle in 1992 when, to quell the outcry of the taxpayer at having potentially to foot the bill for the castle's restoration while the richest woman in the world paid nothing, she volunteered to pay income tax herself. Her family, now living under the permanent gaze of the story-hungry media, is more of a problem.

The traditional Trooping the Colour ceremony – a popular tourist attraction – takes place in June at Horse Guards' Parade, London

During the 1990s, scandals hit the headlines relentlessly. Most stem from the breakup of the marriages of Prince Charles and the late Princess Diana, and Prince Andrew and Sarah Ferguson. The death of Diana aroused yet more controversy, it has also heightened public awareness of the possible consequences of intrusive journalism. It is widely believed that although the Princess was perhaps a victim of her own success, the press cannot be entirely absolved from blame.

In the aftermath of Diana's death, the role of the monarchy is being seriously re-examined, with the royals making an effort to present a more human face to their subjects.

KINGS AND QUEENS OF ENGLAND
(AND LATER BRITAIN/THE UNITED KINGDOM)

HOUSE OF WESSEX
802–39 Egbert
839–55 Ethelwulf
855–60 Ethelbald
860–66 Ethelbert
866–71 Ethelred I
871–99 Alfred the Great
899–924 Edward the Elder
924–39 Athelstan
939–46 Edmund I
946–55 Eadred
955–59 Eadwig
959–75 Edgar
975–79 Edward the Martyr
979–1016 Ethelred II (The Unready)
1016 Edmund II (Ironside)

HOUSE OF SKJOLDUNG
1016–35 Canute
1035–40 Harold I
1040–42 Harthacnut

HOUSE OF WESSEX
1042–66 Edward the Confessor
1066 Harold II

HOUSE OF NORMANDY
1066–87 William I (The Conqueror)
1087–1100 William II (Rufus)
1100–1135 Henry I
1135–54 Stephen

HOUSE OF PLANTAGENET
1154–89 Henry II
1189–99 Richard I (The Lionheart)
1199–1216 John
1216–72 Henry III

1272–1307 Edward I
1307–27 Edward II
1327–77 Edward III
1377–99 Richard II

HOUSE OF LANCASTER
1399–1413 Henry IV
1413–22 Henry V
1422–61 Henry VI

HOUSE OF YORK
1461–83 Edward IV
1483 Edward V
1483–85 Richard III

HOUSE OF TUDOR
1485–1509 Henry VII
1509–47 Henry VIII
1547–53 Edward VI
1553–58 Mary
1558–1603 Elizabeth I

HOUSE OF STUART
1603–25 James I
1625–49 Charles I
1649–60 Commonwealth and Protectorate
1660–85 Charles II
1685–88 James II
1689–94 William III & Mary
1694–1702 William III
1702–14 Anne

HOUSE OF HANOVER/WINDSOR
1714–27 George I
1727–60 George II
1760–1820 George III
1820–30 George IV
1830–37 William IV
1837–1901 Victoria
1901–10 Edward VII
1910–36 George V
1936 Edward VIII (abdicated)
1936–52 George VI
1952– Elizabeth II

A SHORT HISTORY OF BRITAIN

Prehistoric and
Roman times

Stonehenge, Avebury, Maiden Castle: evidence of man's ingenuity and building skills in the later prehistoric periods of the neolithic, Bronze Age and Iron Age widespread, making England a cohesive country for the first time, with a network of roads and prosperous towns like York (see p.188), Colchester (see p.111), Chester (see p.174) and St. Albans (see p.119).

By the end of the 8th century, Viking (Scandinavian) attacks began on places like Lindisfarne; the conquest of England's northern kingdoms followed, establishing Danelaw. Despite the resistance of the Anglo-Saxon king of Wessex, Alfred the Great,

Lindisfarne Castle, on Holy Island, off the Northumberland coast, was built as part of the coastal defenses in 1550

are plentiful in Britain. Julius Caesar invaded what was an outpost of the Roman Empire in 55 and 54 BC, but it was after Emperor Claudius's invasion in AD 43 that the Romans began to settle. The natives were quickly subdued, and Boadicea, Queen of the Iceni, was one of the few to put up any sort of sustained resistance. The Romans' civilizing effects were

The Dark Ages
(410–1066)

Roman rule effectively ended around AD 410 as its forces withdrew to the continent of Europe, and England was unable to withstand attacks by barbarians. The power vacuum was filled by the Angles and Saxons from Germany, as well as the Jutes from Denmark. Prominent figures in this turbulent time include the semi-mythical King Arthur and the flesh-and-blood Saint Augustine, who converted the Anglo-Saxons to Christianity.

by 1016 the Viking Canute became the unchallenged king of England.

In 1066 the throne was taken by the Saxon Harold, only to be lost to William of Normandy at the Battle of Hastings.

Medieval Britain
(1066–1485)

The Normans have bequeathed a host of splendid castles and cathedrals as lasting symbols of their authority over Saxon England. French became the language of the ruling class, Anglo-Saxon that of the ruled class.

The Normans' swift conquest established a feudal system in England, cemented by the *Domesday Book* in 1086, a remarkably thorough census of the population. For much of the Middle Ages kings, bishops and barons jockeyed for position to establish how much power they could feasibly hold. In the contest between church and state, King Henry II made a mess of things with Thomas à Becket, Archbishop of Canterbury, who was murdered in 1170.

In 1215, in the contest between the king and his leading subjects, King John lost out as the English barons compelled him to sign the Magna Carta (the Great Charter) which limited his authority in relation to theirs. This document is seen as a significant step forward towards representative government, and further democracy was gained by the establishment of the model parliament in 1295.

Despite this, much of the history books on the Middle Ages are taken up with fighting: Edward I in his conquest of Wales and Scotland; of the Hundred Years War (1338–1453) between England and France, made famous in Shakespeare's *Henry V*; and the Wars of the Roses (1455–85), in which both the House of Lancaster (the red rose) and the House of York (the white rose) claimed the throne. The matter was only settled by the marriage of Lancastrian Henry VII to Elizabeth of York to begin the Tudor dynasty.

The Tudors
(1485–1603)

This relatively peaceful century is called the Renaissance period for its flourishing culture. Long-serving King Henry VIII and his daughter Queen Elizabeth I make two of the most colorful monarchs. Henry VIII is famous for having had six wives (he beheaded two, divorced two, one died in childbirth and the sixth outlived him) in his pursuit of a male heir, which he gained in Edward VI, only for the boy king to die prematurely aged 16 in 1553. In order to legitimize divorce, Henry broke from the Church of Rome and launched the English Reformation. He established himself as the head of the Church of England and, in 1536 and 1539, carried out the Dissolution of the Monasteries in order to fill his treasury. The monasteries were extremely rich, owning between a quarter and a fifth of all cultivated land in England, and the despoilation of their buildings and rich contents destroyed much of the best medieval architecture and art in the country.

After a brief reversion to Catholicism, Elizabeth I re-established Protestantism and locked up her Catholic rival to the throne, Mary Queen of Scots, for 20 years before eventually executing her. Her reign is perhaps more memorably marked by the likes of Shakespeare, and explorers Raleigh and Drake, who sailed around the world and defeated the Spanish Armada in 1588.

The Stuarts
(1603–1714)

The Scottish dynasty of Stuarts oversaw and contributed to a very turbulent one hundred years. The first half of the century saw a struggle between the power of the monarch and Parliament. It culminated in the Civil War, fought between Charles I, who believed in the monarch's divine autocratic right, supported by his Royalists (or Cavaliers), and Puritan Oliver Cromwell and his Parliamentarians (or Roundheads). Charles lost and was executed; the monarchy was abolished and Cromwell ruled as Lord Protector (he, too, became frustrated by Parliament) until his death in 1658. The interregnum was unpopular, and the monarchy returned in the Restoration in 1660 under Charles II, with a flourishing period for the arts after the strictures of the Puritan years. Charles was succeeded by his brother, James II, who in turn was deposed for his Catholic leanings by his Protestant daughter Mary and her husband, William III.

The Georgians
(1714–1837)

As reflected in the wealth of lovely architecture, the Georgian era was one of elegance. The ineffectuality of the Georgian monarchs led to the rise in cabinet government under Britain's first prime minister, Sir Robert Walpole (1730–41). Overseas, Britain lost the

American colonies, but began to acquire an empire, gaining possession of Canada, India in the Seven Years' War (1756–63), and New Zealand and Australia through the adventures of Captain Cook. Closer to home, in the Napoleonic Wars, Admiral Nelson was victorious at the Battle of Trafalgar in 1805 and the Duke of Wellington defeated Napoleon at Waterloo in 1815. During the last 10 years of George III's reign, his son, George IV, ruled as Regent in what is called the Regency period.

The Industrial Revolution and the Victorian era (1837–1900)

Between 1750 and 1850, Britain became "the workshop of the world," its economy rapidly changing from agricultural to industrial. The Lancashire cotton mills came first, then, with the invention of the steam engine in 1769, factories moved near to coalfields in the Midlands, the North of England and South Wales. A network of canals and railroads were built to transport goods, with the first railroad line in the world between Stockton and Darlington.

This was also the Dickensian age of appalling working conditions, slums and conurbations, where factories belched out smoke and fumes. Yet it was during the Victorian era that Britain became the world's unchallenged superpower, for which Queen Victoria, the longest-serving British monarch, became the very symbol. The success of the

British Empire was founded on the country's commercial and industrial strength.

20th-century Britain

Like virtually every country in the world, Britain has undergone massive upheavals during this century, but the underlying theme to its tribulations has been the diminution of its greatness from its Victorian prime.

The Edwardian era up to World War I was, for the elite at least, like a leisurely swan song. In the Great War, Britain lost 750,000 men. The years between the two world wars were marked by a general strike in 1926, the suffragette movement that gained women the vote in 1928, the Depression in the early 1930s with millions unemployed, and the abdication of Edward VIII following his decision to marry the divorced Wallis Simpson in 1936.

Britain seemed to thrive under adversity during World War II, epitomized by the rousing speeches of the prime minister, Winston Churchill, and the camaraderie during the Blitz, when Britain's cities were battered daily with bombs. After the war, Britain's empire disintegrated. A welfare state was established, and emerging from the war, the British people were told by their prime minister, Harold MacMillan, "You've never had it so good!"

Following the permissive and hedonistic 1960s, recession hit in the 1970s. In 1973, Britain joined the European Economic Community (now known as the

European Union). Throughout the postwar years, there had been what was termed "consensus government." However, the election of the Conservative Party under Britain's first woman prime minister, Margaret Thatcher, in 1979, put an end to that. A weak political opposition, victory in the Falklands War in 1982, and also against the miners in 1984, perpetuated Mrs. Thatcher's power until 1990, when she was ousted by her own party. Despite the effects of recession, the Tories won a fourth successive term in 1992 under a more conciliatory leader, John Major, but in 1997 Britain voted for a Labour term of office.

SCOTLAND

Scotland was never subdued by the Romans, but Scottish tribes were kept at bay by Hadrian's Wall and, for some time, the more northerly Antonine Wall from the Firth of Forth to the Firth of Clyde. The Picts, Scots, Angles and Britons united, helped by Christianity under Saint Columba.

During the Middle Ages, the expansionist aspirations of the English Plantagenet kings and intermarriage between royal households threatened Scottish independence. Edward I declared himself king of Scotland in 1296, but Robert the Bruce won Scotland some 400 further years of independence at the Battle of Bannockburn in 1314. In 1603, in the Union of the Crowns, James VI of Scotland, son of Mary, Queen of Scots, succeeded to the throne of England as James I, but

Violent clashes between civil rights marchers and Unionist extremists in 1968 set the stage for more militant postures from both the Irish Republican Army (IRA) and the Ulster Defence Association (UDA). Terrorism increased and fierce rioting took place, which led to the British army being despatched to Northern Ireland as a peacekeeping force. The tension and violence increased, and after the events of what became known as "Bloody Sunday," Britain suspended Northern Ireland's parliament and imposed direct rule.

The IRA announced a ceasefire on August 31, 1994, and the British military presence in Northern Ireland was substantially reduced. But, however, after 2 years of talks instances of violence still resumed.

The IRA and its political wing, Sinn Fein, both agreed to another ceasefire in July 1997, which led to the resumption of peace talks. An overwhelming majority of voters in both Northern Ireland and the Rupublic of Ireland supported the April 1998 peace agreement in a referendum vote. The accord faced its next test – a June 1998 election for the new 108-seat Northern Ireland Assembly, whose members will assume responsibility for many affairs now handled by the British government.

Scotland retained its own parliament. This finally disappeared in 1707 when it was amalgamated into the English parliament. Scotland's legal and educational systems remained distinct.

The cause of the Stuart dynasty was kept alive by the Jacobite rebellions in 1715, and under Bonnie Prince Charlie, the Young Pretender, in 1745, whose army was crushed at the Battle of Culloden in 1746.

WALES

Wales had evolved separately from England until the Acts of Union with England (1536–43), which imposed English law and administration. King Offa of Mercia built a great dike in the 8th century defining the English/ Welsh border, but the following Norman invasion of England led to the gradual erosion of independent territory and ultimately to its annexation. After persistent Norman incursions Welsh independence was briefly strengthened by leaders such as Llywelyn the Great. But, the last of the dynasty, Llywelyn the Last, died in his campaign against Edward I in 1282.

NORTHERN IRELAND

The colonization of Ireland by Protestant English and Scottish settlers begun in the late 16th century and was most successful in Ulster. The Protestant ascendancy was furthered by the defeat of James II, a Catholic, by William III, a Protestant, at the Battle of the Boyne in 1690, and the implementation of anti-Catholic laws known as the Penal Code.

The Republic of Ireland gained independence from Britain in 1921, while six of the nine counties of Ulster with a Protestant/Unionist majority decided to become part of the United Kingdom. From 1922 to 1972, Northern Ireland was governed by a parliament which met at Stormont Castle.

BRITISH ARCHITECTURE

With the following brief guide through the major styles and leading architects of the last 1,000 years, will hope to give an informative overview of British architecture.

Norman (1066–1190)

There are few remaining examples of Anglo-Saxon architecture, as much was destroyed by the Vikings, and the Normans rebuilt virtually every church and abbey. Norman architecture, also called Romanesque, manifests itself in a host of extant cathedrals and churches with massive walls, round arches and sparse, often geometrical, decoration (carving initially had to be done with axes rather than chisels). As for fortifications, the Normans had built as many as 500 strongholds by 1100; many were of "motte and bailey" design (an earthern mound – the motte – topped by a wooden tower surrounded by an open space – the bailey) and erected in wood, but soon stone was the favored construction material. Best examples are – **Anglo-Saxon churches**: St. Laurence in Bradford-on-Avon, St. Andrew in Greensted-juxta-Ongar in Essex; **Norman cathedrals**: Durham, Ely, Norwich and Southwell; **Norman castles**: Tower of London (White Tower), Chepstow and Rochester.

Gothic (1190–1540)

Gothic architecture is most closely associated with ecclesiastical buildings. The hallmarks of its design are the pointed arch, and a generally lighter, airier feel than in the Norman period. In Gothic churches, stained glass was used on a large scale for the first time, and sculpture became stylized, both serving as the religious textbooks of the illiterate.

The Gothic era breaks down into three periods. The **Early English** period (1190–1300) is marked by the use of ribbed vaulting and lancet windows. More elaboration came in the **Decorated** period (1300–70), for example, in rich tracery in the windows. The **Perpendicular** period (1370–1540), named for its use of strong vertical lines, heralded a phase of superlatively complex roof patterns called fan vaulting. Soaring Perpendicular architecture can be found not only in famous cathedrals, but also in innumerable churches throughout East Anglia and the Cotswolds.

Meanwhile, castles were also being built all over England, Scotland and Wales to more complex patterns, based on a system of multi-layered defenses. Best examples are – **Early English cathedrals**: Wells, Salisbury and Lincoln; **Decorated cathedrals**: Exeter and Ely (octagon); **Perpendicular churches**: King's College Chapel in Cambridge, Winchester Cathedral, Westminster Abbey (chapel of Henry VII) and Windsor Castle (St. George's Chapel); **Castles**: *Wales* – Beaumaris, Caernarfon, Conwy and Harlech; *England* – Tower of London and Dover; *Scotland* – Edinburgh and Stirling.

Tudor (1485–1560), Elizabethan (1560–1600) and Jacobean (1600–25)

During these eras, architecture went through a gradual transition from the Gothic to the simplified classical forms of the Renaissance, which were infiltrating into the country from the Continent, and in particular from Italy. Many magnificent, often red-brick country houses were built.

The Englishman's home no longer needed to be his castle, so gabled windows, ornamental turrets and balustrades took the place of battlements and thick walls, while the interiors became more ornamental, transformed with rich wood and elegant plaster decoration.

While few complete examples of small-scale medieval domestic architecture have survived, there are plenty of stunning timber-framed buildings from these times, particularly in southeast England, East Anglia and the West Midlands. Best examples are – **Tudor country house**: Hampton Court Palace; **Elizabethan country houses**: Longleat in Wiltshire, Montacute House in Somerset and Hardwick Hall in Derbyshire; **Jacobean country houses**: Hatfield House in Hertfordshire and Audley End in Essex; **Domestic architecture**: Chester, Little Moreton Hall in Cheshire and Lavenham in Suffolk.

Classical (1616–1835)

In the early 17th century, **Inigo Jones (1573–1652)** was the first architect to entirely abandon the Gothic for the classical style, and for the next two centuries, columns, temples, pediments and porticoes were all the rage. Jones, influenced by the famous Italian architect Andrea Palladio, managed in the space of a remarkably few buildings to bring the **Palladian** style of architecture to Britain.

However, the universal acceptance of classical buildings came with the freer forms created by the prodigiously productive **Sir Christopher Wren (1632–1723)**, whose style varied from classical simplicity to the extravagantly ornate **baroque**. Shortly after this period, **Nicholas Hawksmoor (1661–1736)** and **Sir John Vanbrugh (1664–1726)** had even greater fun with the baroque idiom. The straight lines and

pleasing proportions of Palladianism returned to favor in the 1720s, revived by Lord Burlington and **William Kent (1685–1748)**. Great classical houses were complemented and even surpassed by their own landscaped grounds and parkland, more often than not created by **Lancelot "Capability" Brown (1716–83)**, who acquired his nickname from often saying "I see great capability for improvement here."

Robert Adam (1728–92), who enriched numerous **Georgian** interiors, modified Palladianism into a more gentle, less austere "**neoclassical**" style, which lasted through to the 1820s. Modest as well as grand red-brick Georgian houses, with their symmetrical sash windows, can be found all over the country, but the most pleasing Georgian townscapes are the planned streets, squares and crescents in Bath and Edinburgh. Best examples are – **Inigo Jones** (early Palladian):

The stunning gardens at Hampton Court are in a mixture of styles

Queen's House in Greenwich, Banqueting Hall in London and Wilton House in Wiltshire; **Sir Christopher Wren**: St. Paul's Cathedral (see p.28), many London churches, Royal Naval College in Greenwich and the library of Trinity College in Cambridge; **Nicholas Hawksmoor** and **Sir John Vanbrugh** (baroque): Castle Howard in North Yorkshire and Blenheim Palace in Oxfordshire; **William Kent** (Palladian): Houghton Hall in Norfolk and Holkham Hall in Norfolk; **Robert Adam** (neoclassical): Harewood House in North Yorkshire, Syon House in London and Kenwood in London; **Georgian townscapes**: Bath and Edinburgh; "**Capability**" **Brown's gardens**: Blenheim Palace in Oxfordshire, Stowe in Buckinghamshire and Bowood in Wiltshire.

19th century

Throughout the 19th century there was a constant battle between classical and Gothic styles. On the one hand, in the 1820s and 30s, **Regency** architecture, exemplified by the townscapes of Nash (1752–1835), followed the classical Georgian tradition, but on the other they allowed for more ornamentation. Also at this time

Sculptural fantasy on the theme of the ocean can be seen at Hay's Galleria on the South Bank

serious, charmless public buildings such as town halls, banks and museums were erected in **Greek Revival** style. Yet in 1818, Parliament voted to spend £1 million on building 214 new Anglican churches, 170 of which were designed in the **Gothic Revival** style, and later had the Houses of Parliament revamped in excessive Gothic style by Sir Charles Barry (1795–1860). This love for fake medievalism is also in the grand baronial houses with turrets, pointed windows and stained glass. The ostentation of the buildings says much about the confidence of the Victorian age.

Best examples are –
Regency townscapes: Brighton, Cheltenham and Regent's Park in London; **Gothic Revival:** Houses of Parliament in London; Albert Memorial in London, Truro Cathedral and Keble College in Oxford.

20th century

There aren't that many 20th-century buildings in Britain that make you want to stop and stare. The Lloyd's building in London, designed by Richard Rogers and built in 1986, is an example of more successful modern British architecture. The South Bank Centre is an example of 1950s architecture which most people would rather forget! The ugly Hayward Gallery and the National Theatre are subject to endless complaints – a recent proposal for recladding may improve their appearance. The Canary Wharf Tower in Docklands (800 feet) is the latest edifice to dominate the skyline, dwarfing the NatWest Tower in the City, previously the tallest building in London. A solid mass, it has been criticized for its uninspiring design. The new complex at London Bridge City and Hay's Galleria is attempting to redress the balance.

Despite the mistakes of the century, the countryside is nevertheless dotted with fine Edwardian country houses that often echo the symmetrical, red-brick, Queen Anne-style mansions of the beginning of the 18th century. Also, **Sir Edwin Lutyens** (1869–1944) produced some memorable country houses in a mix of Arts and Crafts and classical styles. Best examples are – Castle Drogo in Devon and Lindisfarne Castle in Northumberland.

GOVERNMENT

Parliament

Britain has no written constitution. The principles by which the country is ruled have gradually evolved over the centuries from the feudal era, when the Magna Carta defined the barons' obligations and the limits of King John's power, to the parliamentary democracy of today.

Parliament sits at the Houses of Parliament, also known as the Palace of Westminster. There are two houses. Virtually all power lies in the law-making **House of Commons**. It is made up of 651 elected Members of Parliament (M.P.'s), who each rep-resent a geographical constituency. The upper house, the **House of Lords**, scrutinizes bills (proposed legislation) passed by the House of Commons. It is made up of 800 hereditary peers (nobility), 200 life peers (given titles as reward for public service) and 26 bishops. (Many people see it as an outdated institution in need of reform.)

The M.P.'s are either back-benchers (those not holding a senior office who occupy the rear row seats in the House of Commons) or more important ministers for the party in power, or shadow ministers for the main party in opposition. The prime minister appoints ministers who form the Cabinet, the policy-making body of the government. The leader of the opposition also appoints ministers in the same way for his Shadow Cabinet.

Political parties

There are three main parties on the present British political scene. The right-wing **Conservative Party** (also called the Tories) represents the establishment, and is comparable to the Republican Party in the United States. In simple terms, it favors private ownership of services such as transportation and utilities, low government expenditure, and low taxation. The Conservative party was in power from 1979, first under Margaret Thatcher, and later by John Major, who took over from Mrs. Thatcher in 1990. During his time in office Mr. Major was beset by problems within his own party of M.P.'s, who were challenging the Conservative acceptance for strengthening ties with the European Union, and of senior figures being involved in a variety of scandals.

The left-wing **Labour Party** represents democratic socialism, similar in some respects to the Democrats in the United States and is currently seeing its first term of office, headed by Tony Blair, for many years.

The Houses of Parliament were originally built as the Palace of Westminster in 1049 for Edward the Confessor

Since the party's inception at the turn of this century, it has been closely allied to the trade unions. In recent years, and particularly since the election of their new leader, Tony Blair, in 1994, it has attempted to become a more left-of-center party to appeal to more middle-class voters.

The third party, the **Liberal Democrats**, emerged out of the Liberal Party in the 1980s. Generally they have far fewer M.P.'s than either the Labour or Conservative parties. In addition, there are a handful of **Welsh** and **Scottish Nationalist** M.P.'s, and 17 **Northern Ireland** M.P.'s: politicians from the main parties cannot contest seats in Northern Ireland.

Elections

The government in power must call an election before the end of a five-year period. Therefore the present ruling Labour government will have to call a general election in 2002, but may do so at any time prior to this. In 1928, universal suffrage was reached for those over 21, and since 1969, all those over 18 years can vote. Each constituency elects one M.P. in a simple majority system. The advantage of this method is that it tends to produce governments which hold an outright majority. Its drawback can best be appreciated by looking at a few results from the 1992 election. The Conservatives gained power with 336 seats out of the 651 available in the House of Commons, but with only 41.9 percent of the vote. By

contrast, the Liberal Democrats polled nearly 18 percent of the vote, but got only 20 seats.

Britain also has European elections in which it votes for 81 M.E.P.'s – Members of the European Parliament. Of all the member states in the European Union, Britain, performing true to form as an island nation (although

strictly speaking no longer one due to the Channel Tunnel), is probably the most concerned about the seemingly ineluctable developments for increasing political and monetary union; the other states have even pledged to try to achieve nothing less than a common European currency by the end of the century.

ECONOMY

According to the American author John Updike, Britain is "a soggy little island huffing and puffing to keep up with Western Europe." In its Victorian heyday, Britain was the world's leading industrial nation and governed a quarter of the world's surface. By 1950, it was only the world's sixth richest country; 30 years on, it had dropped to 22nd. To take another comparison, before World War I the coal mining industry employed around a million people; by 1991 only 57,000 miners were at work.

Why such a decline? With the loss of its colonies, Britain also lost sources of cheap raw materials and assured worldwide markets (most of its trade is now with the European Union). Also, poor vocational training, poor productivity and low investment made competition from countries like Japan, the U.S. and Germany more difficult to bear. A bonus revenue fell into Britain's lap from the discovery of North Sea oil

and natural gas in the late 1960s, and at the beginning of the 1990s, Britain was the ninth largest oil producer in the world, and the seventh largest producer of natural gas. Production of oil has now peaked, but there is the possibility of further massive rewards in new fields west of Shetland.

Like many countries, Britain has turned to the service industries, which now employ over two-thirds of the workforce. The financial district in London is still one of the leading banking centers of the world, responsible for around 25 percent of bank lending worldwide.

On all statistical measures of personal wealth, British households have never had it so good: 70 percent own their own homes, and nearly as many own a car. Yet, at the same time, many people are still poor, especially in those parts of northern England, Wales, Scotland and Northern Ireland that have lost their supporting industries. Since 1980, between 1½ and 3½ million people have been unemployed.

LONDON

"When a man is tired of London, he is tired of life," said Samuel Johnson. Two centuries later, the city's outstanding museums, palaces, churches, and first-rate music and theater offer endless entertainment

LONDON

London, the largest city in Europe, covers some 610 square miles, with over 40 main streets and a population of nearly 7 million. Take a bus tour or river cruise to familiarize yourself with the city's geography, and pick up a good street map.

But in any case, don't be daunted: London's center is fairly compact and covers the financial district (called **the City**), the

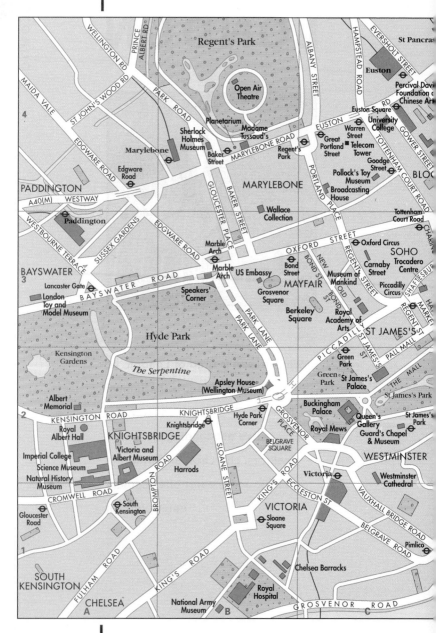

entertainment and shopping area (called the **West End**), and **Westminster**, seat of Parliament and home of royalty.

The *very* center, from which distances are measured, is Trafalgar Square.

London's wealthiest neighborhoods, such as **Knightsbridge**, **Kensington** and **Chelsea**, lie to the west and, beyond, on the capital's fringes, are attractive communities along the River Thames, like **Richmond**. Beyond

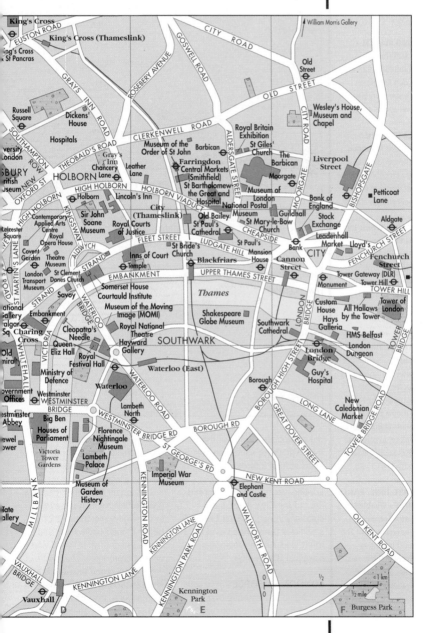

CALENDAR OF EVENTS

EARLY JANUARY –
**International Boat
Show**, Earl's Court
Exhibition Centre.
The largest boat
show in Europe.

MID MARCH –
**Ideal Home
Exhibition**, Earl's
Court Exhibition
Centre. Very popular
and always crowded.

LATE APRIL –
London Marathon.
The world's largest
road race with a great
atmosphere for run-
ners and spectators.

**THIRD WEEK IN
MAY** – Chelsea
Flower Show,
Chelsea Royal
Hospital. Superb
flower and garden
displays.

JUNE – Beating the
Retreat, Horse
Guard's Parade. Col-
orful military display
for the "retreat" or
setting of the sun.
Trooping the Colour.
Starts at Buckingham
Palace, to celebrate
the Queen's official
birthday.

**LATE JUNE/ EARLY
JULY –** Wimbledon
**Lawn Tennis
Championships.** The
most important
event in the tennis
diary. Tickets are
available by lining
up on the day or by
public ballot ∎

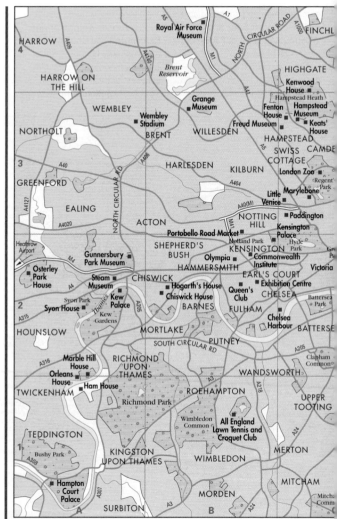

the immediate vicinity of the
river, sprawling south London
holds little of interest for the
visitor, and likewise north
London, apart from **Hampstead**.
East of the City, there is the
culturally intriguing **East End**, the
ambitious **Docklands** development, and, further downriver,
historical **Greenwich**.

LONDON'S PEOPLE
London is so immense that
residents tend to identify with

their neighborhood, or perhaps
the north, south, east and west of
the city, rather than the metro-
polis as a whole.

Londoners have been part of a
great ethnic melting pot ever
since large-scale immigration
began in the Middle Ages and
continued until after World War II,
when Commonwealth citizens
were encouraged to settle here.
The capital is by far the most
multicultural, tolerant and liberal
part of Britain. Close-knit Irish,

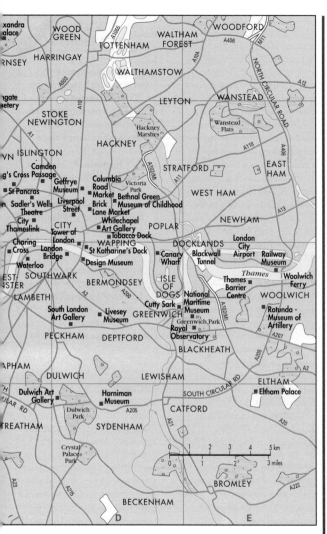

CALENDAR OF EVENTS

THREE WEEKS IN JULY –
Royal Tournament, Earl's Court Exhibition Centre. Military spectacle with pageantry and daring feats.

AUGUST BANK HOLIDAY WEEKEND (*last weekend in August*) – **The Notting Hill Carnival** celebrates West Indian culture and claims to be Europe's largest outdoor festival.

SEPTEMBER 29 –
Election of Lord Mayor of London. A colorful procession marks this occasion.

OCTOBER – Annual Full Tidal Closure. Watch the immense Thames Barrier lift out of the water (see p.49).

NOVEMBER 5 –
Guy Fawkes' Day. Bonfires all over London to commemorate the Gunpowder Plot of 1605. Excellent public displays. **Christmas Lights.** Oxford Street and Regent Street festively illuminated.

DECEMBER –
New Year's Eve, Trafalgar Square. Thousands gather to bring in the New Year ∎

Caribbean, Chinese and Indian communities, to name but a few, live side by side with cockneys (East Enders), Sloanes (the upper-class west London set) and Porsche-driving yuppies.

LONDON'S HISTORY

The Romans founded the settlement of *Londinium* in AD 43 where the present City of London now stands and, as the focus of the Roman road network, it soon became the capital of *Britannia*. In the 11th century, when Edward the Confessor built Westminster Abbey and William the Conqueror was crowned there, London was expanding and becoming the seat of power. By Henry VIII's reign in the early 16th century, the city's population was 50,000, a figure which quadrupled by Elizabethan times a century later. The Great Plague in 1664 killed 100,000 people, while the Great Fire in 1666 destroyed 13,000 houses and 87 churches. A building boom

TICKETS AND LISTINGS

To find out what's on where and when in London, refer to the local "bible," the weekly listings magazine *Time Out.* **The London weekday newspaper, the** *Evening Standard* **is also useful.**

For ticket agencies offering a credit-card booking service, try Ticketron (tel: 0171724 4444) and Ticketmaster (tel: 0171344 4444); both can provide seats for a vast range of sporting events and cultural shows. To avoid a booking fee, contact the venues direct.

The Society of West End Theatre (S.W.E.T.) ticket booth in Leicester Square sells half-price tickets for that day's performance for any theater with spare seats ■

followed, under Sir Christopher Wren, and in the early 19th century, under John Nash, who laid out much of the West End.

With the arrival of the train and, in 1906, the Underground (subway), Londoners became commuters. The city's worst hours came during the Blitz in 1940–1, when German bombing raids reduced much of the city to rubble, damaging or destroying 3½ million buildings and killing nearly 30,000 citizens. Postwar development was often ugly, though postmodernist architecture in the Docklands and along the Thames' embankments is trying hard to improve matters.

EATING AND DRINKING

Britain's reputation as a culinary desert is outdated, nowhere more so than in London. Not only are there a handful of world-class temples to French *haute cuisine*, such as Le Gavroche and La Tante Claire, but also a wide choice of ethnic restaurants. Soho has perhaps the greatest concentration of restaurants, including many Chinese restaurants in Chinatown, Mayfair and St. James's are known for their club-like dining rooms; Bayswater, Chelsea, Islington, Kensington and Notting Hill have restaurants to suit all tastes and pocketbooks.

For a special **breakfast** or **afternoon tea**, head for one of the grand hotels such as the Savoy (see p.32) or the Ritz (see walk on p.44). For **lunch**, the ubiquitous sandwich bars are the most popular choice. Some of the cafeterias in the big museums and galleries, notably at the Tate Gallery and the Victoria and Albert Museum, are excellent. Most **pubs** serve inexpensive food. (pubs with character in each area of London are recommended on pp.27, 31, 41, 44 and 50).

★★★
HIGHLIGHTS

British Museum (► 26)
Buckingham Palace (► 46)
Covent Garden (► 43)
East End markets (► 31)
Greenwich (► 49)
Hampton Court Palace (► 50)
Harrods (► 34)
Houses of Parliament (► 46)
National Gallery (► 46)
Natural History Museum (► 35)
St. Paul's Cathedral (► 28)
Science Museum (► 37)
Tate Gallery (► 48)
Tower of London (► 29)
Victoria and Albert Museum (► 37)
Westminster Abbey (► 48)

SHOPPING

You can shop 'til you drop in London. This guide covers the major shopping streets, famous stores and street markets.

In the West End, major department stores (like Selfridges, John Lewis and Dickins & Jones) lie along **Oxford Street** and **Regent Street**, where you'll also find Liberty and Hamleys. **Tottenham Court Road** specializes in electrical goods, Charing Cross Road in bookstores; **Piccadilly** has the gourmet food emporium, Fortnum & Mason, and expensive **Burlington Arcade; Bond Street** has art galleries and shops merchandizing *haute couture*.

South of Piccadilly in **St. James's**, the shops are ultra-conservative, but around **Covent Garden** you'll find many affordable clothes and gift stores. The upmarket districts of west London have fashionable clothes stores in the chic **King's Road** in Chelsea, and the more exclusive **Kensington and Knightsbridge** (home to Harrods). Lots of bargains are to be had in the sales, beginning after Christmas, and in the summer.

ARTS AND NIGHTLIFE

London's 50 West End **theaters** perform everything from Andrew Lloyd Webber musicals to Shakespeare's *Hamlet*. The Barbican (see p.28) and the National Theatre on the South Bank (see p.42) have a more consistently highbrow repertoire. The most beautiful theatrical setting must be Regent's Park open-air theater (see p.38).

The South Bank has halls for **classical music** – the Royal Festival Hall, the Queen Elizabeth Hall and the Purcell Room. Fun annual classical music events include The Proms (especially the Last Night) in the Royal Albert Hall (see p.36) and lakeside concerts at Kenwood (see p.50).

For **opera**, visit the traditional Royal Opera House; the London Coliseum, where the English National Opera performs works in English; or, for iconoclastic interpretations, the Opera Factory on the South Bank. The Royal Ballet performs at the Royal Opera House, the English National Ballet at the London Coliseum and the South Bank, and the London Contemporary Dance School at The Place. Major visiting companies perform at Sadler's Wells Theatre.

Top **nightclubs** include the Hippodrome on Cranbourn Street WC2 (loud and high-tech) and Stringfellows, 16 Upper St. Martin's Lane, WC2 (glamorous and sophisticated). The city's most famous **jazz** venue is Ronnie Scott's at 47 Frith Street, W1. There are a huge number of **comedy** venues; the best known is the Comedy Store at 1 Oxendon Street, SW1.

PUBLIC TRANSPORTATION

London's public transportation system carries around 5 million passengers a day. It is less slick than in many other capitals, but very comprehensive. Using it is preferable to driving: traffic is heavy at any time, unoccupied parking meters are hard to find, and there's a risk of having your car clamped, which involves a heavy fine.

Tickets Travelcards can be used on the Underground, buses, Docklands Light Railway and British Rail central and suburban services, and offer savings. Day passes can only be used after 9.30 a.m. on weekdays (anytime at weekends), while weekly or monthly passes can be used anytime. Otherwise, buy single tickets for each journey from ticket booths or at machines in the Underground stations, or from the driver or conductor on the buses. You can buy travelcards from some newsagents, and all tube and train stations.

The Underground (subway), also called "the tube," is the quickest way to get around, but it can be claustrophobic during rush hours (weekdays 7.30–9.30 a.m. and 4.30–6.30 p.m.). Trains operate from around 5.30 a.m. to midnight (7 a.m.–11.30 p.m. on Sunday).

Bus A journey by a double-decker bus is often slow, but the views compensate. Buses operate at similar times to the tube; there are also night buses on main routes through Trafalgar Square.

Taxis Black cabs can be hailed in the street when the yellow (For Hire) light is showing. Minicabs, cheaper but less reliable, cannot tout for business on the street; refer to the *Yellow Pages* for phone numbers.

HARRODS SALES

More of a miniature kingdom than a department store, the crowds are larger than usual during the famous January sales at Harrods.

Huge reductions are on offer, and some people are so desperate to secure a bargain that they will actually camp outside the entrance over Christmas. Once inside the store, even the most level-headed people lose all sense of dignity as elbows and fists fly in the race to find their desired item! ∎

most important treasure is the Parthenon frieze, carved between 447 and 432 BC. The array of Assyrian art is as striking as the Greek sculpture, while ancient Egyptian art covers animal and human mummies and the famous Rosetta Stone – historians were able to decode the hieroglyphs by its parallel Greek translation.

The museum also houses most of the important archeological finds made in Britain, such as the Mildenhall treasure of Roman silver tableware and the Sutton Hoo treasure, recovered from a 7th-century buried Viking ship. At the display of historical and literary manuscripts, you can peruse drafts written by Jane Austen and William Wordsworth, the richly illustrated *Lindisfarne Gospels* (dated around AD 698) and two of the four surviving copies of the Magna Carta.

The famous domed Reading Room in the British Museum is currently being refurbished and should be open in the year 2000. The British Library, which until 1998 was housed in the Reading Room, has now moved to 96 Euston Road, next door to St. Pancras Station.

★ Dickens' House 21D4
(48 Doughty Street, WC1)
Tube: Russell Square
The house looks much as it did when the author Charles Dickens lived here from 1837 to 1839 and wrote *Oliver Twist, Nicholas Nickleby* and other works. It contains his desk and chair, and first editions of his works.

CHELSEA 20A1
The chic residential area of Chelsea has a broader acclaim, thanks to its main thoroughfare, the **King's Road**. The road's name – it was a private royal way leading from St. James's Palace to Hampton Court until 1829 –

Ex-army pensioners can apply to live at The Royal Hospital in Chelsea, SW3, where they are looked after. They take great pride in their uniforms (blue in winter, red in summer) and show visitors around the splendid Wren building

BLOOMSBURY 21D4
The massive, 1930s Senate House, focal point for the University of London (with over 64,000 students, the largest in Britain), dominates this area of leafy squares east of Tottenham Court Road. Bloomsbury has long had an academic flavor. In the early 1900s, members of an intellectual circle called the Bloomsbury Set, which included Virginia Woolf, E.M. Forster and D.H. Lawrence, resided here. Blue plaques on many buildings indicate who once lived inside (Virginia Woolf at 46 Gordon Square, WC1, for example).

★★★ British Museum 21D4
(Great Russell Street, WC1)
Tube: Tottenham Court Road
This is one of the largest and most varied museums in the world, outstanding for antiquities. The classical collection includes the Elgin Marbles, controversially taken by the 7th Earl of Elgin from Athens and sold to the British government in 1816; its

belies its more recent reputation, for the King's Road lay at the heart of the Swinging Sixties in London, and the punk movement in the 1970s and 1980s. The street retains its bohemian flavor, with fashion boutiques, shops selling antiques and antiquarian bookstores. You'll also see aged ex-soldiers, called Chelsea Pensioners, resplendent in their colorful frock-coats and triangular caps; they live in and guide visitors around Wren's impressive **Chelsea Royal Hospital**, on Royal Hospital Road, founded by Charles II in 1682.

THE CITY *21F3*

When Londoners ask "Do you work in the City?" they mean "Do you work in finance?". During weekdays, the narrow streets are the hive of activity you would expect from one of the world's leading financial centers; brokers and bankers crowd the wine bars and pubs on the back lanes at lunchtime. On the weekend, all is ghostly quiet, for only a few thousand people live in the area.

The **Square Mile**, as it is sometimes called, comprises a city within a city, its boundaries marked by plinths bearing the city griffin holding the flag of Saint George, patron saint of England. London began on this compact plot of land, and a well-preserved stretch of the Roman wall can be seen by the Museum of London (see p.28). The City's major draw is its ecclesiastical architecture, nestling between tower blocks of varying aesthetic appeal, much of which, under the supervision of

GOOD PUBS

Bloomsbury:
Museum Tavern, 49 Great Russell Street, WC1 (once frequented by Karl Marx)

Chelsea: *Front Page*, Old Church Street, SW3 (newspapers); *Grenadier*, 18 Wilton Row, SW1 (military ambience)

City: *Olde Cheshire Cheese*, 145 Fleet Street, EC4 (dating from 1667; sawdust floors); *Olde Mitre*, 1 Ely Place, EC1 (founded in 1546)

Covent Garden:
Lamb and Flag, 33 Rose Street, WC2 (18th-century inn) ■

WALK

THE CITY: FROM FLEET STREET TO THE TOWER OF LONDON

Start at *Fleet Street*, a synonym for the British press until the mid-1980s when many of the national newspapers moved their offices to the Docklands. Off its eastern end, *St. Bride*, "the journalists' church," dates from Roman times, but was rebuilt by Sir Christopher Wren after the Great Fire in 1666; its spire is shaped like the tiers of a wedding cake, and its crypt has an exhibition on printing.

Off Ludgate Hill, the Central Criminal Court is better known as the *Old Bailey*. The figure of Justice stands on top of the dome, holding a pair of scales. Visitors can watch the proceedings from the galleries in the 18 courtrooms.

Back on Ludgate Hill, Wren also rebuilt St. Martin Ludgate, notable for its woodwork. Past *St. Paul's Cathedral* (see p.28) into Cannon Street, take Bow Lane up to *St. Mary-Le-Bow*, built by Wren over a Norman crypt; by tradition, anyone born within the sound of its bells is a proper "cockney," or true East End Londoner.

King Street takes you on to the medieval *guildhall*, its stained glass covered in the names of hundreds of lord mayors, and its walls and roof embellished with the coats of arms and banners of the City Livery Companies.

Princes Street brings you to *Bank* (see Bank of England p.28), the commercial focus of the city. Go south along King William Street. On the left stands *St. Mary Woolnoth*, an astonishing

building built by Wren's protegée Nicholas Hawksmoor. On the right are two more Wren creations: *St. Mary Abchurch* (Abchurch Lane), with a remarkable reredos by Grinling Gibbons, and *St. Stephen Walbrook* (on Walbrook), considered by many to be Wren's finest (its dome is said to have been a prototype for St. Paul's).

Back on King William Street you soon come to *Monument*, erected in 1677 to commemorate the Great Fire 11 years earlier, and designed by (you guessed it!) Sir Christopher Wren. You can climb to a viewing platform near the top of its 202 feet – the distance from the base of the column to where the fire broke out in Pudding Lane. *The Tower of London* (see p.29) is just a couple of hundred yards to the east ■

Wren, grew out of the ashes of the Great Fire in 1666.

★ Bank of England 21F3
(Bartholomew Lane, EC2)
Tube: Bank
Great classical buildings face each other around a busy junction in an area called Bank, the financial hub of the City.

Mansion House, on the south side, is the official residence of the Lord Mayor of London; the Royal Exchange, to the east, was until recently home to the futures market; the fortress-like Bank of England, on the north side, is responsible for regulating the British banking system and issuing banknotes. Its operations are explained in an excellent museum, where you can also ogle at gold bars and the screens showing the state of play in the international money markets.

★ Barbican Centre 21F4
(Silk Street, EC2)
Tube: Barbican
Completed in 1981, the Barbican doubles as a residential complex and one of London's top arts venues for theater, concerts, film and art exhibitions. Even without tickets, it can be worth visiting for the free foyer concerts, exhibitions and cafés.

★ Leadenhall Market 21F3
(Whittington Avenue, off Gracechurch Street, EC3)
Tube: Bank
The graceful Victorian arcade stocks game, caviar and champagne, in beautiful displays to tempt hungry brokers.

★ Lloyd's Building 21F3
(Lime Street, EC3)
Tube: Bank
This glass-and-steel construction, designed in 1986 by Richard Rogers, is one of the most exciting pieces of modern

CHRISTOPHER WREN
(1632–1723)
England's greatest architect trained as a scientist, and at the age of only 29, he became Professor of Astronomy at Oxford.

Later, he served as a Member of Parliament, but he turned his hand to designing buildings in the wake of the Great Fire of 1666.

He submitted a new vision of London, with Parisian-style avenues and piazzas, and though this was never realized, he was nevertheless commissioned to build a new St. Paul's Cathedral, and also rebuilt 51 city churches (23 of which survived the Blitz).

His use of the classical style and daring designs, particularly in his church steeples, was groundbreaking in England ■

architecture in the City. It houses the world's largest insurance market, Lloyd's of London.

★★ Museum of London 21E4
(London Wall, EC2)
Tube: Barbican
As its name suggests, this is *the* place to come to learn all about London and Londoners through the ages. Clever reconstructions bring to life the Roman city, relics recall the Great Plague and the Great Fire is re-enacted. A 1940s air-raid shelter, along with stores and kitchen furnishings, represent the 20th century. You can also see the dazzling Lord Mayor's state coach, made in 1757 but still used for the Lord Mayor's Show.

St. Bartholomew-the-Great
(Smithfield, EC1) 21E4
Tube: Barbican
London's oldest church was founded in 1123 by King Henry I's jester for the Augustinian canons who maintained the adjacent St. Bartholomew's Hospital. It has fine Norman features and a lovely oriel window.

★★★ St. Paul's Cathedral 21E3
(Ludgate Hill, EC4)
Tube: St. Paul's
One of the best-known images of London, the dome of St. Paul's rising unscathed through the smoke of a World War II bombing raid, became a symbol of the unbroken spirit of the capital. The dome, the third largest in the world, makes this classical-style cathedral so remarkable. It was built by Wren to replace the Gothic cathedral that burnt down in the Great Fire of 1666. A memorial to the architect under the dome expresses his obvious confidence in his achievement: *Si monumentum requiris, circumspice* ("If you are seeking his monument, look around you").

You can ascend the dome to the Whispering Gallery to test the acoustics and view the interior in all its glory, then climb much higher to the Golden Gallery for a panorama of the city. Other highlights include the choir stalls and organ of master craftsman Grinling Gibbons, and the tombs in the crypt, a roll call of "the great and the good."

Smithfield Market *(EC1)*   21E4
Tube: Farringdon
Vegetarians should avoid this rough and ready meat market, where porters in bloodied tunics haul carcasses of beef and pork. The market operates on weekdays and is all over by 10:30 a.m. Local pubs open at dawn and serve hearty breakfasts to hungry workers.

★★ Tower Bridge *(SE1)*   21F3
Tube: Tower Hill
The Gothic towers and their connecting walkway, opened with much ado in 1894, are another well-known image of London. Electrical motors lift the two central spans to allow tall ships to pass through. You can climb the stairs or take an elevator up the towers, walk along the high-level walkway, learn about the bridge from state-of-the-art displays and see the original steam-driven hydraulics.

★★★ Tower of London   21F3
(Tower Hill, EC3)
Tube: Tower Hill
This is the country's most popular historical attraction, with over 2 million visitors annually, it is advised to arrive early in summer to avoid the lines. William the Conqueror's castle, begun in 1078, has served as a royal palace, mint, observatory and a prison. Anne Boleyn and Katherine Howard, two of Henry VIII's wives, lost their heads here. Sir Thomas More and Sir Walter Raleigh were incarcerated here before they went to the scaffold. Executions took place on Tower Green, where the famous ravens live; legend has it that if they fly away the Tower will collapse, so their wings are clipped. The Bloody Tower, over Traitor's Gate, through which prisoners arrived, is presumed to be where the "Little Princes," Edward and Richard, sons of Edward IV, were murdered in 1483.

The Crown Jewels are now displayed in a new Jewel House. The most famous jewel is the

Tower Bridge is one of the most famous of London's many landmarks, with its twin towers and spans that can be raised to allow ships to pass beneath. A comprehensive display describes the history and workings of the bridge

giant *Koh-i-Noor* diamond in the Queen Mother's crown. You can take a guided tour with a Yeoman Warder (or Beefeater) in Tudor uniform, or explore on your own. To watch the Chief Yeoman Warder lock up in the 700-year-old Ceremony of the Keys, you must apply in advance to the Resident Governor, Queen's Jewel House, H.M. Tower of London, EC3N 4AB.

Tower Hill Pageant is a recent attraction combining archeological finds with a multi-sensory ride.

Massive and controversial, Canary Wharf Tower dominates the newest developments in the Docklands area, and can be seen from miles around

LONDON DOCKLANDS VISITOR CENTRE

Situated at Limeharbour, on the Isle of Dogs, the London Docklands Visitor Centre offers an exhibition and video show tracing the area's fascinating history up to today and looking forward to the fulfilment of the regeneration program.

Guided tours of the Docklands can be arranged with prior notice

DOCKLANDS *23E2*

London's port was one of the busiest in the world before World War II, but it no longer exists.

In the 1980s the docklands, stretching from the east end of the city to Woolwich, became a huge development area, with waterside apartments, office blocks and leisure marinas. Now professionals live and work here beside working-class East Enders. In the 1990s, many developers went bankrupt and the Docklands have become a symbol of the recession's effect on the whole country.

You can see the development from a boat trip on the Thames or from the elevated **Docklands Light Railway**, which runs from Bank tube station or from Tower Gateway, opposite Tower Hill tube station, to Island Gardens; you can walk from here through a tunnel under the Thames to Greenwich (see p.49).

You could also take an interesting walk east from Tower Bridge, stopping at the Dickens Inn at St. Katharine Dock, or the Prospect of Whitby pub at Wapping (see p.31). Bus tours of the area leave from the visitor center in Limeharbour on the Isle of Dogs (Docklands Light Railway: Crossharbour), subject to seasonal variations.

★ Canary Wharf *23D2*
(Isle of Dogs, E14)
Docklands Light Railway: Canary Wharf

Docklands' white elephant is the 50-storey tower, One Canada Square, the tallest in Britain. The building dominates London's skyline, but unfortunately it stood largely vacant when it was built in 1992. Now, however, it does seem to be filling up with new businesses. The Canary Wharf area was badly damaged by an IRA bomb in 1996.

★ **St. Katharine Dock** *23D2*
(St. Katharine by the Tower, E1)
Tube: Tower Hill
The dock's 19th-century
warehouses have become luxury
apartments. Yachts and historic
vessels fill the main basins that
once would have seen cargo
ships of tea, spices and ivory.

★ **Tobacco Dock** *23D3*
(The Highway, E1)
Docklands Light Railway/Tube:
Shadwell
This huge shopping and
restaurant complex was
converted from 19th-century
warehouses, there are two
replica sailing ships on display.

THE EAST END

Dickens has bequeathed the
Victorian image of the poverty of
the East End through such novels
as *Oliver Twist*. This part of
London, stretching east from the
City, is still a rough, working-class
area. It has long been a melting
pot, with waves of immigrants,
from Huguenots in the 17th
century to recent groups of
Bangladeshis, Pakistanis and
Indians, settling among the cockneys. Curry houses, *halal* (Muslim) butchers and stores selling
bright fabrics line the streets.

Largely bereft of fine buildings
and museums, the East End is
not obvious sightseeing territory,
but a visit to one of its raucous
and colorful markets (Sunday
morning only, trading starts
extremely early) offers a
fascinating insight into an utterly
different side of London.

★★ **Bethnal Green Museum
of Childhood** *23D3*
(Cambridge Heath Road, E2)
Tube: Bethnal Green
You will find the largest collection
of toys in the world at this
outpost of the Victoria and Albert
Museum (see p.37): dolls'

houses, dolls, trains, teddy bears,
musical contraptions from every
continent and dating from the
17th century. The museum also
presents exhibitions related to
the social history of childhood.

Brick Lane Market *(E1) 23D3*
Tube: Shoreditch
In this vast, sprawling market you
will find every type of household
object under the sun. Some
goods are so threadbare it is hard
to imagine anyone would want to
buy them. Vendors sell hi-fi equipment and crates of crockery with
an amazing cockney sales patter.

★★★ **Columbia Road** *23D2*
Market *(E2)*
Tube: Shoreditch
Even if you don't want to
purchase any trees or house
plants, it is still charming to
wander along this colorful street
early on Sunday mornings – it is
impossible to come away without
a large bunch of flowers.

★★★ **Petticoat Lane** *21F4*
(Middlesex Street, E1)
Tube: Liverpool Street
In the 17th century, this was the
place where the local poor could
buy cast-off clothing from their
richer neighbors. Today it is the
biggest attraction of the East End
markets. It still sells clothes, but
mostly deals in household items,
including antiques.

★ **Whitechapel Art Gallery** *23D3*
*(80–82 Whitechapel High
Street E1)*
Tube: Aldgate East
This interesting 1901 art-nouveau
building puts on some of the best
modern art exhibitions throughout
the capital. With a name for
presenting provocative
exhibitions, it has gained an
international reputation. Check
with *Time Out* magazine to see
what is on.

**MORE
GOOD PUBS**
Docklands: *Prospect
of Whitby*, 57
Wapping Wall, E1
(haunt of Samuel
Pepys, Turner and
Whistler); *Dickens
Inn*, St. Katharine's
Way, E1 (converted
18th-century brew-
ery); *Mayflower Inn*,
117 Rotherhithe
Street, SE16 (Pilgrim
Fathers' departure
point; sells U.S.
postage stamps)
Holborn: *Cittie of
York*, 22 High
Holborn, WC1
(longest bar in
Britain with,
cozy cubicles ■

AN AMERICAN VIEW OF LONDON

"In London ... you have plays performed by good actors. That, however, is, I think, the only advantage London has over Philadelphia." Benjamin Franklin, 1786 ∎

LONDON ADDRESS CODES

The codes such as WC2 and SE16 denote a particular location in the city. All codes have one or two letters which refer to whether they are north, south, east, west, northwest, (no northeast codes), southwest or southeast in the city. The only exceptions are "WC" meaning West Central and "EC" meaning East Central. The numbers go from 1 to about 20 and refer to the distance from the center of London (measured from the City area), thus High Holborn, in central London, is WC1, and Wimbledon, which is far from the center, is SW20 ∎

HOLBORN and THE STRAND   *21D3/4*

Connecting the West End with the City, this area is the heart of legal London. It is home to the four medieval Inns of Court, each similar in style to Oxford or Cambridge university colleges with a dining hall, chapel and library, and lawyers' offices (called "chambers") grouped around courtyards and gardens. The inns have the exclusive right in England and Wales of making law students into barristers (advocates in the higher courts), and they can be seen traversing the grounds in their black gowns.

★★ Courtauld Institute Galleries   *21D3*
(The Strand, WC2)
Tube: Aldwych
Housed in grand Somerset House, this collection began with an educational purpose. In 1931, Samuel Courtauld donated to the institute some of the world's most famous French impressionist and postimpressionist paintings for art students to study. Artists represented include Manet, Degas, Renoir, Pissarro and Van Gogh, and specific masterpieces include Manet's *Bar at the Folies-Bergère* and a small version of *Déjeuner sur l'Herbe*, and Van Gogh's *Self-portrait with Bandaged Ear*. Further galleries hold many Renaissance works and paintings by Rubens.

★ Gray's Inn   *21D4*
(High Holborn, WC1)
Tube: Chancery Lane
This Inn of Court was badly damaged in the Blitz, but has been well restored.
   Shakespeare's *Comedy of Errors* was first performed in its hall in 1594. Its fine gardens were laid out by the great Renaissance man and scientist, Sir Francis

Bacon, in 1606. His statue stands in South Square.

★★ Lincoln's Inn   *21D4*
(Chancery Lane, WC2)
Tube: Chancery Lane
Lawyers were operating from this site as long ago as 1292. Fig trees and wisteria climb over the fine buildings in 17th-century New Square. John Donne, the poet, preached in the chapel, and Dickens set the case of Jarndyce v. Jarndyce in *Bleak House* in the Old Hall, which used to be the Court of Chancery.
   The adjacent and attractive Lincoln's Inn Fields is the largest square in central London and is a peaceful place to sit for a while away from the city streets.

The Savoy   *21D3*
(The Strand, WC2)
Tube: Charing Cross
Arguably London's best-known and grandest hotel, the Savoy was built late last century on the proceeds of D'Oyly Carte's productions of Gilbert and Sullivan operettas, performed at the Savoy Theatre next door.
   Drop in for afternoon tea, a cocktail in the American Bar, or a glass of champagne and oysters in the seafood bar, or perhaps rub shoulders with politicians in the paneled Savoy Grill in the evening (see p.290).

★★ Sir John Soane's Museum   *21D3*
(13 Lincoln's Inn Fields, WC2)
Tube: Chancery Lane
The architect Sir John Soane (1753–1837) designed the interior of this house around his collection of sculpture, drawings, paintings and *objets d'art*, using mirrors to dramatic effect. Sir John insisted the house remain as he left it, so it is crammed full of the treasures in chaotic fashion. Of special interest are

Hogarth's paintings *A Rake's Progress* and *An Election*, and an ancient Egyptian sarcophagus.

★★ Temple   *20D3*
(Fleet Street, EC4)
Tube: Temple
Across the street from the Royal Courts of Justice, where civil cases are tried, the alleys and courtyards of the Temple contain two of the Inns of Court, the **Inner Temple** and the **Middle Temple**. Temple Church was founded in 1185 by the Knights Templar. The original part of the church, called the Round, has a set of striking early medieval figures of armored knights, while the later chancel, the Oblong, is one of the finest examples of Early English architecture. Elizabethan Middle Temple Hall has a stunning hammerbeam roof; the serving table is said to have been made from the timbers of Sir

Francis Drake's ship, the *Golden Hind*. William Shakespeare acted in a performance of *Twelfth Night* here in 1601.

HYDE PARK and   *20A2/3*
KENSINGTON GARDENS
Christened "the lungs of London" in Victorian times, **Hyde Park**, the vast, recreational swath that divides the West End from Kensington, is the largest of London's central parks.

The park centers around The Serpentine, a lake where there are boats to rent, and the bandstand where music is played in the summer. To the south is Rotten Row, a corruption of *route du roi*, where Kings would ride along into the park to hunt deer; it is now used by the Household Cavalry to exercise their horses.

In the northeast section of the park, across the road from Marble Arch, soapbox demagogues and

GRUESOME DUELLING GROUND
Hyde Park became well known as a duelling ground, as so many were contested here.

In 1712 the Duke of Hamilton fought "one of the arrantest rakes in town," Lord Mohun, and so violent was their confrontation that they neglected the rules of the art and killed each other ■

hecklers slug it out in a war of words every Sunday at Speaker's Corner. The entertainment can be so compelling that George Orwell once called it "one of the minor wonders of the world."

Marble Arch was moved here from its original site in front of Buckingham Palace, as it was allegedly too narrow for the royal carriages to pass through. Even today, only members of the royal family are allowed to drive through the span.

The western side of the park becomes the more formal **Kensington Gardens**, where you can find the Serpentine Gallery, with changing exhibitions of modern art, and a statue of Peter Pan, smoothed over the years by loving strokes from small hands.

★★ Apsley House   20B2
(*Hyde Park Corner, W1*)
Tube: Hyde Park Corner
The site of Apsley House was no doubt somewhat quieter in the early 19th century when the Duke of Wellington, conqueror of Napoleon at the Battle of Waterloo in 1815, lived here. The grand rooms display his fine art collection and his many campaign relics.

★★ Kensington Palace   22B2
(*Kensington Gardens, W8*)
Tube: South Kensington
This surprisingly modest-looking palace was purchased in 1689 by William III, who hoped that the air around this country retreat would help his asthma. It served as the reigning monarch's home until 1760. Since then, it has been a residence for members of the extended royal family, most famously Princess Diana up until her death in 1997, and is presently home to Princess Margaret, Prince and Princess Michael of Kent and the Duke and Duchess of Gloucester.

You can visit some of the sumptuous, Italianate state apartments, with painted ceilings and works of art from the Royal Collection.

KNIGHTSBRIDGE   20A2
and KENSINGTON
These very exclusive areas mean primarily two things to visitors: the three gargantuan **museums** in South Kensington (the Science Museum, the Natural History Museum and the Victoria and Albert Museum), and **shopping**.

In Knightsbridge, you'll find designer boutiques on and around Knightsbridge and Brompton Road, and in a concentration of trendy stores on Beauchamp (pronounced "Beecham") Place. Sloane Street has items for expensive and more conventional tastes. Kensington High Street has mainstream stores, while Kensington Church Street is lined with antiques shops.

★ Commonwealth   22B2
Institute
(*Kensington High Street, W8*)
Tube: South Kensington
The institute arranges lectures and has displays on the Commonwealth countries and people, often taking the form of three-dimensional tableaux. These appeal to children, who can also take part in music, dance and drama workshops.

★★★ Harrods   20B2
(*87–135 Brompton Road, SW1*)
Tube: Knightsbridge
Britain's most famous store has over 300 departments and 4,000 staff. It is summed up by its motto: *omnia, omnibus, ubique* ("everything, for everyone, everywhere"). Don't miss the displays in the superb food halls, and the many bargains to be had at the popular sales held in January (see p.25).

(see p.25).

AN AMERICAN VIEW OF LONDON

"An American in London ... cannot but be impressed and charmed by the city. The monumentality of Washington, the thriving business of New York, the antique intimacy of Boston, plus a certain spacious and open feeling reminiscent of Denver and San Fransisco – all these he finds combined for his pleasure ..." John Updike, 1976 ■

★ London Toy and Model Museum
20A3

(21–23 Craven Hill, W2)
Tube: Lancaster Gate
Two Victorian buildings are filled with over 3,000 toys and models dating from the 18th century to the present: planes, trains, a miniature railway, boats, bears, and arcade machines in 20 themed galleries. Young children can ride the 1930s carousel and steam railway in the garden.

★★★ Natural History Museum
(Cromwell Road, SW7) *20A2*
Tube: South Kensington
This vast and elaborate Victorian building, with its terracotta facing showing relief mouldings of animals, birds and fishes, covers an area of four acres.

People associate the Natural History Museum with its giant dinosaur skeletons, and they are definitely the big attraction, but with more than 67 million items in the collection, it holds quite a few other highlights as well.

Make a beeline for the section of the 1,335-year-old sequoia tree, the Creepy Crawlies exhibition and the Hall of Human Biology exhibit that simulates the experience of a fetus in the womb and during birth.

When Harrods department store is lit up at night it looks like a fairytale castle, and for many the sumptuous displays inside are just as fantastic

*Portobello Road
Market grows
from a few
humble vegetable
stalls during the
week to a massive
display on
Saturdays, which
almost resembles
a carnival – not
only are there
antique bargains
to be found,
but there is
street enter-
tainment, and
food stalls abound*

★ Portobello Road Market
(W10–W11) *22B3*
Tube: Notting Hill Gate
At the heart of the trendy ethnic neighborhood of Notting Hill, north of Kensington, colorful Portobello Road Market serves as a magnet for thousands of tourists and locals alike. Saturday is the big day, when bric-a-brac and antiques are sold along with an array of odds and ends, from crafts to food and outright junk, with stalls stretching for over a mile. From Monday to Thursday fruit, vegetables and clothing can be purchased, with general goods sold on Friday.

Royal Albert Hall *20A2*
(Kensington Gore, SW7)
Tube: South Kensington
This vast, domed building, completed in 1871, is named for Prince Albert, Queen Victoria's beloved husband. To raise money for the project, 1,300 of its 8,000 seats were sold at £100 each, allowing the purchasers to attend shows for 999 years. Sporting events and rock concerts are held here, but the best-known events are the annual **Promenade** concerts (held from mid-July to mid-September), which culminate in a frenzy of patriotism on the last night of the series. It is

Elsewhere, you can marvel at early engines such as George Stephenson's *Rocket*, the oldest locomotive in the world; the Apollo 10 capsule in the Space Gallery and airplanes galore, including the first to fly across the Atlantic Ocean.

★★★ Victoria and Albert Museum *(Cromwell and Exhibition Road, SW7)*   20A2
Tube: South Kensington
In its 7 miles of galleries, the "V and A," as everyone calls it, houses an extraordinarily large and diverse collection of mostly decorative art. Glass, furniture, jewelry, textiles, carpets, metalwork, sculpture and paintings are just some of the media represented, from all cultures around the world and from every era of civilization. It is impossible to see it all in a single visit, so study the museum's plan and be selective.

Popular sections include the superb collections of Japanese, Indian and Chinese art, the medieval art exhibits, the dress collection, the Raphael cartoons and Constable landscapes, as well as the 20th-century galleries, with the latest thoughts on contemporary design. Its most talked-about piece is the *Three Graces* by the Italian neoclassical sculptor, Canova, for which over £7 million was paid in 1994 to outbid an offer by the Getty Museum in California.

MARYLEBONE and REGENT'S PARK   20B4
Marylebone comprises the grid of handsome, 18th- and 19th-century streets between Oxford Street and Regent's Park. Well-known addresses include Harley Street, where many private medical specialists practice, as well as Baker Street, where the fictional Sherlock Holmes lived.

STREET MARKETS
London's street markets, each very individual in character, are great fun to wander through while listening to the sales banter, even if you've no intention of haggling for anything.

The most atmospheric are the raucous East End markets of Petticoat Lane, Brick Lane and the flower market of Columbia Road (see p.31); trendy Portobello Road (see p.36); the weekend Camden Market, which specializes in secondhand clothes, crafts, antiques and jewelry; and the weekly antiques fair at New Caledonian Market (see p.41) ∎

possible to visit the hall on a guided tour, which is available from May to September.

★★★ Science Museum *(Exhibition Road, SW7)*   20A2
Tube: South Kensington
As entertaining as it is educational, the Science Museum is a favorite with children.

Interactive displays let you experiment in the Launch Pad Gallery and explain about modern food technology in the Food for Thought exhibition, but the most popular part of the museum is dedicated to computers and silicon-chip technology.

THE BBC

The BBC is an anomaly in the world of late 20th-century broadcasting, in that it is financed by a license fee. By law, every television-owning household in the country has to buy a television license.

No advertising revenue is used to fund the corporation, and no commercials appear on its television or radio channels.

Indeed, the BBC was set up in 1927 to stop radio broadcasting from becoming commercialized as it had done in the United States! ■

★ Broadcasting House 20C4
(Portland Place, W1)
Tube: Regent's Park
This 1930s building contains the original studios from which the British Broadcasting Corporation (the BBC) began transmitting radio programs in 1932. It imitates the shape of All Soul's Church alongside, the only church built by John Nash, which is used by the BBC for live lunchtime and evening concerts.

★★ London Zoo 22C3
(Regent's Park, NW1)
Tube: Regent's Park
In the collection and presentation of its wildlife, the long-established London Zoo is essentially a traditional, large urban zoo. However, since funding problems have beset it in recent years, it has fostered a more educational and conservational face to encourage more visitors.

The new **Children's Zoo**, at a cost of £1 million, is the first stage in the zoo's 10-year, £21 million redevelopment plan.

★★ Madame Tussaud's 20B4
(Marylebone Road, NW1)
Tube: Baker Street
The world's largest and most famous waxworks is incredibly popular, with 2½ million visitors annually and unfortunately, long lines in summer.

The collection, begun in 1802, is updated continuously to portray likenesses of pop stars, politicians and other famous people. The exhibits are enhanced by authentic clothes and personal effects, from the Beatles' suits to Margaret Thatcher's handbag.

Highlights also include the Chamber of Horrors and the new Spirit of London show, a hectic, 5-minute ride in a black cab through London's history.

★★ Planetarium 20B4
(Marylebone Road, NW1)
Tube: Baker Street
Next to Madame Tussaud's (combined admission ticket available) and every bit as popular, a beautiful vision of the sky at night is projected onto the underside of a vast dome. The accompanying exhibition imaginatively tells of the latest astronomic discoveries.

★★ Pollock's Toy Museum
(1 Scala Street, W1) 20C4
Tube: Goodge Street
In a Former bohemian district just west of Tottenham Court Road called Fitzrovia, this small museum is crammed full of Victorian toy theaters and other antique playthings. A delight for children, it is designed with them in mind, with eye-level displays and occasional Punch and Judy shows. Robert Louis Stevenson wrote about it: "if you love art, folly or the bright eyes of children, speed to Pollock's."

★★ Regent's Park *(NW1)* 20B4
Tube: Regent's Park
Architect John Nash laid out this massive park, beginning in 1812. Italianate villas and grand terraces were supposed to be built throughout the park, but the plan was never fully realized and the elegant, Regency-style residences are concentrated along its eastern side, providing some of the most prestigious addresses in London. Alongside the boating lake, the Inner Circle encloses rose gardens and the Open-Air Theatre, where Shakespearean plays are performed in summer.

The **Grand Union Canal** runs westward through London Zoo (see above) down to the fashionable residential area of **Little Venice**, where there are waterside pubs and houseboats.

★ Sherlock Holmes Museum

(239 Baker Street, NW1) 20B4
Tube: Baker Street
The supersleuth's home is re-created with his personal possessions and memorabilia. His fictional address was No. 221B, just down the road; a savings bank that occupies the site has to employ a full-time member of staff solely to deal with correspondence addressed to Holmes.

Telecom Tower 20C4

(Howland Street, W1)
Tube: Goodge Street
Many Londoners still refer to the pencil-like tower, finished in 1964, as the Post Office Tower, from when the post office used to own the telephone system. Some Londoners remember using the revolving restaurant near its 619-foot summit, before a bomb scare incident in 1975 denied public access.

★★ Wallace Collection 20B4

(Hertford House, Manchester Square, W1)
Tube: Marble Arch
Compared to the big London galleries, few people visit this outstanding collection of art, which is displayed on an intimate scale in an elegant mansion, once the home of the Marquis of Hertford. Eighteenth-century French furniture and art, bought on the cheap after the French Revolution when they were understandably unfashionable, make up the core of the collection, which includes Sèvres porcelain, Limoges enamels and works by Boucher, Fragonard and Watteau. There are also Renaissance pieces, fine 17th-century Dutch works such as Frans Hals' *The Laughing Cavalier*, a portrait by Rembrandt of his son Titus, Rubens' *Rainbow Landscape* and Poussin's *Dance to the Music of Time*.

Dame Edna Everage is just one of thousands of household names that are immortalized in wax at Madame Tussaud's on Marylebone Road. An essential aspect of this gallery of imitations is being able to touch and be photographed with heroes and villains of your choice

SOUTH BANK of the THAMES

The south bank of the river has a clutch of outstanding museums, but it is not one of central London's more attractive parts. It begins opposite the Houses of Parliament and runs east along the Thames to just beyond Tower Bridge.

★ HMS Belfast 21F3
(Morgan's Lane, off Tooley Street, SE1)
Tube: London Bridge
This vast World War II battleship is permanently moored on the Thames. One of the largest battleships ever built for the British Navy, it was saved from

The retired naval battleship HMS Belfast is now permanently moored on the south bank of the Thames, and is open to the public

The redeveloped waterfront area of so-called **London Bridge City** is sleek and fashionable, however, in such pockets as Hay's Galleria, an imaginative shopping complex in a Victorian warehouse conversion on Tooley Street, the area remains rather deserted. The other area of interest in this part of London is the South Bank Centre (see p.42), but the area adjacent to the center, south of Waterloo Bridge, is known as "Cardboard City" because of the large numbers of homeless who live under the railway arches in makeshift shelters.

the scrapyard in 1971. On November 21, 1939 she was almost destroyed by a magnetic mine and had to be rebuilt. She played an important role in the D-Day landings of June 1944.

★ Design Museum 23D2
(Butler's Wharf, SE1)
Tube: London Bridge
The museum, founded by Terence Conran, showcases commonplace 20th-century objects which epitomize the best in modern design. It forms the core of an imaginative warehouse conversion, with stylish restaurants and stores.

Florence Nightingale *21D2*
Museum *(2 Lambeth Palace Road, SE1)*
Tube: Westminster
The "Lady with the Lamp" founded the school of nursing at St. Thomas's Hospital in 1860. The museum shows her work in the Crimea and the slums of London.

★★ Imperial War Museum
(Lambeth Road, SE1) *21E2*
Tube: Lambeth North
The history of British involvement in 20th-century warfare is sensitively and thoroughly documented in a building that was formerly a lunatic asylum known as "Bedlam."

There is a huge range of military hardware, from tanks, submarines and planes to missiles such as the German V2 rocket. Reconstructions vividly bring to life the horror of the two world wars, of life in the trenches and in London's bombed-out streets during the Blitz, while a flight simulator recreates the experience of a bombing raid. Works of art by official war artists add another dimension to the museum.

★★ London Dungeon *21F2*
(28–34 Tooley Street, SE1)
Tube: London Bridge
Prepare to be thoroughly scared by the grisly tableaux of victims being hanged, flogged, boiled alive and disemboweled. Adults may squirm, but kids will love it.

★★ Museum of the *21D3*
Moving Image (MOMI)
(South Bank, SE1)
Tube: Waterloo
MOMI offers hours of infallible entertainment for movie and TV enthusiasts. Staff dressed as famous stars put on shows, and help you to read the news, be a chat show interviewee or audition for a Hollywood musical. The exhibits, using plenty of TV and movie footage where appropriate, deal with the history of the moving image from its 4,000-year-old origins to the latest satellite technology, explore the ethical issues of program making, and look at the works of famous moviemakers such as Alfred Hitchcock.

New Caledonian Market *21F2*
(at the junction of Long Lane, Bermondsey Street and Tower Bridge Road, SE1)
Tube: London Bridge
Also known as the Bermondsey Antiques Market, this claims to be the biggest of its kind in Europe, and only operates on Friday mornings.

Professional dealers trade in the dark, long before dawn; the general public arrive later, between 7 and 11a.m., in search of fine antique furniture, jewelry, porcelain, *objets d'art* and bric-a-brac.

**MORE
GOOD PUBS
Kensington:** *Anglesea Arms,* Selwood Terrace, SW7 (comfortable, traditional early Victorian pub)
Mayfair: *Bunch of Grapes,* Shepherd Market, W1 (traditional and salubrious)
St. James's: *Red Lion,* 2 Duke of York Street, SW1 (civilized Victorian pub; mahogany paneling)
South of the Thames: *George Inn,* 77 Borough High Street, SE1 (mentioned in Dickens' *Little Dorritt;* last galleried coaching inn in London); *Mayflower,* 117 Rotherhithe Street, SE16 (pretty riverside pub, on the site where the *Mayflower* departed for America) ∎

LONDON

SIGHTSEEING TOURS

Double-decker bus tours are an excellent way to get an overview of the city.

Try the Original London Transport Sightseeing Tours; they leave regularly from Victoria Station, Baker Street Station, Marble Arch and Piccadilly Circus.

In summer, take a river cruise from Westminster, Charing Cross and Tower of London piers.

Walking tours can be themed: for example, Jack the Ripper Haunts, and The Beatles' Magical Mystery Tour. Original London Walks (tel: 0171 624 3978) offer a wide variety ■

★ Shakespeare Globe Theatre and Museum *21E3*
(New Globe Walk, Bankside, SE1)
Tube: London Bridge
The original foundations of Shakespeare's Globe Theatre, where *Hamlet, King Lear* and *Macbeth* were first performed, were discovered in 1989. A replica, completed in 1996, has been created close by. You can tour the new Globe, which stages Shakespearean productions, and the neighboring exhibition center.

★★ South Bank Centre *21D2*
(SE1)
Tube: Waterloo
Sprawling along the south side of the Thames by Waterloo Bridge, this postwar, concrete complex wins few fans for its aesthetic appeal. Yet the country's most important arts center holds the three theaters of the Royal National Theatre, three concert halls (the Queen Elizabeth Hall, the Royal Festival Hall and the Purcell Room), the National Film Theatre, the Museum of the Moving Image (see p.41) and the Hayward Gallery, which puts on some of the capital's best art exhibitions. Free exhibitions and music events take place in the main foyers and on the terraces.

★ Southwark Cathedral *21F3*
(Borough High Street, SE1)
Tube: London Bridge
Inconspicuously set among railway viaducts and traffic, the small cathedral has 12th-century

A present-day Fair Lady sells flowers from a basket on the busy piazza in the middle of Covent Garden

origins but was heavily restored in the 19th century. One of its many monuments commemorates John Harvard, founder of Harvard University.

THE WEST END

Few Londoners agree on the precise boundaries of the West End; indeed, it is almost more of a concept than a geographical area. It is the capital's center for entertainment and shopping, where you'll find dozens of theaters and cinemas, and the widest range of shopping, from affordable boutiques around Covent Garden to exorbitant ones in Mayfair, and famous department stores along Oxford Street and Regent Street.

Charing Cross Road *20D3* *(WC2)*

Just about every other store on this street sells books: new, secondhand and antiquarian. Foyles, at No.113–19, claims to be the largest bookstore in the world but is notorious for its confusing layout, arranged alphabetically by publisher. Smaller stores specialize in detective novels, art and design books, or environmental books. Cecil Court, off Charing Cross Road, has a number of antiquarian bookstores. Stanfords, nearby at No.12–14 Long Acre (towards Covent Garden), is the best-stocked map and travel bookstore in the country.

★★★ Covent Garden *21D3*

Tube: Covent Garden
Historical Covent Garden is encapsulated in the scene from Shaw's play *Pygmalion* (or its spin-off musical and movie, *My Fair Lady*), where the cockney heroine Eliza Doolittle sells flowers to the wealthy emerging from the Royal Opera House in the portico of St. Paul's Church.

The old **vegetable and flower market** moved away in 1974, and since then Covent Garden has become something unique in London – a traffic-free **piazza** where you can dine or drink *al fresco*, watch slick street performers and browse in the specialist stores in the Victorian arcaded central market, the craft markets and the maze of little streets around.

St. Paul's Church, designed by architect Inigo Jones, sits at the western end of the piazza. It is known as "the actors' church" because of its close proximity to many of the capital's great theaters, and because Charlie Chaplin, Vivien Leigh and Noel Coward are buried or commemorated inside.

Leicester Square *(WC2)* *21D3*

Tube: Leicester Square
With the Swiss Centre on its northern side, and surrounded by cinemas, this is the entertainment center of the West End, constantly bustling with people deciding what to do for the evening, buying tickets or already on the way to their chosen destination. A statue of William Shakespeare looks somewhat lost in the middle.

At night the lights and throngs of people give Leicester Square a party-like atmosphere

WALK

MAYFAIR: FROM PICCADILLY CIRCUS TO THE RITZ

Start at *Piccadilly Circus* (see p.45). As you head down Piccadilly, you soon come to a craft market, on your left (Thursday and Friday), in the courtyard in front of Wren's *St. James's church* (his favorite creation). Its lavish interior has an organ case, font and altarpiece designed by the sculptor Grinling Gibbons.

Further along on the same side, *Fortnum & Mason* is London's top food store, famous above all else for its indulgent hampers; Mr. Fortnum and Mr. Mason, who founded the grocery shop in 1707, bow to each other on the hour on the face of the clock above the entrance to the store.

Across the street, the *Royal Academy of Arts,* in the courtyard of the Palladian Burlington House, holds art exhibitions featuring masterpieces of world renowned artists, as well as the Summer Exhibition (June to mid-August), in which some 1,000 works by living (and often amateur) artists can be seen and bought.

Turn right into *Burlington Arcade,* a Regency shopping mall with high-class galleries and boutiques. Beadles in top hats keep order, and notices forbid hurrying or whistling. Continue into *Cork Street,* whose commercial art galleries specialize in contemporary works.

Turn left into Clifford Street to reach *Bond Street,* the epitome of Mayfair with a plethora of dealers in fine art, jewelry and antiques, interspersed with fashion stores of names like Gucci and Gianni Versace. Of course, the prices are all sky high, but window shopping is free. *Sotheby's* auctioneers, at No. 34–5, has viewings and sales on most days.

Return along Old Bond Street back to Piccadilly and turn right: the Parisian-style *Ritz Hotel* is about 100 yards along on your left. If it's the right time of day and you're suitably attired (no jeans), why not treat yourself to full, traditional English tea? (Book in advance if possible, tel. 0171 493 8181) ∎

MORE
GOOD PUBS
Trafalgar Square:
Sherlock Holmes, 10 Northumberland Avenue, WC2 (Sir Arthur Conan Doyle drank here; Holmes' memorabilia and re-creation of his study)
Westminster:
Albert, Victoria Street, SW1 (frequented by civil servants and M.P.s) ∎

★★ London Transport Museum *(The Piazza, Covent Garden, WC2)* 21D3
Tube: Convent Garden
Kids enjoy the London Transport Museum, housed in the old flower market, where you can climb aboard buses and trams, pretend to drive Underground trains and work the signals on overground trains.

Mayfair *(W1)* 20B3
Enclosed by Oxford Street, Regent Street, Piccadilly and Park Lane, with its plush hotels, Mayfair is the suave and sophisticated corner of the West End. Exclusive art galleries and fashion stores are located on **Bond Street**. The architecture is at its most elegant around Berkeley and Grosvenor squares, the latter bordering the American Embassy. Nearby are the famous hotels of Claridge's and the Connaught.

The atmosphere is more villagey around **Shepherd Market**, where there are stores, restaurants and pubs. These narrow streets and alleys were built in 1735 by Edward Shepherd on the site of the May Fair.

Museum of Mankind 20C3
(6 Burlington Gardens, W1)
Tube: Green Park
The ethnography department of the British Museum has lively, changing exhibitions about various non-European cultures of the world. You might see, for example, a reconstructed Borneo longhouse.

Oxford Street *(W1)* 20C3
Tube: Oxford Circus
Oxford Street has discount stores, clothing chain stores and flagship department stores along its 1½ miles, offering the densest concentration of shopping in

LONDON

London. Its centerpoint is busy Oxford Circus.

As a general rule, blocks to the east towards Tottenham Court Road are lined with smaller souvenir and clothing stores, and blocks to the west towards Marble Arch contain the large department stores. Of these, Marks & Spencer has a reputation for relatively inexpensive but high-quality goods, while Selfridges is Harrods' (see pp.25 and 34) main competitor. John Lewis's slogan is "never knowingly undersold."

Piccadilly Circus *(W1)* 20C3
Tube: Piccadilly
Though Piccadilly Circus has come to represent the very essence of London to the rest of the world, it is, in reality, an extremely busy junction at the hub of the West End, characterized by neon advertising and a statue of Eros, God of Love, looking somewhat marooned to one side of the never-ending traffic.

Next to it is the underground shopping and entertainment complex of the **Trocadero**, with trendy stores and eating places.

Regent Street *(W1)* 20C3
Tube: Oxford Circus
Classy clothes stores and department stores can be found all along the sweeping curve of grand Regent Street. Hamleys claims to be the largest toy shop in the world and Liberty is famous for its luxurious printed fabrics.

Soho *(W1)* 20C3
Tube: Oxford Circus
Bounded by Oxford Street, Charing Cross Road, Leicester Square and Regent Street, Soho was formerly a red-light district of strip shows and sex shops. While the sleaze is still evident,

the area has been gentrified and made more fashionable with movie, TV and advertising offices on Wardour Street and Dean Street. Dean, Frith, Greek and Old Compton streets have one of the greatest concentrations of good **restaurants** in the whole of London, catering to every taste and pocket.

Directly south of the theater district along Shaftesbury Avenue, Gerrard Street lies at the heart of London's **Chinatown**, complete with requisite pagoda-shaped telephone boxes and a multitude of Chinese restaurants.

★★ Theatre Museum 21D3
(Russell Street WC2)
Tube: Covent Garden
This thoroughly engaging museum is crammed full of props, models and costumes from the 16th century onward, with everything from Noel Coward's monogramed dressing gown to Mick Jagger's jump suit. It even presents make-up demonstrations.

WESTMINSTER and ST. JAMES'S
Westminster signifies the center of British government with the Houses of Parliament, the prime minister's home at No.10 Downing Street, and the departments of state along Whitehall – in fact, the administrative arm of government is often simply called Whitehall.

St. James's stands for royal London, not only in Buckingham Palace, but also in further regal residences off the Mall, and in the upper-crust tone of the streets behind.

Eros, the Greek God of Love, with his bow and arrow, stands jauntily on one leg above the roar of Piccadilly Circus, now a synonym for anything overcrowded or chaotic!

The hours in Westminster are struck on a mighty bell known as Big Ben, which hangs inside the 316-foot clock-tower of the Houses of Parliament

Mews holds the lavish state carriages and horses (both open certain days all year). The **Changing of the Guard** takes place at 11:30 a.m. daily April to August, and every other day during the rest of the year.

★★★ Houses of Parliament

(Parliament Square, SW1) 21D2
Tube: Westminster
Despite a notorious attempt on November 5, 1605 by Guy Fawkes to blow up Parliament, the old Palace of Westminster survived until 1834, when it burned down. Today's late-Gothic pile, bristling with pinnacles and towers, is the work of Augustus Pugin and Charles Barry. The famous clock-tower holds Big Ben, possibly named for Sir Benjamin Hall, who was in charge of building when the bell was hung.

Members of Parliament sit in the often raucous **House of Commons**, while peers meet in the considerably more sedate **House of Lords**.

To see these debating chambers in action, you need to wait in line; you'll stand a better chance of getting in after 5:30 p.m. Monday to Thursday, and early on Friday morning (line up at the St. Stephen's entrance). For public information, tel: House of Commons; 0171 219 4272; House of Lords; 0171 219 3107.

★★★ Buckingham Palace

(The Mall, SW1) 20C2
Tube: Victoria
Dating from 1703 but remodeled and extended several times, this has been a royal residence since Queen Victoria acceded to the throne in 1837. To help finance repairs to Windsor Castle after the fire in 1992 (see p.104), the palace doors have been opened to the public for the first time, but only in August and September when the queen is absent (the Royal Standard is flown when she's at home). Expect very long lines. Just 18 of the hundreds of rooms are on show, including some state apartments: the Throne Room, the State Dining Room and the Picture Gallery, lined with works from the Queen's art collection.

More masterpieces from the collection are displayed in the **Queen's Gallery**, at the rear of the palace, while the **Royal**

★★★ National Gallery

(Trafalgar Square, WC2) 21D3
Tube: Charing Cross
The National Gallery has one of the world's finest collections of European art from the Renaissance to the early 20th century. There are lectures and guided tours, and a leaflet detailing the most popular masterpieces.

The controversial Sainsbury Wing (completed in 1991)

houses Renaissance works such as da Vinci's cartoon *Virgin and Child*, Piero della Francesca's *The Baptism of Christ* and works by Van Eyck, Botticelli, Uccello and Bellini.

Elsewhere, look for works by Michelangelo, Titian's *Bacchus and Ariadne*, *Self Portrait* by Rembrandt, works by Gainsborough, Turner and Constable (including *The Haywain*), and a splendid array of impressionist and postimpressionist art by Cézanne, Degas, Manet, Monet, Gauguin and Van Gogh.

★★ National Portrait Gallery
(St. Martin's Place, WC2) 21D3
Tube: Charing Cross
The National Portrait Gallery has 7,000 paintings, drawings, sculptures and photographs. The catalog of famous Britons runs from the Middle Ages to the present day, from likenesses of Chaucer and Richard II, Elizabeth I and Shakespeare, Byron and Wordsworth to Prince Charles and the late Princess Diana.

St. James's *(W1)* 20C2
Tube: Green Park
This area, between Piccadilly and St. James's Park, is something of a conservative male bastion. Even today, most of the private clubs along Pall Mall and St. James's Street only accept men as members. The stores, particularly along Jermyn Street and St. James's Street, cater to the needs and tastes of gentlemen, with displays of panama hats and pipes, and there are custom-made tailors and shoemakers. Some stores are allowed to show a royal coat of arms, indicating that they have been patronized by the Queen, the Queen Mother, the Prince of Wales, or the Duke of Edinburgh in the last three years.

St. James's Park *(W1)* 20C2
Tube: St. James's Park
The bridge across the middle of the lake has views of Buckingham Palace in one direction and Whitehall in the other. Wildfowl have made their home on and around the water. (For St. James's Palace and Clarence House, see walk below.)

WALK

WESTMINSTER: FROM THE HOUSES OF PARLIAMENT TO BUCKINGHAM PALACE

Start outside the *Houses of Parliament* (see p.46). Head north into Parliament Street and turn left down King Charles Street, with the Treasury offices on one side and Foreign Office departments on the other. At the end of the street, the bomb-proof, underground *Cabinet War Rooms* look as they did in World War II: the Map Room shows where Allied campaigns were charted, and the Transatlantic Telephone Room, the hot line by which Churchill could contact Roosevelt.

Return to Parliament Street and continue north to the *Cenotaph*. Designed by Sir Edwin Lutyens in 1919, it now serves as a memorial to the dead of both world wars. Go up Whitehall; iron gates seal off *Downing Street*, on the left, where the Prime Minister and the Chancellor of the Exchequer live at nos.10 and 11 respectively. Further up Whitehall on the left, between 10 a.m. and 4 p.m., sentries from the Household Cavalry in ceremonial dress guard *Horse Guards*. Opposite, *Banqueting House*, designed by Inigo Jones and the only survivor of Whitehall Palace, shows a restrained classical exterior, but the ceilings inside have superb paintings by Rubens.

At the top of Whitehall, at *Trafalgar Square*, you've reached the center of the city. As you leave the square via *Admiralty Arch*, a memorial to Queen Victoria in the southwest corner, a marvelous vista appears down *The Mall* to Buckingham Palace. On state occasions, royal carriages proceed along this great avenue, lined with fine Regency buildings. In Charles II's day, a hybrid form of croquet and golf called "pell mell" was played along The Mall and parallel Pall Mall – hence their names.

Between the two thoroughfares, the brick mansion of *St. James's Palace* was the official residence of the sovereign until the reign of Queen Victoria, and the Queen Mother lives in *Clarence House* (no public access to either). From Clarence House it is a short walk to *Buckingham Palace* (see p.46) ∎

★★★ Tate Gallery 21D1

(Millbank, SW1)
Tube: Pimlico
The Tate holds British paintings from the 16th century to the present, and international art from the impressionists to the present. The domestic collection is on permanent display. Most major British artists are represented: Constable, Reynolds, Gainsborough, Pre-Raphaelites, and 20th-century artists such as Spencer, Bacon and Hockney. The modern **Clore Gallery** is devoted to 300 paintings and 20,000 drawings, sketches and notebooks of J.M.W. Turner.

The modern foreign art is rotated, but you can rely on seeing paintings by Picasso and Matisse, and sculpture by Rodin, such as *Le Baiser (The Kiss)*.

One-armed and one-eyed, Admiral Lord Nelson stands loftily above the pigeons on his 172-foot column in the middle of Trafalgar Square, named for his famous victory

Trafalgar Square *(WC2)* 21D3

Tube: Charing Cross
Pigeons, demonstrators and New Year's Eve revelers flock to London's most famous square. Lord Nelson, victor at the Battle of Trafalgar, stands at the top of the 172-foot column, flanked by lions by Sir Edwin Landseer. The National Gallery (see p.46) runs along its northern side.

The church of **St. Martin-in-the-Fields**, built by Gibbs in 1726, served as a template for many early American churches. Concerts are held here.

★★★ Westminster Abbey 21D2

(Parliament Square, SW1)
Tube: Westminster
Every monarch since William the Conqueror has been crowned in Westminster Abbey – the present Coronation Chair was made in 1300 – and every monarch from Henry III to George III was buried here. Their tombs are magnificent, including those of Edward the Confessor, who began building the abbey in 1050; Henry III, who rebuilt the church in Gothic style in the 13th century as a shrine to the Confessor; and Henry VII, in a superb, fan-vaulted 16th-century chapel. There are also some thousand monuments to great statesmen, musicians and poets. Yet the most moving is the **Tomb of the Unknown Warrior**, the last resting place of an unidentified soldier buried here on November 11, 1920 in soil brought from the battlefields of France and Belgium to represent the dead of World War I.

Outside the church, there are lovely cloisters, the octagonal Chapter House (EH) where parliament convened between 1257 and 1547, and the Abbey Treasures Museum (EH) in the Norman undercroft, with royal death masks and wax effigies.

DAY TRIPS

Central London offers an incredible amount of entertainment, but can be very exhausting. A good way to revive the batteries is to spend a day or two in its attractive village suburbs, which are not only more sedate, but also have some outstanding sights. Kew, Richmond, and, further afield, Hampton Court are all located in southwest London along the River Thames, and could be visited together; likewise, Greenwich and the Thames Flood Barrier are close together, eastward along the Thames, and could be visited at the same time.

★★★ Greenwich   23D2

Getting there: the best ways are along the Thames (boats leave from Westminster, Charing Cross and Tower Bridge piers) or by the Docklands Light Railway; alternatively take a train from Charing Cross

Surrounded by majestic buildings and boasting a fascinating royal and naval history, this attractive village suburb (pronounced "Grennich") becomes very busy on the weekends, especially in the summer, as its multifaceted markets and old-fashioned riverside taverns draw the crowds away from the center.

At the water's edge you can board the *Cutty Sark*, a tea clipper that sailed at record speed between London and the Far East in 1871, and Sir Francis Chichester's *Gipsy Moth IV*, in which he sailed around the world single-handed from 1966 to 1967.

Also at the riverside stands the monumental **Royal Naval College**, now used for naval officer training. It was built by Sir Christopher Wren originally as a seamen's hospital, with superb baroque paintings on show in its Painted Hall.

The college was laid out so as not to obstruct the view of the **Queen's House** from the river. Set on the edge of Greenwich Park, this building by Inigo Jones was erected for James I's queen and was the first in England to be designed in Palladian style. The state apartments have been dazzlingly restored to show how they would have appeared in the 17th century.

Later wings house the **National Maritime Museum**, a fascinating, comprehensive collection of nautical artifacts, from the bullet-holed jacket Nelson wore when wounded at the Battle of Trafalgar to the Prince of Wales's state barge, dated 1732.

For many, the most interesting part of the museum is its annex on the hill above. Here, in Wren's **Old Royal Observatory**, the apartments look as they did when the first Astronomer Royal lived here 300 years ago, and galleries contain a plethora of fanciful timekeeping and stargazing instruments. The Gate Clock measures Greenwich Mean Time, and you can straddle the Greenwich Meridian, the dividing line between the eastern and western hemispheres.

Hampstead and Highgate   22C3/4

Getting there: take the Northern Line tube to Hampstead or Highgate

Pretty **Hampstead village** has long been associated with its literary and liberal residents. Its M.P. is the actress Glenda Jackson. John Keats lived here from 1818 to 1820, in what is now **Keats' House** on Keats' Grove; it houses his letters and manuscripts. Sigmund Freud passed his final months at 20 Maresfield Gardens, now the **Freud Museum**, where you can see his famous couch, along

THAMES FLOOD BARRIER

Getting there: take a boat from Westminster or Greenwich

Built to protect London against particularly high tides, the world's biggest moveable flood barrier, spanning the River Thames, is an impressive sight, consisting of ten massive, steel water gates. A visitor's center, the Thames Barrier Centre, explains how it operates ■

POPULAR HEATH

Hampstead Heath has always been popular. Up to 100,000 visitors in one day have been recorded on a public holiday.

At Easter and other public holidays, fairs are still held following a long tradition.

There is also horse riding available along with other sporting activities ■

with books and letters. The William-and-Mary-style **Fenton House** (NT) on Windmill Hill serves as a repository for fine period furnishings, porcelain and early musical instruments. Hampstead is a popular weekend destination, with plenty of cheerful stores, restaurants and cafés along the high street.

Semi-rural **Hampstead Heath** commands great views of the capital, and attracts walkers, kite-fliers and swimmers in its ponds. On its northern edge, **Kenwood House** (EH), finely proportioned by Robert Adam, displays an important collection of paintings by English and Dutch masters. On Saturday evenings in summer, crowds congregate here for outdoor lakeside concerts.

Beyond the eastern side of the heath, **Highgate Cemetery** comes in two parts. The most famous resident in the eastern half, which is always open, was Karl Marx. You can only visit the overgrown western half, crowded with catacombs and mausoleums, on a tour. Highgate also is a pleasant village.

★★★ Hampton Court Palace   22A1

Getting there: the leisurely way is by a 3–4 hour cruise down the Thames from Westminster (April–October); the quick way is by train from Waterloo to Hampton Court

Cardinal Wolsey began building this extravagant, 1,000-room palace in 1515, but he gave it to Henry VIII 10 years later to curry the king's favor (although it didn't work!).

The king added the Great Hall, magnificent for its hammerbeam roof, above the Tudor kitchens (now with a display of medieval food and herbs). Some 150 years later, Sir Christopher Wren, who wanted to build the whole palace

anew, ended up just adding the state apartments, now adorned with priceless Renaissance paintings, furnishings and tapestries. The hundreds of acres of glorious grounds include an Elizabethan knot garden, Tudor pond garden and famous triangular maze.

★★ Kew Gardens   22A2

Getting there: take the District Line tube to Kew Gardens, or a boat from Westminster

With over 45,000 species of plants, trees and shrubs from around the world, the scale of the Royal Botanic Gardens at Kew is hard to appreciate. In spring and summer, flowers of every hue carpet the formal gardens and the grounds laid out by "Capability" Brown (see p.138). A winter visit is highly recommended, too, for the Victorian greenhouses are always blooming with tropical growth. Be sure to take in the glorious iron and glass **Palm House**, and the **Princess of Wales Conservatory**, opened in 1987 and divided into vastly differing computer-controled climatic zones under one roof.

Richmond upon Thames   22A2

Getting there: take the District Line tube or a boat from Westminster

This affluent riverside town has several good pubs overlooking the Thames, and alleys full of antique stores and boutiques. The major attraction is **Richmond Park**; the largest of the Royal Parks and enclosed by Charles I as a royal hunting ground; deer roam its 2,500 acres.

A footpath from handsome Richmond Bridge follows the Thames to **Ham House** (NT), a Jacobean mansion remarkable for its period furniture and portraits by Reynolds.

THE WEST COUNTRY

From the open plains of Wiltshire,
through the gentle patchwork
countryside of Dorset and
Somerset, past the moors and
estuaries of Devon, to Cornwall's
tapering peninsula, the west and
southwest are England's premier
vacation regions

CALENDAR OF EVENTS

MAY TO JUNE –
Bath Festival.
One of the most
prestigious in Britain,
this includes a
program of concerts,
ballets, plays,
lectures and
exhibitions.

JUNE –
Royal Cornwall
Show, near
Wadebridge. The
premier agricultural
show in Britain.
Championship cattle
are on show along
with hundreds of
trade stands.

SEPTEMBER –
Widecombe Fair,
Devon. Made famous
through the
song Widdicombe
Fair (sic), featuring
Uncle Tom Cobley.
Ponies and sheep
from Dartmoor are
for sale.

NOVEMBER 5 –
Tar-barrel rolling at
Ottery St. Mary,
Devon. A fair, bonfire
and the racing of
blazing tar-barrels
through the streets
by rolling or carrying
on the shoulders of
the biggest (and
most insane) men
they can find! ∎

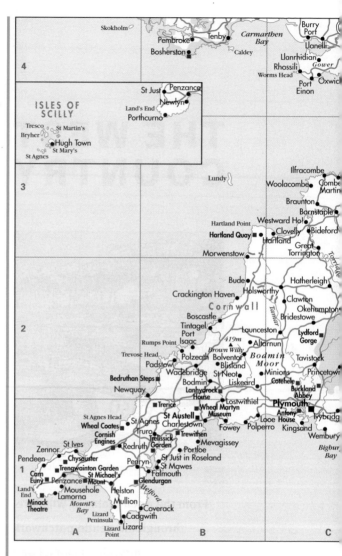

THE WEST COUNTRY

From dizzying cliffs to dazzling
beaches, no other part of Britain
can match the West Country for
its diversity of scenery. It has a
peerless range of man-made
attractions, in its resplendent
country houses, thatched villages
and fishing ports.

Cornwall's Celtic pedigree
lives on in its place names and
many prehistoric monuments,
while the remnants of deserted
mines recall its once important
copper and tin industries. Tourism
rules the roost today, as
vacationers descend down the
narrow lanes in their droves
during summer to Cornwall's 300
miles of coastline, the longest of
any English county. The county's
seaboards have two distinct
faces: towering cliffs, hardy little
ports like Boscastle and Port
Isaac, pristine sandy strands and

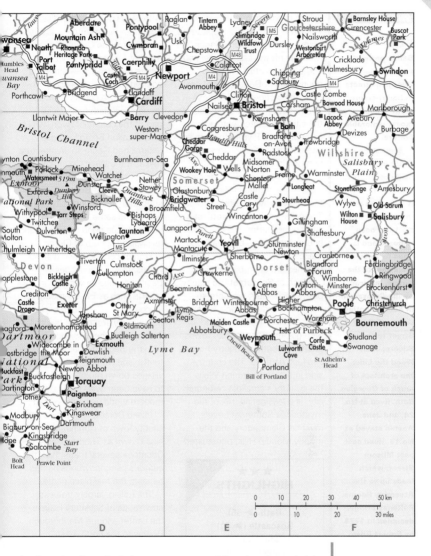

family and surfing-oriented resorts such as Newquay and arty St. Ives mark the grand Atlantic coast from Bude to Land's End. The south coast, tempered by the Gulf Stream, becomes gradually more sheltered, lush and populated as it progresses from Land's End eastward. Here, a myriad of craft moor in wooded river valleys and creeks below colorful harbors like Falmouth and Fowey, exotic plants thrive in ornamental gardens (come in late spring if you can), and picturesque fishing villages nestle between the rocks, above sandy coves.

Of the six West Country counties, **Devon** is by far the largest and most scenically varied. North Devon includes a chunk of lovely Exmoor and becomes the Golden Coast further west, so called for its superb sandy beaches. Age-old country pubs and thatched

WALK

BATH

Bath's perfectly proportioned Georgian streets in honey-colored stone are its most memorable feature.

Start at Royal Crescent. Though made up of 30 separate houses, it looks like one grand residence. No.1 has been restored and is open to view. Walk east to the Circus, inspired by the Colosseum in Rome. Continue south via Gay Street to Queen Square; John Wood the Elder, the architect of much of Georgian Bath, lived at No. 24, and Jane Austen stayed at No.13. Head east past Milsom Street, which leads up to the Assembly Rooms. Pulteney Bridge, designed in 1774 by Robert Adam and based on the Ponte Vecchio in Florence, leads to grand Great Pulteney Street ■

cottages with windows set into whitewashed cob walls epitomize many of inland Devon villages. Many lie off the beaten track, but some come within the boundaries of Dartmoor National Park, the last great wilderness in southern England. Devon also has the cities of Exeter, with a lovely cathedral, and Plymouth, with an interesting nautical history, both bombed in World War II.

The south coast's traditional resorts are at their liveliest along the English Riviera around Torbay. The coastline is at its prettiest around the Dartmouth and Kingsbridge estuaries – both yachting meccas – while the best of the beaches are at Bigbury Bay.

Much of **Somerset** is a sleepy, pretty backwater, no more so than in the cider-making Taunton Vale, and in the south, studded with golden-stone market towns, grand Elizabethan country houses and lush gardens. The countryside in the north around Wells, the country's smallest cathedral city, is a fascinating mix of the mysterious Somerset Levels, mystical Glastonbury and the moody Mendip Hills, punctuated

with caves and gorges. West Somerset has a clutch of lovely churches in the Quantocks, and most of Exmoor National Park, where moorland meets the sea, and fertile coombs climb up to moorland. The county's jewel, however, is Bath (until recently part of the county of Avon, which is now called Bristol), whose untarnished Georgian architecture makes it the West Country's most enticing city.

The county of **Bristol** surrounds the frenetic city and port of the same name, worth visiting for its good museums and its civilized suburb of Clifton.

Dorset comes in two distinct halves. Many tourists seek a traditional seaside vacation in resorts such as Bournemouth on its coastline, or come to explore the geology around the Isle of Purbeck and the fossil-rich cliffs of Lyme Regis. Yet largely agricultural inland Dorset, where rustic villages down muddy lanes seem to have been overlooked by the modern world, is hardly visited.

Inland Dorset, centering on the county town of Dorchester, is also known as Thomas Hardy Country – several maps mark the author's pseudonymous names beneath the real place names.

The rolling, largely treeless downlands of Salisbury Plain in the center and the Marlborough Downs to the north, best characterize **Wiltshire**. Carved into chalk hillsides are several outsize figures, mostly of horses, while Avebury and Stonehenge testify to the area's prehistoric significance. On the county's fringes lie a few outstanding country houses and gardens – notably Longleat, Stourhead and Wilton – and Salisbury Cathedral, apogee of the Early English style. The gentler Cotswold countryside of Wiltshire's northwestern corner makes for better exploring.

The Roman Baths in Bath were built around the only natural hot springs found in Britain. The waters have been both drunk and bathed in for centuries as an aid for many different ailments

★★ AVEBURY, WILTSHIRE 53F3

The standing stones at Avebury date from around 2500 BC and constitute one of Britain's most significant prehistoric sights. Before walking around the circle of 100 sarsen stones that encompass the village, drop in at the **Alexander Keiller Museum** (NT) to bone up on their configuration and the area's history. As at Stonehenge (see p.78), the astrological or religious significance of the stones is much debated. Connected to the main circle is an avenue of 100 pairs of parallel stones which leads to a burial site called **the Sanctuary**. From the main parking lot, a path heads to **Silbury Hill**. It covers over five acres, rises to 130 feet, and is probably Europe's largest prehistoric, manmade mound. The path continues to **West Kennet Long Barrow**, one of the finest examples of an ancient burial chamber, predating Avebury's stones by more than 500 years.

★★★ BATH, SOMERSET 53E3

The city's name explains its origins. Hot springs were discovered here at least 5,000 years before the Romans created an elaborate bathing complex in the 1st century AD. In the 18th century, Bath became the hub of English high society: the likes of Queen Anne, Jane Austen, Dr. Johnson and Admiral Nelson came, not only to indulge in the baths, but also to meet at balls and parties arranged by Beau Nash, the city's famed master of ceremonies, who laid down codes of etiquette for refined behavior. Meanwhile, attempting to recreate the architectural splendor of Roman times, John Wood the Elder and Younger (father and son) built harmonious, Palladian-style colonnaded terraces, most famously in the **Circus** and **Royal Crescent**. Nowadays, Bath is indisputably Britain's most elegant Georgian town, with a vibrant university and shopping center.

THE GHOSTS OF BATH

As there are so many ghosts in Bath, conducted tours of their favorite haunts are available.

The most well-known ghost is the Man in the Black Hat, who is seen around the Assembly Rooms, while the Grey Lady haunts the Theatre Royal and the Garrick's Head ■

At Bath Industrial Heritage Centre you can still taste the soft drinks made by J.B. Bowler

BECKFORD'S TOWER

This eccentric local landmark, 2 miles northwest of Bath, is an early 19th-century folly commanding wonderful views over the city and across the Severn towards Wales. It has 156 steps up to a belvedere ■

The feast of glorious streetscapes encourages visitors to wander around (see walk on p.54); Bath is the sort of place where you might happen across a ceiling lavish enough to grace a palace when you pop into a bank to cash a traveler's check.

As for its sights, the **Roman Baths** are Britain's finest Roman remains, with baths, cold plunges and the caldarium, with its under-floor heating system. Also on view are archeological finds such as a head of Minerva, goddess of wisdom, mosaics and carved stones. While the baths encapsulate the city's ancient history, in the ornate, 18th-century **Pump Room** overlooking the baths you can capture the town's Georgian spirit, drinking tea or a glass of health-giving water to the strains of chamber music.

Nearby **Bath Abbey** is England's last important pre-Reformation church. Its west front represents the dream which inspired Bishop Oliver King to rebuild the abbey in 1499, and there is magnificent fan vaulting to see inside the building.

The city is also awash with interesting museums. The **Assembly Rooms**, gutted in World War II by incendiary bombs but restored to their Georgian stateliness, house the **Museum of Costume**, one of the best of its kind in the world.

The brass foundry and engineering works of the **Bath Industrial Heritage Centre** tell of a more sober era in English history. The works closed down in 1969, but you can still taste the fizzy soft drinks that the family business produced here.

Equally worth seeking out are: the **Building of Bath Museum**; the eccentric canvases in the **Museum of English Naive Art**; the **National Centre of Photography** for its interesting displays on the early days of the camera; the **Holbourne Museum** for its rich display of old masters, furniture and ornaments; and **Herschel House**, home to the famous 18th-century astronomer and scientist.

★ BODMIN MOOR 52B2
CORNWALL

Cornwall's moorland is a smaller and less frequented version of Dartmoor, and can feel even more bleak. The A30 road bisects the moor, but venture down the lanes to appreciate it properly. Walks from the hamlet of **Minions**, Cornwall's highest village, to the stone circles of the **Hurlers** and to the **Cheesewring**, a wind-sculpted heap of granite slabs, provide panoramic views.

Drive on to **St. Neot** to see the medieval stained glass in the parish church, then head north past **Dozmary Pool**, mythological resting place of King Arthur's sword *Excalibur*, to **Jamaica Inn** at Bolventor. Daphne du Maurier's eponymous smuggling tale was written after a visit here in 1930, and you can still see how the slate-hung building inspired her. The adjacent **Mr. Potter's Museum of Curiosity** is a bizarre Victorian collection of mainly stuffed animals, some arranged in anthropomorphic set pieces, such as guinea pigs at a cricket match. The A30 leads on to **Launceston**, a sleepy market town with a largely intact Norman keep (EH) and the remarkable church of St. Mary Magdalene, thickly coated with carvings. The A30 takes you southwest to **Lanhydrock House** (NT), just outside Bodmin, a grand country house with remarkable plaster ceilings.

★★ BRADFORD-ON-AVON 52F3
WILTSHIRE and the
SOUTH FRINGES OF THE
COTSWOLDS

Rows of soothingly-colored terraced homes dating from medieval to Georgian times rise from the River Avon in pretty Bradford-on-Avon. Some are mansions built by wealthy cloth merchants, others are modest weavers' cottages. A medieval bridge spans the river, and a domed chapel also served as a diminutive jail. The **Church of St. Lawrence**, an almost complete example of Saxon ecclesiastical architecture, lay forgotten until 1856, when a vicar picked out the shape of the old church amongst the surrounding buildings.

The town makes a good base for exploring the southern fringes of the Cotswolds. The beautifully preserved village of **Lacock**, 9 miles northeast, belonged for generations to the Talbots, who bequeathed it to the National Trust in the 1940s. Its cottages, dating back to the 13th century, run the gamut of domestic styles: half-timbered, red-brick, stone and whitewashed.

Lacock Abbey (NT) was built in 1232 as a nunnery, and converted into a Tudor mansion after the Reformation, though its cloisters, chapter house and sacristy remain. William Henry Fox Talbot, the inventor of photography, lived here, and a museum commemorates his pioneering work with cameras and photos.

The Elizabethan manor house of **Corsham Court**, 3 miles west of Lacock, has grand state rooms added by "Capability" Brown in 1760, but it is best known for its contents, which include a roll call of paintings by many old masters from Van Dyck to Rubens. North, at the pretty village of **Castle Combe**, a brook flows under stone footbridges and past simple stone houses.

"Capability" Brown is also linked to **Bowood House**, 5 miles east of Lacock. The extensive gardens, which he landscaped between 1762 and 1768, form one of the finest parks in England, complete with formal gardens, an artificial lake, cascades and grottoes. Robert Adam had a hand in the design of the magnificent Georgian house.

THE WEST COUNTRY

LUNDY ISLAND

The island's name comes from the Icelandic word for puffin, *lunde.*

These delightful birds only come here to breed in spring, but ornithologists are attracted to the cliffs throughout the year to study many other species. The island's puffin stamps are always for sale.

This simple, car-free, tiny island, roughly 3 miles long and half-a-mile wide, has just a single store and a pub.

Situated in the Bristol Channel, 12 miles north of Hartland Point, the island can be reached by ferry from Bideford, and from Ilfracombe in summer. You can visit on a day-trip or stay overnight. Accommodations must be booked in advance through the Landmark Trust; part of the National Trust (see p.283) ∎

★★ BRISTOL, BRISTOL 53E4

The West Country's largest city was badly bombed in World War II, so its most aesthetically interesting part is, in fact, a suburb called **Clifton,** where you'll find elegant Georgian squares and crescents, as well as a gentrified atmosphere in its bars and boutiques. Soaring **Clifton Suspension Bridge,** spanning the Avon gorge, was designed by the famous 19th-century engineer, Isambard Kingdom Brunel.

The city was once an extremely important port. Long John Silver, of Robert Louis Stevenson's *Treasure Island* fame, sailed from here, as did John Cabot on his way to North America in 1497. At the **Llandoger Trow Inn** in King Street, Daniel Defoe is said to have met the real-life Robinson Crusoe. A long **floating harbor** was created in 1809 by diverting the River Avon, but after the new docks were built at Avonmouth in 1879, Bristol's port languished. The harbor has now been revivified into an attractive leisure area, with cobbled wharves, floating restaurants and boat trips. On the southern side, the fascinating **Bristol Industrial Museum** pays homage to the city's contributions to the development of transport. Further along, Brunel's **SS *Great Britain**,* the first ocean-going propeller-driven ship, stands once again in its original dry dock.

Also on the southern side of the water is the **Church of St. Mary Redcliffe**. Elizabeth I called it "the fairest, the goodliest, and most famous parish church in England." Outside the south door lies a feline tomb to a devout cat which attended all the church services. North of the harbor, the **cathedral**, founded as a church for Augustinian canons in 1140,

has 16th-century misericords in the choir, an organ case carved by the virtuoso woodcarver Grinling Gibbons, and a fine Norman chapter house. **John Wesley's New Room**, in Broadmead shopping precinct, is the oldest Methodist chapel in the world.

Secular parts of Bristol worth discovering include the handsome Georgian **Corn Exchange** on Corn Street, outside which stand four bronze tables, or "nails," where Bristol merchants would settle cash transactions (hence the phrase "paying on the nail").

Nearby **Christmas Steps** is a picturesque alleyway built in 1669 by a wealthy wine merchant, and you can learn more about the importance of wine, particularly sherry, at **Harveys Wine Museum**. Up the hill lies the **City Museum and Art Gallery**, specializing in glassware, including examples of the delectable Bristol Blue, and **Red Lodge**, whose rooms are riotously paneled in Italian Renaissance style.

Cabot Tower, built by the Victorians to commemorate the navigator, provides panoramic views over the city.

★★★ CHEDDAR GORGE 53E3 and WOOKEY HOLE, SOMERSET

The Mendip Hills are honey-combed with limestone caverns.

Near the village of **Cheddar** (many of whose stores specialize in selling Cheddar cheese) are the most accessible and spectacular gorge and caves. Near the foot of the 450-foot gorge are cave systems with spectacular stalactites and stalagmites (**Gough's Cave** is the best), and the start of the **Jacob's Ladder** staircase, hundreds of steps long, which leads up to the plateau and viewpoint above.

Stone Age finds are on display in the **Cheddar Showcaves Museum** and include the skeleton of a young man from Gough's Cave, where he was buried around 9,000 years ago.

More weird and wonderful rock formations can be seen in **Wookey Hole caves**, 6 miles southeast. The best known is supposed to represent the Witch of Wookey, and the theory of a resident witch is supported by the discovery of a woman's bones and an alabaster ball and comb in the caves, now on show in a museum in Wells (see p.78).

On a more cheerful note, an old-fashioned amusement center has turn-of-the-century fairground exhibits, Edwardian penny-in-the-slot machines and a mirror maze.

★ **CLOVELLY and** 52C3
HARTLAND QUAY, DEVON 52B3
Clovelly, a photogenic village on Devon's north coast, is a victim of its own beauty in high season, when it is packed with visitors. So steep are the cliffs above the harbor that the houses virtually stand on top of each other, and the main street, descending in cobbled steps, is much too steep for cars. You can approach the village along a scenic 3-mile toll road called Hobby Drive, built by a 19th-century squire.

Hartland Quay to the west was swept away by storms 100 years ago. The cliffs to the lighthouse on top of 325-foot **Hartland Point** are some of the most awesome in the West Country.

Clovelly Harbour dries out at low tide. Today it is largely home to pleasure craft, though a few inshore fishing boats remain

BRONZE AGE DARTMOOR

Grimpspound is a striking example of a Bronze Age settlement with 24 hut circles. Above the Erme Valley is a stone-lined processional route, some 2 miles long, and just outside Merrivale is another. Near Gidleigh are 23 upright stones which form Scorhill Stone Circle ■

DART ESTUARY   53D1
DEVON

The meandering River Dart, with its thickly arboreal banks, is navigable up as far as Totnes, and undoubtedly the high point of a visit to the area is to take a cruise. Pleasure boats run between Dartmouth and Totnes, and circular trips leave from Dartmouth. There is plenty of wildlife to see – look out for herons, kingfishers and seals – and Dartmouth's colorful tiered terraces, set beside a waterway bristling with sails and masts, are best seen from the water.

The port has been significant from the days of the Crusades

butter), where there is a small maritime museum. **Dartmouth Castle** (EH) commands the narrow estuary entrance.

Totnes, 12 miles upstream, is a compact, ancient town made wealthy in Tudor times from the export of wool and tin. It too has a **butterwalk**, along with many attractive, slate-hung and gabled houses on its main street, where every other establishment seems to be a bookstore or has an ethnic, health or New Age theme.

The **Elizabethan House** and **guildhall** are both of great interest, but the main attraction is the classic motte and bailey **castle** (EH).

The clapper bridge at Post-bridge on Dart-moor is typical of the very ancient granite slab bridges found around the moors. Many have been plundered for their stone over the years, but this one is intact

through to World War II; nowadays, it is home to the Britannia Royal Naval College and hosts the annual Royal Regatta in late August. The Pilgrim Fathers stopped off at the quaint, cobbled quayside of **Bayard's Cove** in 1620 on their way to America. Many of the timber-framed houses stand on reclaimed land, such as the **butterwalk** (its arcade stopped the sun from melting the traders'

★★★ DARTMOOR   53C2
DEVON

This 365 square miles of national park is the largest lung of untrammeled countryside in southern England, inhabited by just 30,000 people, but visited by up to 8 million vacationers annually. It is effectively a massive lump of granite covered in moorland and bog, out of which rise craggy outcrops known as *tors*, where piles of boulders have been eroded over the millenia by wind and rain into often mysterious shapes.

Sheep, cattle and shaggy Dartmoor ponies, descended from prehistoric wild horses, graze on the open moors. Other features include stone crosses, marking the route of ancient byways and protecting travelers against unfriendly spirits, and some 400 letterboxes, often remotely sited. Each has a visitor's book, rubber stamp and an inkpad, the idea being that a self-addressed postcard would be left to be picked up and sent by the next walker.

Though Dartmoor demands to be explored on foot or horseback, the windswept uplands can be particularly bleak if the weather is bad, when you'd do better to hole up in a cozy thatched cottage in the fertile valleys below.

Easily accessible **Haytor**, on the eastern side, is a good viewpoint. Below nearby **Hound Tor** are the remains of a deserted medieval village.

Widecombe-in-the-Moor is Dartmoor's best-known village, thanks to the folksong *Widdicombe Fair* (the fair is still held on the second Tuesday in September). Its church is so vast that it's called "the cathedral of the moor." The clockface of pretty **Buckland-in-the-Moor's** church is inscribed with the words "MY DEAR MOTHER," instead of the usual numerals.

Medieval clapper bridges of flat granite stone crop up frequently on Dartmoor's rivers, and you can see one at **Dartmeet**, where the rivers West and East Dart join forces to form the River Dart . The hill-and-valley countryside around here, surveyed by **Combestone Tor**, is delightful. Downstream, there was a monastery at **Buckfast Abbey** before the Norman Conquest, but

the present abbey church was only completed in 1938. **Buckfastleigh** also has a butterfly farm and otter sanctuary, and steam trains run from its station along the River Dart to Totnes.

The B3212, west of Dartmeet, crosses the middle of the moor. Foreboding **Princetown**, at 1,400 feet, is the highest town in England, but it is better known for its high-security prison, built to house French prisoners of war in 1806. North along the B3212 takes you to **Postbridge**, with an impressive clapper bridge, constructed in the 13th century from huge slabs.

North Bovey is a lovely ensemble of a pretty green, stone cross, village pump and thatched cottages. **Chagford** is larger but sleepy too, and the old market town of **Moretonhampstead** has a row of thatched, 17th-century almshouses. The River Teign wends its way through a forested gorge. **Castle Drogo** (NT), looming over the valley, looks like a medieval castle from the outside, but then reveals itself to be an Arts and Crafts *tour de force*, built by Sir Edwin Lutyens between 1910 and 1930. The main entrance is near **Drew-steignton**, which has a charming village square.

The high and remote northwest corner of the moor is used for army training. On some days, including most weekends, you can drive along the **army road** from Okehampton Camp.

Okehampton has a Museum of Dartmoor Life, housed in a Regency watermill which tells of early tin and copper mining.

The chief allure of the moor's western fringes lies in **Brent Tor**, where a church ruin sits on top of an isolated hill that commands spectacular views, and **Lydford Gorge**, a famous and much-visited beauty spot.

WALKS

DARTMOOR
Walking on the more exposed parts of Dart-moor, north and west of Post-bridge in particular, is not to be taken lightly.

Tors such as Haytor (see opposite) and Hound Tor (see opposite) are more accessible, and for a milder taste of woods, moorland and prehistoric sites, explore south of Postbridge around Bellever.

As on Exmoor, there are scenic riverside walks, such as in the Teign Valley, where a beautiful circular walk from Castle Drogo (see opposite) takes you through Drewsteignton to the picturesque, packhorse Fingle Bridge. At the Lydford Gorge (see opposite), a 1½-hour trail takes you along a densely wooded ravine to a waterfall and whirlpool ∎

DRIVE

THE HAMSTONE TOWNS OF SOMERSET AND DORSET

130 miles (allow 3 days)

The tour takes in an unspoiled and little-visited part of the West Country, with wooded hills, snug valleys and rolling downlands, peaceful market towns of honey-colored stone, and Tudor manor houses.

THE FLYING DONKEY

There has been a church on the site of St. Mary Magdalene Church in Taunton since 1488. The impressive 163-foot tower was rebuilt to its original design in 1862 using Quantock Red Stone.

In order to raise the stones during construction, they walked a donkey down the street using a pulley system. When the rebuild was finished, the donkey was hauled to the top of the tower to see the view he had created! ■

Leave Bridgwater on an unclassified road to Enmore. Continue to Bishop's Lydeard, then turn left onto the A358 to Taunton.

1 Taunton, Somerset

From Enmore in the Quantock Hills (see p.75), the fertile Vale of Taunton Deane is laid out before you. Somerset's county town, Taunton, is known for its large cattle market and its cricket: the West Indies' Viv Richards and England's Ian Botham played here. The small but devoted **Somerset Cricket Museum** is next to the ground.

After the Battle of Sedgemoor in 1685, in which the Duke of Monmouth unsuccessfully tried to wrest the throne from James II, Judge Jeffreys held his notorious Bloody Assizes in towns across the West Country. In the Great Hall of Taunton's Norman **castle**, he condemned to death more than 500 of Monmouth's supporters.

Hammett Street frames the 16th-century **Church of St. Mary Magdalene**. The vale is known for its apples. Outside town, visit **Sheppy's Cider Farm**, and buy its cider and the rougher and stronger scrumpy.

Leave Taunton on the B3170 heading south. Shortly after crossing the M5, turn left for Staple Fitzpaine. Continue on unclassified roads towards Buckland St. Mary and the A303. Turn left onto the A303, then right onto the B3168 to Ilminster.

2 Ilminster, Somerset

The small market town of Ilminster glows golden from the hue of the local limestone, called Hamstone. The **church** boasts an ornate tower based on the tower of Wells Cathedral.

Just north of the town, the main attraction at the Elizabethan manor house of **Barrington Court** (NT) is the lovely ornamental and kitchen gardens.

From Ilminster go south on an unclassified road, turning right onto the A358 to Chard.

3 Chard, Somerset

Chard claims to be the birthplace of both modern flight and artificial limbs, explained in the excellent local **museum**.

Along the road to Crewkerne at **Cricket St. Thomas Wildlife Park**, llamas, camels, bison and wallabies roam in the parkland of a 19th-century mansion; there is also a scenic railway, milking parlor and aviary.

Leave Chard on the A30 in the direction of Crewkerne (5 miles).

4 Crewkerne, Somerset

This market town has long had a reputation for making sails: those for Nelson's HMS *Victory* came from here, as well as those used for some of the contenders for the Americas Cup.

From Crewkerne on the A356, signposted

*Dorchester/Bridport, turn
right onto the A3066 for
Beaminster (4½ miles).*

5 Beaminster, Dorset

The hilly, wooded countryside
around Beaminster (pronounced
"Bemminster") is unspoiled, rural
England at its best.

The honey-colored town centers on a triangular square and tall
church, built in 1503. The nearby
Elizabethan manor of **Parnham**
has become a center for outstanding modern furniture design.

*Continue south on the
A3066 for 6 miles
to Bridport.*

6 Bridport, Dorset

The width of the town's streets is
explained by the fact that the
strands of flax ropes were once
laid out along them: ropes and
nets have been made here for
many centuries, and Bridport is
still Europe's largest netmaking
center.

With the sea on one side and
chalky downs and valleys on the
other, the views along the B3157
on the way to Abbotsbury are
really awesome.

*Leave Bridport heading for
West Bay, then turn onto
the B3157 for 8 miles
to Abbotsbury.*

SINISTER EXPRESSION

**The ancient town
of Bridport was
so well known for
its rope-making
industry around
the time of
sailing ships that
"being stabbed by
a Bridport
dagger" became
a well-known
expression for
saying that
somebody had
been hanged ∎**

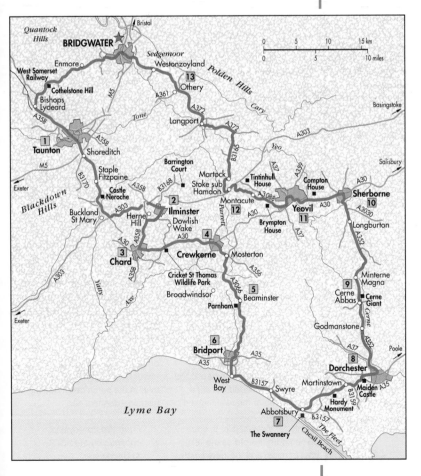

THE MYSTERY OF CHESIL BEACH

Experts on coastal geology have never been able to explain how the billions of pebbles that make up this huge bank of shingle are graded from west to east and become gradually bigger towards the Isle of Portland.

Reaching higher than 40 feet in places, it has been the reason for many sailing ships being wrecked when gales swept across the bay ∎

7 Abbotsbury, Dorset

The thatched, limestone village gets its name from a Benedictine **abbey**, dissolved in 1541. Virtually all that remains is its magnificent **tithe barn**. You can also visit the **swannery**, founded by the monks to supply meat for the table. This lies at one end of **the Fleet**, a marshy lagoon known for its birdlife, behind the extraordinary natural phenomenon of **Chesil Beach**. A narrow, unsignposted road leads over Black Down Hill past the **Hardy Monument**, an obelisk commemorating Vice Admiral Hardy who knelt at the dying Nelson's side at the Battle of Trafalgar.

Leave Abbotsbury uphill on an unclassified road to Martinstown; then turn left onto the B3150 for Dorchester.

8 Dorchester

(see p.65)

From Dorchester head north on the A352 for Cerne Abbas.

9 Cerne Abbas, Dorset

On the way to Cerne Abbas, look for the tiny **Smith's Arms**, at Godmanstone. Cerne Abbas has timber-framed and stone and flint buildings, but the main attraction here is the 180-foot **giant** etched through the grass into the chalk hillside. It is plain to see why he is a fertility figure.

Continue north on the A352 to Sherborne.

10 Sherborne, Dorset

Two Saxon kings are buried in the **abbey** here, founded in 705; a spider's web of fan vaulting and multicolored bosses cover the ceiling. Sir Walter Raleigh once owned both the **old castle** (EH), now in ruins, and the **new castle**, where it is said he was doused by a servant with a flagon of ale as he smoked the newly-discovered tobacco.

Leave Sherborne on the A30 heading west for 6 miles to Yeovil.

11 Yeovil, Somerset

Bombed in World War II, Yeovil is a busy modern town. The only old building of any significance is the impressive 14th-century **church**.

Leave Yeovil on the A30 and turn right onto the A3088, turning left in 3 miles for Montacute.

12 Montacute, Somerset

The Tudor mansion of **Montacute House** (NT) was built by Sir Edward Phelips, who prosecuted Guy Fawkes in 1605 for his plan to blow up the Houses of Parliament. Paneling, elaborate plaster friezes and tapestries complement the fine furnishings and a collection of period portraits on loan from the National Portrait Gallery. Houses at **Tintinhull** (NT), with a small but glorious garden, and **Brympton D'Evercy**, with the country's smallest distillery, date from the same era.

From Montacute take the A3088 to Stoke-sub-Hamdon, then the A303 and right onto the B3165. Join the A372 heading for Westonzoyland.

13 Westonzoyland, Somerset

Westonzoyland's **church** was used as a prison after the Battle of Sedgemoor (see Taunton). The tower overlooks the fenland and a map in the porch describes the historical connection.

From Westonzoyland continue on the A372 to Bridgwater.

★ **DORCHESTER and**   *53E2*
HARDY COUNTRY, DORSET

Dorset's county seat is known first and foremost as being the Casterbridge of Thomas Hardy's novels, and although it is not outstandingly attractive, it offers much of interest.

On its southwest edge, **Maiden Castle** is Britain's most impressive Iron Age fort, a vast plateau surrounded by deep, defensive ditches. In the 1st century AD, the Romans overran the fort and established the colony of *Durnovaria* where Dorchester now stands. The remains of a **Roman town house** show an underfloor heating system and a mosaic floor.

Within the district council offices, the **Old Crown Court** has been preserved to look as it was when the Tolpuddle Martyrs were sentenced here in 1834 to six years' transportation to Australia, essentially for the crime of forming a trade union. A small museum set up by the Trade Union Congress in the village of **Tolpuddle,** east of Dorchester on the A35, tells the full story.

The **Dorset County Museum** in Dorchester offers an excellent introduction to the region, with much Hardy material, including a re-creation of his study with original items, and Iron Age and Roman artifacts and fossils.

Hardy was born in 1840 in **Higher Bockhampton,** just east of Dorchester, in a thatched cottage (NT) built by his grandfather; it lies on the edge of Egdon Heath as mentioned in his writings, now largely forested. To view the interior, which contains period but not original furnishings, the National Trust advises you to make an appointment (tel. 01305 262366), though they may let you in without one. The novelist's heart is buried in nearby **Stinsford Church** alongside his relatives, though his body lies in Westminster Abbey.

★ **EXETER, DEVON**   *53D2*

Much of the medieval city was wiped out in a "Baedeker" air raid (one specifically aimed at the destruction of historic sites) in World War II. However, parts of the hulking, red medieval walls can still be seen, and the sumptuous **cathedral** was spared. Its finest feature is its soaring, vaulted nave; at 100 yards from end to end, it is the longest of its design in the world.

While inside, also search out the 15th-century astronomical clock in the north transept, the dozens of superb misericords in the choir stalls, and the 50-foot-high bishop's throne. In the cathedral library, the *Exeter Book* contains the country's largest surviving collection of Anglo-Saxon poetry. Two massive Norman towers dominate the cathedral's exterior, while rows of kings, apostles, angels and prophets adorn the west front.

Old houses in the surrounding **close** were also missed by the bombs, such as the Elizabethan Mol's Coffee House, where Sir Francis Drake would have sought sustenance, and, up a side alley, the low-beamed Ship Inn where he alleviated his thirst.

For more attractive buildings, head for Georgian **Southernhay** and take in the **guildhall**, the oldest in England, and its display of city regalia. For something a little different, consider a guided tour around the 13th-century **underground water system**, from which citizens hauled up buckets of water through holes in the tunnel roof (the entrance is in Princesshay shopping center).

The city's best museum is the **Maritime Museum** in the old canal basin. Some of the 200 craft on display, including

WALKS

THE SOUTHWEST COAST

Much of the Southwest Peninsula Coast Path, some 560 miles from Poole in Dorset to Minehead in Somerset, produces clifftop hikes as dramatic as you're likely to find anywhere.

Many of the most superb sections are only accessible on foot, leaving them relatively unfrequented and entirely unspoiled.

In Dorset, the path is at its finest around Lulworth Cove (see p.74) and the Golden Cap, east of Lyme Regis.

South Devon's coastline is spectacular either side of the Kingsbridge Estuary – from Bolt Head to Bolt Tail and around Prawle Point and Start Point – and is primarily accessible only on foot ∎

THE WEST COUNTRY

WHY SOMERSET IS CALLED SOMERSET

The name Somerset comes from "land of the summer-farm dwellers."

The county was once covered in marshland, out of which protruded hills like Glastonbury Tor. The farmers' flocks would have to winter on the hills, and could only graze on the "levels" (as the flood plains west of Glastonbury are still called) when they had dried out in the summer ∎

coracles, a Chinese junk, an Arab *dhow* and early steamships, are afloat and can be boarded.

★★★ EXMOOR   *52C3*
SOMERSET/DEVON

Exmoor, England's smallest national park, packs in a great variety of scenery, from towering cliffs along the coast, to lush, wooded combes riven by sparkling streams, to gentle farmland in the east and wilder moorland in the center and south. You'll be very lucky to spot any of the resident red deer, but you will certainly meet a few hardy, dun-colored Exmoor ponies on your travels. To set the scene, you might want to read R.D. Blackmore's historical novel, *Lorna Doone*, based on stories about a group of 17th-century

outlaws who lived in a beautiful part of the park now commonly known as Doone Country.

Coastal Exmoor

The moorland comes right up to the clifftops for much of Exmoor's coast and this is the most interesting part.

In the northwest corner, the medieval **Church of St. Petrock** at Parracombe has remained unaltered over generations.

The sedate Victorian resort of **Lynton** sits on a cliff 400 feet above its twin resort of **Lynmouth**, and is connected to it by a late Victorian, water-powered cliff railway. Lynmouth, set round a small harbor, was also a favored Victorian bolthole, put on the map by such notable visitors as Shelley, Wordsworth and Coleridge.

The heathland of Exmoor starts abruptly at around 1,000 feet above sea level, leaving behind lush wooded valleys and productive farmland well sheltered from the prevailing westerly winds

Watersmeet describes the tumbling together of two rivers, where there is a café converted from a fishing lodge and waterfalls and oak woods complete the picturesque scene. The gorse-clad cliffs at nearby Countisbury Common rise to nearly 1,000 feet and provide tremendous views across to South Wales.

From Malmsmead, a path leads into Doone Country along Badgworthy Water. The heroine Lorna was married at the lovely little church at Oare. The medieval church at Culbone, found in a remote wood near the sea, is one of the smallest churches in regular use in the country. Porlock, set in a bowl below the disturbingly steep Porlock Hill, was a port before the sea subsided into marshland. Porlock Weir became a small harbor in the 19th century. Two of Exmoor's most charming villages lie just east: Allerford boasts a double-arched packhorse bridge and an interesting rural-life museum in its old school, while Selworthy has a cluster of thatched, white-walled cottages and a 16th-century church with a fine wagon roof.

Just beyond the vacation resort of Minehead is Dunster, once an important medieval cloth center, which still has an octagonal yarn market, nunnery, tithe barn, dovecot, packhorse bridge and working watermill (NT) amid its mellow, ancient houses. It would do well in a competition for England's finest historical small town. Pride of place goes to the Norman castle (NT) whose interior was restored and made considerably more comfortable during Victorian times.

Inland Exmoor

Open moorland and rolling farmland mix across much of inland Exmoor. For a mini driving tour, start at the moor's highest point, Dunkery Beacon, an easy to climb hill with fabulous views. Head on to Exford, a pretty group of cottages around a village green often busy with the sounds of the staghounds kenneled here.

The scenic route continues across Winsford Hill from Exford to Dulverton, a compact, pretty and not too touristy shopping center, and then on to Twitchen along the south boundary of the park. East of Winsford Hill, Winsford might well be judged the prettiest village, due to its seven bridges; west and upstream from Withypool, Tarr Steps is the local name for one of Britain's finest clapper bridges, rebuilt many times in its 1,000-year-long history.

WALKS

EXMOOR
A fantastic length of the North Devon and West Somerset coastline, from Combe Martin to Minehead, falls within Exmoor.

Don't miss the Valley of Rocks, a splendid walk from Lynton through a land of misshapen *tors* populated by feral goats.

Close to Lynton are gentle, wooded, riverside trails: to the west along the River Heddon down to Heddon's Mouth, to the east along the River Lyn from Watersmeet and from Malmsmead into Doone country.

Also recommended are walks around famous beauty spots like Dunkery Beacon and Tarr Steps ■

KERNOW

While there is little talk of devolution in Cornwall, some Cornish people still regard anyone from Devon and beyond as foreigners.

Historically, Kernow (Celtic for Cornwall) has more affinity with Celtic Brittany and Wales than with England.

The Celtic tradition lives on in place names with prefixes such as "Tre" (meaning homestead), "Pol" (a pool) and "Pen" (a headland or hill) such as Trelissick, Polperro and Penzance.

Many surnames also begin with these same three letters; a local rhyme goes "By Tre, Pol and Pen, ye shall know Cornishmen."

The Cornish tongue is no longer spoken except by language students. The last monoglot, Dolly Pentreath from Mousehole, died in 1777 ■

★★★ FAL ESTUARY   52B1
CORNWALL

More commonly, and intriguingly, called Carrick Roads, this vast and beautiful natural harbor, surrounded by densely wooded banks and colorful little villages alongside spindly creeks, is always full to the brim with boats of every type and size.

The waterway is best appreciated from the water: numerous **boat trips** run up, across and around the estuary from Falmouth and Truro. At the estuary entrance, the twin castles of **Pendennis** (EH) and **St. Mawes** (EH), built by King Henry VIII against a possible French invasion, offer superb views.

The large resort town of **Falmouth** was once a very important port from which sailing packets would carry mail to the far outposts of the British Empire, and an interesting little maritime museum tells the story.

Truro, Cornwall's unofficial capital, is not unduly alluring despite its Georgian architecture and its 19th-century cathedral.

Southern Cornwall's mild climate explains the presence of so many lovely gardens in this region, and a visit to at least one of the following gardens is a must, particularly if you're here in spring or early summer.

Subtropical plants fill the churchyard of **St. Just in Rose-land**, right on the water's edge. The woodland garden of **Trelis-sick** (NT), with paths down to the waterside, is famous for its dozens of varieties of hydrangea. **Trewithen's** gardens, around an elegant Georgian manor, specialize in huge banks of rhodo-dendrons, camellias and magnolias. Side by side overlooking the tranquil River Helford, **Glendurgan** (NT) and **Trebah** are glorious and romantic with exotic species in lush valley settings.

At the head of the River Helford at Gweek, the **Cornish Seal Sanctuary** serves as a hospital and convalescent home for injured seals, dolphins and birds.

★★ FOWEY and AROUND   52B1
CORNWALL

A major port since the Middle Ages, Fowey (pronounced "Foy") is a classic expression of southern Cornwall, with a harbor and estuary scene packed with yachts, fishing boats and ocean-going ships loaded with china clay, and narrow streets running down to the quays from tiered terraces. It is at its liveliest during the regatta in August.

Polperro, 9 miles east of Fowey via the car ferry to Bodinnick, is one of Cornwall's most photogenic fishing villages. It retains a refined, civilized air despite the onslaught of visitors in summer, and non-residential traffic is kept out of the village.

Glastonbury Tor has been associated with all kinds of myths, from an entrance point to the Underworld to an Arthurian hill fort, a ceremonial spot covered in a pre-Christian maze, and a magnet for UFO's!

THE ONCE AND FUTURE KING

The West Country has many places which lay claim to links with King Arthur – a legendary British Celtic King who fought Germanic Saxons around the 5th century AD.

Legend has it that Arthur was born at Tintagel Castle (see p.71), and the magician Merlin lived in the cave below.

Camelot could have been at Cadbury Castle, in Somerset, or at Colchester in Essex.

After being mortally wounded in his last battle, Arthur sailed to the Islands of the Blest (the Isles of Scilly) or to Avalon (Glastonbury). Yet, as the "Once and Future King," he was ready to return when his people called ■

Smuggling once contributed handsomely to the villagers' income, and you can discover the story in its small museum.

West of Fowey, **Charlestown** is a fascinating little port still used by the china clay industry. At the open-air **Wheal Martyn Museum**, 2 miles north of St. Austell, you can learn about the industry. A trail takes you to working pits through a moonscape created from the extraction of the material.

Tourism has superseded, but not ousted, fishing in **Mevagissey**, which is so commercialized that it may seem a caricature of itself when seething with day-trippers. Yet, when peaceful, it is extremely picturesque, and there are fishing trips and family-oriented attractions.

In complete contrast, the rocky harbor of minute **Portloe**, further west, is one of Cornwall's few almost unspoiled gems, thanks to its relative inaccessibility. It is worth venturing inland to **Veryan** to see its five strange, 19th-century roundhouses with their thatched, conical roofs topped by a cross.

★★ GLASTONBURY   53E3
SOMERSET

Mystic shops and healing centers on the main street of this ancient town hint at the presence of Glastonbury's mysteries. The story goes that Joseph of Arimathea came here with the chalice from the Last Supper (the Holy Grail) and established the first Christian foundation in Britain, on the site of the present, and substantial, medieval **abbey ruins**. King Arthur and Queen Guinevere were allegedly buried here and a plaque marks the grave. The grail is supposed to be hidden at the Chalice Well, at the base of **Glastonbury Tor**, a 500-foot green hillock that used to be an island when the sea covered the surrounding Somerset Levels.

THE WEST COUNTRY

WALKS

THE CORNISH COAST

Long stretches of the Cornish coast make particularly thrilling walking.

Head for the Lizard Peninsula, around Kynance Cove (see opposite) and the Penwith Peninsula south and east of Land's End (see p.73) around Porthgwarra.

The North Cornish Coast, notably around Morwenstow (see p.71), between Crackington Haven and Tintagel (see p.71), and above the Camel Estuary around Rumps Point and Pentire Point, won't disappoint.

The West Country's offshore islands, the Scilly Isles (see p.77) and Lundy Island (off the north Devon coast – see p.58), are a ramblers' paradise ■

LIZARD PENINSULA *52A1* CORNWALL

Rugged cliff scenery, stacks of multicolored serpentine rock (so called because of its snakeskin markings), nestling coves and a flat interior criss-crossed by a maze of lanes distinguish the Lizard. Lizard Point is as far south as Britain reaches, and mild, southerly climes allow rare species of clover and Cornish heather to grow on the peninsula.

On the western cliffs, the **Marconi Memorial** near Poldhu Point commemorates the first successful transatlantic radio signal, sent in 1901 to Newfoundland. **Kynance Cove** displays the serpentine at its best: red, green, purple and blue shades ornament the pillars and pyramids that rise in spectacular fashion from the beach. The village of **Lizard**, meanwhile, is a center for making ornaments from serpentine.

On the eastern coast, **Cadgwith** and **Coverack**, once notorious for smuggling, are the prettiest peninsular villages, with thatched cottages overseeing, respectively, a stony strand and harbor. In between, **Kennack Sands** is wide, firm and easily accessible, the best family beach in the area.

Flambards Village Theme Park, just outside Helston, has attractions such as hair-raising rides, a Concorde flight deck and a reconstructed Victorian village. It is also possible to tour **Poldark Mine**, north of Helston. Cornwall once led the world in copper and tin production, but the many derelict engine houses scattered across the countryside tell of the industry's decline.

★★ LONGLEAT *53F3* WILTSHIRE

The family home of the Marquis of Bath does not fulfill traditional expectations of an English stately home. Its parkland, designed by "Capability" Brown, became the first drive-through wildlife safari park in the country, opened in 1966. Despite other commercial attractions, the ornamental gardens are lovely and there is a large maze. The Elizabethan house, much of which was transformed in the 19th century to an Italianate style, is one of England's most sumptuous, a receptacle for tapestried walls, painted ceilings, marble fireplaces, portraits and rare manuscripts. The Victorian kitchens give an idea of what life was like "below stairs" in the servants' quarters.

★ LYME REGIS, DORSET *53E2*

The fame of this lovely Regency seaside town has reached far and wide in recent years, thanks to the most memorable scene from the movie of John Fowles' novel, *The French Lieutenant's Woman*, in which Meryl Streep stands forlornly on the wave-pounded, curved stone breakwater called the Cobb. The resident Fowles is said to be an authority on fossils, which are found in abundance here in England's foremost fossil area. For safety and conservation reasons, extractions from the surrounding cliffs are discouraged, but many fossils, most commonly huge ammonites, can be seen in garden walls, in specialist stores and in two good local museums.

★★ MILTON ABBAS *53F2* DORSET

Dorset's most remarkable village came into being as a result of the ruthlessness of Lord Milton who, at the end of the 18th century, demolished the existing settlement to make room for a new mansion. What you see is the surreal-looking housing estate he built for the evicted villagers, a street lined with quaint, whitewashed and thatched cottages, each virtually identical to its neighbor. The lord's mansion is now a private school, standing in parkland alongside medieval **Milton Abbey,** which, impressive as it is, forms just the chancel of the planned church.

NORTH CORNISH COAST   52B2

This is a land of towering cliffs, majestic golden beaches and tiny ports, hidden from the force of the destructive Atlantic rollers in natural inlets. The Victorian Reverend Robert Hawker settled in lonely **Morwenstow**, close to the Devon border; a short walk from his lovely medieval church, the driftwood shack where he smoked opium nestles above awesome cliffs. **Bude** is by no means beautiful, but its fine beach attracts surfers in their droves. Past the cove of **Crackington Haven**, squashed between strangely lined cliffs and the dizzying views from Cornwall's highest cliff at **High Cliff**, comes **Boscastle ★★★**, a somewhat precious village behind a long, sinuous harbor inlet. The disturbing relics in the Witches House may make you re-evaluate your opinion of tales of sorcery.

Though stories of Arthurian associations with **Tintagel's castle** (EH) are tenuous, and little of the fortress remains, neither matters since its setting is magnificent, above a flight of stone steps on a virtual island. In **Tintagel ★★★** itself, the eccentric King Arthur's Halls, built in the 1930s by a millionaire custard manufacturer, give an insight into the legend's significance in British culture. The tiny medieval manor house of the Old Post Office (NT) seems to look on aghast at all the stores that milk for all they are worth Tintagel's mystical connections.

The village of **Port Isaac ★★★**, by contrast, has so far escaped the worst ravages of tourism. Among its whitewashed cottages is the descriptively named Squeezebelly Alley, while cars can only just squeeze along its main street. When the tide is out it is possible to park on the beach.

Close by the windsurfing beach of Daymer Bay; lovable **St. Enodoc's Church** was

The long curve of Boscastle Harbour is behind a wall at the mouth of a deep cleft in the rock, almost impossible to see from out at sea and a difficult entry in any weather for the fishermen of old

threatened with submersion under the dunes last century. The late poet laureate, John Betjeman, wrote a well-known poem about it; he is buried in the sandy graveyard.

Padstow doubles as a fairly substantial working port and a restrained resort. You can inspect the day's catch in the dockside warehouses, or have your

Approaching Land's End from the south the cliffs are dramatic and dangerous. The coast path follows the edge at a respectful distance, the views are superb and it's the best way to get to the point itself

THE 'OBBY 'OSS AND THE FURRY DANCE

Every May Day Padstow celebrates the 'Obby 'Oss.

Pantomime horses prance through the streets to the tune of accordion players, all the while hassled by a "teazer" with a club. It's said to be all about pagan fertility rites.

In Helston, a celebration to welcome spring occurs every year on May 8, when men in top hats and tails and women in billowing party dresses dance formally through the streets in the Furry (or Flora) Dance ■

seafood prepared in the town's excellent fish restaurants. Above the town, Prideaux Place is a fine, lived-in Elizabethan mansion whose interior reveals all sorts of architectural flourishes.

South of Padstow, the coast is more built up with vacation development, but has a concentration of sandy beaches. At Bedruthan Steps, the huge granite offshore rocks were, according to legend, stepping-stones used by the giant Bedruthan.

Surfers congregate at many of these beaches, but Newquay's 7 miles of fantastic sandy strands are their most popular haunt; the resort is Cornwall's biggest and most brash. Elizabethan Trerice Manor (NT), south of town, is considerably more sedate, having changed little since it was built in 1573. Remarkable plasterwork covers its ceilings.

★★★ PENWITH PENINSULA, CORNWALL   52A1

It is well worth making the effort to travel to Cornwall's western extremity, where a lonely moorland is encased in a memorable granite coastline.

St. Michael's Mount ★★★ (NT) is Cornwall's most romantic sight, a perfect little granite island topped by a castle and reached by a snaking causeway at low tide or, in summer, by a ferry from Marazion at high tide. It looks remarkably like a smaller version of its namesake, Mont St. Michel (across the Channel in Normandy, France), and in the Middle Ages it was controlled by the Benedictine order, who built the church on the summit. After the monastery was dissolved in 1539 it was absorbed into the castle; 100 years later the complex became Saint Aubyn's family residence, as it still is today. Guided tours take you around the intriguing maze of rooms, which have been much altered through the centuries.

The resort of **Penzance** looks across Mount's Bay to the island, and has pleasant Georgian areas, such as Chapel Street, where you can also see the riotously styled Egyptian House and visit the out-of-the-ordinary maritime museum, with a walk-through section of a man o' war. The National Lighthouse Centre tells you all you could possibly want to know about the guardians of the entire coast of Britain.

Mousehole (pronounced "Mouzal"), with its granite houses and working harbor, presents a very pretty scene, as does **Lamorna's** handful of cottages, tiny harbor and rocky beach. Cliffside, open-air **Minack Theatre**, with the ocean as its backdrop, is spectacularly sited. Shows are presented from May through September (for details tel. 01736 810471).

Each year over one million visitors journey to **Land's End** ★ ★ ★, mainland Britain's southwest tip. Come at sunset or in clear weather, when you can spot the offshore lighthouses and maybe even the Isles of Scilly, 28 miles out to sea. Don't worry about the crowds or the insensitivity of a

theme park being sited here: you can leave them all behind on a short walk along the cliffs.

Sennen Cove gives access to Whitesand Bay, the best beach in the area, while more striking cliff vistas unfold around the northern shores of the peninsula, such as at Cape Cornwall. The church at **Zennor** is famous for its mermaid carved onto a bench end. The story goes that she lured a squire's son to the murky depths.

Fishing port, beach resort and artists' colony, **St. Ives** ★ ★ ★ is appealing for many different reasons. It is easy to see how its various faces, from the colorful harbor to the atmospheric, narrow back streets and alleys, to a trio of lovely sandy beaches, could be the source of artistic inspiration. The St. Ives School developed in the late 1930s around sculptor Barbara Hepworth and painter Ben Nicholson, leading figures in the development of British abstract art. Today, you can browse among contemporary works at many galleries. Hepworth's studio and garden is now a museum dedicated to her sculpture. The **Tate Gallery St. Ives** displays more works of the St. Ives School in a setting that makes the most of its position above Porthmeor Beach.

Prehistoric remains are scattered thoughout inland Penwith. If you visit just one, go to **Chysauster** (EH), the best-preserved Iron Age hamlet in Cornwall, showing excavated houses opening off a central courtyard. **Carn Euny** has an example of a "fogou," a passage whose significance is uncertain; **Chûn Castle** is an Iron Age fort; Lanyon Quoit is a Bronze Age burial chamber; and **Men-an-Tol** is a stone with a hole which was thought to relieve infertility in those who crawled through it.

NAVY CITY

Plymouth actually means "the navy," and special navy days are held every other year in August.

These give the public the rare chance of going on board vessels as well as seeing exciting air displays and events taking place on the river.

Sir Francis Drake was the first Englishman to sail around the world. He is best known for his great victory over the Spanish Armada, although the weather played a major part in this achievement as a third of the Spanish fleet was shipwrecked! ■

★ PLYMOUTH and the RIVER TAMAR , DEVON   *52C1*

Since the 16th century, Plymouth's vast natural harbor has played a significant role in Britain's maritime affairs. Sir Francis Drake sailed from Plymouth to defeat the Spanish Armada; its harbor was the last port of call for the Pilgrim Fathers on their way to America; centuries later, it was one of the embarkation points for American troops for the D-day landings, and for the British fleet in 1982 on its way to the Falkland Islands. Bomb damage during World War II decimated the city, but the cobbled streets and timber-framed houses of an old district called the **Barbican**, west of Sutton Harbour, escaped damage; a plaque here commemorates the Pilgrims' departure.

Nearer the center, the **Merchant's House** is a particularly fine timber building and a local museum. The promenade of the **Hoe**, where Drake famously refused to allow the sight of the Spanish fleet to disrupt his game of bowls, commands the best views over the nautical comings and goings in Plymouth Sound; alongside are an excellent **aquarium**, a vast 17th-century **citadel** (EH) and **Plymouth Dome**, a high-tech introduction to the city.

Boat trips from Plymouth visit the **Royal Naval Dockyard**, go up the **River Tamar**, and cross the Sound to the relatively uncommercialized villages of **Kingsand** and **Cawsand**. **Antony House** (NT), on the Tamar's west bank, is a fine classical mansion, finished in 1721.

Upstream, the absorbing, fortified medieval manor of **Cotehele** (NT) has altered remarkably little over the centuries, and neither have its estate workshops; alongside the quay rests the last surviving Tamar barge. The quay at **Morwellham**, once a busy copper-loading port, now forms part of an industrial museum.

Buckland Abbey (NT) was built by Cistercian monks in 1278, but was converted into a lavish secular dwelling by Sir Richard Grenville, who then sold it to Sir Francis Drake in 1581. The house has some relics from Drake's famous ship, *The Golden Hind*, such as his drum and banners.

PURBECK, ISLE OF DORSET   *53F2*

This promontory of Dorset downs and heathland is an island only by name. Its chief sight is **Corfe Castle** (NT), a jumble of jagged Norman graystone ruins set dramatically on a hilltop. It survived a long siege in the English Civil War, after which the Parliamentarians under Oliver Cromwell used mines and gunpowder to blow it up.

On the coast north of the resort of Swanage stand the chalk stacks of the **Old Harry Rocks**, and the long, dune-backed sandy beaches of **Studland Bay**. West of Swanage, beyond the steep streets and stone cottages of pretty **Worth Matravers**, a simple Norman chapel stands on the lofty clifftop of **St. Aldhelm's Head**. The army uses a swathe of coastline west of Kimmeridge as a firing range, though access is usually possible at weekends. Inland, at Bovington Camp near Wareham, the **Tank Museum** displays more than 250 fighting vehicles from around the world.

The popular beauty spot of **Lulworth Cove** is a fine example of the sea winning its battle against the cliffs, which in this case are made of crumbly chalk. At **Durdle Door**, the sea has gnawed away to form a spectacular natural arch.

In 1789, King George III braved the waters at **Weymouth** in a bathing machine as the band played *God Save The King*, setting the Georgian tone for this traditional, yet gentrified resort and attractive port. Its outstanding attraction is the **Time Walk Museum**, set in an old brewery, where the town's nautical history is given life in a series of multi-sensory tableaux.

★ QUANTOCK HILLS
SOMERSET   53D3

This moorland plateau of thickly wooded slopes, wild ponies and resident red deer, has much in common with its western neighbor, Exmoor. A dense, confusing maze of narrow, high-hedged lanes surround the slopes and, as testament to a time when the wool trade brought prosperity, manor houses and fine churches dominate the sleepy, red sandstone villages.

Some churches, such as those at **Broomfield, Spaxton, Crowcombe** and **Bicknoller**, have beautiful 16th-century carvings on the ends of the pews.

The poet Samuel Taylor Coleridge lived in a cottage (NT) in **Nether Stowey** from 1797 to 1800, during which time he wrote *The Rime of the Ancient Mariner*. The cottage now contains some of his mementoes and early editions of his work. William Wordsworth and his sister Dorothy came to keep him company, staying at Alfoxton Park in the neighboring village of **Holford**. Setting off from Bishop's Lydeard (near Taunton), the steam and diesel trains of the **West Somerset Railway** pass through here on their way to Minehead. Just south of Watchet, the remains of Cistercian **Cleeve Abbey** are distinctive for having so much of their living quarters still standing.

Corfe Castle stands on the site of a hunting lodge where Edward the Martyr was killed in 978. The castle itself was reduced to the ruins you see today by Oliver Cromwell's forces during the English Civil War

THE SALISBURY GIANT

This is a large wooden replica of a man, and was used in the days when the guilds used to march in procession on worthy civic occasions along with the Merchant Tailors.

They called the giant Saint Christopher and would parade him with pride accompanied by his sword and mace-bearers, morris dancers and a hobby horse named Hob-Nob.

They can be viewed at the Salisbury and South Wiltshire Museum, housed in the King's House (see opposite) ∎

SALCOMBE and AROUND, DEVON   53C1

Many visitors to this civilized little yachting mecca come in their own boats, but you can rent a craft to explore the peaceful, tentacled **Salcombe** estuary or take the ferry up to **Kingsbridge**.

Overbecks (NT), on the outskirts, is an Edwardian house named after a research pharmacist who lived here in the 1930s. It has a glorious subtropical garden high above the mouth of the estuary. The south-facing coastline either side of the estuary delights in majestic **cliffs**, generally accessible only on foot. To the west, around Bigbury Bay, the villages of **Hope**, **Thurlestone** and diminutive **Bantham** are of picture-postcard quality: thatched cottages are a common sight, and the beaches are wide and golden.

On the western side of the River Avon, when the tide prevents you from walking across the sands to **Burgh Island**, climb aboard the amphibious tractor. The views from the top of the island are superb, cocktails await in the sumptuous art-deco hotel, and a pint of beer beckons in the Pilchard Inn, a 14th-century smugglers' haunt.

★★★ SALISBURY   53F3
WILTSHIRE

Salisbury **Cathedral's** spire is the tallest in the country. Rising above the water-meadows, as painted by John Constable, it is a classic image of England. The cathedral was built in just 40 years, beginning in 1220, although the 404-foot spire dates from the 14th century. As a result, its Gothic style is remarkably uniform. An 18th-century architect named James Wyatt denuded the interior of much of its decoration, and his ruthlessness earned him the

sobriquet "the Destroyer." Yet there is much to see: England's oldest functioning clock, roof tours up to the base of the spire, and a memorable medieval frieze of Old Testament stories in the chapter house. The library over the cloisters contains the best preserved of the four surviving manuscripts of the Magna Carta, the famous charter of rights signed by King John in 1215.

Wyatt's posthumous reputation is salvaged by his design for the largest cathedral **close** in England, a lovely ensemble of lawns, mature trees and softly colored stone and brick houses from the 14th to 18th centuries. Some have been converted into museums: the medieval **King's House** has prehistoric exhibits from Stonehenge, the 13th-century **Wardrobe** house holds a regimental museum, and the Queen Anne **Mompesson House** (NT) offers a remarkable display of English drinking glasses.

Stonehenge (see p.78) is probably the best-known prehistoric monument in the world; it certainly does have a particular grandeur.

Beyond the close, the streets with half-timbered houses are also worth exploring.

Magnificent **Wilton House**, 3 miles west, is at its most dazzling in its state apartments, fashioned by Inigo Jones in the mid-17th century. Most memorable is the utterly grand Double Cube Room, specially designed for its collection of Van Dyck portraits.

★★ SCILLY, ISLES OF 52A3

The archipelago of the Scilly Isles, 28 miles west of Land's End, numbers around 150 islands, but only five are inhabited by people; many others are home to colonies of seals and seabirds. These islands share a mild yet windbeaten climate, lovely white beaches, clean, yet chilly seas, much birdlife and a profusion of flowers, both wild and commercially grown daffodils and narcissi. Otherwise, they are distinctively individual.

Most people live on **St. Mary's**, at up to 3 miles wide the largest island. Passenger launches depart for the other islands from the little capital, Hugh Town. Star Castle, now a hotel, was built in Tudor times against the Spanish and can be explored. Paths allow you to follow the bays and headlands of the beautiful coastline – Peninnis Head is the most dramatic feature – and to search out the many prehistoric burial chambers further inland. **Tresco** is a car-free private estate, with forts and pristine beaches, but its main draw is the subtropical garden around the remains of an abbey, home to many plant species unique in Britain. Treeless, gorse-covered **St. Martin's** has spectacular golden beaches and a sailing and scuba-diving school. A 17th-century lighthouse towers over **St. Agnes**, the smallest inhabited isle; a maze of pebbles said to have been laid out in 1729 by a lighthouse keeper with time on his hands. **Bryher** is the least populated and wildest of the

ISLAND HOPPING

The Scilly Isles, situated west of Land's End, can be reached by helicopter from Penzance heliport, by airplane from Land's End aerodrome, or by a 2½-hour boat journey to St. Mary's.

There is a good boat service between all the other islands ■

STONEHENGE – THE STRUCTURE

The sheer size of Stonehenge can only really be appreciated up close.

Thirty giant stones form a circle which measures 108 feet across.

A second circle of 16 stones stands within that, and a horseshoe of 10 stones within that. Right in the middle is another horseshoe of 19 stones, and at the heart lies the great "altar stone."

The stones weigh around 4 tonnes each and the gigantic sarsen stones weigh between 25 to 50 tonnes! How they got there is anybody's guess! ∎

group. Its west coast, with place names like Hell Bay, bears the full brunt of the Atlantic.

There are a number of ways to reach the islands: a 2½-hour boat trip; a 20-minute helicopter ride from Penzance; or a 15-minute fixed-wing flight from St. Just Aerodrome near Land's End, or from Newquay, Exeter or Bristol.

★★★ STONEHENGE 53F3 WILTSHIRE (EH)

This circle of vast, standing stones in the midst of the chalk downlands of Salisbury Plain (off the main A303 road) is probably the most famous prehistoric monument in Europe. Despite poor facilities, no direct access to the stones themselves, and absolutely hordes of visitors, the sight is still unforgettable.

It is known that the monument originally formed just a bank and ditch around 2800 BC. Some 700 years later, so-called bluestones from south Wales, either brought by man or by Ice Age glaciers to Wiltshire, were erected in a double ring. Between 2000 BC and 1500 BC the structure was rearranged into the form that it resembles today, with a circle of sarsen stones around a horse-shoe of bluestones.

The site aligns with the midsummer sunrise, suggesting it had astronomical and calendrical significance, while the many nearby burial mounds attest to its sacredness. Each year around the summer solstice many people, including Druids and New Age Travelers, are refused access to the site and for several years pitched battles with the police have ensued. Despite a plethora of theories to explain the stones' significance – more fanciful ones suggest a bird trap, a model of the solar system or an inspiration from outer space – Stonehenge remains a mystery.

★★ STOURHEAD 53E3 WILTSHIRE

Stourhead's grounds (NT) are a masterpiece of landscape design. They were begun in the 1740s by Henry Hoare after he had been inspired by travels in Italy and the Arcadian vistas of classical paintings. Around an artificial lake lie temples, rotundas, bridges, grottoes and magnificent trees, all arranged to be seen from particular viewpoints. The Palladian mansion plays second fiddle, but has Chippendale furniture specifically designed for the house.

WELLS, SOMERSET 53E3

Many believe the 800-year-old tiny cathedral ★★★ of this Somerset city to be the most beautiful in England. The most outstanding feature is its west front, a huge screen adorned with some 300 angels, saints and kings. This unparalleled concentration of medieval sculpture would have looked even more spectacular at the time, when it was vividly painted. The interior's highlights include the colossal, innovative "scissor arches" which support the tower, a remarkable 14th-century astronomical clock, fascinating secular carvings on the capitals and corbels, and an octagonal chapter house supported by a palm-like pillar at the top of centuries-old stone stairs.

The fortified 13th-century residence of the Bishop of Bath and Wells, the **Bishop's Palace**, is sometimes open. In the surrounding moat, by the draw-bridge, swans traditionally rang a bell with their beaks at feeding time. Among Wells' handsome streets of old limestone houses, **Vicar's Close** is the pick of the bunch, cobbled and lined with 14th-century cottages in which the clergy used to live.

SOUTH &
SOUTHEAST
ENGLAND

Home to the world's largest
inhabited castle, the south of
England has always been alluring
with its mild climate, venerable
cathedrals of old, seaside piers,
stately homes and even vineyards
and fruit orchards

CALENDAR OF EVENTS

THROUGHOUT THE YEAR –
New Forest Round-ups. The wild ponies in the New Forest are rounded up by the local people for health checks.

FEBRUARY –
Pancake Race, Olney, Buckinghamshire. It has been a tradition since 1445 to race with a pancake in a pan between the market place and the church.

MAY TO JUNE –
Dickens Festival, Rochester, Kent. The locals take to the streets to celebrate the famous novelist's love affair with the city.

FIRST WEEK OF JULY –
Henley Royal Regatta. One of Britain's most famous and prestigious boating events. It's one of the places at which to be seen on the "social" calendar.

EARLY NOVEMBER –
London to Brighton Car Run. Cars built before 1904 start in Hyde Park and attempt to make it to the finish at Brighton ∎

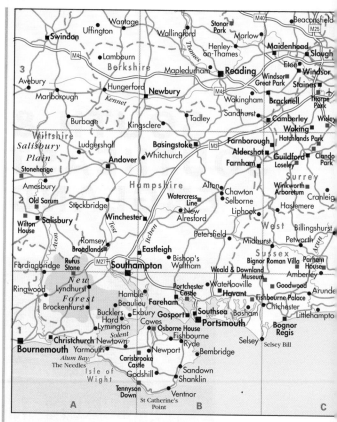

SOUTH AND SOUTHEAST ENGLAND

The southeast of England is the tamest part of Britain – affluent and heavily populated. Its countryside, with its undulating patchwork fields, seduces rather than stuns. The same can be said of its coastline, in the main a long necklace of traditional seaside resorts and busy ports. But the region does have its magnificent castles, stately homes and dazzling gardens, as well as several small historic cities, like Canterbury, Winchester and Chichester.

You can visit many of the region's most popular places on a

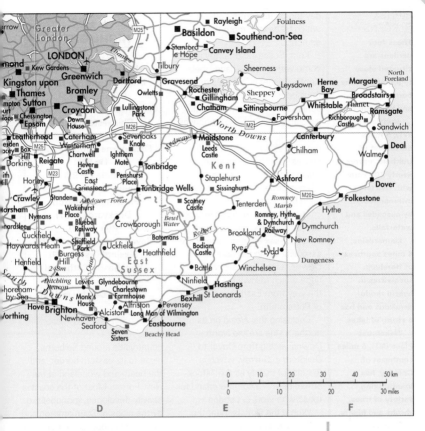

The red-brick and tiled oast houses of Kent were originally added to farmhouses and used to dry the hop crop. Many today have been rebuilt and converted into interesting houses

SOUTH AND SOUTHEAST ENGLAND

SUSSEX GARDENS

These four gardens are situated close together near the borders of East and West Sussex.

Sheffield Park (NT), 5 miles northwest of Uckfield, covers nearly 200 acres, with five lakes interconnected by cascades and waterfalls.

Leonardslee, 4 miles southeast of Horsham, specializes in hybrid rhodo-dendrons and has a string of lakes.

Wakehurst Place (NT), 5 miles southeast of Crawley, has a breathtaking variety of trees, shrubs and plants, arranged geo-graphically.

Nymans (NT), 5 miles south of Crawley, has a series of inter-linked gardens designed by Gertrude Jekyll ■

day-trip by train from London, which takes little more than an hour.

Kent, Sussex and Surrey all come with a ready-made label. Kent's epithet is "The Garden of England," for here you'll find apple orchards, hop fields and vineyards, as well as oast houses, built as kilns to dry the hops, but now often converted into homes. Kent lies in an area called the Weald, offering pretty villages of timber-framed, pantile-hung buildings.

The Weald extends seamlessly into Sussex, though East and West Sussex are more scenically associated with the South Downs, a long, grassy, chalk ridge which follows the coast all the way from Eastbourne to north of Portsmouth.

Enclosing the Weald on its northern side are the North Downs, arcing from Dover to Guildford in Surrey, which is thought of mainly as the "stock-broker belt" – a commuterland for those who work in London.

Where the Downs meet the sea near Eastbourne and at Dover, the coastline is dramatic and unspoiled. More typical, however, is the continuous trawl of old-fashioned resorts along the Sussex coast; good places to spy on the eccentricities of the English at leisure. Also, since this coast was the first stop for invading Romans and Normans, there are fortifications from nearly every era in the last 2,000 years.

Berkshire, west of London, is not the most interesting of counties save for the famous castle at Windsor (see p.104) and the famous school at Eton (see p.104), across the river. It also shares the Thames with Bucking-hamshire and Oxfordshire.

As for Hampshire, there are pockets of real rural beauty to discover here, such as the

---

★★★ HIGHLIGHTS

Beachy Head (► 93)
Brighton and the Royal Pavilion (► 85)
Canterbury Cathedral (► 86)
Chichester (► 88)
Eton College (► 104)
Fishbourne Roman Palace (► 89)
Knole (► 93)
Leeds Castle (► 94)
Portsmouth Historic Dockyard (► 97)
Rye (► 98)
Seven Sisters cliffs (► 93)
Sissinghurst (► 99)
Winchester Cathedral (► 102)
Windsor Castle (► 104)

---

countryside around Selborne, close to its eastern border, and the heath and woodland of the New Forest. Most of the coast is heavily developed, monopolized by the cities of Southampton and Portsmouth, both great maritime centers. Portsmouth, with its historic dockyard, is considerably more appealing, but Southampton is a thriving university city with a busy commerical port.

The Isle of Wight, a brief ferry or hovercraft ride from the mainland, is a tranquil vacation island with sedate resorts, clifftop walks and a world-famous sailing scene for yachting aficionados.

★★ ARUNDEL and AROUND, WEST SUSSEX   80C1

Guarding a gap in the South Downs created by the River Arun, fairytale Arundel Castle, its heavy, gray walls medieval in origin, but Victorian in appearance, dominates this handsome town, along with a neo-Gothic, Catholic cathedral.

The castle's grand state apartments hold a fine collection of furniture and portraits. For over 700 years it has been the seat of the dukes of Norfolk, the country's leading Catholic laymen. The parish church, on the boundary of the castle grounds, contains the dukes' private, **Fitzalan Chapel**. At one time it was separated from the rest of the church by brickwork, but now an iron grille does the job. Just north of town, over a thousand species of wildfowl reside in the riverside reeds and ponds in a **nature reserve**.

wildfowl habitats. A blacksmith, potter, printer and boatbuilder – traditional local industries – work with old-fashioned tools in the open-air **Amberley Museum**; there's also a narrow-gauge railway, and steam engines and vintage buses to view.

At the foot of the Downs, east of Amberley, **Parham** is a lovely Elizabethan mansion set in a sweeping deer park. Most impressive are the splendidly proportioned Great Hall, its 160-foot Long Gallery, and its fine displays of paintings, furniture and needlework.

Arundel Castle, which rears above the village below, was originally founded as far back as the 10th century; a 12th-century keep remains, but the majority of the present-day castle was rebuilt from ruins in the 19th century

Amberley, to the north, is one of the loveliest villages of the South Downs, a charming hodgepodge of vernacular dwellings in old stone, flint, timber and thatch behind creeper-hung walls and cottage gardens. Next to its ruined castle (now a luxury hotel) lie the water-meadows of **Amberley Wild Brooks**, protected for their

Bignor Roman Villa, north west of Amberley, was discovered in 1811 by a tilling plowman. This farm estate, though less grand than that at nearby Fishbourne (see p.89), sits in a prettier position at the foot of the Downs, and has even more impressive mosaics, set under attractive thatched and white-washed cottages.

SOUTH AND SOUTHEAST ENGLAND

WALKS

THE SOUTHEAST COAST

There are pleasant walks along the cliffs east of Hastings to Fairlight Cove. Continuing eastward, you could walk across Romney Marsh along the Royal Military Canal close to the line of the original coastline, and more clifftop walking beckons from Dover along to Deal.

West of Eastbourne, the coastline is unremittingly built up until you reach Chichester Harbour, whose sand dunes and salt marshes are at their best around East Head near West Wittering. (See also The South Downs Way walk on p.93) ∎

★ BATTLE, HASTINGS 81E2/81E1
and PEVENSEY 81D1
EAST SUSSEX

Battle's name derives from the most famous scrap fought on English soil, the Battle of Hastings. William, Duke of Normandy defeated King Harold here in 1066 and thereby changed the course of English history. William celebrated his victory by building **St. Martin's Abbey** (EH). Its high altar is supposed to stand on the site where Harold fell. According to an interpretation on the 11th-century Bayeux Tapestry, on show in Bayeux in Normandy, France, he was pierced in the eye by an arrow. The substantial abbey ruins, which postdate William's works, house a museum on the history of the site. Plans, placed at significant points over the **battlefield**, outline the course of the engagement.

Hastings is a mix of fishing port and unpretentious resort. Fishermen winch their boats onto the shingle beach below tall black sheds called *deezes*, where their nets are stored. Behind, weatherboard houses on narrow alleys characterize the **old town**. A Victorian funicular railway takes you up to the ruins of a massive castle built by William, where the events of the Norman invasion unfold in **The Story of 1066,** housed in a fake siege tent. The animated figures of the **Smugglers' Adventure**, set in caves once used for storing contraband, are also entertaining. The adjoining Regency resort of **St. Leonards** is a must for those with a fondness for backstreet antique shops.

Pevensey, further down the coast, was where William landed. Here, his half-brother Robert built a **castle** (EH) with a moat and keep within the existing walls of a 4th-century Roman fort.

★★ BLUEBELL RAILWAY 81D2
WEST SUSSEX

Steam trains pulling Victorian carriages puff their way along the 9 miles of track from Sheffield Park (see panel p.82) to Horsted Keynes and on to Kingscote. The trip is especially lovely in late spring when bluebells cover the countryside.

This was the first of many standard-gauge steam railways in the country to be reopened for tourists. The stations have been restored to their Victorian glory, complete with period advertising, fire buckets and gas lamps, and they also have on show a large collection of old locomotives.

★★★ BRIGHTON 81D1
EAST SUSSEX

In the middle of the 18th century, Dr. Richard Russell published a book proclaiming the virtues of sea bathing at the fishing village of Brighthelmstone. The upper classes took to the waters in bizarre bathing contraptions. The raffish Prince Regent, who

became King George IV, visited first in 1783. By the end of the century, thanks to royal patronage, Brighthelmstone had become Brighton, "the most frequented and, without exception, one of the most fashionable towns in the kingdom." W.M. Thackeray in *Vanity Fair* called it "a clean Naples ... that always looks brisk, gay and gaudy, like a harlequin's jacket." With the arrival of the railway in 1841, day-trippers of all classes could afford to visit. The town earned the nickname of "London-by-the-Sea" and a reputation as the classic rendezvous for adulterers.

The Brighton of today is a mix of traditional seaside resort, elegant well-to-do Regency town, major conference venue, and a top nightclubbing scene. Each May a broad-ranging, eclectic international arts festival takes place, The **seafront** is the place to come for fish and chips and a snooze in a deckchair. Poking out of the shingle beach is the decrepit West Pier and the quarter-mile-long **Palace Pier**, with souvenir stalls, fortune-tellers, fairground rides and the **Sea Life Centre**, an excellent aquarium. Volk's Electric Railway takes you along the seafront.

Behind the front lie some handsome Regency terraces, such as **Regency Square**, **Brunswick Square** in adjoining Hove, and in the planned streets of **Kemp Town**.

The Regency period's *pièce de résistance* is the **Royal Pavilion ★ ★ ★**, one of Britain's most inventive and enjoyable pieces of architecture. The **Brighton Art Gallery and Museum**, in the pavilion's old royal stables, has a superb collection of art-deco and art-nouveau furniture and furnishings.

Close by, the brick-paved alleyways of the original fishing village are known as **The Lanes**. Here you'll find ritzy galleries, jewelry and antique stores, open-air cafés and several of the town's 400 restaurants.

ROYAL PAVILION

This extraordinary pleasure palace, converted for the Prince Regent from the bones of an ordinary farmhouse by the architect John Nash, is in a loose pastiche of Chinese and Indian styles.

A riot of domes and minarets determines its unmistakable outline – "like a collection of stone pumpkins and pepperpots," according to the essayist William Hazlitt ■

The Royal Pavilion at Brighton, which was originally built between 1784 and 1820, has recently been restored, allowing the brilliant coloring, gilt and chandeliers to shine once again

WALK

AROUND CANTERBURY

Start at Christ Church Gate, head down medieval Mercery Lane and cross over High Street to St. Margaret's Street. Canterbury Tales relives Chaucer's works in tableaux, while Hawk's Lane leads to the Heritage Museum, a high-tech look at 2,000 years of history. Back on High Street, Eastbridge Hospital is where medieval pilgrims stayed. Take St. Peter's Street across the river to the Tudor houses built for Huguenot refugees. Across the end of the street, West Gate (in the city walls) holds a display of arms and armor ■

The great central tower of Canterbury Cathedral is known as Bell Harry Tower or Angel Steeple and was added between 1495 and 1503; many of the stained-glass windows date from the 12th and 15th centuries

CANTERBURY, KENT   81F3

Canterbury has been the center of the English Church since AD 597 when Saint Augustine converted King Ethelbert of Kent to Christianity and subsequently became the first archbishop. The cathedral became a center of pilgrimage after Thomas à Becket was murdered under its roof in 1170, by assassins who had misinterpreted King Henry II's plea: "Will no one rid me of this turbulent priest?"

Pilgrims came from all over Europe to seek miraculous cures at the tomb of the sanctified Becket, some from the Tabard Inn in Southwark (now part of London), as recounted in Chaucer's *Canterbury Tales*, where each tells a story to enliven the journey.

Though the city was heavily damaged in 1942 by an air raid and a rash of ugly postwar buildings sprang up, there is much of historical interest in the center. A number of museums bring to life the city's history in an entertaining fashion.

The great **cathedral ★ ★ ★** managed to avoid wartime damage. The present church was originally built by Lanfranc, the first Norman archbishop, but with the aid of revenues from pilgrims it grew considerably in the next 300 years in a variety of architectural styles. In the northwest transept a simple memorial marks the site where Becket was murdered. The martyr's shrine, in the Trinity Chapel, was destroyed by Henry VIII, but notice how the steps up to the chapel have been worn over the centuries by pilgrims' knees. Here, also are the magnificent tombs of Henry IV and the Black Prince.

In addition, it is worth seeking out the Norman crypt for the carvings and items from the cathedral treasury, along with the cloisters and monastic buildings. The adjacent **King's School** was founded on the site of a 7th-century monastery and the Elizabethan playwright Christopher Marlowe was a pupil.

As well as the sights covered in the walk around Canterbury (see opposite), you should also visit the **Roman Museum** in Butchery Lane, with reconstructions of Roman buildings and displays of swords, silver spoons and other artifacts. Just beyond the ancient **city walls,** east of the city center, stands **St. Augustine's Abbey** (EH). It was established by the saint in 597; foundations of a later Norman church and medieval monastery are apparent. Further on, you'll come to **St. Martin's Church** which was in use even before Saint Augustine arrived on the scene.

If you've come to the city in your own vehicle, drive on to **Chilham,** 6 miles southwest of Canterbury. The half-timbered Tudor and Jacobean houses surrounding its square make it one of Kent's showpiece villages. The castle, a combination of 17th-century mansion and Norman keep, hosts medieval banquets and jousting and falconry displays in the summer.

★★ CHARTWELL, KENT   81D2

Sir Winston Churchill lived at Chartwell (NT) from 1924 until his death in 1965. It is not grand, but more of a comfortable, country home. His rooms, such as the study where he wrote much of his historical and autobiographical work, remain largely as he left them. There is a plethora of the statesman's possessions, from walking sticks and uniforms to his paintings in the garden studio

The National Trust enforces timed ticketing in summer to alleviate long lines.

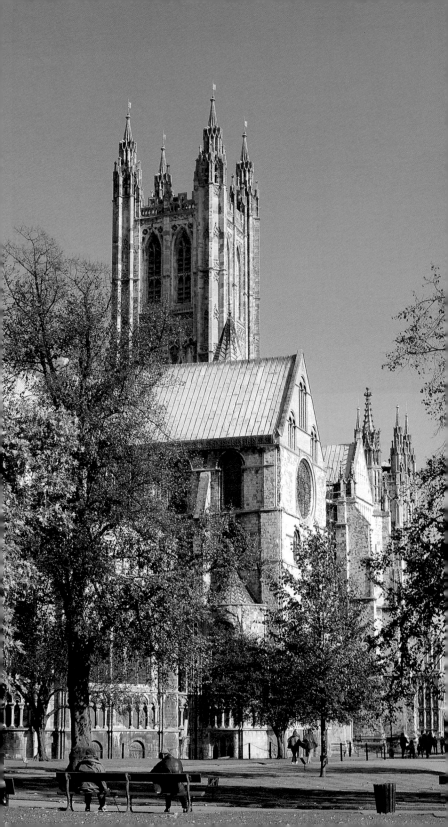

The idyllic Hampshire village of Selborne, seen from The Hanger, a vantage point on the Downs

THE TIDES AT BOSHAM

Locals say that it was on the shores of Bosham that the Danish King Canute (994–1035) proved his inability to control the waves. The evidence that he was here, they say, lies in the fact that his daughter is buried in the lovely Saxon and Norman church ■

CHAWTON and SELBORNE, HAMPSHIRE

80B2

The novelist Jane Austen lived for most of the last years of her life, from 1809 to 1817, in a modest, red-brick house in the attractive little village of **Chawton**. Here she wrote *Mansfield Park*, *Emma* and *Persuasion*. Today, the house is furnished in appropriate early 19th-century style and has many of the author's possessions, such as a homemade patchwork quilt, desk and bureau, and, in the bakehouse, the donkey cart on which she rode to town.

Beech trees and mellow stone cottages distinguish the village of **Selborne**, a little further south. It was the home of the naturalist, Reverend Gilbert White. In 1789 he finished *The Natural History and Antiquities of Selborne*, a wonderfully evocative field study of an unassuming corner of rural England. His house, the Wakes, has been preserved as a memorial to him.

★★★ CHICHESTER and AROUND, WEST SUSSEX

80C1

Chichester, a prosperous port in the 1700s, is still today a lovely Georgian town. Yet it is laid out on the original Roman streets, which meet at a fine 16th-century market cross (or Butter Cross). The Georgian streetscape is best seen in the area called **the Pallants. Pallant House** is a gallery specializing in modern British art.

Other places worth seeking out are the medieval **St. Mary's Hospital** in St. Martin's Square, converted into its present use as almshouses for the aged poor in the 16th century, and the **Mechanical Music and Doll Collection**, for its operational, quirky machines.

The largely Norman **cathedral** is remarkable for its detached bell tower, unique in England, and for a pair of sculpted Romanesque stone panels. Its notable 20th-century artworks include a painting by Graham Sutherland, a tapestry by John Piper and a stained-glass window by Chagall. Every summer the town hosts a drama festival of high repute.

The most interesting of the many sightseeing options outside Chichester is the largest and richest Roman palace yet found in Britain, at **Fishbourne ★★★**. Discovered in 1960 by a trenchdigger, it is thought to have been the home of one Cogidubnus, a pro-Roman British king. You can study at close quarters the splendid mosaics and the underfloor heating system, while the gardens have been laid out and planted with interesting species in keeping with Roman times.

Southwest of the town, within the yachting haven and marshy inlets of Chichester Harbour, lies the pretty village of **Bosham**. Its waterside brick cottages and sheltered waters make for a much-painted scene and a magnet for retired yachtsmen.

Inland, in wooded parkland, the 18th-century, flint **Goodwood House** is a treasure trove of porcelain, tapestries, furniture and fine art, notably by Van Dyck, Reynolds and Canaletto. The equine studies by Stubbs are appropriate for a house whose fame is overshadowed by the racecourse on the downs above. Known as Glorious Goodwood, it is for many the most beautiful racecourse in the country.

Not far away, near Singleton, 35 local buildings dating from medieval to Victorian times have been rescued and re-erected at the **Weald and Downland Open Air Museum**. They include a farmhouse, school, blacksmith's, watermill and even a charcoal burner's hut. In summer, you can watch demonstrations of traditional crafts and farming.

★ DOVER, DEAL and WALMER, KENT   *81F2*

To millions of vacationers, **Dover** is no more than a large, workaday port below white cliffs, which constitute an evocative first and last sight of Britain. While wartime bombs deprived the town of much charm, it has been the most significant cross-Channel port since Roman times and there are a number of interesting historical sights. Magnificent **Dover Castle** (EH) looks out to France, just 17 miles away and easily visible on a clear day. Its 12th-century keep, built by Henry II, is surrounded by Victorian barracks and ramparts. In the complex of tunnels underneath, called Hellfire Corner, the evacuation of troops from Dunkirk in 1940 was masterminded. Within the castle walls is the shell of the **pharos**, a Roman lighthouse used as a bell tower by the Saxon church of **St. Mary de Castro**.

In the town center, the **Roman Painted House** has a central heating system, and the oldest, best-preserved wall paintings north of the Alps. Also diverting are the **White Cliffs Experience**, a high-tech history lesson on the port, and the **Old Town Gaol**, a re-creation of Victorian prison life using televisual talking heads.

Deal, 8 miles along the coast, is a low-key town with a shingle beach, pier and old fisherman's quarter. Henry VIII built **Deal Castle** (EH), in the shape of a Tudor rose, along with over 20 other forts on the southeast coast; an exhibition inside tells why. One of the others was **Walmer Castle** (EH), which was converted into a stately home in the 18th century as the residence of the Lord Warden of the Cinque Ports. The Duke of Wellington died here, and a number of his possessions are on display.

THE CHANNEL TUNNEL

The Chunnel was first mooted back in 1802, designed with air shafts protruding above the waves.

Digging actually began in 1882 at both the English and French ends, but was abandoned because of British security fears.

Work was again halted in the 1970s on economic grounds, and the present project, begun in 1987, was completed in 1994 at a cost of £10 billion ($15 billion).

You can now take your car through the tunnel on *Le Shuttle* between Folkestone and Calais, or take a non-stop Eurostar passenger train from London Waterloo to Paris, Lille and Brussels.

The Eurotunnel Exhibition Centre at Folkestone has an overview ■

DRIVE

THE BEST OF THE WEALD

122 miles (allow 3 days)

In the "Garden of England," gentle valleys, woods and even vineyards compete for attention with tile-hung, clapboard houses, as well as a wealth of fine buildings with fascinating historical and literary associations, and a number of glorious gardens.

HEVER CASTLE FACTS

Henry II, who ruled between 1154 and 1189, ordered that no baron was allowed to build a castle without permission from the king.

In 1272, Sir Stephen de Penchester obtained a license to convert his house at Hever to a castle.

Further alterations were made by William de Hever around 1340. The castle was bought by the Boleyn family in 1462 and was the scene of King Henry VIII's courtship of Anne Boleyn. Its delightful grounds include an Italian walled garden that is filled with sculpture ∎

Leave Tunbridge Wells on the A264, then take the B2188 north to the village of Penshurst.

1 Penshurst, Kent

Penshurst Place (see p.101), complete with lovely walled gardens, stands in this pretty village of neo-Tudor cottages.

Take the road past the church and follow the B2176, turn left on the B2027 and follow unclassified roads for 6 miles to Hever.

2 Hever, Kent

Chiddingstone, just east of Hever, has delightful overhanging and beamed buildings along its main street. Its castle was remodeled in the Gothic style in the 19th century. At 16th-century **Haxted Mill**, west of Edenbridge, you can see working waterwheels and mill machinery.

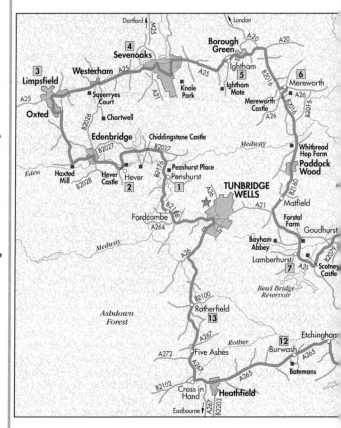

*From Haxted Mill take
unclassified roads north
to Limpsfield.*

3 Limpsfield, Surrey

The composer Frederick Delius is
buried in the churchyard here,
and there is the lovely 15th-
century hall house, De Tillens.

Two miles east is **Quebec
House** in Westerham, General
Wolfe's childhood home. There is
more Wolfe memorabilia at
nearby **Squerryes Court**, a
William and Mary house.

For much of his life, Winston
Churchill lived at **Chartwell** (NT,
see p.86), 2 miles south of
Westerham.

*Follow the A25
to Sevenoaks.*

4 Sevenoaks, Kent

Knole (NT, see p.93) is the
largest private house in England.

*Leave Sevenoaks on the
A225, and rejoin the A25
to Ightham.*

5 Ightham, Kent

Pronounced "item," the village
has half-timbered, medieval
cottages and an old oast house,
forge, coaching inn and church.
Ightham Mote (NT, see p.94) lies
2½ miles south.

*Continue east on the A25
(A20), then turn south onto
the B2016, turning east
for Mereworth.*

6 Mereworth, Kent

The original village of Mereworth
was destroyed by Lord West-
moreland to make way for his
opulent **castle** (no admittance,
privately owned), built in the early
1700s as a copy of a Palladian
villa in Italy. The village church is
built in matching style.

South on the way to Lamberhurst, the **Whitbread Hop Farm**
at Beltring has craft workshops in
Victorian oast houses, and tells
the history of growing hops.

*From Mereworth return to
the B2016 via the A26.
Continue south on the
B2016, B2015, B2160
and A21 for 14 miles
to Lamberhurst.*

7 Lamberhurst, Kent

The Owl House is a half-timbered
building in lovely grounds, but the
main road disturbs the old village.

The well-preserved, 13th-
century remains of **Bayham
Abbey** (EH), 2 miles west, are
more peaceful, as are the
gardens of **Scotney Castle**
(NT) situated just south of
the village.

**FAMOUS
RESTING
PLACE**

**Admiral Lucas,
the first person
to be awarded
the Victoria
Cross, is buried
at Mereworth.**

**He won it
during the
Crimean War in
1854 for
"conspicuous
bravery in the
face of the
enemy."**

**The medal was
instituted by
Queen Victoria,
and is the
highest military
decoration
achievable ■**

WILLIAM MORRIS and EDWARD BURNE-JONES

William Morris, a Pre-Raphaelite British designer, artist and poet, started his firm of decorators and designers in 1861.

He designed stained glass, carpets and furniture and his wallpaper designs are still used today. Much of the inspiration for the 19th-century Arts and Crafts movement was drawn from his work.

Edward Burne-Jones, a painter and designer, established his reputation in an exhibition in 1877. His work for Morris included illustrating the works of Chaucer (1896) ■

From Lamberhurst continue southeast on the A21, taking the unclassified road on the left after 1½ miles, through Kilndown. Turn right on the A262 to Goudhurst. After 1½ miles turn right onto the B2085, then left to Cranbrook on meeting the A229.

8 Cranbrook, Kent

Cranbrook was a wealthy wool-making and trading center in the 15th century. It has an 18th-century working windmill. Three miles northeast are the gorgeous gardens of **Sissinghurst** (NT, see p.99).

Continue on the A262, then the A28 for 9 miles to Tenterden.

9 Tenterden, Kent

Tile and weatherboard buildings with Georgian storefronts line the high street of this lovely Wealden town. When the town was a wool-trading and shipbuilding center, the church tower was used as a beacon for ships; in the 16th century, nearby Smallhythe was its port. From 1899 to 1928 the actress Dame Ellen Terry lived in **Smallhythe Place** (NT), a half-timbered, harbormaster's house; it contains her mementoes. You can travel from Tenterden along the Rother Valley on the **Kent and East Sussex Steam Railway**.

Follow the A28 for 8 miles to Northiam.

10 Northiam, Kent

Elizabeth I is said to have stopped for breakfast under the great oak on the village green, in 1573 on her way to Rye. While there, she took off her shoes and left them behind as a memento. **Great Dixter**, ½ mile west, is a beautiful and intriguing place.

The architect Sir Edwin Lutyens enlarged the half-timbered, 15th-century manor by incorporating an old hall house, brought timber by timber from nearby. The gardens have amusing topiary.

Return towards the main road, taking the narrow road, first on the right, and follow country lanes to Bodiam.

11 Bodiam Castle, East Sussex

Robertsbridge, 5 miles southwest, is a classic Wealden village, with half-timbered, weatherboard cottages along its high street.

From Robertsbridge, follow the unclassified road past the station to Etchingham, then the A265 to Burwash.

12 Burwash, East Sussex

Brick-faced cottages and shops line the main street of this lovely village. The Weald was once a major source of iron ore and Burwash was a center for the industry. The church holds an early cast-iron tomb, and **Bateman's** (NT, see p.101) was built by a local ironmaster.

Take the A265, turning right onto the A267 past Heathfield. Turn left onto unclassified roads shortly after Five Ashes and follow signs to Rotherfield.

13 Rotherfield, East Sussex

At the edge of the Ashdown Forest, the village church contains medieval wall paintings and splendid stained glass by the Arts and Crafts duo, William Morris and Edward Burne-Jones.

Return via unclassified roads to the A26. Turn right, return to (Royal) Tunbridge Wells.

★ EASTBOURNE 81D1 and the EASTERN END OF THE SOUTH DOWNS EAST SUSSEX

Eastbourne is one of the most genteel and sedate resorts on the south coast. Popular with the elderly, its tone is set more by the bandstand and floral displays that color the 3-mile seafront above its shingle beach than by the fun and games on its lovely Victorian pier.

There is a glorious stretch of coast west of the town. The chalk cliffs at Beachy Head ★ ★ ★ rise above a small lighthouse to a dramatic 534 feet, the highest point on the south coast. Further west, switchback downland meets the sea spectacularly in abrupt chalk cliffs called the Seven Sisters ★ ★ ★. They are best seen on foot (see opposite), or from Birling Gap or Cuckmere Haven, where the river heads through water-meadows.

Inland, in the Cuckmere Valley, the village of Alfriston bustles with visitors: it has medieval timber-framed inns, flint cottages, tea and antique shops. The timbered and thatched Clergy House (NT), built for parish priests in Chaucer's time, was, in 1896, the first building to be acquired by the National Trust. Nearby, carved into the chalk of the Downs, is the Long Man of Wilmington, a 227-foot figure, probably of Anglo-Saxon origin.

★ ★ HEVER CASTLE, KENT 81D2

This manor was the home of the Bullen family, notably of Anne Boleyn (she gentrified the spelling), second wife of Henry VIII and mother of Elizabeth I. The fortified and moated house dates from the 13th century, but much of its present appearance – fake paneling and plasterwork, a village of Tudor-style cottages in the grounds, a beautiful Italian garden – is the result of 20th-century work undertaken by the American multimillionaire, William Waldorf Astor. It also contains exhibitions on the Astors, Henry VIII and Anne Boleyn, and a fine array of Tudor portraits.

★ ★ ★ KNOLE and 81D2 IGHTHAM MOTE, KENT

Knole (NT), at Sevenoaks, is an enormous house, with a court for every day of the week, a corridor for every week in the year and a

WALK

THE SOUTH DOWNS WAY

The entire 80 miles of the South Downs Way winds along the ridge of the chalk downs from near Petersfield on the Hampshire/Sussex border all the way to Beachy Head near Eastbourne.

Much of the well-signposted route takes in views of country-side and sea. Undoubtedly, the most exciting and unspoiled section is where the rolling downs meet the sea at the Seven Sisters Country Park.

From the information center near Cuckmere Haven there is also a forested walk ■

Fortified and moated Hever Castle dates from the 13th century, and a feature of the Italianate garden is the extraordinary topiary

SOUTH AND SOUTHEAST ENGLAND

GLYNDEBOURNE

Just outside Lewes, the country house of Glyndebourne presents a spectacle of well-to-do English society at play each summer, as ladies and gentlemen in evening dress enjoy champagne picnics and some of the best opera in the country.

The festival has been running since 1934, when John Christie built a theater in the grounds of his ancestral home. Needless to say, tickets are hard to come by. The box office is open May to October, tel: 01273 813813. The season runs from May to August ■

room for every day of the year. Its significant history began in 1456, when Thomas Bourchier, Archbishop of Canterbury, rebuilt the medieval manor. In 1533, it passed into royal hands; it was subsequently bought and remodeled by the Sackville family in 1603, whose descendants still live here. The poet, novelist and friend of Virginia Woolf, Vita Sackville-West, grew up here and wrote of the house. The apartments contain fine plasterwork, tapestries, 17th-century English furniture and portraits by Reynolds, Gainsborough and Van Dyck. Formal walks weave around the 26 acres of gardens and beyond is a vast deer park.

Ightham Mote (NT), 2 miles east, is on a different scale. This small, medieval, stone and timber manor, is set around a courtyard and encircled by a moat. Its great hall and two chapels, one 14th-century, the other Tudor, are remarkably well preserved.

★★★ LEEDS CASTLE   81E2
KENT

If you visit just one medieval castle in England, Leeds Castle, 4 miles east of Maidstone, would make a good choice. Its setting, on two small islands in a lake, surrounded by 500 acres of parkland landscaped by "Capability" Brown, is magical. Sometimes called "Ladies Castle," it was home to eight medieval queens. Plush, 1930s drawing rooms belie the gaunt exterior; there is a Norman cellar, Henry VIII's banqueting hall and a collection of dog collars. In the grounds are woodland and cottage gardens, a maze and even an aviary.

★ LEWES and AROUND   81D1
EAST SUSSEX

The best view of East Sussex's charming county town of **Lewes** (pronounced "Lewis"), strategically placed in a pass through the downs, is from the keep of the Norman **castle**. Laid out before you are the red roofs of Georgian houses and snug cottages, arranged along steep streets and narrow alleys. Look more closely at the High Street and cobbled Keere Street.

The most photogenic building in town is **Anne of Cleves House**, on Southover High Street. It was one of the properties Henry VIII gave Anne as alimony, and it now houses a folk museum.

Every November 5, costumed, torch-carrying figures parade the streets and bonfires burn effigies, not only of Guy Fawkes, but also of the Pope, in commemoration of 17 Protestant martyrs who were burned at the stake in the mid-16th century.

The Bloomsbury Group set up around Lewes during World War I. Just south of Lewes at Rodmell, Leonard and Virginia Woolf lived at the **Monk's House** (NT, very limited opening times). Virginia drowned herself in 1941 in the nearby River Ouse. Vanessa Bell (Woolf's sister), her husband Duncan Bell and her lover Duncan Grant lived in **Charlestown Farmhouse**, 5 miles east of Lewes. The walls and furniture are painted in their abstract and naturalistic designs. They also painted murals in the church at **Berwick,** at the end of a lane under the downs.

★ NEW FOREST   80A1
HAMPSHIRE

The 144 square miles of the New Forest is neither new nor a forest. It was set aside by William the Conqueror in 1079 as a royal hunting ground. "Forest" then meant anywhere where deer were hunted. "Verderers" have managed the forest since at least the 14th century, initially

protecting the crown's interests, nowadays more often protecting the rights of "commoners" to graze animals on the land. Deer are still common, though you're more likely to meet wild ponies. Despite many wooded enclosures, the typical landscape is scrubby, lowland heath, particularly on the west side of the park.

Head initially for **Lyndhurst**, "The Capital of the Forest," with the area's main information center and the New Forest Museum. North of Lyndhurst, off the A31 near Minstead, the **Rufus Stone** marks the spot where the unpopular King William II, known as William Rufus, was killed in suspicious circumstances by an arrow while he was out hunting.

The forest's most scenic routes are along **Bolderwood** and **Rhinefield** ornamental drives, west and southwest of Lyndhurst; laid out during Victorian times with exotic trees. Bolderwood also has a deer sanctuary and the Knightswood Oak, at 700 years old, is reputedly the oldest in the forest.

To the southeast, the village of **Beaulieu** lives up to its French name (it means "beautiful place" in French). Nearby are the attractions of the Montagu family's estate. Its centerpiece is the **National Motor Museum**, with over 250 vintage, racing and record-breaking cars, such as *Bluebird*, which held a land-speed record of 404 mph during the 1960s. There is also simulated rally driving; a tour of the grounds on an overhead monorail; the remains of what was once the largest Cistercian abbey in the country; and the Montagu stately home, originally the abbey gatehouse.

The pretty hamlet of **Bucklers Hard** was one of the foremost shipbuilding centers of the 18th century. Cottages re-create living conditions from the period, and the Maritime Museum tells of the famous ships built here, including some of Nelson's fleet.

Across the River Beaulieu, **Exbury Gardens** has a fine collection of hybrid rhododendrons, as well as a splendid array of azaleas and camellias.

The New Forest is an ancient woodland and heathland environment particularly famous for its wild ponies

WALKS

IN THE NEW FOREST
The heathland and wooded enclosures of the New Forest offer interesting rambles. The parking lots at Beaulieu Road Station, Hatchet Pond and Fritham make convenient starting points, and there are forest trails from the Bolderwood and Rhinefield drives ∎

SOUTH AND SOUTHEAST ENGLAND

WALK

THE NORTH DOWNS WAY

The North Downs Way runs along the North Downs from Guildford to Dover's white cliffs. The countryside is at its best in National Trust land around Dorking in Surrey, at Box Hill and Leith Hill – at 1,029 feet the highest point in the southeast – and at Black Down near Haslemere ■

★★ PETWORTH *80C2*
WEST SUSSEX

The Sussex town of Petworth, with half-timbered and Georgian houses on its winding, narrow streets, is attractive in its own right, but **Petworth House** (NT) steals the show. This grand 17th-century mansion, surrounded by a 700-acre deer park which was landscaped by "Capability" Brown and is enclosed by a 14-mile-long wall, bears more than a passing resemblance to a great French château. More like an art gallery than a comfortable home, it holds a spectacular collection of works, many by J.M.W. Turner, a frequent visitor, and several by Van Dyck, as well as incredible carvings by Grinling Gibbons.

★ POLESDEN LACEY *81C2*
and AROUND, SURREY

In the affluent commuter-belt country in northwest Surrey around Guildford, Woking and Dorking are a number of fine National Trust-owned houses and gardens.

Polesden Lacey (NT), a Regency villa set in 1,000 acres of parkland 3 miles northwest of Dorking, is the best known. An Edwardian society hostess remodeled the house to display paintings, tapestries and furniture, and King George VI and Queen Elizabeth (now the Queen Mother) spent part of their honeymoon here.

Hatchlands Park (NT), in nearby East Clandon, has fine

Admiral Lord Nelson's flagship, HMS Victory, is now preserved in dry dock for visitors to examine her decks and see the spot where her commander fell at the Battle of Trafalgar

interiors by Robert Adam and a restored Gertrude Jekyll garden.

Nearby **Clandon Park** (NT) is a superb Palladian mansion with baroque plasterwork in finely proportioned rooms. More decorated ceilings can be seen at Elizabethan **Loseley House**, 2 miles southwest of Guildford, along with Tudor paneling, a chalk fireplace and period furniture. Within the 250 magnificent acres of **Wisley Gardens**, 7 miles northeast of Guildford, are many rare species, propagated by the Royal Horticultural Society.

PORTSMOUTH   *80B1*
HAMPSHIRE

Large, industrial Portsmouth has a vast natural harbor that is one of the cradles of English maritime history. Henry VII constructed the first dry dock here, and the port has been an important naval base ever since. The South Atlantic Task Force sailed from here to the Falkland Islands in 1982.

At the **Historic Dockyard** ★ ★ ★ you can tour HMS *Victory* and see the spot where Nelson fell, the awful living conditions of the crew, and the Victorian HMS *Warrior*, the first iron-hulled warship. Henry VIII's flagship, the *Mary Rose*, was rescued from the seabed in 1982. Its treasures give a unique insight into Tudor life. The Royal Naval Museum, alongside the ships, covers British naval history, with figureheads, models and a display on the Battle of Trafalgar.

Visit the **Charles Dickens' Birthplace Museum** on Commercial Road, then leave for the Edwardian resort of **Southsea**. Here, the **D-Day Museum** tells the story of the biggest seaborne invasion in history and displays the 272-foot *Overlord Embroidery*, which depicts the major events of the war up to the Normandy landings.

The **Royal Marines Museum** has displays on their role in recent conflicts, and a junior commando course for aspirants.

Many forts surround the waters of the Solent which separates the Isle of Wight from the mainland. Some, like Southsea's, were built by Henry VIII, others to combat the Napoleonic threat. The oldest and most striking is **Portchester Castle** (EH). Standing on the water's edge at the back of Portsmouth Harbour, its massive outer Roman walls surround a 12th-century moated castle and priory church.

★★ ROCHESTER and   *81E3*
CHATHAM, KENT

The industrial sprawl of the Medway Towns in northern Kent looks unlikely sightseeing territory, but has, in old Rochester and Chatham Dockyard, two clumps of historic buildings.

Rochester's cathedral is one of the oldest in the country. It has a striking Norman west front with blind arcading. A 13th-century wall painting, *The Wheel of Fortune,* decorates the choir. Climb the massive keep of the **castle**, built in 1127, a fine example of a Norman military building. The 17th-century **guildhall** houses an instructive museum, while the **Dickens Centre** introduces the town where the author spent many years; Rochester features in scenes in *Great Expectations* and *Pickwick Papers.*

Naval luminaries such as Sir Francis Drake and Admiral Lord Nelson sailed from **Chatham Dockyard**, founded in 1547. In 1984, the dockyard closed to become a tourist attraction that shows the history of shipbuilding in its 18th-century warehouses, the enormous Sail and Colour Loft, and the ¼-mile Ropery.

SOUTH AND SOUTHEAST ENGLAND

BATTLE OF TRAFALGAR

In 1805, Napoleon's army was lined up along the coast of France ready to invade Britain, but could not do so while the British navy controlled the English Channel.

On October 21, the two fleets met at Trafalgar, near the Straits of Gibraltar. The flags on Admiral Nelson's ship H.M.S. *Victory* **spelled out the message: "England expects that every man shall do his duty." A British victory followed, thanks to aggressive tactics employed by Nelson and the speed at which his ships could fire broadsides – one every 80 seconds.**

Nelson died in the battle (famously saying to his captain "Kiss me, Hardy!"), but the threat of invasion had passed for another 135 years ■

SOUTH AND SOUTHEAST ENGLAND

CINQUE PORTS

Edward the Confessor (1042–66) established an association of Kent and Sussex ports, which, in return for considerable privileges such as tax exemption, were expected to supply ships and men for England's maritime defense.

As well as the original five towns of Dover, Sandwich, Hythe, Romney and Hastings, Rye and Winchelsea later joined the fold.

The Lord Warden of the Cinque Ports, whose official residence is Walmer Castle, survives as an honorary title, held presently by the Queen Mother ■

ROMSEY, HAMPSHIRE   81A2

The small town of Romsey boasts a splendid Norman **abbey church**. It avoided destruction at Henry VIII's Dissolution of the Monasteries when the townspeople purchased it for £100. Lord Mountbatten, admiral and last viceroy of India, who died as the victim of an IRA bomb in 1979, is buried within.

An exhibition on his life is on show at **Broadlands**, where he lived. It was here in the harmonious, art-filled rooms of this imposing Palladian mansion on the banks of the River Test, that the Queen and Prince Philip began their honeymoon.

RYE and WINCHELSEA, EAST SUSSEX, and   81E2 ROMNEY MARSH, KENT

Though it is now 2 miles away, the sea used to practically encircle **Rye ★ ★ ★** in the 16th century, when it was one of the original Cinque Ports (see opposite).

Rye today is a much-visited, classic medieval town with a stone gateway. Timber-framed and tile-hung houses stand along cobbled streets, of which Mermaid Street is the prettiest. At the top of the town, one of the few buildings to survive a French-induced fire in 1377 was the Ypres Tower. St. Mary's Church, opposite, has a delightful old clock and great views from its tower. Enthusiasts of the American novelist Henry James, who described Rye as being "huddled and neighborly," should visit Lamb House (NT), where he lived from 1898 to 1916.

Just south of Rye, is **Winchelsea**, another Cinque Port that has also lost its coastline, along with any sense of its importance, and is now little more than a pretty village. Edward I built the "new"

Winchelsea – "old" Winchelsea was washed away – on a hillock using a grid plan, unusual for its day. Old houses with vaulted wine cellars, the remains of a church sacked on a French raid and three medieval gateways recall a former era.

Romney Marsh, now a mysterious flat and wet land populated by birds, frogs and well-fed sheep, was completely covered by water 2,000 years ago. You cannot miss the escarpment of the old shoreline. Below it runs the **Royal Military Canal**, an elaborate defense against possible Napoleonic invasion, which travels for 25 miles from Rye to Hythe. The remains of 74 Martello towers, which were built all along the south coast in the face of the perceived French threat, lie on the coastal edge of the marshes. The tower at **Dymchurch** (EH) has been fully restored, with an original 24-pounder gun placed on its roof. At **Dungeness**, a power station dominates the shingle promontory, which would be a desolate, eerie place even without it. There is a visitor center and tours of the reactor for the curious. At the northern end of this sweep of shoreline, unspoiled and picturesque **Hythe** is more welcoming. The crypt of St. Leonard's Church is somewhat spooky, containing over 500 skulls. A good way to take in the coast is on the small trains and carriages that run along the **Romney, Hythe and Dymchurch Railway** for 14 miles from Hythe to Dungeness.

★ SANDWICH, KENT   81F3

Sandwich was one of the original Cinque Ports, but since the River Stour silted up it has been stranded 2 miles inland behind sand dunes. The small town lies behind earthen ramparts along the river, and its intact medieval center is focused around three churches, a barbican and guildhall. Just to the northwest, **Richborough Castle** (EH), with parts of its walls and foundations still clearly visible, protected an important Roman port. It was here that Emperor Claudius's forces landed in AD 43.

★★★ SISSINGHURST *81E2*
KENT

These famous gardens (NT) were fashioned in the 1930s by Vita Sackville-West (see Knole, p.93) and her husband, Sir Harold Nicolson, around the remains of an Elizabethan manor.

Such is its fame and its smallness (just 6 acres) that crowds, and possibly a wait for admission, are par for the course in summer (to ease the problem, the National Trust enforces timed ticketing). Red-brick walls and thick hedges enclose a series of beautiful, self-contained gardens. In one, called the White Garden, only plants with white flowers or silver leaves grow. You can also visit Vita's glory-hole of a study in the Tudor tower.

SOUTHAMPTON *80A2*
HAMPSHIRE

Since Roman times, Southampton has been an important port. The *Mayflower* stopped off here on its way to America, and the *Titanic* set off for its maiden voyage from these docks. The city is now largely modern, industrial and commercial. However, ranged around the Norman city walls are old buildings that avoided World War II bombs: the **Tudor House**, now a museum of domestic life; the **Wool House**, a medieval warehouse converted into a maritime museum with relics from the *Titanic*, and **God's House Tower**, part of the fortifications that now houses a museum of archeology.

The **Hall of Aviation** has examples of famous airplanes designed by R.J. Mitchell, such as the Spitfire.

Church Square in Rye displays the typical half-timbered architecture of this part of Kent, with mellow terracotta rooftiles and diamond-paned windows

The Pantiles in (Royal) Tunbridge Wells, Kent, is an elegant, covered arcade from Regency times, now home to expensive boutiques and tea shops, as well as offering the health-giving waters that made the spa famous in the 18th century

THANET, ISLE OF, *81F3* KENT

Now an island only in name, in Roman times Thanet was a proper island, separated from the mainland by a mile-wide stretch of water. Its sands have been attracting pleasure-seekers ever since Benjamin Beale invented the covered bathing machine in 1753 in Margate.

Any of its three resorts are fun destinations for a traditional day out at the seaside. **Margate** has a gaudy seafront of amusement arcades and a funfair. **Broadstairs**, smaller, quieter and the prettiest of the three, has a fishing harbor and seven tiny, sandy coves below low cliffs. Charles Dickens came here for frequent sojourns. At the house where he wrote *David Copperfield*, now called Bleak House, you can see his possessions and furniture. **Ramsgate**, neither as kitsch as Margate nor as genteel as Broadstairs, is a working port but it does boast some fine Regency terraces.

★ TUNBRIDGE WELLS *81D2* and AROUND, KENT

Health-giving mineral springs were discovered in **Tunbridge Wells** in 1606. By the 18th century, Tunbridge was a flourishing spa, fashionable with royalty and dandies in much the same way as Bath (see p.55); indeed, Bath's social organizer, Beau Nash, was master of ceremonies here.

You can still drink the medicinal waters at the **Pantiles**, an elegant Regency colonnaded arcade with classy stores. The local **museum** specializes in Tunbridge Ware: boxes and trinkets decorated with a mosaic of tiny pieces of wood.

Tunbridge is a good base for exploring the castles, country houses and gardens of the Weald, such as Hever (see p.93), Chartwell (see p.86), Knole and Ightham Mote (see p.93), and Sissinghurst (see p.99).

Penshurst Place, just northwest of the town, dates from around 1340. It has a magnificent great hall, supported by chestnut beams and carved figures. Descendants of the 16th-century owners, the Sidney family, still live there; the family became the Earls of Leicester, and in the village you'll find the original Leicester Square.

Standen (NT), just outside East Grinstead, is a fine example of a house of the Arts and Crafts period. It was built in the 1890s by Philip Webb, friend of the leading artist/designer of the period, William Morris, and displays Morris textiles and wallpapers and original electric light fittings.

Southeast of Tunbridge, **Scotney Castle** (NT) has one of the country's loveliest gardens.

Bodiam Castle (NT), further south, was built in the 14th century to protect the Rother Valley against the threat of a French invasion. Parliamentarians destroyed the castle in the Civil War. Nonetheless, the battlements are remarkably intact and, from across its lily-filled moat, you could hardly hope to see a more perfect realization of a medieval fortress.

Bateman's (NT), at Burwash to the west, presents an altogether gentler face. The 17th-century house was home to the writer Rudyard Kipling from 1902 until his death in 1936. His study looks as it did when he wrote *Puck of Pook's Hill*, which lovingly evokes the neighborhood, and the famous poem, *If*.

WATERCRESS LINE 80B2
HAMPSHIRE

Steam-powered trains of the Mid-Hants Railway, supervised by staff in period costume, run for 10 miles from New Alresford to Alton through rural Hampshire.

It is better known as the **Watercress Line**, as over half the country's watercress comes from the fields surrounding the track. Unsurprisingly, watercress soup is served on the evening train!

WALKS

IN THE ASHDOWN FOREST

If you're looking for somewhere to stretch your legs in shouting distance of London, you might consider the heath and woodland of the Ashdown Forest at the heart of the Weald.

This is A.A. Milne's *Winnie The Pooh* country. South of Hartfield, off the B2026, you'll find both Poohsticks Bridge and the Enchanted Place described in *The House at Pooh Corner* ∎

WALK

THE ISLE OF WIGHT

Across the waters of The Solent on the Isle of Wight, the National Trust owns chalk downlands inland as well as 15 miles of coastline. The best cliffs are at Tennyson Down and along the southwest side of the island.

It is a popular opinion that among the best things on the Isle of Wight are the downs.

They command wonderful views, and the air, which comes straight from the sea, is most invigorating ■

★★ WIGHT, ISLE OF   80A1

A short ferry ride brings you to this demure island, favored as a retirement home and a family summer vacation destination. You can tour the island comfortably in a day, but if you stay over you'll be able to make the most of the breezy clifftops and chalk downlands, and relax at the island's Victorian-style resorts and sandy beaches. To reach the island, take the ferry (from Lymington to Yarmouth, Portsmouth to Fishbourne, or Southampton to East Cowes), the Hovercraft (Southsea to Ryde), or catamaran (Portsmouth to Ryde, Southampton to West Cowes).

Cowes is a world famous yachting center. It is most vibrant during the Round-the-Island yacht race in late June, and during the regatta, called Cowes Week, in July/August. Heading anti-clockwise round the coast, attractive, low-lying marshes and creeks characterize Newtown Creek. Yarmouth is a pleasing small port with a castle built as part of Henry VIII's coastal defences. Alum Bay boasts striking, multihued sandstone cliffs, while the 100-foot chalk ridges of the Needles, the island's best-known landmark, rise out of the sea offshore. The poet Tennyson walked virtually every day along the splendid chalk cliffs of Tennyson Down, as a monument here confirms. Precipitous cliffs continue to the island's most southerly headland, St. Catherine's Point, where you can visit a lighthouse; from St. Catherine's Hill behind, a panorama extends across much of the island.

Ventnor, the island's most attractive resort, extends in terraces over the cliffs like an amphitheater. A succession of rather less alluring resorts takes up most of the east coast:

genteel Shanklin, with its 300 foot-deep gorge of Shanklin Chine; brasher Sandown; the yachting center of Bembridge; and the major vacation center of Ryde. Just outside East Cowes, Osborne House (EH) constitutes the island's top sight. The Italianate villa was built in the 1840s for Queen Victoria and Prince Albert. From Albert's death in 1861 until her own death at the house in 1901, Victoria kept everything as it had been in his lifetime. You can view some state and private rooms and a host of personal effects.

Inland, near Newport, Carisbrooke Castle (EH) dates from Norman times, though it has been thoroughly strengthened in subsequent centuries. As well as mementoes of Charles I, who was imprisoned here before his execution, you can see a donkey working a donkey wheel in the wellhouse. Godshill, the island's outstandingly attractive thatched village, can be swamped by visitors in season.

★★ WINCHESTER   580B2
HAMPSHIRE

A statue of King Alfred (AD 871–901) stands in the center of this lovely, compact city, a reminder that in Saxon times Winchester was the capital of the kingdom of Wessex as well as of the whole of England.

Though externally squat and unimposing, the medieval cathedral ★★★ is superb, the longest of its period in Europe. Though construction began in 1079, much of its best architecture, in Perpendicular style, dates from the 14th century. There are impressive chantries off the nave, tomb chests of Saxon kings and a shrine to Saint Swithun, a 9th-century bishop. On July 15, 971, his body was moved from outside the cathedral to a more honored spot inside, against his expressed wishes. As a consequence, an almighty rainstorm came down and, by tradition, if it rains on St. Swithun's Day it will rain for the next 40 days!

More memorable features include the country's oldest choir stalls, priceless treasures in its library, and a fine Norman crypt. Its **close** has some charming old buildings, and the extensive ruins of **Wolvesey Castle** (EH), the old bishop's palace, more than hint at the city's wealth and pre-eminence in medieval times.

The **High Street**, with more historic buildings, has one end at Westgate, a fortified medieval gateway; in rooms above is a small museum of objects from the city's past. Nearby, the **Great Hall** is the only surviving part of a Norman castle; the superb room would be worth visiting in its own right, but attention focuses on a large painted table hanging on a

Winchester cathedral incorporates every style of medieval English architecture from Norman to Perpendicular

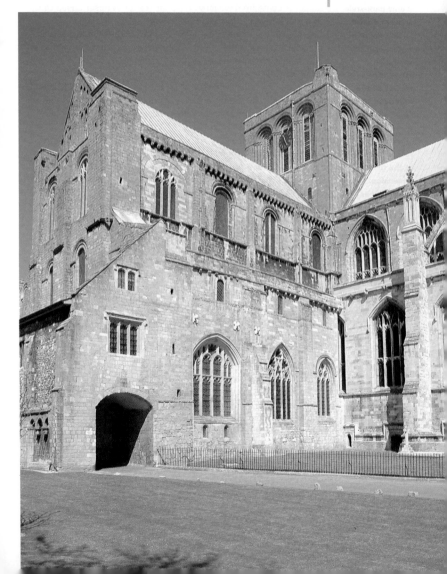

CHESSINGTON WORLD OF ADVENTURES and THORPE PARK

Chessington, 5 miles south of Kingston-upon-Thames, and Thorpe Park, 3 miles south of Staines, are traditional family attractions, with theme park-style areas and rides.

Chessington combines a zoo with such attractions as a version of the American Wild West, a walk through a computer screen to a fantasy world of the fifth dimension, and rides such as the Terror Tomb and Dragon River.

Huge Thorpe Park specializes in getting you wet on scary water rides ∎

wall, a medieval fake of King Arthur's Round Table. To the east, High Street becomes **Broadway**, leading past Alfred's statue to the half-timbered, 18th-century **City Mill** (NT).

South of the cathedral, the famous public school of **Winchester College** was founded in 1382 by Bishop Wykeham (pupils are called "Wykehamists") to provide education for poor scholars. The tradition continues, but now most students come from wealthy families. Between March and September, you can tour its precincts, including the quadrangle, chapel and hall, all redolent of Oxford and Cambridge university colleges.

A 1½-mile walk south across the water-meadows brings you to the serene **St. Cross Hospital**, established in 1136 as the country's oldest charitable institution, where you can still claim the Wayfarer's Dole of beer and bread.

★★ WINDSOR and ETON, BERKSHIRE *80C3*

The twin towns of Windsor and Eton, facing each other across the Thames, are synonymous with two great bastions of English privilege: Windsor Castle and Eton College.

Towering above the pleasant town of Windsor, **Windsor Castle ★★★** has been inhabited by royalty since William the Conqueror's time and has grown to be the largest lived-in fortress in the world. Its most outstanding building is St. George's Chapel, one of the finest examples of Perpendicular architecture in existence. The chapel holds the tombs of 10 monarchs and the decorated, 15th-century stalls of the Knights of the Garter, England's oldest and most prestigious order of chivalry.

Some of the castle's grand state apartments were gutted by a disastrous fire in 1992, but have now been restored at unimaginable cost. Numerous old masters are on display, and even more absorbing is Queen Mary's Dolls' House, designed by Sir Edwin Lutyens in 1923; everything, down to books and paintings by contemporary authors and artists, is fashioned at one-twelfth size. As an inhabited royal palace, opening times for Windsor Castle can vary: tel: 01753 831118.

Windsor town features a **waxworks exhibition** at the train station and a display of the queen's presents and state carriages in the **Royal Mews.** The **guildhall** on the High Street designed by Sir Christopher Wren, whose columns intentionally do not reach the ceiling, is also impressive.

Within the 2,000 acres of **Windsor Great Park**, skirted by a magnificent avenue of chestnut and plane trees called the Long Walk, lie formal rose gardens and woodlands. Alongside, on what was once the Windsor Safari Park, there has been a **Legoland** theme park developed, based on the original in Denmark.

Go across the River Thames via Windsor Bridge to **Eton, where** school boys in tail coats and wing collars are a common sight. **Eton College**, founded by Henry VI in 1440, is Britain's most famous and exclusive school, having spawned 20 prime ministers. Like many private fee-paying schools in England, it is paradoxically called a "public" school. At most times of year you can visit its Perpendicular college chapel, schoolyards, the Museum of Eton Life, and see the playing fields where, according to the Duke of Wellington, the battle of Waterloo was won.

EASTERN
ENGLAND

This predominantly flat and
off-the-beaten-track region
embraces Cambridge, the East
Midlands and the scenic parts of
East Anglia

CALENDAR OF EVENTS

WHOLE OF MAY –
Lincoln Festival
of the Arts. Events
held all over the city
include pop,
rock and jazz music,
concerts, poetry, film
and theater.

MAY BANK
HOLIDAY (first
Monday in May) –
Maypole Dancing,
Wellow, Notting-
hamshire. The village
has a permanent
maypole and
The May Queen
is elected by
the locals.

JUNE – Aldeburgh
Festival of
Music and the Arts.
One of the most
prestigious in the
international
calendar, this festival
was founded by the
famous British
composer, Benjamin
Britten.

JULY – Ely Folk
Weekend. Presents
traditional folk song
and folk dance, in an
area of the country
which was once
a stronghold of
these arts ■

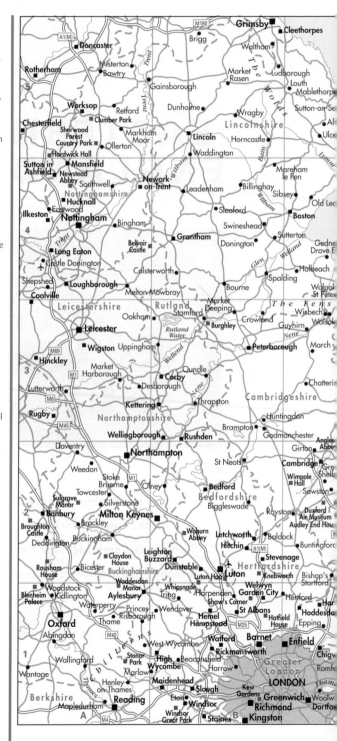

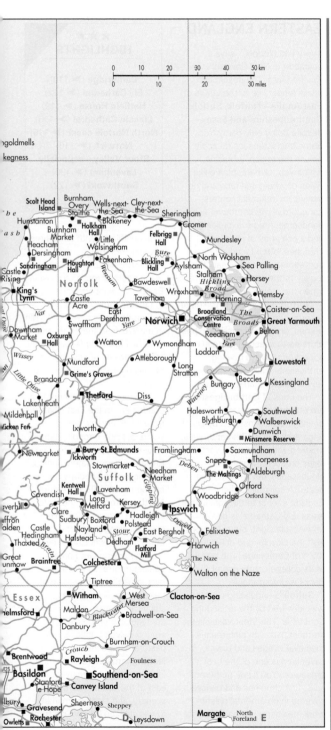

CALENDAR OF EVENTS

LATE JULY –
King's Lynn Festival.
This has been a
regular event in the
charming old town
since 1951. Early
classical
and avant-garde
music are featured.

SEPTEMBER –
Burghley House
Horse Trials,
Stamford,
Cambridgeshire. A
major occasion in the
horse trials calendar,
held over three days.

OCTOBER – Norfolk
and Norwich
Festival. Held in
Norwich, this is one
of the oldest festivals
in the country.
Started in 1821,
it has been
interrupted only by
world wars.

DECEMBER
(Christmas Eve) –
Festival of Carols
and Lessons, King's
College Chapel,
Cambridge. This has
become a familiar
part of the season on
radio and television.
It was first held
in 1918 ■

GEORGE
BERNARD
SHAW

**In 1906, the great
Irish playwright
George Bernard
Shaw moved into
the early 20th-
century New
Rectory in Ayot
St. Lawrence,
near Welwyn.**

**He renamed the
house, with
characteristic
lack of modesty,
Shaw's Corner
(NT). It is stuffed
with personal
effects and looks
as if he's just
stepped out for a
moment.**

**He wrote in
verse that though
Ireland was his
birthplace: "This
home shall be my
final earthplace,"
and he died there,
aged 94, in 1950.**

**His last
published work
was a booklet of
poems about the
little hidden
village of Ayot
St. Lawrence ■**

EASTERN ENGLAND

"Very flat, Norfolk," says a character in Noel Coward's *Private Lives*. The description sticks limpet-like to the whole of East Anglia – Norfolk, Suffolk, Cambridgeshire and Essex – despite being only partly true. Some characteristics do apply across the region: a bracing, windswept climate; prairie-like fields of wheat and rape and no significant industrial centers. Languorous market towns with handsome, medieval buildings and a rich array of parish churches, often faced in flint and sometimes thatched, mark the legacy of the medieval wool trade when the region prospered.

Norfolk is loveliest in the quiet resorts, bird reserves, stately homes, dunes and sand marshes of its north coast. The Broads appeal primarily to boating enthusiasts. Norwich receives far fewer visitors than it deserves.

The Fens of **Cambridgeshire** are utterly flat, criss-crossed by drainage canals installed by Dutch engineers in the 17th century and bristling with windmills. Vast skies produce magnificent cloudscapes and sunsets. The peat-rich soil makes this one of England's most fertile agricultural areas. Ely Cathedral is one unmissable sight, but at all costs. visit the bicycle-mad university town of Cambridge. The beauty of its college courts and of the Backs is unforgettable.

Suffolk's undulating country was idealized by the artist John Constable. The Stour Valley is the prettiest part with picturesque medieval villages and towns, Lavenham is one of the best preserved. You'll see timbered halls, fine churches and houses covered in ornamental plaster-work. Its charming coast is partly fringed with reeds and topped

★★★
HIGHLIGHTS
Cambridge (▶ 110)
Ely Cathedral (▶ 112)
Hatfield House (▶ 119)
Lincoln Cathedral (▶ 115)
North Norfolk coast (▶ 116)
Norwich (▶ 116)
**Stour Valley – especially
Lavenham (▶ 120)**
Southwold (▶ 122)

with heathland, with small-time soothing resorts.

The Roman town of Colchester is the principal reason for visiting **Essex**, the least attractive county.

Lincolnshire (not properly part of East Anglia) is green and rolling in the Wolds to the north, and flat in its bulb-growing fenland to the south. The city of Lincoln has one of the country's most stunning cathedrals.

The counties directly north of London and in the East Midlands have a few notable sights if you're passing through. Hatfield House in **Hertfordshire** is one of England's finest stately homes, and more grand country houses can be found in **Bedfordshire. Northamptonshire**, the Victorian county of "squires and spires," is pleasant along the Grand Union Canal and in its northern reaches around Rockingham Forest. **Leicestershire** is industrial in the east, as is the county town of Leicester, which also has a significant Roman and medieval heritage. Eastern Leicestershire, around Belvoir Castle, is more pastoral. Remnants of **Nottinghamshire's** Sherwood Forest can still be enjoyed. The east of the county has the best scenery, and pleasant market towns such as Newark-on-Trent and Southwell.

The Boston parish church of St. Botolph is one of the largest in the country. Its 288-foot tower, the famous "Boston Stump" is visible from a radius of 40 miles across the surrounding flat fenland

BOSTON   *106C4*
and SPALDING   *106B4*
LINCOLNSHIRE

At the heart of the Lincolnshire Fens, **Boston** is now just a modest market town, but in the 13th century it was one of England's largest ports. William Brewster and other Pilgrim Fathers were tried and imprisoned in its guildhall for attempting to flee the country in 1607. Its church is notable for its colossally tall tower, nicknamed "the Boston Stump" due to its lack of a spire.

Surrounded by dikes and streams, and counting seven bridges in its town center, **Spalding** has a Dutch feel, reinforced by tulip fields in Springfield Gardens and its Flower Parade in early May.

BURY ST. EDMUNDS   *106D2*
SUFFOLK

This charming market town has much Georgian and medieval architecture, arranged on an original Norman layout. Bury (pronounced "berry") developed around its **abbey** (now in ruins but with pretty gardens) which was founded in AD 945 to house the shrine of King Edmund, who was martyred by Danish invaders in AD 869. **St. Mary's Church**, with its magnificent hammer-beam roof, is more noteworthy than the cathedral. Also worth seeking out are the 15th-century **guildhall**, the **town hall** by Robert Adam, the Georgian **playhouse**, and the **Queen Anne manor house**, which has a large collection of watches and clocks.

DICKENSIAN ASSOCIATIONS
To the front of the abbey in Bury St. Edmunds is a sloping plain called Angel Hill, where the Angel Hotel can be found.

This was made famous by Charles Dickens, as his character Mr. Pickwick stayed here in the novel *The Pickwick Papers* ■

WALK

CAMBRIDGE

This walk takes in the most beautiful colleges. For guided walks around the city, ask at the tourist office on Wheeler Street.

Start at the Fitzwilliam Museum. Head up Trumpington Street past Peterhouse and Pembroke. Turn left down Silver Street, cross the River Cam with Queens' on your right, and take a path to the right along the Backs.

Cross the Cam via Garret Hostel Lane: Trinity Hall is on your right, Trinity College is on the left with St. John's College behind. Go down King's Parade to King's College Chapel and Corpus Christi College ∎

The punt is the traditional form of transport on the Backs, but poling is a skill which takes time to learn. Alternatively, take a stroll along the banks in spring when daffodils line the banks

Ickworth (NT), 3 miles southwest, is no ordinary stately home, but a 104-foot elliptical rotunda. Its sumptuous state rooms include fine art by Titian, Hogarth and Velasquez.

★★★ CAMBRIDGE 106C2
CAMBRIDGESHIRE
Cambridge University swamps the town. As one of the world's most famous and oldest universities, founded when students were driven out of Oxford by rioting in the early 13th century, its medieval colleges are simply superlative. King's College Chapel is the loveliest single building, the apogee of the Perpendicular style with delicate fan vaulting and outstanding stained glass; listen to the incomparable choir at evensong.

The Backs (the backs of the colleges), where lawns reach down to the River Cam, is very picturesque and best experienced on a punt (a flat-bottomed boat propelled by a long pole).

Nosing around the colleges' hidden courts and gardens, and searching out ancient libraries, refectories and chapels is the most pleasurable part of a visit. Be bold, but sensitive: the colleges are places of study (many are closed around exam time from April through June).

Most Cambridge colleges have their special highlights. The library at Magdalene (pronounced "Maudlin") was bequeathed by former student Samuel Pepys. Trinity, founded by Henry VIII, has Christopher Wren's library and the largest court, made famous in the movie *Chariots of Fire*. Former students form an illustrious list including Isaac Newton, Lord Byron, Alfred Lord Tennyson, and the present Prince of Wales. St. John's boasts nine courts with dazzling architecture from the 16th to the 20th centuries and the Bridge of Sighs, modeled on the Venetian prison bridge. William Wordsworth was a former student.

Trinity Hall has a beautiful main court, while **Clare College** has a formal composition, like a Renaissance palace. **King's**, founded by Henry VI, has the dazzling King's College Chapel (see p.110). **Queens'** has a half-timbered court, striking painted hall and the Mathematical Bridge, originally held together by geometrical principles alone! **Peterhouse** is the oldest college, founded in the 1280s. **Pembroke** has a 14th-century entrance and chapel by Christopher Wren. Christopher Marlowe attended **Corpus Christi**; its Old Court is the oldest in Cambridge. **Christ's** contains the beautiful Fellows' Building and Fellows' Garden. Former students include John Milton and Charles Darwin. Samuel Taylor Coleridge attended **Jesus**, founded in the 15th century on the site of a nunnery.

Fitzwilliam Museum houses an outstanding collection in a grand, neoclassical building. There are Egyptian, Greek and Roman antiquities and superb paintings, including early Renaissance and impressionist masterpieces. **Kettle's Yard** has a collection of 20th-century art. The roof of **Great St. Mary's Church** commands a fine view over most of the colleges.

Georgian **Wimpole Hall** (NT), 8 miles southwest of Cambridge, is the county's grandest house, with a landscaped park. Wimpole Home Farm (NT) nurtures rare breeds of sheep and cattle, while the Great Barn holds 200 years' of agricultural implements.

Duxford, 7 miles south of Cambridge, has a collection of civil and military aircraft, while **Anglesey Abbey** (NT), 6 miles northeast, was built in 1600, with lovely gardens. The 600-acre wetland reserve of **Wicken Fen** (NT), 17 miles northeast, shows what undrained fens were like.

COLCHESTER, ESSEX *107D2*

Famous for its oyster beds and its long history, Roman Colchester, *Camulodunum*, was sacked in AD 62 by Boadicea, female leader of the Iceni tribe. Sections of the Roman wall can still be seen, and the massive keep of the Norman castle houses an array of Roman finds. More Roman brickwork can be found in **St. John's Abbey** gatehouse and in the ruins of **St. Botolph's Priory**. There are also interesting half-timbered buildings, once occupied by Flemish weavers in the old Dutch Quarter.

★ KING'S LYNN and AROUND, NORFOLK *107C4*

King's Lynn has for centuries been a prosperous trading port, and wharves line the riverbanks of the River Great Ouse.

There are a number of interesting buildings to search out including the 17th-century **Custom House**; and around the Saturday market place the twin-towered **St. Margaret's Church**, **Old Gaol House** and **Trinity Guildhall**, whose Regalia Rooms include the King John Cup. On King Street is **St. George's Guildhall** (NT), a theater built in 1420 where Shakespeare is said to have performed.

Houghton Hall, 13 miles east, is a great Palladian house, built for Britain's first prime minister, Sir Robert Walpole. **Castle Acre**, 13 miles southeast, has impressive castle remains and the ruins of a Cluniac priory (EH).

The outstanding feature of the moated, lived-in and fortified 15th-century manor **Oxburgh Hall** (NT), 18 miles south, is its 80-foot Tudor gatehouse. Of the Seven Churches of the Marshland, between King's Lynn and Wisbech, each in Perpendicular or Early English style, the loveliest are at **Walpole St. Peter** and **Walsoken**.

EARLY AMERICAN CONNECTIONS

Eastern England has strong associations with the United States.

Dedham (see p.122) had more people on the *Mayflower* than any other community. Its church has commemorative pews to the people of Dedham (Massachusetts) and to the first manned landing on the moon.

Boston (Massachusetts) is named after the town in Lincolnshire (see p.109).

Many early emigrés studied at Emmanuel College in Cambridge, including John Harvard, whose life is commemorated in the Wren chapel.

Thomas Paine, a colonial patriot, was born in Thetford (see p.113), and Sulgrave Manor is the ancestral home of George Washington ■

DRIVE

A TASTE OF NORFOLK'S FENS, FARMLAND AND NORTH COAST

151 miles (allow 2 days)

This varied tour passes through the Fens to the magnificent cathedral of Ely. It then turns east through forested Breckland, before heading north via delightful, sleepy market towns and wheatfields to stately homes, and Norfolk's atmospheric north coast.

WISBECH IN BLOOM

Wisbech is the colorful center of a rich flower and fruit-growing area. The town, encircled by bulb fields and orchards, is bustling with activity during the fruit-picking season.

In spring "blossom routes" are signposted through the orchards ■

From King's Lynn take the A47 for 14 miles to Wisbech, entering the town via the B198.

1 Wisbech, Cambridgeshire
Fine Georgian houses and warehouses distinguish this elegant town, once the port for Peterborough. They look their best along the **Brinks**, on either side of the River Nene. **Peckover House** (NT), has notable woodwork and plasterwork, and an interesting Victorian garden. The town's local museum provides an introduction to the surrounding Fenland.

Follow the A1101, then the A1122 to Downham Market for 13 miles.

2 Downham Market, Norfolk
There's not much to see in this quiet market town, but a visit to **Denver Sluice** (2 miles away), where the River Great Ouse and the artifically created Old and New Bedford rivers are regulated to prevent flooding, helps you to understand the Fens.

Leave Downham Market eastwards to join the A10, turn south and follow to Ely.

3 Ely, Cambridgeshire
Before the Fenland was drained in the 17th century, Ely was an island, from the safety of which the Anglo-Saxon nobleman, Hereward the Wake, put up a last-ditch resistance against the invading Normans.

Ely's **cathedral ★ ★ ★**, one of England's ecclesiastical masterpieces, rises like a beacon from the featureless countryside, and overpowers this modest market town. Its substantially Norman architecture is best seen in the west front and in the stupendous nave.

Its most striking feature resulted from a disaster in 1322 when the central tower collapsed and a vast, but delicate octagonal lantern was installed. At the same time, the sacristan Alan de Walsingham created the beautifully vaulted Lady Chapel.

There is also a stained-glass museum, ruined cloisters and precincts to explore, which include the buildings of the King's School whose origins date back to the time of Alfred the Great.

Leave Ely on the B1382 through Prickwillow, then take the A1101 to Kennyhill, turning left onto an unclassified road to Lakenheath. Pick up the B1112 as far as Hockwold cum Wilton, and finally take another unclassified road to Weeting.

4 Weeting, Norfolk
On reaching Weeting you've entered an area of East Anglia called Breckland, partly sandy heathland, partly forested, and partly requisitioned as an army training ground.

Just east of Weeting there are **forest trails** from Santon Downham, and in the conifer forest of Thetford Warren lie **Grime's Graves** (EH), which are

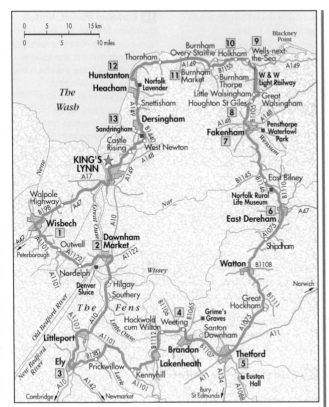

not in fact burial places but hundreds of 4,000-year-old flint mines. One of the shafts has been opened to the public.

Follow the B1106 and A1065 to Brandon, then the B1107 for 8 miles to Thetford.

5 Thetford, Norfolk

Now the main town of Breckland, Thetford was in pre-medieval times East Anglia's premier settlement and in the Middle Ages a religious community with five monasteries. It has a notable **castle** mound surrounded by Iron Age earthworks and the remains of a 12th-century Cluniac **priory**.

Leave Thetford on the A1075 heading northward to East Dereham.

6 East Dereham, Norfolk

East Dereham has a well named after Saint Withburga, the daughter of an Anglo-Saxon king who founded a convent here in the 7th century, and 16th-century **Bishop Bonner's Cottage** with fine pargeting (now the local museum). Three miles north at Gressenhall, the **Norfolk Rural Life Museum** stocks rare breeds of farm animals and instructs on local farming practices.

From East Dereham continue northward on the B1110, then the B1146 to Fakenham.

7 Fakenham, Norfolk

This charming, old market town has a pair of coaching inns in the market place and the **Museum of Gas and Local History**, the only

"TURNIP TOWNSHEND"

Just 3 miles southwest of Fakenham is *Raynham Hall*.

It is famous for being the home of the 18th-century politician and agriculturalist, the 2nd Viscount Townshend. Known as "Turnip Townshend" for his encourage-ment in the growth of turnips, but more importantly he evolved the system of crop rotation ■

surviving small-town Victorian gasworks in Britain.

Cross the A148 and follow the B1105 for 4 miles to Houghton St. Giles.

8 Houghton St. Giles, Norfolk

Slipper Chapel, at Houghton St. Giles, is so-called because pilgrims on their way to **Little Walsingham** would remove their shoes here for the last part of the journey. The shrine came about after a vision of the Virgin Mary seen in 1061. Though destroyed, along with two priories in the Dissolution, new shrines have returned this century. The lovely flint-faced **shirehall** tells the story in its museum. Nearby, **Great Walsingham** has a textile center.

Return to the B1105 from Great Walsingham and follow to Wells-next-the-Sea.

9 Wells-next-the-Sea, Norfolk

A narrow-gauge steam **railway** runs from Little Walsingham to Wells, an appealing port which overlooks salt marshes, and specializes in whelks (marine mollusks). Colorful buildings line the high street, and fine Georgian houses surround the **Buttlands**, a large shady green.

Follow the main coast road, the A149, west for 2 miles to Holkham.

10 Holkham, Norfolk

Holkham Hall, a monumental Palladian mansion in extensive parkland landscaped by "Capability" Brown, is famed for its Marble Hall, neoclassical sculpture and an array of fine art by Poussin, Rubens and Titian.

Continue further along the A149, then left onto the B1155 to Burnham Market.

THE GARRATT STEAM LOCOMOTIVE

The Wells and Walsingham Light Railway covers 4 miles of 10¼ inch gauge track, which is the longest track of this gauge in the world.

The line passes through some beautiful countryside, noted for its wild flowers and butterflies.

The Garratt steam locomotive was specially built for this track ■

11 Burnham Market, Norfolk

Burnham Market, around a handsome green, is head of a family of 7 Burnham hamlets and villages.

Burnham Overy Staithe is the prettiest, with a windmill, watermill and brick and flint cottages overlooking the mill.

Horatio Nelson was born at **Burnham Thorpe** in 1758; the church's cross and lectern were made from the timbers of HMS *Victory*, and the names of the pubs in the district bear witness to the famous Admiral.

Return to the A149 for 12 miles to Hunstanton.

12 Hunstanton, Norfolk

The attractions of this Victorian seaside resort include striking striped-chalk cliffs, good beaches and an interesting walk-through aquarium. Just south, **Norfolk Lavender** is England's only lavender farm.

Head south on the A149, then the B1440 from Dersingham to Sandringham, and further south, via West Newton, to Castle Rising.

13 Sandringham, Norfolk

This royal estate was a 21st-birthday present to the Prince of Wales from his mother, Queen Victoria, in 1862. Now a royal vacation home, the neo-Jacobean house, grounds and museum are open when the royals are not in residence. The **church of St. Mary Magdelene**, within the grounds, is full of royal gifts.

At **Castle Rising**, you can't miss the impressive, restored Norman keep (EH), standing on top of extensive earthworks.

Take the B1439 back to rejoin the A149, then follow an unclassified road back to King's Lynn.

LINCOLN 106B5
LINCOLNSHIRE

With little else of outstanding interest in Lincolnshire, you'll probably have to travel out of your way to reach the small, backwater city of Lincoln. But you'll be rewarded by one of England's most splendid cathedrals, its colossal towers soaring above the flat countryside.

Historic Lincoln occupies the uphill part of the city, above and separate from the modern and commercial center.

Though it was an important Roman outpost, visible signs of *Lindum Colonia* are patchy, and best represented in the **Newport Arch** on Bailgate.

Lincoln's medieval heritage is considerably better represented. A wealth of distinguished, old edifices line **Steep Hill**, which certainly lives up to its name. The best known is the Jew's House, said to be the oldest domestic residence in the country. Many also now house secondhand book and craft stores.

At the top of Steep Hill, on one side of the square called Castle Hill, stands the Norman castle. Within its walkable ramparts, you can visit the chapel of a former prison where pews were arranged to prevent prisoners from seeing each other. You can also study a copy of the Magna Carta (see p.11) and its good accompanying exhibition.

The other side of the square leads to the west front of the cathedral ★ ★ ★, breathtaking for its size and with an abundance of arcading. Though part of the facade is Norman, the bulk of the church is a masterpiece of Gothic architecture, from the penumbral nave to dazzling stained-glass windows in the transept, and from St Hugh's Choir, with its beautifully carved stalls and misericords, to the

Angel Choir, named for the many carved angels between the arches. The Lincoln Imp, emblem of the city, is also to be found between a pair of arches. Don't miss the Chapter House and the Medieval and Wren libraries. Cathedral tours (including roof tours) are highly recommended.

None of Lincoln's museums make for compulsive viewing. With time to kill, however, head for: the **Usher Hall Gallery** for paintings of Lincolnshire, pocket watches, portrait miniatures, coins and the effects of locally-born Alfred Lord Tennyson; the **Museum of Lincolnshire Life**, for its large display of domestic and agricultural bygones; and the **National Cycle Museum**.

Lincoln Cathedral is one of the most magnificient in Britain, with its 271-foot central tower carrying Great Tom, a bell weighing 5½ tons

NORWICH CHURCHES

Norwich has 32 medieval churches. Some have been converted to antiques and craft centers, theaters and even a sports hall. St. Peter Mancroft is the most impressive, with a lovely roof and a museum of church art.

St. Andrew's and Blackfriars' Halls, linked in a vast structure off St. George's Street, were once the chancel and nave of a Dominican church.

St. Peter Hungate on Princes Street has a lovely roof and is now a little museum of church art.

Nearby, St. Michael at Plea now sells antiques.

Three more, as well as a 17th-century meeting house and the elegant Unitarian Octagon Chapel, lie along Cole-gate, north of the River Wensum. The best of the four churches along St. Benedict's Street is St. John Maddermarket ■

★ NORFOLK BROADS   107E3

The Norfolk Broads are made up of a vast wetland teeming with birdlife, corn mills and wind pumps. England's most recently designated **national park**, in a triangle between Norwich, Lowestoft and Sea Palling, comprises 125 miles of navigable waterway, made up of shallow reed-fringed lakes (the Broads themselves) formed by the flooding of ancient peat diggings connected by a network of rivers. Thus, it is naturally best explored by boat. Most visitors rent residential craft from centers such as Wroxham, but motor launches for day rental are also available.

If you are in a car, head for a nature reserve, such as the **Broadland Conservation Centre** at Ranworth, **Hickling Broad,** and the **Horsey Mere** (NT).

★★★ NORTH NORFOLK COAST   107D4

The unspoiled coastline from Cromer in the east to Hunstanton in the west is a bewitching landscape of vast, sandy strands, salt marshes, nature reserves and muddy creeks worming their way inland to low-key flint villages. The driving tour on p.112 covers the sights along the coastline west of Wells-next-the-Sea.

Cromer and **Sheringham** are atmospheric resorts from the Edwardian era. Cromer retains a small but important crab fishing industry. Inland are two of the region's top country houses: **Fel-brigg Hall** (NT), a 17th-century manor with its original 18th-century furniture, and, further south, **Blickling Hall** (NT), a splendid Jacobean house whose highlight is its 127-foot plastered ceiling in the Long Gallery.

Back on the coast, **Cley-next-the-Sea** is made picturesque by its windmill. The important bird

reserve at **Cley Marshes** has a huge number of waders as well as herons, spoonbills and bitterns. More birdlife, and even seals, can be seen around the long, shingle-and-sand spit of **Blakeney Point**, reached on a lengthy walk from Cley or by boat from the quay at **Blakeney**, a pretty yachting center. More nature reserves can be visited at **Scolt Head Island**, breeding site for terns, oystercatchers and ringed plovers (accessible by boat from Brancaster Staithe), and around **Holme-next-the-Sea**.

★★★ NORWICH NORFOLK   107D3

Overlooked by most tourists, this compact city, made rich in the Middle Ages by the wool trade, has enough sightseeing to fill a long weekend, as well as interesting shopping (especially along St. Benedict's Street), excellent restaurants, and a

vibrant arts scene due, in part, to the presence of the University of East Anglia (U.E.A.).

Exploration naturally starts at the **Market Place**, permanently covered by the striped awnings of a large, open-air market.

All around lie a host of flint-faced churches (see panel on p.116), as well as medieval streets such as cobbled **Elm Hill**, lined with overhanging and brightly plastered buildings.

But the top sight has to be the **cathedral**, which features a magnificent display of over 1,000 multicolored roof bosses depicting dramatic scenes in miniature along its grand nave and around its cloisters. The large, serene cathedral **close**, with elegant Georgian houses, feels like a well-kept village. Medieval gates open out from the Upper Close; the Lower Close leads to lovely Hook's Walk and down to the medieval gate of **Pull's Ferry**.

Norwich has no shortage of museums. The largest, in the **castle** complex, excels in its enormous teapot collection and galleries of works by John Crome and John Sell Cotman, outstanding landscape artists of the well-respected Norwich School. You can also visit the dungeons and battlements of the heavily restored Norman keep.

The Sainsbury Centre for the Visual Arts, at U.E.A.'s campus, holds an unmissable art collection, innovative for its eclecticism (works by Degas and Francis Bacon intermingled with Egyptian and Iraqi sculpture) and for the modern building which houses it.

Also enjoyable, though more conservative, are the **Bridewell Museum** (Bridewell Alley), a nostalgic look at Norwich's industries, and **Strangers' Hall** (Charing Cross), a rambling, old merchant's house.

WALKS

EAST ANGLIA
The best walks are along the coast, where the many nature reserves have profuse birdlife.

In northern Norfolk, head for Holme-next-the-Sea, Burnham Overy Staithe, Holkham Gap and Cley.

A path runs the length of the Suffolk coast. Aldeburgh, Thorpeness, Dunwich (for the Minsmere Reserve) and Southwold make good departure points.

There are good strolls through the Broads – try around Horsey Mere ■

Sherwood Forest Visitor Centre makes much of the tales of Robin Hood and his Merry Men

WALKS

THE INLAND SHIRES

In Hertfordshire, walk on the chalk downland of Ivinghoe Beacon, northeast of Tring on the edge of the Chilterns. Just across the border in Bedfordshire, you can hike along Dunstable Downs close to Whipsnade Zoo.

In Northamptonshire, combine a visit to the Canal Museum at Stoke Bruerne (5 miles south of Northampton at the heart of the canal system) with a walk along the towpath. There are more canalside walks along the Grand Union Canal in Leicestershire, for example, at Foxton Locks near Market Harborough.

In Nottinghamshire, your best bets are Clumber Park, and Sherwood Forest near Edwinstowe ∎

NOTTINGHAM and AROUND, NOTTINGHAMSHIRE   *106A4*

Don't be seduced by tales of Robin Hood and the Sheriff of Nottingham: Nottingham today is a busy, industrial city. Its Norman **castle** has virtually disappeared, replaced by a much later mansion housing a good museum and art gallery. Of equal interest are the tours of the **passages** below the castle's rock. In the 18th century, Nottingham expanded rapidly as a lace-making center, and the industry flourishes to this day.

Near the castle, visit the **Museum of Costume and Textiles,** and the **Lace Centre,** where you can buy lace items for every purpose imaginable. Redbrick Victorian warehouses at the Lace Market round Stoney Street are redolent of the city's past.

Sherwood Forest is a pale shadow of its former self. However, in the **Sherwood Forest Country Park,** near Edwinstowe north of Nottingham, you can wander among old oaks and be entertained in the visitor center with fanciful legends connected with the ever-popular philanthropic outlaw. Tradition tells that Maid Marian married Robin Hood at Edwinstowe's St. Mary's Church.

Clumber Park (NT), further north, has a further 4,000 acres of park and woodland.

Nottinghamshire has literary connections as well. Ten miles north of Nottingham, **Newstead Abbey,** a house incorporating a priory church, was the Byron family home and houses manuscripts and memorabilia of the poet.

"Whoever stands on Walker Street, Eastwood, will see the whole landscape of *Sons and Lovers* before him," wrote D.H. Lawrence. The terraced house in which the author lived in the old mining town of **Eastwood,** north west of Nottingham, has been furnished to depict working-class life in Victorian times.

PETERBOROUGH   *106B3*
CAMBRIDGESHIRE

This expanding town has a massive and remarkably complete Norman **cathedral.** The interior is powerfully simple, with a row of unadorned pillars under a superb ceiling painted with figures of saints, kings and monsters, while the glorious triple-arched Early English west front makes a successful break from the Norman cohesion.

★ SAFFRON WALDEN   *106C2*
ESSEX

This delightful, small town found wealth from the growing of saffron for medicine and dyes. Its 200-foot-long flint **church** is the largest in the county, and its high street has examples of pargeting (ornamental plasterwork).

Nearby **Audley End** (EH) was the country's largest Jacobean house when it was built by the lord treasurer to James I, though it was considerably reduced in size in the 18th century by Sir John Vanbrugh and Robert Adam. Its magnificence lies foremost in its great hall and state rooms.

★ ST. ALBANS and AROUND, HERTFORDSHIRE

106B1

St. Albans is named after a Roman soldier, Alban, who was beheaded for sheltering a priest and thus became the first English Christian martyr. The site of his execution was a shrine, then a rich abbey, and now a largely Norman **cathedral** (making use of Roman bricks). As well as Saint Alban's shrine, look for medieval wall paintings, the rood screen and the choir's painted ceiling.

To the west of town lie the extensive excavations of Roman *Verulamium*, once the most important town in Britain. It includes an amphitheater, city walls, house foundations, a temple, and an interesting museum of discoveries.

St. Albans itself has several old streets and inns which are also worth investigating.

Hatfield House ★ ★ ★, to the east of St. Albans, is a giant Jacobean palace, one of the country's showpiece stately homes. Queen Elizabeth I spent much of her childhood under house arrest in the old palace, of which only one wing survives. Items of her clothing, a large amount of fine art, tapestries, ornate plasterwork, a magnificent grand staircase and marble hall all make the house memorable.

Luton Hoo (south of Luton) isn't in the same architectural league, but houses the superb Wernher art collection, including Dutch old masters and art connected with the Russian imperial family.

The houses of Saffron Walden exhibit a wide range of architectural styles, many dating back several centuries

JOHN CONSTABLE (1776–1837)

Constable's paintings have brought fame the world over to the pastoral English landscape. Many represent scenes in Dedham Vale, which even in his lifetime was dubbed "Constable Country."

He was born in East Bergholt (an early studio is now just part of a garage), but it was the old family home and business at nearby Flatford Mill that provided the inspiration for some of his best-known works, such as *The Haywain*.

The National Trust (NT – see p.283) owns the buildings here, and tours of the painter's viewpoints match paintings with the little-altered subject matter. Other sights on the Constable trail include his school in Dedham, and a rare religious painting in the church at Nayland ∎

★ SOUTHWELL 106A4
NOTTINGHAMSHIRE

The glory of this small market town is its great **minster** (church). In the main it takes an early Norman style, in its triple towers, stern, simple nave and transept. But it is at its most remarkable in the late 13th-century octagonal chapter house, covered in exquisitely sculpted leaves and blossoms of every persuasion.

★★ STAMFORD 106B3
LINCOLNSHIRE

Mellow-stoned Stamford is sometimes referred to as the most handsome town of its size in England. It has been around for a long time, being one of the original 9th-century Danelaw towns. It was an important religious center and, temporarily, an alternative seat of learning to Oxford in the Middle Ages.

Its four medieval churches are worth a look, as are the Elizabethan almshouses of **Lord Burghley's Hospital** and 15th-century **Browne's Hospital**. Its period as an important coaching stop is well represented by the superbly atmospheric **George coaching inn**.

A mile south of town stands **Burghley House**, built by the chief minister to Elizabeth I and bristling with towers, turrets and chimneys. Baroque ceilings run rampant inside, amid an art collection of more than 700 works. Annual horse trials are held in the grounds.

★★★ STOUR VALLEY 107D2
SUFFOLK

In essence, little has changed visually from the countryside of Constable's youth: "Its luxuriant meadow flats sprinkled with flocks and herds, its well-cultivated uplands, its woods and rivers, with numerous scattered villages and churches, farms and picturesque cottages," was how he described it.

But he undersells the valley's gorgeous settlements. Even the smallest invariably boasts an incongruous, but impressive flint-faced "cloth" church (so called because in the Middle Ages it would have been built with proceeds from the cloth industry). More sizeable places also have a glorious half-timbered guildhall.

Lavenham ★★★, a medieval gem, is the prize town in this area. Among its 300 listed buildings are: the guildhall (NT), with an introduction to cloth manufacturing; the Little Hall, progressively a wool hall; a

merchant's house that more recently has been partly converted into an artists' dormitory. As you explore the timbered buildings that litter Lavenham's back streets, look for the ancient priory, converted into a family home, and don't miss the superb church.

A main road deprives neighboring **Long Melford** of real charm, but there are an incredible number of antique shops in which to browse, a magnificent church (note the benefactors' names on the exterior walls) and two Elizabethan stately homes. Finely furnished Melford Hall (NT) is somewhat stuffy, at least in comparison to its neighbor, Kentwell Hall, a relaxed, lived-in affair that lays on large-scale, painstaking historic "recreations" during much of the summer.

From Long Melford, the River Stour heads westward to pretty **Cavendish**, with thatched cottages around its green, and **Clare**, with more antique stores and timbered shops. To the south, **Castle Hedingham** has a superb Norman keep and enchanting back lanes. **Sudbury**, the valley's main center, is missable but for Gainsborough's House, where the prolific painter Thomas Gainsborough (1727–88) was born. Portraits of local squires and their families, as well as a number of landscapes and drawings, now hang on the walls.

WALKS

MORE EAST ANGLIA WALKS

From Cambridge, there's a delightful 2-mile walk through the water-meadows to Grantchester, a village associated with the poet Rupert Brooke.

The best way to approach Constable's Flatford Mill is on a meandering 2-mile amble along the banks of the River Stour from Dedham.

In Lincolnshire, the unspoiled chalk hills of the Lincolnshire Wolds around Louth provide the most stimulating walks.

Wicken Fen has a boardwalk past bog oaks, a birdwatchers' hide, and a longer nature trail ■

The guildhall at Lavenham in Suffolk is a typical example of many of the splendid half-timbered buildings in the town

ALDEBURGH FESTIVAL

While absconding from World War II in America as a conscientious objector, the Suffolk composer Benjamin Britten read an article by E.M. Forster about the Aldeburgh poet George Crabbe.

His best-known poem, *The Borough*, which describes the harsh life of Suffolk coastal folk, proved to be the basis for Britten's first and best-loved opera, *Peter Grimes*.

The Aldeburgh Festival was founded in 1948 to showcase British opera, and due to its ever-growing popularity, in 1967 the barley-processing Snape Maltings were converted into a superb concert hall. The festival takes place in June (for more details tel. 01728 453543) ∎

Head east from Sudbury to **Hadleigh**, its eminence as a wool town borne out by its fine church, guildhall and eccentric red-brick Deanery Tower, grouped strikingly together. The facades along its high street showcase the plastered and pargeted local styles of decoration.

Despite strong competition, **Kersey**, just outside Hadleigh, is undoubtedly the most adorable village in these parts, a scene of ancient inns, thatched and timbered weavers' cottages and often a family of ducks in its shallow ford. The keenest competition comes from a clutch of villages to the south, such as **Boxford**, **Polstead**, **Stoke-by-Nayland** and **Nayland**.

Most tourists make a beeline for tea, gifts and boats for rent in more commercialized **Dedham**, at the heart of Constable Country (see p.120). On the edge of Dedham at Castle House, you can view many works by the late Alfred Munnings, a distinguished painter best known for his studies of race horses.

SUFFOLK COAST   107E2

The Suffolk coastline has plenty of sleepy, old-world charm. Its shingle beaches, low cliffs and marshes fight a constant battle with the sea's eroding power.

Before **Orford** was placed inland by a growing spit of land, it was an important seaport, hence the magnificent 90-foot **castle** keep (EH).

Aldeburgh, firmly on the map as a musical mecca (see opposite), is otherwise a low-key fishing portand resort with a half-timbered moot hall next to a strip of shingle beach (400 years ago there were three roads between the hall and the sea).

Thorpeness is a unique vacation village of pseudo-old weatherboard and half-timbered buildings, laid out early this century around an artificial lake. You can't miss its lofty former water tower, delightfully named the House in the Clouds.

Beyond the controversial Sizewell nuclear power station comes the **Minsmere Reserve**, sheltering over 100 species of bird such as the avocet, a winter visitor, and the rare marsh harrier, which breeds here.

A whole medieval port, once one of the most prosperous in the country, lies under the water beyond the cliffs of now tiny **Dunwich**; visit the excellent little museum to hear the sad story. The lost city includes nine churches, the last to go falling into the sea in 1918. A solitary gravestone from its churchyard may still be visible when you visit.

At the most attractive, civilized resort of **Southwold** ★★★, red-brick and flint cottages are built around seven greens that came into being after a great fire in 1659. The Tudor cannon on Gun Hill, the gleaming white lighthouse in the center of town, and the parish church with a memorable painted and gilded interior all add to the town's appeal.

Sandy **Lowestoft** combines a mainstream seaside resort with a large, commercial fishing port. There are guided tours of the fish markets and docks in summer.

★ WOBURN ABBEY   106B2

Woburn has two attractions in one: the biggest drive-through safari park in Britain, where you can observe tigers, rhino and other wild beasts from the comfort of your car, and one of the world's finest private collections of paintings in the state rooms of its Palladian stately home. There are rooms devoted to Canaletto and Reynolds, and Dutch paintings including portraits by Rembrandt.

THE HEART OF ENGLAND

The Heart of England is a curious
blend - the stunning architectural
glory of the university city of Oxford,
contrasting with simple dry-stone
cottages in the Cotswolds of
Gloucestershire and the stark,
industrial Black Country of the
Midlands

CALENDAR OF EVENTS

APRIL –

Shakespeare's Birthday. Celebrated on April 23 with a procession through the streets to lay a wreath on the Bard's tomb.

MAY –

May morning festivities in Oxford.

AUGUST –

Three Choirs Festival. This is held alternately at Worcester, Hereford and Gloucester cathedrals and is Europe's oldest music festival.

SEPTEMBER –

Burton Beer Festival. Local, national and international breweries bring their beers, lagers and ciders to this three-day event.

SEPTEMBER and OCTOBER – Walsall Illuminations. Draws around 300,000 visitors to the town as thousands of light bulbs shimmer and sparkle after dark ■

THE HEART OF ENGLAND

Few parts of England are as varied in nature yet as quintessentially English as this region, stretching from the outskirts of London west to the Cotswolds, across to the Welsh border and up to the industrial landscapes around Birmingham.

★★★ HIGHLIGHTS

Black Country Museum (► 129)
Bourton-on-the-Water (► 134)
Great Tew (► 135)
Henley-on-Thames (► 141)
Hidcote Manor (► 135)
Ironbridge Gorge (► 143)
Oxford (► 146)
Painswick (► 133)
Shrewsbury (► 148)
Stratford-upon-Avon (► 148)

Everyone's ideal English village, with stone cottages, flower-filled gardens, an ancient church and stream running by, is multiplied a hundredfold in the **Cotswolds**. Even more "English" is the image of black-and-white timbered buildings from the days of the Tudors; hundreds still survive, especially in Shropshire, Worcestershire and Hereford-shire. The university city of **Oxford**'s "dreaming spires" may seem a moviemaker's cliche, but it is hard not to feel a surge of emotion as you glimpse them from hills to the east. Even the industrial **Black Country** and Ironbridge Gorge have a romantic side: the area is the birthplace of the Industrial Revolution, which went on to transform not only Britain but the world.

The homes of two statesmen, George Washington and Sir Winston Churchill, are among many widely contrasting, historic mansions to seek out, while the town of **Stratford-upon-Avon** is associated with the great playwright William Shakespeare.

Less well known, but arguably as great in his own way, was Abraham Darby of Coalbrookdale,

father of the Industrial Revolution, whose story is told at Ironbridge Gorge. Don't avoid the Black Country, perhaps put off by the name; it is far greener and more interesting than you might ever imagine, and the gritty realism of its industrial history provides a bracing contrast to an overdose of Cotswolds prettiness.

The countryside of the Heart of England was not always so peaceful. During the Civil Wars of the mid-17th century, major battles were fought at Marston Moor and Worcester between the Royalist Cavaliers and Parliamentarian Roundheads, and many families were split apart by their political differences. Earlier still was the turmoil of the

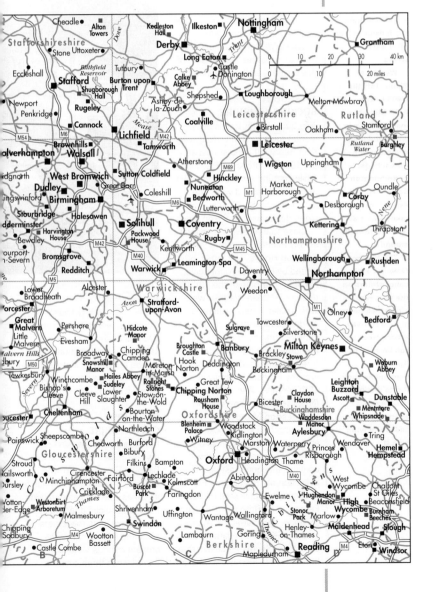

WALKS

CHILTERN WOODLAND

The 85-mile Ridgeway runs along the top of the Chiltern escarpment, with fine views and prehistoric interest. The beech woods clothing the hillsides also offer excellent walks.

Wendover Woods (off the A4011 near Aylesbury) has marked trails in woodland once owned by the Rothschilds.

Boddington Bank is an Iron Age hillfort which takes about 30 minutes to walk around.

The two-hour Firecrest Trail concentrates on the tiny, rare bird which nests high in Norway spruce trees and can be seen from April to September; look for its distinctive orange cap, white eye-stripe and white wing-bars ■

Middle Ages, which explains the existence of many castles; War-wick and Berkeley are among the most impressive.

But these castles are youthful compared to the Iron Age hillforts of the **Malvern Hills**, the 4,000-year-old **Icknield Way**, running along the ridge of the **Chiltern Hills** on its way to Stonehenge, or the atmospheric **Rollright Stones**, as important to Neolithic peoples as Stonehenge itself. A walk on the breezy hilltops is perhaps the best way of all to get a true "overview" of this beautiful part of England.

AYLESBURY   *125D1*
BUCKINGHAMSHIRE

A frequent visitor to this busy market town east of Oxford was King Henry VIII, who stayed at the 15th-century Kings Head inn while courting Anne Boleyn, who became his second wife. The parish church, St. Mary's, is much older, dating back to Saxon times.

Close to the town are several stately mansions, among them **Claydon House** (NT), often visited by Florence Nightingale, nurse and heroine of the 19th-century Crimean War; **Stowe**, with its elaborately landscaped gardens (NT) dotted with 18th-century temples, grottoes, monuments and bridges; and three great mansions built by the wealthy Rothschild family in the 19th century – **Ascott House** (NT), **Mentmore Towers** and **Waddesdon Manor** (NT). Waddesdon, a French-inspired architectural extravaganza of the "no expense spared" variety, contains an equally astonishing collection of 18th-century French decorative art collected by Baron Ferdinand de Rothschild. Carved paneling, royal furniture, Aubusson and Savonnerie carpets and tapestries, Sèvres porcelain, rare books, Dutch, Flemish and Italian

paintings, and portraits by Gainsborough, Reynolds and Romney are displayed in such abundance that they almost cause visual indigestion, which can be relieved by a stroll around the terraced gardens, aviary and extensive parkland.

BANBURY   *125C2*
OXFORDSHIRE

Immortalized in the nursery rhyme "Ride a cock horse to Banbury Cross" (see p.139), Banbury is also locally famous for its cakes – sweet pastry rounds filled with spiced dried fruit – which have been made here since the 16th century. The present cross is Victorian; Banbury had three crosses

originally, but all were taken down by enthusiastic Puritans in the early 17th century. The flower-bedecked town center, with its bustling street markets on Thursdays and Saturdays, displays handsome buildings, many of 18th-century origin or older.

At the museum in Horsefair (one of many street names recalling Banbury's importance as an agricultural market center), you can also find out about "chapbooks," by which the Rusher family, 19th-century local printers, made literature available to a wider audience. There is also historical information here about the cross and its rhyme (see p.139).

BERKELEY CASTLE   *124B1*
GLOUCESTERSHIRE

In this magnificent Norman castle, begun in 1153 and the home of the Berkeley family ever since, King Edward II of England was murdered in 1327; he is buried in Gloucester Cathedral (see p.137). The cell in which he was imprisoned makes a stark contrast to the splendor of the apartments, with their fine tapestries, paintings and furniture. The gardens have been replanted in Elizabethan style.

The castle overlooks an attractive small town which was the birthplace and home of Dr. Edward Jenner, who pioneered smallpox vaccination; he is buried in the local churchyard.

The present Banbury Cross is Victorian and stands ignominiously in the middle of a traffic circle in the town center

The Gas Street Basin, in Birmingham, is home to many colorful barges. Birmingham is part of an extensive canal network, a good escape from the jungle of roads and intersections

BIRMINGHAM 125B3
WEST MIDLANDS

Birmingham, Britain's largest city after London, cannot be called beautiful: wrecked by city "planners" of the mid-20th century, it is a mess of flyover roads, industrial parks and sprawling suburbs. But it also has more canals than Venice (created as an early mass-transport system at the height of the Industrial Revolution in the late 18th and early 19th centuries) and a few splendid Victorian buildings, the legacy of its 19th-century wealth and industrial importance.

The massive **City Museum and Art Gallery** contains the world's best collection of 19th-century Pre-Raphaelite paintings (by Ford Maddox Brown, Edward Burne-Jones, Dante Gabriel Rossetti and Holman Hunt, among others) and the Holy Grail tapestries designed· by Burne-Jones and made by the William Morris Arts Workers' Guild.

The early 18th-century cathedral has fine plasterwork and jewel-like east windows by Burne-Jones and William Morris. In the City Library, itself architecturally unimpressive, is a comprehensive collection of Shakespeariana: over 50,000 books and illustrations relate to the playwright.

The **Jewellery Quarter Discovery Centre** tells of the city's importance as a center for gold- and silversmiths: over 200 still work here, carrying on a tradition established in medieval times. The city has had its own assay office (to check the purity of the metal) since the mid-15th century, with an anchor as its assay mark.

At **Bournville**, another major industry opens its doors to visitors: **Cadbury World** offers the chance to look around a chocolate factory established by the Cadbury family during the 19th century.

While in Birmingham, do not pass up a chance to hear the top-quality City of Birmingham Symphony Orchestra in its home at the Symphony Hall (details from the tourist information office).

industries which flourished here. Go underground "into the thick" at the colliery, or watch the sparks fly at the Castlefields Ironworks, where chain-making, nail-making, forging and metal-working are still living skills.

Watch the great replica *Newcomen* engine, first built in 1712 to pump water from mines on Lord Dudley's estates; its steam power was quickly utilized by the early industrialists.

Trams and trolley-buses, horse-drawn delivery carts, and locally made early cars all travel the streets, while narrowboats offer trips right beneath the Castle Hill to see impressive limestone caverns. Canals are a feature of the Black Country, with pleasant canal path walks, wharves and handsome warehouses, and elegant ironwork bridges.

But Dudley is not only concerned with the 19th century. Overlooking the town is a great Norman **castle** with an adjoining range of 16th-century apartments, all gutted by fire in 1750 and now an impressive ruin.

Elsewhere in the Black Country, there are some other surprises. Great Barr is the site of **Asbury's Cottage**, boyhood home of one of the earliest Methodist preachers, Francis Asbury. At John Wesley's request, Asbury sailed to America in 1771, where over the next 45 years he traveled over 250,000 miles on horseback, preaching the Methodist gospel. He became a bishop in 1784 and, after a lifetime of preaching nearly 18,000 sermons, died in 1816. A statue of him stands in Washington D.C.

At Walsall is the **Garman Ryan Collection**, a superb assemblage of paintings and sculpture given to the town by the widow of New York-born sculptor Sir Jacob Epstein, and including works by Van Gogh, Picasso, Constable

THE BLACK COUNTRY *125B3*
WEST MIDLANDS

North and west of Birmingham stretches the Black Country, a birthplace of the Industrial Revolution, and named for the smoking factory chimneys, mining spoil heaps and devastated countryside which resulted. Land reclamation work has brought about a much greener present-day landscape than the name might suggest.

The tale unfolds in Dudley at the excellent **Black Country Museum ★★★**, which describes life in an industrial community in the 19th century. Industrial buildings and dwellings from elsewhere in the area have been re-erected and peopled with living, costumed inhabitants. The village pub, the Bottle and Glass, serves Black Country ale and authentic faggots and peas (a cheap and filling meat dish made of the less popular parts of a pig).

With its Methodist chapel, a hardware store, bakery and candy store, the village center is surrounded on its 26-acre site by working examples of the

CANALS

The building of canals was part of the Industrial Revolution. The first canal linked St. Helens with the River Mersey in the 1750s.

In the 1760s, the Bridgewater Canal was built to carry coal into Manchester and later to Liverpool. Canals linking the River Trent and Mersey, the Thames and Severn, followed, creating a network between London, Liverpool, Birmingham, Hull, and Bristol. By the 1850s there were 4,250 miles of canal.

The coming of the railways started the canals' decline, which was compounded by the arrival of motor transport. However, some 4 million tons of goods are still carried by water, in addition to the canals' important recreational use ■

THE HEART OF ENGLAND

WALK

WYRE FOREST

This mixed wood-land, near Bewdley, is rich in wildlife, especially butterflies. A 4-mile walk starts at the visitor center.

Take the track to the right, then follow the left-hand, uphill path at the red/green post. At the T-junction turn right and right again, following red markers through the woods.

At Park House, turn right on the old railway track where you might spot rare fritillary butterflies.

After the cutting, turn right before a bridge, then left onto a bridlepath; there will be fungi to spot below the trees in the fall.

The path eventually turns left where two paths cross, past a pool, uphill and back to the parking lot ∎

and Turner. Walsall also has a prize-winning **Leather Museum**, dedicated to the industry for which the town is famous, with craftsmen demonstrating their skill, and, near St. Matthew's Church, a huge **open-air market** with several bargains to be found.

The Black Country is also known for its glassmaking, and several crystal glass companies still operate in the Stourbridge area; glass can be purchased at the factory shops. The Broadfield House Glass Museum at Kingswinford displays much older glass, some dating back to Roman times.

★★ BLENHEIM PALACE   125C1
WOODSTOCK, OXFORDSHIRE

This vast baroque mansion, home of the Churchill family and birthplace in 1874 of Sir Winston Churchill, the great British leader during World War II, occupies seven acres of ground.

It was built for the first Duke of Marlborough in 1722, on land given to him by Queen Anne as a reward for his military victory against the French at Blenheim in 1704.

Designed by Sir John Vanbrugh, assisted by Nicholas Hawksmoor, with stone carvings by the great Grinling Gibbons, the state rooms overflow with paintings by Van Dyke, Reynolds, Romney and Kneller, elaborate gilding, richly carved furniture, tapestries and damasks. Sir Winston Churchill is commemorated in the Churchill Exhibition, which is situated close to the room in which he was born.

The surrounding gardens and parkland have been altered over the years; some of Vanbrugh's formal, symmetrical designs were swept away by landscape gardener "Capability" Brown later in the 18th century. Brown was responsible for the present lake;

the centerpiece of the magnificent view which opens out as visitors enter the park through the triumphal arch from Woodstock. Early in the 20th century, formal gardens were restored close to the house, re-creating the setting which Vanbrugh had originally envisaged.

★ BRIDGNORTH   125B3
SHROPSHIRE

If you suffer from vertigo, do not go to Bridgnorth: its site on a sandstone cliff high above the River Severn has necessitated steep and winding steps, paths and lanes – and even a cliff railway – to join High Town and Low Town. The town center blends half-timbered and deep-red brick buildings in a satisfying mixture of styles and dates, centering on the town hall of 1652. The remains of Bridgnorth's Norman castle, which can be seen from Castle Walk at the clifftop, lean alarmingly sideways, seeming to defy gravity.

Bridgnorth is the northern terminus of the **Severn Valley Railway**, which operates steam-hauled trains south to Kidderminster via Bewdley through a green and leafy river valley. You might be lucky enough to see as many as five or more preserved steam locomotives at the engine sheds along the route, hissing and puffing as if they had stepped straight out of the past.

It is well worth stopping off at **Bewdley** to see its fine, brick-built, 18th-century town center, with some earlier half-timbered, 16th- and 17th-century buildings. Drop into the Old Shambles Museum (where butchers once traded) to see an operational brass foundry, workshops and demonstrations of local crafts, including charcoal burning and the making of clay pipes, ropes and glass. The **Wyre Forest**, west of the town, is a national nature reserve of broadleaved woodland, with waymarked trails.

★ CHELTENHAM   125B2
GLOUCESTERSHIRE

Cheltenham is the epitome of gentility. Its heyday was as a spa town in the early 19th-century Regency period, and it still preserves fine 18th- and 19th-century terraced housing embellished with wrought-iron balconies and balustrades. The town flourished on its mineral spring, which was discovered in 1715. You can try the water for yourself at the **Pittville Pump Room** (like most noncommercial, true mineral water, it is an acquired taste), where there is also a costume collection to admire. The town's original pump room (where the spring water was pumped up for consumption), called the Rotunda, is in Montpellier Street.

Gustav Holst (composer of *The Planets*) was born in Cheltenham in 1874; his birthplace can be visited. An international Festival of Music every July and a Festival of Literature in October still bring musicians, composers and writers to the town. Equally famous is the National Hunt Festival Meeting, the main event in the steeplechasing calendar, which takes place each March at the racecourse.

★ CHILTERN HILLS   125D1
OXFORDSHIRE

To the east of Oxford, from the River Thames as far northeast as Luton, stretch the chalk hills known as the Chilterns. Along the top runs the prehistoric Icknield Way, part of a 4,000-year-old track leading eventually to the great neolithic monuments at

Avebury and Stonehenge. Cutting through the hills are the Roman Watling Street (now the A5) and Akeman Street (now the A41). An Iron Age earthwork known as Grim's Ditch runs across the hills, possibly a boundary or defensive in nature. Stone Age barrows (burial mounds) and Iron Age forts crown the hilltops. History steeps the beechwood-clad hillsides and breezy tops.

Burnham Beeches, south of Beaconsfield, is perhaps the most famous of the woodlands; here, centuries of coppicing (cutting off the tree trunks about 6 feet from the ground to encourage multi-stemmed growth suitable for firewood and wood-turning) have resulted in huge gnarled and twisted trees, best viewed in their fresh spring growth or rich autumn colors. Above the woods stretch acres of springy-turfed downland with magnificent views over the vales of both Oxford and Aylesbury.

The towns and villages in and around the Chilterns are popular with the wealthier middle classes, leading to some suburban sprawl, but thatched, half-timbered, or brick and flint cottages and handsome houses are still to be found in the Chiltern towns and countryside.

Mapledurham, by the River Thames, offers an Elizabethan house topped by a forest of typically tall chimneys, and the river's only remaining working watermill. Further up the Thames is **Wallingford**, with a magnificent, medieval 19-arched bridge, three medieval churches and a wealth of 16th- to 18th-century buildings in its attractive town center. Visit **Ewelme**, a tiny village northeast of Wallingford, to see perfectly preserved 15th-century almshouses, a school and a church built by the Earl of Suffolk and his wife Alice,

GUSTAV HOLST (1974–1934)

Of Swedish ancestry (which explains the un-English name of a very English composer), Holst originally intended to be a concert pianist.

Instead, he first became an orchestral trombone player, then taught as a music master.

He is perhaps best known for his suite in seven movements, *The Planets*, composed between 1914 and 1917.

His *St. Paul's Suite for Strings*, written in 1913, was inspired by English folk songs, while *Egdon Heath* (1927) and *Concerto for Two Violins* (1929) are among his better-known later works.

His grave can be seen in Chichester cathedral ■

THE HEART OF ENGLAND

THE WINDSOR CHAIR

Windsor chairs have been made around High Wycombe for at least 300 years.

Popular in inns and coffee houses, they feature a solid, molded seat. The work of a woodturner ("bodger") rather than a joiner, the sticks are turned using a pole lathe, then driven into holes bored in the seat.

Different woods might be used: elm for the seat and beech for the legs, but yew, birch or ash for arms and back. The center back was often filled by a "splat," a wider plank with decorative piercing.

Windsor chairs were made also in America, but without splats; Thomas Jefferson sat in a Windsor chair in 1776, when signing the Declaration of Independence ∎

granddaughter of the Canterbury *Tales* poet, Geoffrey Chaucer. Set on a terraced hillside, all three buildings still perform their original functions. The tomb of Alice, with an angel-carved canopy and alabaster effigy, can be seen in the church.

Near High Wycombe, once the center for manufacturing Windsor chairs and still associated with furniture-making, are Stonor Park and Hughenden Manor. **Stonor Park** looks 18th century, but beneath the brick facade lies a much older house, home of the Stonor family for 600 years.

Nineteenth-century **Hughenden Manor** was the home of Benjamin Disraeli (1804–81) one of Britain's most famous prime ministers.

High Wycombe itself is typically 18th-century, with its handsome market house (known locally as the "pepperpot") and guildhall. Here, once a year, the medieval ceremony of weighing in the town mayor and charter trustees takes place. The origin of this practice was to determine whether town officials had grown fat at the taxpayers' expense during their term of office. The beautiful parish church dates from the 11th to 13th centuries.

Nearby **West Wycombe**, with buildings from the 17th and 18th centuries and almost entirely owned by the National Trust, is associated with the notorious Sir Francis Dashwood (1708–81), who lived at West Wycombe Park. Sir Francis established the Hell-Fire Club, whose members dabbled in black magic, but were better known as drunks and lechers – the delinquents of their day. They met, among other places, in the **West Wycombe Caves**, chalk caverns now open to the public, and in the hollow golden ball at the top of St. Lawrence's Church.

East of High Wycombe, at Chalfont St. Giles, a **cottage museum** recalls the poet John Milton (1608–74), who stayed in the village in 1665. Having left London to escape the great plague, which was killing off inhabitants in their hundreds, Milton completed *Paradise Lost* here and started work on *Paradise Regained*. At the **Chiltern Open-Air Museum** nearby, traditional buildings are on show, saved from dereliction or demolition and moved here.

★★★ THE COTSWOLDS   125B1
GLOUCESTERSHIRE

The towns and villages set around the Cotswold escarpment – a swath of golden, creamy or gray-colored stone, stretching from Stratford-upon-Avon south-west to Cirencester and beyond – owe their beauty to sheep, or rather, the wool on their backs.

In medieval times, the wealth created by the wool industry built stately, large-windowed, light-filled churches in every town and country parish. Their congregations lived, and still live, in mullion-windowed cottages, with roofs encrusted with golden lichen, set in flower-filled gardens beside tumbling rivers or streams; in villages such as Bourton-on-the-Water, the overall effect is almost too chocolate-box perfect. Naturally, visitors flock to see such pretty places, but there are still communities where the roads and sidewalks stay uncrowded even in high summer.

The Cotswolds divide naturally into two halves: the southwestern communities cluster around Cirencester, while the northeastern towns and villages look more to Chipping Norton as their center.

Cirencester itself (locally pronounced "Sister") is a

substantial, busy market town, centered on the splendid St. John the Baptist parish church, with its fan-vaulted porch and soaring interior. Take a walk along Dollar Street to enjoy old-fashioned, bow-windowed facades, or Cecily Hill, leading to Cirencester Park around a stately mansion. In the 1st century, Cirencester (or Corinium as it was called) was a great Roman city, second only to London in importance. The **Corinium Museum** tells the story, while at **Chedworth**, north of the town, an excavated Roman country villa, with handsome mosaic floors, underfloor central heating and baths, shows that they knew how to live in style.

Northwest of Cirencester, **Painswick ★ ★ ★** is a beautiful old cloth-weaving town with gray-stone houses and cottages set on a sloping site around a 14th-century parish church; the graveyard contains 99 yew trees and a wealth of 16th- to 19th-century tombstones. The 17th-century Court House, a manor house built for a cloth merchant, and the 18th-century Painswick House are both worth seeing. A climb to the top of Painswick Beacon above the town opens up magnificent countryside views.

East of Painswick is one of the prettiest Cotswold villages, **Sheepscombe**, its cottages scattered along a valley with beech woods to shelter them.

To the south of Painswick are **Dursley**, with its pillared, bell-turreted Market House of 1738; **Wotton-under-Edge**, beneath the Cotswold escarpment, once famous for woolen and silken cloths and with the beautiful 13th-century St. Mary's parish church; **Nailsworth**, a handsome mill town with many surviving mill buildings now converted to other uses; and the hilltop market town of **Minchinhampton**, which

has been in existence since Norman times.

For a superb view, and a trip back to prehistoric times, climb up to **Uley Bury**, a 2,000-year-old Iron Age hillfort near Dursley; to the north is Hetty Pegler's Tump, a neolithic burial mound which dates from about 2800 BC.

It is probable that the countryside all around here has been farmed since Roman times, 2,000 years ago.

East of Cirencester is the archetypical Cotswold village of **Bibury**. Full of pretty cottages and flower-filled gardens, it is famous for Arlington Row, a terrace of former weavers' cottages reached by a pictures-que three-arched footbridge over the River Coln. The 17th-century, water-powered Arlington Mill, now housing a museum, stands on a site recorded in the 11th-century Domesday Book. Among its exhibits are items by William Morris (1834–96), leader of the Arts and Crafts Movement, poet, writer and active socialist, who moved to **Kelmscott Manor** a few miles east in 1871, and whose ideas for house decoration

Arlington Row, in the attractive Cotswold village of Bibury, was built to house weavers whose history is told in nearby Arlington Mill Museum

The 17th-century facade conceals a Tudor house at Snowshill Manor, which contains Charles Paget Wade's eclectic collection of craftsmanship

and furnishing were very influential in late-Victorian Britain.

Fairford, south of Bibury, boasts a splendid "wool church" with late 15th-century stained-glass windows. Nearby, at Filkins, the **Cotswold Woollen Weavers** operate a working woolen mill in 18th-century buildings, continuing the Cotswold tradition. At Northleach, tradition is also on display, this time in a house of correction (country jail, complete with restored courtroom and cellblock) where the **Cotswold Countryside Collection** focuses on agricultural history exhibits.

Tradition of a different sort can be seen on many Saturdays or Sundays on village greens or outside country pubs throughout the Cotswolds: the centuries-old dances of the **Morris Men**. Many local villages have their own "sides" of dancers, those of Bampton being perhaps the best known; a particular step-and-jump

used in many dances is called a "Bampton caper."

Further east is **Burford**, built on a hill with its wide, main street sloping down to a medieval stone bridge crossing the River Windrush. Its many inns saw the hustle and bustle of passengers in the days of stagecoaches; their modern equivalents bring crowds of summer visitors to admire the Church of St. John the Baptist, Warwick Almshouses, the grammar school, Tolsey Museum and several other attractions.

Bourton-on-the-Water ★★★, northeast of Burford, is just as busy, even prettier, and packed with visitor attractions, including a 1937 scale model of the village. It is best visited either very early or very late in the day.

Lower Slaughter and nearby Upper Slaughter are not at all bloody, much less frequented than some of the other Cotswold villages, and rewarding to wander through, with their typical stone cottages, old mill and stream.

Chipping Norton, market center for the northern half of the Cotswolds, means just that: "northern market." The area has been inhabited since before Roman times judging by the **Rollright Stone Circle**, a late neolithic (*about* 3000 BC) henge of standing stones, which can be found northwest of the town. There was a substantial Saxon, then Norman, community at Chipping Norton, but it really flourished on the medieval wool trade, evidenced by its handsome guildhall, almshouses, and 14th-century St. Mary's Church with earlier Norman features. Its vicar, Henry Joyce, was hanged from the tower in 1549 when local people rioted following the introduction of Archbishop Cranmer's English Prayer Book to replace the Latin Mass. The mid-19th-century Bliss Mill is a survivor of the town's continuing importance as a textile center through the centuries. It is now converted to apartments.

The village of Hook Norton is famous for its delicious ale which you can sample in many Cotswold pubs. Nearby **Great Tew** ★ ★ ★, with its thatched cottages and sheltering trees, is one of the loveliest villages in the area; its parish church contains a treasury of wall paintings, linenfold paneling, a 15th-century font and three-decker pulpit (for parson, reader and clerk).

To the west lies **Stow-on-the-Wold**, 800 feet up on the Cotswold escarpment, with handsome stone houses and antique shops fronting a broad square; and **Winchcombe**, with its gargoyle-encrusted church, and folk and railway museums. **Cleeve Hill**, nearby, gives fine views west to the Malvern Hills, while ruined **Hailes Abbey** to

the east was established by Cistercian monks in the 13th century.

Sudeley Castle, southeast of Winchcombe, was the home of Katherine Parr, sixth wife of King Henry VIII. She survived him (by just one year) and was buried here. The 12th- to 15th-century castle contains paintings by Rubens, Van Dyck and Turner

The handsome market town of **Chipping Campden** (don't pronounce the "p" in Campden) is centered around its wide main street and market hall of 1627. The 14th-century Woolstaplers Hall museum is nearby, as is a fine parish church containing the largest memorial brass in Gloucestershire. North of town, at **Hidcote Manor** (NT) ★ ★ ★, is a beautiful garden laid out from 1907 by an American, Major Lawrence Johnstone. A keen gardener and plant collector, he traveled all over the world to find specimens for his garden "rooms," such as the Poppy Garden and White Garden.

The beauty of **Broadway** attracts the crowds. Golden-stone houses and cottages – gabled, stone-tiled or thatched, in 16th- and 17th-century style – fringe the broad main street. The 16th-century Lygon Arms, once a private mansion, hosted both King Charles I and Oliver Cromwell (the head of the Parliamentarian forces responsible for the king's death in 1649). Overlooking the village is Broadway Tower, 1,000 feet above sea level, built as a folly in 1800.

Snowshill Manor, to the south, is a beautiful 16th-century house containing an interesting collection of clocks, toys, musical instruments, bicycles, weavers' and spinners' tools and Japanese armor! The nearby villages of Buckland and Stanton are both full of charm.

COTSWOLD MORRIS DANCING

Morris dances are part of a tradition found all over England.

In 1911, the English Folk Dance Society was set up to preserve and promote the dances "in their true traditional form." Many of the sides (teams) seen in the Cotswolds stem from this revival, but the origins of the men of Bampton, Headington Quarry and Chipping Campden are much earlier.

Six dancers dressed in white, with sashes, flowered hats, ribbons and bells, white handkerchiefs and sticks are accompanied by a fiddler or accordionist and hindered by a "fool" with a pig's bladder on a stick ■

THE HEART OF ENGLAND

EMBROIDERED HISTORY

Hardwick Hall is famous for its collection of 16th- and 17th-century embroideries.

Some of these are closely associated with Hardwick's founder – Elizabeth, Countess of Shrewsbury, more popularly known as "Bess of Hardwick" – and others with Mary, Queen of Scots, who was the Countess' prisoner for 14 years.

At least one embroidery is probably Mary's work; it shows her personal monogram beneath a crown, against a background of thistles (symbol of Scotland), lilies (France) and roses (England).

All the embroideries demonstrate the Elizabethans' love of nature, bright colors, strong design and humor; some have been in the house since 1601 ■

COVENTRY 125C3
WEST MIDLANDS

The main reason to visit the car-manufacturing city of Coventry is to see its **cathedral**, designed by Sir Basil Spence and built between 1954 and 1962 beside the ruins of its 1,000-year-old predecessor, which was destroyed by bombing during World War II. With vivid stained-glass windows by John Piper, a dramatic tapestry by Graham Sutherland, sculpture by Sir Jacob Epstein and an engraved glass screen by John Hutton, the memorable postwar building crowned by a lantern tower is filled with the best modern religious art of the time. Transport enthusiasts will want to visit the Museum of British Road Transport, where there are many vintage vehicles on show, together with *Thrust 2*, holder of the World Land Speed Record.

DERBY and AROUND 125C4
DERBYSHIRE

Derby is a dreary place, relieved only by its displays of Derby porcelain in the City **Museum and Art Gallery** and **Royal Crown Derby Museum**, but in its vicinity lie some splendid stately homes. Ten miles south, the baroque mansion of **Calke Abbey** (NT) is billed as "the house where time stood still," looking much as it did when the reclusive last baronet died in 1924.

Palladian **Kedleston Hall** (NT), 5 miles northwest of Derby, is one of Robert Adam's masterpieces, particularly its interior, with the dazzling Marble Hall and the domed Saloon. **Hardwick Hall** (NT), close to the M1 southeast of Chesterfield, stands as one of England's great Elizabethan houses, its highlight being the magnificent High Great Chamber decorated with a plaster frieze and period tapestries.

FOREST OF DEAN 124A1
GLOUCESTERSHIRE

An ancient royal forest, later a major coal, iron-ore, stone and charcoal producing area, the Forest of Dean is still a mix of industrialization amid attractive woodlands. Once the area almost ruled itself: the "free miners" had historic rights set out in the medieval Book of Dennis; the growing and living things of the forest – the "vert" and venison – were looked after by the verderers, first appointed early in the 11th century.

This early self-government still survives in part: the miners' rights continue to the present day, while the people of Gloucestershire now elect the verderers, who meet four times a year in Speech House at the forest's center and have a role to play in environmental decisions.

Find out more about the area and its independent-spirited people at the **Dean Heritage Centre**, in a converted mill at Soudley. Travel the Dean Forest Railway behind a steam locomotive or go down into the **Clearwell Caves**, an iron-ore mining complex worked for nearly 2,000 years which is now a museum. Visit Newland church to see, in the Greyndour Chapel, the Miner's Brass, showing a medieval forest miner holding pick and hod with a candle in his mouth.

Northward, up the Wye Valley, is **Symonds Yat**, a famous rocky viewpoint overlooking the Wye. There is a path along the riverbank below, through one of the prettiest parts of the gorge. West of the forest, on the banks of the Wye, stands **Tintern Abbey**, a medieval Cistercian foundation, roofless but with walls still standing to their full height, which inspired both the painter J.M.W. Turner and the poet Wordsworth.

★ **GLOUCESTER** *125B2*
GLOUCESTERSHIRE
Though it has many bland modern buildings, Gloucester, founded by the Romans nearly 2,000 years ago, still retains a medieval heart and cathedral worth exploring. On Westgate Street, the Folk Museum occupies a row of 16th- to 17th-century half-timbered houses. The cathedral precincts center on the impressive **cathedral** itself, founded in the 12th century and added to over succeeding centuries in a pleasing mix of styles. It has a magnificent east window of medieval stained glass. The *Tailor of Gloucester* show a picturesque building which now houses a Beatrix Potter Museum.

In complete contrast to the medieval heart are Gloucester's 19th-century inland docks, where red-brick warehouses now house shops, restaurants and offices. Here the **National Waterways Museum** tells the history of Britain's canals, while the Regiments of Gloucester Museum covers 300 years of military history. The **Robert Opie Collection of Advertising and Packaging** has a huge variety of boxes, packages and leaflets which survived the trash can.

The Robert Opie Packaging Museum is a treasure house of ephemera arranged thematically, as in this old chemist's shop

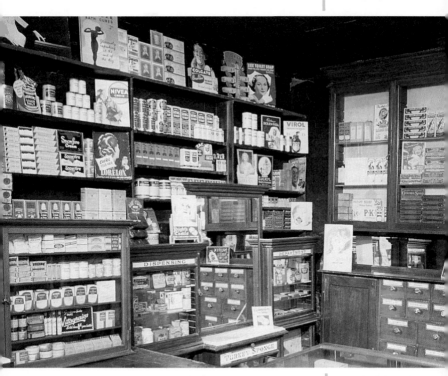

cloisters, around a peaceful garden, are roofed with some of the finest 14th-century fan vaulting in Europe.

Gloucester has another claim to fame: Beatrix Potter's illustrations for her story *The*

South from Gloucester heading down the M5 is **Slimbridge Wildfowl and Wetlands Trust**, established by Sir Peter Scott, where a huge number of birds can be seen from hides, particularly in winter.

DRIVE

THE NORTH COTSWOLDS

99 miles (allow 2 days)

This circuit, through the lesser-known half of the Cotswolds, features stone-walled fields, stone-built villages and handsome churches, as well as prehistoric standing stones.
The family homes of two great statesmen, Sir Winston Churchill and George Washington, are highlights of the tour.

"CAPABILITY" BROWN

Lancelot Brown (1715–83) began as a kitchen gardener in Oxfordshire. He was a pupil of William Kent, and became a destroyer of the formal Dutch style of garden.

His nickname arose because he claimed always to see "the capability of improvement." He planted thousands of trees, and was largely responsible for the idea of "English parkland." He worked at Stowe, and was made Royal Gardener at Hampton Court. Later schemes included Croome Court and Blenheim. A monument to him was erected at Croome in 1809 ■

Leave Oxford on the A44 (A34) north and turn left onto an unclassified road towards Cassington. At Cassington, turn north onto an unclassified road; at the A4095 turn right to Bladon, then left on the A44 to Woodstock.

1 Woodstock, Oxfordshire
Pause at Bladon churchyard to see the starkly simple grave of Sir Winston Churchill, British prime minister during World War II (and the graves of his wife and parents), then continue into stone-built Woodstock. In the town center is the Oxfordshire County Museum, telling of the local history and landscape from the Stone Age to the present. But most people head straight for Blenheim Palace, at the end of the main street (see p.130). The surrounding parkland will tempt you out for a walk after sampling the treasures of the palace itself.

From Woodstock take the A44 north, turning left onto the B4437 to Charlbury and then the B4026 to Chipping Norton.

2 Chipping Norton, Oxfordshire
The woolen trade has left a legacy of interesting buildings in this town, which include: the splendid church of 14th- to 15th-century origin, the guildhall, substantial stone houses and shops and the impressive 19th-century Bliss Tweed Mill, marked by a tall chimney.

Continue north on the B4026, then turn left onto the A3400 for just over a mile and turn left onto an unclassified road signed Little Rollright.

3 Rollright Stones, Oxfordshire
This stone "henge" was probably as important to neolithic people as Stonehenge or Avebury. The stones, nicknamed "The King's Men," measure 100 feet across. The King Stone, a monolith, is just across the road, while the Whispering Knights (the remains of a prehistoric burial chamber) are gathered a few yards down the road.

Return to the A3400 and go south before turning left onto the A361. Just beyond Bloxham turn left onto unclassified roads to Broughton.

4 Broughton, Oxfordshire
Broughton Castle is the magnificent moated home of Lord Saye and Sele, whose family has lived here since 1451. The original manor house was fortified by William de Wykeham (1324–1404, founder of New College, Oxford) to withstand the frequent unrest of 14th-century England. In about 1600, the Fiennes family "modernized" the old house to create the stylish Elizabethan mansion seen today.

BEHIND THE RHYME

Ride a cock-horse to Banbury Cross, To see a fine lady upon a white horse, With rings on her fingers and bells on her toes, She shall have music wherever she goes.

A "cock-horse" is a child's hobby-horse. The "fine lady" may be Celia Fiennes, who traveled around the countryside on horseback in the 1690s and wrote of her experiences in her diaries.

Another possibility is the "earth goddess" of traditional May Morning rituals (represented by a flower-bedecked young girl).

Rings were a sign of wealth and rank, while bells were often sewn as decoration onto clothing and footwear in medieval times ■

Celia Fiennes, 17th-century diarist and traveler, was the sister of the third Viscount Saye and Sele, and is possibly the original "fine (Fiennes) lady on a white horse" to be seen at Banbury Cross.

Drive 3 miles east along the B4035 to Banbury.

5 Banbury, Oxfordshire

Banbury town center retains its medieval street plan and is a good place for a rewarding stroll (see p.126). The round-towered church (uncommon in Britain) replaced one destroyed in the 17th century. Banbury once manufactured fine plush cloth; the industry is recalled at the museum in Horsefair (which also has plenty of information about the famous nursery rhyme). Banbury is also the site of Europe's largest cattle market.

The Oxford Canal (1790) is to be found nearby.

Head eastward along the A422, turning left after 2 miles onto the B4525 and along an unclassified road to Sulgrave.

6 Sulgrave, Northamptonshire

Houses of attractive gray stone make up this village, famous for its manor house, the ancestral home of George Washington. His forebear, Lawrence Washington, a wool merchant, bought the manor in 1539 and the family lived here until 1659. A brass monument to Lawrence and his wife Anne can be seen in St. James's Church. Mementoes of George Washington on display in the manor house include his portrait by Gilbert Stuart (used on

ROMAN BRITAIN

In the century following Julius Caesar's "visits" to Britain with his army in 55 and 54 BC, Roman merchants gradually settled in southern England and exported slaves, grain and iron.

In AD 43, Emperor Claudius' army annexed Britain for Rome, but only southern Britain fell wholly under Roman rule.

Well-built roads joined the Roman garrison towns (such as Cirencester and Gloucester – "cester" comes from "castra," a camp) to London, and the _Pax Romana_ of the next three centuries brought prosperity, at least to the merchants and town dwellers of the south.

When the Empire started disintegrating in the late 4th century, Picts and Scots invaded the north and Saxons the east of England. The garrisons were finally withdrawn early in the 5th century, Roman towns fell into ruins and their civilization was forgotten ■

American bank notes), a chair from Mount Vernon and a piece of Martha Washington's wedding dress. American visitors should look above the entrance porch to see a familiar sight: the Stars and Stripes – or rather, the family's own coat of arms.

Take the unclassified road through Helmdon, heading south to join the A43 towards Brackley. A short distance after Brackley, turn right onto the B4031 to Aynho.

7 Aynho, Northamptonshire

Built of limestone, Aynho is famous for its wall-trained apricot trees, which flourish in the limestone soil. The Cartwrights of Aynho Park, lords of the manor from 1615 to 1954, used to be paid rent partially in apricots. The village stands on a hill, with steep lanes and alleyways around St. Michael's Church (18th century, with a fine 15th-century tower).

From Aynho, go west for 3 miles along the B4031 to Deddington.

8 Deddington, Oxfordshire

With handsome buildings centered on the spacious market square, Deddington flourished as a market town from medieval times until the late 19th century. Leadenporch House is a medieval hall with its original doorway, while Castle House (once the rectory) is 14th century, with 17th-century additions. The church (13th century) has an eight-pinnacled, 17th-century tower. The Norman castle is long gone, but its mound, banks and defensive ditch still remain.

Drive southward for 5 miles along the A4260 and then left onto an unclassified road to Steeple Aston.

9 Steeple Aston, Oxfordshire

Immaculate cottages and trim gardens characterize Steeple Aston. Nearby Rousham House (1635) was built by Sir Robert Dormer, whose family still owns the house. Architect William Kemp enlarged the building in the 18th century and designed the gardens which were first laid out in 1738 – they are still intact.

Another unclassified road leads south onto the B4030. Turn left at the B4030, which becomes the A4095 to Bicester.

10 Bicester, Oxfordshire

The history of Bicester (pronounced "Bister") dates back at least to Roman times. The Roman city of Alchester has been excavated south of the town, showing occupation from the middle of the 1st century to the early 5th century. There are some newer excavations too, in the shape of Bicester Village, a shopping complex with stores selling designer clothes at knock-down prices.

Take the A41 east, following an old Roman road. Turn right along the B401, then sharp right to Boarstall.

11 Boarstall, Buckinghamshire

Near Brill, on the edge of Otmoor, Boarstall is a tiny village totally dominated by Boarstall Tower – the intimidating 14th-century stone gatehouse to a long-vanished fortified house, moated, with crossloops which could be used for crossbows. Nearby is the 18th-century Boarstall Duck Decoy in 13 acres of woodland.

Take unclassified roads via Horton-cum-Studley along the edge of Otmoor for the return journey to Oxford.

★ HAY-ON-WYE 124A2
HEREFORD

Hay-on-Wye is the secondhand book capital of Britain, founded by bookseller Richard Booth in 1961. There are literally millions of books, on miles of shelving, housed in various converted buildings, attracting bibliophiles from all over the world. A Festival of Literature is held every year.

★★★ HENLEY-ON-THAMES
OXFORDSHIRE 125D1

Henley-on-Thames, set on a mile-long stretch of the Thames, is famous for its **regatta**, founded in 1839 and held every year in early July. At regatta time the banks are lined with hospitality tents and well-dressed spectators parade up and down.

The river is also the focus for another annual event: **swan-upping**, in late July. For 800 years the cygnets born to swans on the Thames have been caught and marked to distinguish their ownership: most of the swans belong to the Queen, but some belong to the Vintners or the Dyers, two of the City of London's medieval merchant guilds.

Henley itself, which grew around a 12th-century river crossing, has a very attractive and compact town center with lots of half-timbered or soft-toned brick buildings of the 15th to 18th centuries. Look too for the flint and stone-checked 16th-century tower of St. Mary's Church, and the adjoining 15th-century Chantry House, timber-framed with jettied upper floors. Near the town is Quarry Wood, a mixed woodland, predominantly beech trees, which was the inspiration for the wild wood in Kenneth Grahame's children's story *The Wind in the Willows*.

Marlow, the next settlement downstream, is a pretty Georgian town with a fine suspension bridge built in the 1830s. The novelist Mary Shelley wrote the classic horror story *Frankenstein* at Albion House, West Road in 1818, while in St. Peter's Street stands the Two Brewers pub where, in 1889, Jerome K. Jerome wrote *Three Men in a Boat* – a comical account of a trip up the Thames from Kingston-upon-Thames to Oxford, which was fraught with disasters.

Hay Castle Bookshop, one of dozens of secondhand bookstores in Hay-on-Wye

PRESIDENTIAL APPROVAL

Written in 1908, *The Wind in the Willows* was not at first well-received. But the adventures of Mole, Rat, Toad and Badger gradually won admirers, most notably President Roosevelt.

He wrote enthusiastically to Kenneth Grahame in 1909: "I have read it and reread it ... [and] I felt I must [tell] you how much we had all enjoyed your book" ∎

The iron bridge at Coalbrookdale is surprisingly elegant and delicate-looking, and was the first bridge in the world to be constructed of iron

★ HEREFORD   124A2
HEREFORDSHIRE

This small cathedral city, set in the rich agricultural land of the Wye Valley, was established by the Saxons as the capital of their kingdom of Mercia.

The Normans started work on the handsome, red, sandstone **cathedral** in 1107, while examples of later medieval prosperity still remain along the city center's streets. The 13th-century building housing St. John Medieval Museum at Coningsby, in Widemarsh Street, is one example, while another is Old House in High Town (1621), a fine half-timbered building furnished in keeping with its period. The cathedral itself contains many treasures, including the peaceful 13th-century Lady Chapel, 14th-century bishop's throne, and the rare chained **library** of over 1,600 books and manuscripts dating from around the 8th to 15th centuries. Be sure to see the *Mappa Mundi*, a world map drawn by Richard de Bello in 1289, which predates the discovery that the world is round and includes such items as *Noah's Ark*, the *Garden of Eden* and *Lot's wife*.

Herefordshire is particularly famous for two things: Hereford cattle and cider-making. Both are surprisingly evident even within the city, where a livestock market is held weekly, and a Cider Museum (in Pomona Place, off Whitecross Road) tells the story of cider from the 13th century onward and also distills cider brandy. Some 6,000 acres of commercial apple orchards cover the surrounding countryside.

Southwest of the city at **Abbey Dore** are the remains of a vast Cistercian abbey church. Nearby at **Kilpeck** is a much

smaller but truly wondrous Norman church, one of the finest in Britain. It is decorated inside and out with carvings of birds, angels and mythical beasts, some rather ribald in nature, which a moralistic Victorian "clean-up" attempt overlooked.

Travel north from Hereford to discover the **Black and White Villages Trail**, circling from Leominster through some of the region's many beautiful half-timbered villages. Weobley, with a 14th-century church, is said to be the breeding place of the first Hereford cattle. Pembridge, with its medieval pillared market hall set in a triangular market place beside the ancient New Inn of 1311, has an unusual detached timber-braced bell house at St. Mary's Church, and ancient almshouses. Eardisland has timbered cottages grouped around a little river.

Leominster is itself a most appealing town, with the massive priory church (the town was a religious center long before Hereford took over the role), a splendid array of medieval timber-framed buildings, especially in High Street and Draper's Lane, and equally fine 18th- to 19th-century houses in Church Street.

★★★ IRONBRIDGE GORGE SHROPSHIRE   125B3

Here in the wooded gorge of the River Severn, the Industrial Revolution was born in 1709 when Abraham Darby discovered that by smelting iron ore with coke instead of charcoal, iron could be mass-produced. Thus Britain became the world's first industrial nation.

The world's first iron bridge (1779) is just one of the Ironbridge Gorge Museum's sites, which are spread over six square miles; buses run between sites in the summer months. In the western part of the gorge, near the bridge, is the **Museum of the River** and a visitor center, in a warehouse built to store the Coalbrookdale Company's iron products. Darby's actual furnace is on show at the **Museum of Iron**, which explains the history of iron-making and of the Coalbrookdale Company.

Blists Hill Open Air Museum is a re-created 1890s town covering 50 acres, with gas-lit streets, iron furnaces, a colliery, sawmill, candle factory, stores and a pub (with beer).

Nearby are the **Coalport China Museum**, showing manufacturing techniques and examples of Coalport wares made in this building until 1926, when the firm moved to Stoke-on-Trent; and the **Jackfield Tile Museum**, housed in the former Craven Dunhill works, with examples of locally made decorative tiles.

CIDER IN HEREFORDSHIRE

A traditional farmhouse drink for centuries, cider is first mentioned in Hereford in the 13th century.

Apples with names like *French Longtails, Cowley Crabs, Hereford-shire Styne*, and *Foxwhelp* would be crushed, then the pulp parceled up in horsehair mats and pressed until it was dry "pummace" (fed to the pig) and the juice ready for cask and fermentation.

True farmhouse "scrumpy" is now rare. Pubs in Hereford serving traditional cider include the Black Lion, Old Harp, Saracen's Head and the Sun ∎

THE HEART OF ENGLAND

SIR EDWARD ELGAR (1857–1934)

Born at Lower Broadheath (see p.150), Elgar was acknowledged as a composer and conductor by his early twenties, but he taught the violin to earn a living.

The *Enigma Variations* (1899), was the first composition to bring him international recognition. The *Dream of Gerontius* (1900) was performed at the Three Choirs Festival (see panel on p.150) in 1902. The *First Symphony* (1908) and the *Pomp and Circumstance Marches* (1901–30) were widely popular.

After a period in London, Elgar returned to Worcester in his old age. He lived on Rainbow Hill, where he was inspired by the view of the Malvern Hills ■

★ LICHFIELD 125C4
STAFFORDSHIRE

Three pink, sandstone spires, known as "Ladies of the Vale," soar above the handsome 14th- to 16th-century houses and 17th-century bishop's palace lining the cathedral close at Lichfield.

Founded by the Saxons, **Lichfield Cathedral** as it now stands is largely of 12th- and 13th-century origin. The spires are not its only unusual feature. The west front has 113 (badly eroded) statues, including representations of 24 English kings. Within, beautiful triple-shafted columns with leaf-carved capitals soar upward from the nave. Equally uncommon are the tall windows of the 14th-century Lady Chapel, reminiscently French and filled with 16th-century glass taken from the Abbey of Herkenrode in Belgium.

A bookseller's son, born in Lichfield and educated at the grammar school, was later to become the nationally famous lexicographer, poet and critic, **Dr. Samuel Johnson** (1709–84). Another native of Lichfield was Elias Ashmole (1617–92), the antiquarian who, in 1682, presented the University of Oxford with the collection which formed the basis of the Ashmolean Museum (see p.146).

Northwest of Lichfield is **Shugborough**, the home of Lord Lichfield, cousin of the Queen and well-known photographer. This late 17th- to 18th-century stately home, surrounded by parkland scattered with follies and temples, is in the care of the National Trust and has fine plasterwork and furnishings.

Housed in the former kitchens, coachhouse, brewhouse and laundry is the **Staffordshire County Museum**, with displays of domestic implements, costumes and crafts.

★★ LUDLOW 124A3
SHROPSHIRE

Ludlow is a market town set on a cliff above a bend of the River Teme. Chosen by King Henry VII (1456–1509) as the headquarters of the Council of the Marches (the border region) to control Wales and the troublesome Marcher Lords, the defensive site is crowned with a red sandstone **castle** begun in 1085 by Roger Montgomery, Earl of Shrewsbury. The inner bailey (court) is entered through an Elizabethan gateway beside the massive keep. Within is the 12th-century St. Mary Magdalene's Chapel, which is round, with Norman decoration; and the Great Hall and domestic buildings, where many royal visitors were accommodated. Each June and July, during the Ludlow Festival, performances of Shakespeare's plays are given in the inner bailey.

On High Street is the Buttermarket (1746), close to fine 15th-century buildings at the corner of Broad Street. **St. Laurence's Church**, whose size demonstrates Ludlow's medieval wealth from the wool trade, has an unusual hexagonal entrance porch, a superb east window with glass showing the life and miracles of Saint Laurence, equally fine glass in the window of the Palmers' Chapel, and enchanting carved, 15th-century *misericords* beneath the choir stalls (these ledges enabled the occupants to lean back and rest their legs during long services – the name comes from the Latin for "tender-hearted"). In the churchyard are the 13th-century Reader's House and the grave of poet A.E. Housman (1859–1936); *A Shropshire Lad* is perhaps his best-known work. Take a rewarding wander around Broad Street, with the Angel Inn; Mill Street, with the guildhall and old

The Feathers Hotel, on Old Street in Ludlow, is an extraordinarily ornate example of a timbered building dating from 1603

TIMBER-FRAMED HOUSES

Timber-framed houses of the 15th to 18th centuries are still relatively common in Britain; a few survive even from the 12th century.

The most commonly used timber was oak. The panels between the frames were filled with wattle and daub (hazel or willow rods covered with a mixture of clay, dung and horsehair, then plastered) or with brickwork.

In western England, timbers were set in squares; in the east and north vertical timbers were preferred. Timber-framed buildings are easy to dismantle and re-erect, which has allowed many to be preserved on new sites, for example, at the Chiltern Open-Air Museum ∎

grammar school; and Old Street, on the Roman road with the outstanding timbered Feathers Hotel (1603) at the top and even older Bull Inn opposite.

To the northwest of Ludlow, near Craven Arms, is **Stokesay Castle** (EH), a fine 13th-century fortified manor house.

★★ MALVERN HILLS   *125B2* HEREFORD AND WORCESTER

The Malvern Hills offer superb views for miles from the hilltop paths. Iron Age man realized the defensive possibilities of these hills 2,500 years ago, and fortified both the highest point, Worcestershire Beacon, and Herefordshire Beacon to the south.

The Benedictine monks of the medieval priories at Great Malvern and Little Malvern used spring water from the hills as a curative. The priories were shut down by Henry VIII in 1541, but the water continued its popularity into the 18th century, when Malvern became a spa; the water is bottled today and sold worldwide.

Great Malvern still has a medieval priory church, with soaring verticals, delicate tracery and 15th-century stained glass, but most of the buildings date from its 19th-century heyday as a spa town. There are four other Malverns: Malvern Link and Malvern Wells (the composer Sir Edward Elgar had houses in both villages); Little Malvern (in whose churchyard Lady Elgar was buried); and West Malvern.

Southwest of the hill ridge is **Ledbury**, with its broad main street and a 16th-century timbered market house; the town was the birthplace of poet John Masefield (1878–1967).

THE CIVIL WARS 1642–51

In the mid-17th century, Charles I was at odds with his Parliament. The balance of power was shifting away from the Crown as a new, wealthy class of people wanted a share in government.

Many were of Puritan faith and war broke out in 1642, with the Catholic King and Royalists or Cavaliers on one side and the Puritan Parliamentarians or Roundheads under Oliver Cromwell on the other.

The king finally surrendered in 1646 and was beheaded in 1649. Cromwell died in 1658, and Charles II returned as king in 1660 ■

One of the most peaceful ways to enjoy Oxford is by walking along the riverbanks, watching the rowing eights at practice and occasionally glancing up at the "dreaming spires" on the skyline

★★★ OXFORD   *125C1*
OXFORDSHIRE

First, a word of warning: do not take a car into Oxford; the one-way system, will drive you crazy, as will finding a parking space. Use the excellent "park and ride" system, or the train or bus.

All main sights are within easy walking distance of the city center. Unfortunately, there is no one-way system for pedestrians; to avoid the worst sidewalk crushes, try not to visit in July or August. April/May or September/October are more pleasant, though still busy.

The University of Oxford, like that of Cambridge, has no single campus as such, but is made up of individual colleges (and a few university buildings), which lie mostly behind high walls as if to cut off the noise and bustling streets of this busy commercial city. The wealth of historic buildings (over 600) has the added benefit of greenery nearby: most colleges have gardens, small or large, while Christ Church Meadow, Magdalen Deer Park, the Botanic Garden, Marston Meadows and acres of playing fields are within view of the city center. Climb to the top of the tower of the university church, St. Mary the Virgin (High Street), for the best view of the patchwork layout of buildings, quadrangles and winding lanes, with green hills in the distance.

The older, main university buildings are off Broad Street: the **Sheldonian Theatre** (1664), designed by Sir Christopher Wren, where degree ceremonies are held; and the **Bodleian Library**, which houses 5½ million plus volumes – it is a copyright library, entitled to receive a free copy of every book published in Britain. The sculpted heads topping the nearby railings represent Roman emperors.

The **Ashmolean Museum** (Beaumont Street) contains the university's outstanding collection of art and antiquities, while the

University and Pitt Rivers Museums (in the Science Area) contain natural science, anthropology and ethnology collections. The Museum of the History of Science (Broad Street) is less known but full of fascinating early scientific apparatus. Nearby is the Oxford Story Exhibition, a commercial and gimmicky, but fact-filled, introduction to the city's history, as you are carried along sitting at a replica medieval desk.

Seek out Magdalen College, from whose tower choristers sing at dawn on May Morning each year. At Christ Church ("The House"), the Great Tom bell booms out from Tom Tower, which overlooks the vast Tom Quad. It has an exquisite fan-vaulted chapel, which is also Oxford's cathedral, and a fine picture gallery. The chapel at New College (new in 1379), contains a statue of Lazarus by Sir Jacob Epstein, and there are extensive gardens where parts of

the medieval city walls can be seen. St. Edmund Hall (Teddy Hall) is small and extremely old (built about 1220), with a well at the center of its very pretty quad. Merton has an ancient library, while Queen's and Worcester both have fine 18th-century buildings. Keble is a fantasy of High Victorian architecture featuring a chapel with a kaleidoscope of colour, and St. John's has beautiful gardens. Most colleges open partially to visitors in the afternoons, but access may be restricted at examination time (late May/June). Please remember at all times that colleges are lived in by undergraduates: peering into windows and loud talking are not appreciated by students trying to study.

Other places to see include the Martyrs' Memorial (St. Giles), commemorating Archbishop Thomas Cranmer and bishops Hugh Latimer and Nicholas Ridley, who were burnt at the stake for their religious beliefs in 1555–6 (the scorch marks caused by heat from the fires can still be seen on the doors of Balliol). The Covered Market (Market Street, off Cornmarket) is well worth a visit. For drinking, try the Turf Tavern on Turl Street (off High Street) or the Eagle and Child (St. Giles) – both will probably be crowded with students. Also visit the parks and meadowland beside the River Thames (here called the Isis) and River Cherwell; in late May the rowing races of Eights Week are held: a display of determination as boats "bump" each other in their bid to become "Head of the River."

South of Oxford is the fertile Vale of the White Horse. The horse itself overlooks Uffington, cut into the chalk hillside. No one knows how old it is, but it may date from the Iron Age.

WALK

OXFORD
Start from Magdalen Bridge. Turn left down Merton Street, past Merton, then Corpus Christi and Oriel colleges. Walk up Oriel Street, cross High Street and pass left by the University Church to see the Radcliffe Camera and Bodleian Library, past Brasenose (left) and All Souls' (right) colleges.

Walk down Catte Street into Broad Street for the Sheldonian Theatre and History of Science Museum, then backtrack and go down New College Lane/ Queens Lane or Holywell Street/ Longwall Street to return to Magdalen and Magdalen Grove, or the Botanic Garden across the street ∎

THE HEART OF ENGLAND

WILLIAM SHAKESPEARE (1564–1616)

Recognized as England's greatest playwright, Shakespeare was probably educated at the Grammar School in Stratford, before marrying and moving to London.

His earliest work was probably written in the late 1580s or early 1590s. His plays (some 37 are attributed to him) can be broadly divided into histories (*Henry IV, Henry V, Richard III*), tragedies (*Hamlet, King Lear, Macbeth*), comedies (*Much Ado About Nothing, As You Like It*) and lyric plays (*A Midsummer Night's Dream, Romeo and Juliet*).

He also wrote much poetry, including *Venus and Adonis, The Rape of Lucrece*, and sonnets ∎

★★★ SHREWSBURY SHROPSHIRE *124A4*

Almost completely surrounded by a loop of the River Severn, Shrewsbury was recognized by the Normans as a superb defensive site: they built a castle at the one vulnerable point. The castle is still standing and is now a museum. Close by is Castle Gates House, one of the town's abundant timber-framed buildings. Shrewsbury has over 1,000 listed buildings of architectural importance, the result of wool trade prosperity.

Narrow alleyways (called "shuts") prevent car access, and thus make the town center a pleasure for pedestrians. St. Mary's Church, with its fine spire and stained glass, is close to Bear Steps, a group of 15th- to 16th-century buildings with a hall built in 1389 for wool merchants, and Butcher Row. Nearby are Ireland's Mansion, Owen's Mansion and the Market Hall, also from around the 16th century. At Clive House, in College Hill, lived Robert, Lord Clive (of India), who was the local Member of Parliament in the 1760s; his statue is in the square. The late 17th-century guildhall stands in Dogpole. Across the English Bridge is the massive Norman **abbey church**, once part of a Benedictine monastery and founded in 1083.

Close to the town walls are many handsome 18th-century buildings including St. Chad's Church, with a circular nave, gallery and "wedding cake" tower. A much older building, Rowley's House, of 16th- and 17th-century origin, houses a museum containing finds from the excavated Roman city of *Viriconium*, just east of the town.

The **South Shropshire Hills** are a must for walkers: from Church Stretton (with an excellent information center in Church Street; St. Laurence's Church is also worth a look) it is easy to reach the Long Mynd, where outcrops and deep ravines (called "batches") reveal rocks 700 million years old. Caer Caradoc is best reached on foot from Hope Bowdler. West of the Long Mynd are the Stiperstones, quartzite outcrops on a windy ridge above Snailbeach, where old iron workings can be seen.

★★★ STRATFORD-UPON-AVON, WARWICKSHIRE *125C2*

Famous as the birthplace and final home of playwright William Shakespeare, Stratford has suffered from an overdose of visitors for decades. There are five sites associated with Shakespeare and his family; all are connected by an open-topped bus which tours at 15-minute intervals (board at any point on the route). A discounted one-day ticket gives entry to all the properties (start early).

Three sites are within walking distance of each other in the town center: **Shakespeare's Birthplace** is entered through a visitor center and cottage garden. Purchased as a national memorial in 1847 for £3,000, a copy of the auction notice is on display; **Hall's Croft** was the home of Shakespeare's elder daughter, Susanna, and her husband, Dr. John Hall. It is furnished in Tudor style, with an exhibition on Dr. Hall's career and medicine in his day; **Nash's House**, home of Thomas Nash, husband of Shakespeare's granddaughter, has Tudor furniture and exhibits on Stratford's past. Next door was New Place, where Shakespeare died. Only the foundations remain, with an Elizabethan-style knot garden.

Out of town are two further sites: **Anne Hathaway's Cottage**

at Shottery, where Shakespeare's wife lived as a child; and **Mary Arden's House** at Wilmcote, the childhood home of Shakespeare's mother. This farm, which is now a museum, has rare farm animal breeds and displays recalling rural life in the 19th century.

Back in Stratford, **Holy Trinity Church** has a memorial bust of Shakespeare holding a quill pen. The **Memorial Theatre** is home to the Royal Shakespeare Company, with regular productions of Shakespeare's plays; the **R.S.C. Collection** displays props and costumes made for past productions. (The company's London base is at the Barbican (see p.28.) The **World of Shakespeare** is a jazzy, 25-minute romp through sights and sounds of Shakespearean England.

For those uninterested in the Bard, Stratford also has **Harvard House**, home of Catherine Rogers (mother of John Harvard, who founded Harvard University);

a Butterfly Farm, with 1,000 tree-flying species; and the National Teddy Bear Museum.

North of Stratford is **Packwood House**, a brick and timbered Tudor mansion with tall chimneys, which is famous for its topiary garden of clipped yew trees, representing the Sermon on the Mount. Also nearby is medieval **Baddesley Clinton**, a moated manor house with many original features including fine paneling and several priest holes, where persecuted Roman Catholic priests hid during the 16th and 17th centuries.

★ TEWKESBURY 125B2
GLOUCESTERSHIRE

Tewkesbury, at the meeting point of the Rivers Severn and Avon, is a handsome, black-and-white timbered town. Its Norman **abbey church** of the 12th to 14th centuries is one of the finest in England. Dedicated to Saint Mary the Virgin, it was saved from

Anne Hathaway's cottage, at Shottery, was the home of Shakespeare's wife when she was a child

RARE BREEDS

Longhorn cattle and Cotswold sheep are among the animals kept on the farm at Mary Arden's House, just as they would have been 500 years ago. Old breeds were multi-purpose: cattle were not only milked, but pulled the plough; sheep were milked (to make cheese) as well as shorn for their wool ■

THE HEART OF ENGLAND

THE THREE CHOIRS FESTIVAL

Since the 18th century, the three cathedral choirs of Gloucester, Hereford and Worcester have had an annual Music Meeting, now a major music festival held during the last week of August each year.

The original intent was to raise money for widows and orphans of clergy of the dioceses.

Handel's *Messiah* was given its first cathedral performance at Hereford in 1759, and since then many famous 20th-century composers have been linked with the festival, including Elgar, Vaughan Williams, Holst, Berkeley, and Britten. In addition, musicians of world standing frequently perform ∎

dissolution in 1539 when the townspeople raised £453 to purchase it from the king. In the Despenser chantry chapel is the earliest known example of fan-vaulting in Britain.

★★ WARWICK   *125C3*
WARWICKSHIRE

Warwick, county town of Warwickshire, is a pleasant blend of 16th- and 17th-century timbered buildings with 18th-century brick. In the town center, partially rebuilt following a fire in 1694, Court House and Landor House stand out, and two medieval stone-built town gateways survive.

The chapel of Westgate is part of the timbered, 15th-century **Lord Leycester Hospital**. **St. Mary's Church** has fine fan-vaulting in the Beauchamp Chapel, with elaborate tombs of the earls of Warwick, and a Nor-man crypt. The County Museum in the market square has a model of Warwick and an ancient tapestry map of Warwickshire.

The magnificent 14th-century **castle,** beside the River Avon, is both medieval fortress and palatial mansion, set within a Victorian rose garden with peacocks and extensive parkland (designed by "Capability" Brown during the 18th century).

Exhibits range from medieval weapons and armor to opulently furnished state rooms. Two waxwork presentations bring the history of the castle to life: Kingmaker – A Preparation for Battle, 1471 and A Royal Weekend Party, 1898.

Kenilworth Castle, north of the town, is now a huge, Norman, red sandstone ruin, but was once the home of Queen Elizabeth I's favorite, the Earl of Leicester. He entertained the Queen here, but his wife, Amy Robsart, met her death falling

down the stairs – was it accident, suicide or murder?

★ WORCESTER   *125B2*
WORCESTERSHIRE

The city's motto is *Civitas in bello et pace fidelis* ("the city faithful in war and peace"), and Worcester (pronounced "wooster") is famous for its Royalist stand during the Civil Wars (see panel p.146). King Charles II had his headquarters at the Commandery (now a Civil War visitor center) before the decisive Battle of Worcester, which he lost.

Worcester Cathedral was founded in AD 680, though the present building is Norman with a 14th-century tower. King John (1167–1216), of Magna Carta fame, and Prince Arthur (eldest son of King Henry VIII, who died before him) are buried near the high altar. The splendid Guildhall (High Street) of 1721–3, has an elaborate main entrance and assembly room in fine Queen Anne style. Edgar Tower, restored by King John, has a set of early 13th-century wooden gates. Much of the Old Palace (Deansway) is also 13th-century.

Worcester is also famous for Royal Worcester **porcelain**; visit the factory, and the associated Dyson Perrins Museum.

Just outside Worcester, **Lower Broadheath** was the birthplace of composer Sir Edward Elgar (see panel p.144). The cottage where he was born is a museum, with manuscripts, photographs and memorabilia relating to his achievements and interests.

Southeast of the city, the River Avon flows through both **Pershore**, its 18th-century town center balanced by the 13th-century abbey church, and **Evesham**, famous for its surrounding orchards full of blossom in spring, and with another ancient abbey at its heart.

WALES

Wales has its own unique culture and
style - a rich legacy of music and
literature is the basis of festivals
thoughout the country. Superlative
scenery ranges from the mountains
of the Cambrians, to the rugged
coastline of the Gower Peninsula.
For centuries armies fought over
these lands, and mighty castles still
form distinctive landmarks

CALENDAR OF EVENTS

MARCH 1 –
St. David's Day.
A service in St. David's Cathedral honors the patron saint of Wales.

MAY BANK HOLIDAY –
Victorian Extravaganza, Llandudno. Parades in 19th-century costume, buskers, fairground and carriage rides.

JUNE – Three Peaks Yacht Race, Barmouth. A race to Scotland scaling Snowdon, Scafell Pike, and Ben Nevis.

JULY – Eisteddfodau, Llangollen. 12,000 performers from 30 countries compete in this music event (see p.158).

AUGUST – Race the Train, Talyllyn Railway. Charity runners attempt to beat the train over 14 miles – some do it!

SEPTEMBER –
Swansea Festival of Music and Arts, centers on orchestral concerts – the main professional arts festival in Wales.

NEW YEAR'S EVE –
Nos Galon Race, Mountain Ash, Aberdare. Running race held at midnight over 9½ miles ■

WALES

No passport is needed to enter Wales, but once you've crossed the border you soon know you're in another country. Ever since the act of union in 1536, Wales has shared all of England's institutions of authority – the monarchy, government and legal system – but its culture, and even its language, has remained palpably discrete. Its seemingly impenetrable ancient Celtic language manifests itself not only in unpronounceable place names, but in signs such as *Croeso i Cymru* (Welcome to Wales); everyone speaks English, but many locals speak Welsh as their first language.

★★★ HIGHLIGHTS

Beaumaris Castle (➤ 156)
Big Pit Mining Museum, Blaenavon (➤ 168)
Caernarfon Castle (➤ 161)
Conwy Castle (➤ 160)
Erddig (➤ 158)
Pembrokeshire Coast National Park (➤ 161)
Portmeirion (➤ 166)
St. David's (➤ 165)
Snowdon (➤ 167)
Tintern Abbey (➤ 168)

Devolution has long been a political hot potato: the Welsh Nationalist Party, Plaid Cymru, presently has four Members of Parliament at Westminster. More radical elements paint graffiti over anglicized signs, and there are occasional periods when active discontent erupts. But the Welsh identity is more commonly, if stereotypically, expressed in its plethora of Protestant chapels, its male voice choirs, its national sport of rugby

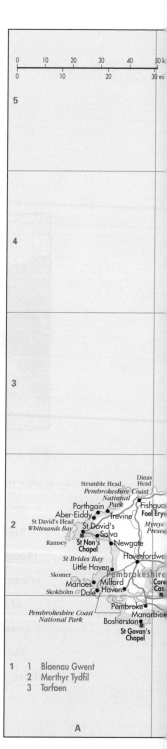

1 Blaenau Gwent
2 Merthyr Tydfil
3 Torfaen

A

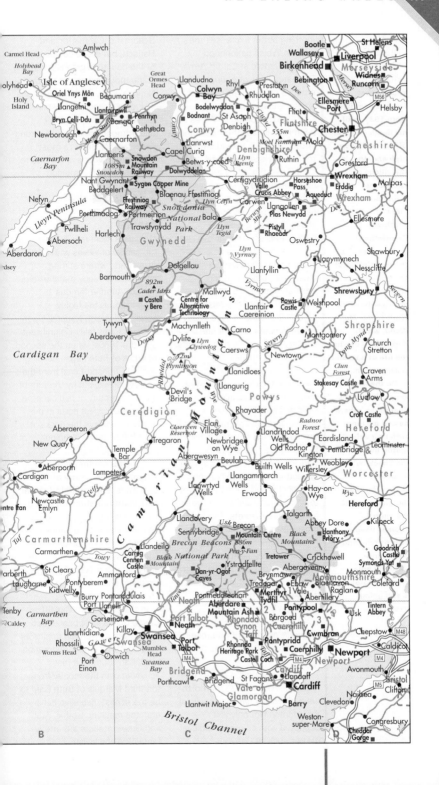

WALES

DYLAN THOMAS (1914–53) and LAUGHARNE

Wales' most famous poet lived from 1937 until his death "on and off, up and down, high and dry" in the village of Laugharne (pronounced "larn"), southwest of Carmarthen.

The place fits the description of the fictional Llaregub (spell it backwards) of his work *Under Milk Wood*, which describes a day in the life of a small seaside town.

On the estuary are preserved the Boathouse, where he and his long-suffering wife Caitlin lived, and the Shack, where he wrote.

He is buried in the graveyard of the church. Thomas liked a beer or two, and his favorite watering hole, Brown's Hotel, is still going strong ■

(nothing better expresses the pride in Welsh nationhood than the crowd at Cardiff Arms Park) and its *eisteddfodau*, emotive celebrations of Welsh artistic endeavor.

A high proportion of Wales' 2.8 million inhabitants live in the **south**. They are spread between the country's small capital of Cardiff (worth visiting for its museums), and Swansea, an "ugly, lovely town" according to native-born poet Dylan Thomas, and in the working-class settlements of "The Valleys" across a massive coalfield. Here, some of the now defunct mines have been turned into top-class attractions. To the east, defining the English/Welsh border, the wooded Wye Valley is a tight concentration of fine scenery and historic monuments. To the west, the remote Pembrokeshire Coast National Park majestically winds its way around memorable inlets, coves, cliffs and beaches.

The hinterland of **mid-Wales** is upland country, covered in hill farms where farmers with traditional and modern aids from sheepdogs to motorbikes tend their flocks, and dormant market towns come to life once a week for livestock markets. The high, grassy plateaus of the Brecon Beacons National Park define its southern limits, north of which lie Wales' peculiar spa towns. To the west, stunning drovers' routes weave across the lonesome Cambrian Mountains. The coastline of Cardigan Bay is not as scenic as that of Pembroke-shire nor as interesting as the north coast.

If you've only time to visit one region of Wales, go to the **north-west**, the most nationalist part of the country. Not only is it peppered with colossal medieval castles such as Conwy,

Beaumaris, Caernarfon and Harlech, but it also contains some of the country's grandest scenery in the mountains of Snowdonia National Park. Further attractions include a plethora of nostalgic railways, tours through the underground mines, and a strong candidate for Britain's most picturesque village is the bizarre settlement of Portmeirion.

★ CARDIFF   *153D1*

and AROUND CARDIFF

Outsiders most readily associate the capital of Wales with Cardiff Arms Park, where stirring international rugby matches are played. Another famous association is the highly acclaimed Welsh National Opera.

Cardiff was fairly insignificant until the 1830s, when the second Marquis of Bute began building docks to transport coal from the nearby valleys, but by the turn of the 20th century, it had become one of the busiest ports in the world. Nowadays the docks at Cardiff Bay are undergoing massive regeneration.

A **visitor center** offers an insight into the history of the docklands, the **Welsh Industrial and Maritime Museum** provides a full-scale introduction into the coal and iron-ore industries through an exhibition on power and displays of old locomotives and boats, and **Techniquest** is an excellent and interesting hands-on science center.

In the city center, **Cardiff Castle** draws its appeal not so much from its Norman origins as from its 19th-century restoration by William Burges, a feat achieved with the money from the third Marquis of Bute (said to be the richest man alive in his era); the resulting Gothic, Arab and Greek interiors are utterly fantastical and lavish.

In the **National Museum of Wales**, part of the fine Edwardian civic center, you can see works by Welsh artists and a good selection of archeological finds, as well as Rodin sculptures and an important collection of French impressionist and postimpressionist art.

Medieval **Llandaff Cathedral**, on the northwest outskirts, suffered heavy bombing during World War II. Jacob Epstein's statue of *Christ in Majesty* dominates the restored building.

West of the city at St. Fagans, the vast **Welsh Folk Museum** comprises re-erected buildings, including a farmhouse, tollhouse, Victorian school and miners' cottages. In the summer months, you can watch a blacksmith, cooper and baker at work.

Castell Coch (Cadw), 5 miles north of Cardiff, was another madcap collaboration between the Marquis of Bute and William Burges. The fairy-tale, fake medieval castle's rooms match those you'll see in Cardiff Castle for their ostentation.

A couple of miles north, **Caerphilly Castle** (Cadw), the second-largest castle in Britain after Windsor, was built between 1268 and 1271 within giant water barriers. Its concentric defense system set a pattern for Edward I's castles in North Wales.

The Octagonal Room at Castell Coch is a fine example of its opulent interior. The castle's eccentric architect, William Burges, was a drug addict, and tended to wander around with a parrot on his shoulder

The Black Mountains rarely live up to their name except perhaps when the skies are black with rain clouds!

THE DRUIDS OF ANGLESEY

Druids were wiped out in most of Britain by the Romans; Anglesey was their last stand.

The Roman historian, Tacitus, in the *Annals of Imperial Rome*, gives a dramatic description of the assault on the island in AD 61: "The enemy lined the shore in a dense armed mass. Among them were black-robed women with disheveled hair like Furies, brandishing torches. Close by stood Druids, raising their hands to heaven and screaming dreadful curses ... it was their religion to drench their altars in the blood of prisoners and consult their gods by means of human entrails" ■

ABERYSTWYTH 153C3
CEREDIGION

This is the largest resort on Cardigan Bay, with a shingle beach, a long promenade, a bandstand and a pier. There are panoramic views, also seen through a camera obscura, from **Constitution Hill**, which you can ascend on a cliff railway. Aberystwyth is also a university town and home to the **National Library of Wales**, where a permanent exhibition shows old Welsh and Celtic manuscripts.

★ ANGLESEY 153B5

Low-lying and agricultural, the island of Anglesey seems, on first impression, rather dull in comparison with the splendid scenery on the other side of the great suspension bridge (constructed by the Scottish engineer Thomas Telford in 1826) across the Menai Strait. Yet it has a beautiful coastline, a fair number of historic sights and is one of the most resolutely Welsh parts of the country.

If you just feel like a day on the beach, head for **Newborough** in the southwest, or **Amlwch** in the northeast. **Holy Island**, connected to Anglesey by a half-mile causeway, is topped by the small Holyhead Mountain, where there is an Iron-Age hillfort. The industrial port of Holyhead, however, is unappealing.

For an overview of the island's history, make for **Oriel Ynys Môn** museum near Llangefni. The island's top historic sights are grouped close to the Menai Strait. The most impressive and easily visited prehistoric sight is **Bryn Celli Ddu**, a 4,000-year-old neolithic burial mound.

Close by, the neo-Gothic stately mansion of **Plas Newydd** (NT) was built for the first Marquis of Anglesey, who commanded the cavalry at the Battle of Waterloo. You can even see the wooden leg he acquired as a result of his exploits. In the 1930s, the artist Rex Whistler added a beautiful and amusing 60-foot *trompe l'oeil* mural in the dining room.

Edward I built the last castle in his chain of fortifications at **Beaumaris** ★ ★ ★ (Cadw), a peerless example of medieval military architecture in geometrical

concentric design, with a moat originally linked to the sea.

It would be a pity not to pick up a platform ticket from the train station of Llanfairpwllgwyngyllgogerychwyrndrobwllllantysiliogogogoch before you leave the island. The longest place name in Britain, known to locals just as Llanfair PG, came about as a 19th-century hoax to draw tourists, but it stuck.

★★ BRECON BEACONS NATIONAL PARK, POWYS *153C2*

The least visited of the Welsh national parks comprises a hilly, pastoral landscape. It is an easily misunderstood region because of its confusing and misleading names. For example, of its four distinct ranges, only the central mountains, the actual Brecon Beacons, are true peaks; the rest of the upland is grassy plateaus or smooth, grassy flanks rising to sharp ridges. Naturally, walking is the best way to enjoy the park, though horse-riding is very popular, too. There are also good scenic drives (see p.162).

The easternmost range, the Black Mountains, runs along the

Wales/England border and is a lush green color most of the year. Ridges enclose deep valleys, the most enjoyable of which runs from Hay-on-Wye (see p.163) over Gospel Pass, down past the ruins of the 13th-century Llanthony Priory (now a characterful hotel). Tretower (Cadw) combines the shell of a medieval fortress with an atmospheric old manor house.

The Usk Valley divides the Black Mountains from the Brecon Beacons. Pen-y-fan, at 2,906 feet, is the highest point in South Wales. Brecon has ancient buildings with timber gables, bow windows and color-washed fronts vying for attention in its town center. The Brecknock Museum has local historical artifacts, including intricately-carved Welsh love spoons, used to symbolize betrothal. The Brecon Beacons Mountain Centre lies out of town near Libanus.

Moving west, Fforest Fawr is actually a tract of virtually treeless hills. The prime attraction here is the limestone district south of Ystradfellte, known as Waterfall Country for the falls found in the Nedd, Hepste and Mellte gorges. You can walk behind the curtain of water of the Sgwd yr Ira on the Hepste. Further west off the A4067, the large and dramatic Dan-yr-Ogof Caves are open to visitors. One is named "the Cathedral" for its mighty proportions, another re-creates a Bronze Age dwelling.

The westernmost segment of the national park is called the Black Mountain (not to be confused with the Black Mountains), much of it a barren moorland terrain only accessible to hardy walkers. It is worth traveling far to see Carreg Cennen Castle, a magnificently sited ruin close to Llandeilo on the edge of a sheer limestone crag.

WALKS

BRECON BEACONS NATIONAL PARK

You can climb the highest point in the Brecon Beacons National Park, Pen-y-fan, most directly from near the Storey Arms on the A470 on a fairly gentle ascent.

Walks from Pontneddfechan or Ystradfellte take in a tremendous series of waterfalls.

More waterside walking is possible alongside the Monmouth and Brecon Canal, all the way from Brecon to Pontypool.

A long-distance path follows the whole length of Offa's Dyke, an 8th-century defensive earthwork erected by King Offa that closely follows the present-day boundary between England and Wales. One of the most enjoyable sections traverses the Black Mountains (above Llanthony) ∎

EISTEDDFODAU

The *eisteddfod* (meaning literally "the sitting down place") is a celebration of Welsh language and culture in contests for music, literature, poetry, song and dance. Local *eisteddfodau* take place all over the country.

The *Royal National Eisteddfod*, Wales' most important cultural gathering, takes place during the first week in August at a different venue each year. It is presided over by the Gorsedd of the Bards in druid robes and is full of patriotic pageantry.

The *International Musical Eisteddfod* takes place every first or second week in July at Llangollen, and covers everything from amateur choral competitions to appearances by Pavarotti ■

★★ ELAN VALLEY and   *153C2-3*
THE CAMBRIAN MOUNTAINS
POWYS, CEREDIGION and
CARMARTHENSHIRE

Through the sparsely populated Cambrian Mountains, a couple of spectacular roads follow old tracks once used by drovers to take herds of cattle and sheep to market. The Elan Valley, the Lakeland of Wales, has a series of vast reservoirs constructed to provide water for Birmingham. The visitors' center at the estate village of Elan provides the history and details of local walks.

A road continues across bleak moorland to Devil's Bridge, which is in fact the earliest of three bridges, probably the work of monks from nearby Strata Florida Abbey. From the bottom of steep steps called Jacob's Ladder leading to the river, there is a great view of magnificent waterfalls. You can also reach Devil's Bridge on a steam railway from Aberystwyth (see p.156).

Further south, one of Britain's most dramatic drives runs from Tregaron east through an uninhabited wilderness on the drovers' route to Abergwesyn and on to Llanwrtyd Wells, where you can observe the manufacture of Welsh tweed and buy products in the Cambrian Factory. This drive can be linked with the Elan Valley drive to make a fine circular tour.

★★★ ERDDIG   *153D4*
WREXHAM

A visit to this late 17th-century mansion (NT) gives a complete insight into the "upstairs-down-stairs" social history of a country house. The Yorke family lived here from 1733 to 1973, when the last squire donated it, in a state of dereliction due to subsidence caused by coal mining, to the National Trust. Offsetting the customary state rooms and fine furniture are portraits of genera-tions of domestic staff in the servants' quarters and poems to them by the philanthropic Yorkes, as well as a set of service buildings such as the sawpit, the smithy and the laundries.

★★ GOWER PENINSULA
SWANSEA   *153B1-C1*

The clenched fist of the Gower Peninsula delivers some of Wales' prettiest coastline. The northern seaboard is marshy, but there are cliffs and sandy beaches on the west and south coasts. If you're just passing through, the place to head for is Rhossili Bay in the far west; it is one of Wales' most spectacular beaches, especially when seen from Worms Head, a rock of an island accessible at low tide, or from Rhossili Downs above. Along the south coast, village resorts match up with beaches at Port Einon and Oxwich, while the Mumbles, curling around into industrial Swansea, is far more developed and brash.

★ LLANDRINDOD WELLS   *153C3*
POWYS

Medicinal properties were discovered of the sulfurous waters in the mid-Wales spa towns of Llandrindod Wells, Builth Wells, Llangammarch Wells and Llanwrtyd Wells in the 1730s. But it was the arrival of the railway in the 1860s that brought the towns prosperity. Llandrindod Wells is the only spa to have remained active: you can drink a glass of its famous water at the Victorian pump room. The wrought-iron arcades and tree-lined streets are redolent of its Edwardian and Victorian heyday. If you come in August, you can experience the nine-day Victorian Festival, when the whole town undergoes a transformation.

Shop windows are dressed in 19th-century items, only carriages and a horse bus are allowed on the main street and residents go about their business in full Victorian dress.

West of Llandrindod Wells, **Old Radnor's church** is said to be the finest in the principality. It has a font over 1,200 years old, medieval choir stalls and a 15th-century screen and organ case.

★★ LLANGOLLEN   *153D4*
 VALE OF, DENBIGHSHIRE
The friendly little town of **Llangollen** makes a good a base

Horsedrawn barge trips take you along Thomas Telford's **Llangollen Canal**, but not as far as his vertiginous Pontcysllte Aqueduct, 4 miles east, where the canal is carried in a cast-iron trough 120 feet above the River Dee. Meanwhile, a **steam railway** puffs its way west.

A stiff climb up to the impoverished ruins of **Castell Dinas Bran** above Llangollen is rewarded by panoramic views. **Valle Crucis Abbey** (Cadw), north of town off the A542, is more easily accessible and its remains, notably the west facade,

Llangollen railroad station has been preserved as it was in its Victorian heyday. Steam trains run along the length of the valley

for North Wales. In and around the deep, narrow limestone valley that hems in the River Dee are a concentration of attractions.

South of the village, **Plas Newydd** is a cottage enlarged and "gothicized" with carved, wooden paneling. Its eccentric inhabitants, Lady Eleanor Butler and Miss Sarah Ponsonby (the "Ladies of Llangollen") were famous enough to have such visitors as the Duke of Wellington and Sir Walter Scott.

vaulted chapter house and carved grave slabs, are more beautiful and substantial. The road passes the abbey to climb up to the **Horseshoe Pass** for more stunning views.

For a much longer excursion, you could meander through the foothills of the Berwyn Mountains, towards **Pistyll Rhaeadr**, where water tumbles down the hillside for over 230 feet, making it the tallest waterfall in Wales.

WALK

PEMBROKE-SHIRE COAST PATH

The Pembroke-shire Coast Path follows the coastline of the national park for nearly 200 miles. If you want bite-sized sections with self-made circular routes, tackle walks around the headlands and peninsulas, such as (from south to north) St. Govan's Head, the Marloes Peninsula, St. David's Peninsula, Strumble Head and Dinas Head ∎

THE THREE BRIDGES

**Three bridges span the River Conwy, each designed to complement the castle.
The graceful suspension bridge was built by Telford in 1826, the tubular bridge by Stephenson in 1848, and the road bridge was finished in 1858 ∎**

MACHYNLLETH, POWYS 153C3

This small market town is unremarkable, save for being the place where Owain Glyndwr (see panel on p.168) briefly set up a parliament: the **Parliament House** has an exhibition on the Welsh hero.

Hippies have made their homes in the surrounding Dyfi Valley. Alternative lifestylers run the **Centre for Alternative Technology**, 2 miles north, accessed by a water-powered cliff railway. The center, established in 1974, demonstrates environmentally sound ways of generating, conserving and using energy, including water, wind and solar power, and insulation techniques. There's plenty of advice on hand on how to cut your heating bills and make your garden more organic.

THE NORTH COAST 153C5

The north coast of Wales is distinguished by two utterly different aspects. Firstly, it has a concentration of mighty castles built by Edward I. Secondly, it is lined for much of its length with rather gaudy seaside resorts like Prestatyn, Rhyl and Colwyn Bay.

The lovely resort of **Llandudno** stands out by comparison. Its 2-mile promenade around a gently curving bay has lost little of its Victorian splendor, with its pier and Punch and Judy puppet shows on the sands. Take a cable car or the funicular railway up the Great Orme, the headland which separates the town's two beaches, for a spectacular view. On the west shore stands the White Rabbit Memorial, commemorating Lewis Carroll's walks along the seafront with Alice Liddell, the inspiration for his famous story, *Alice in Wonderland*. The **Alice in Wonderland Visitor Centre** elaborates on the story.

Taking Edward's fortifications from east to west, the first of real appeal is **Rhuddlan Castle** (Cadw), south of Rhyl. A new channel for the River Clwyd was dug to give the castle navigable access to the sea. Within today's empty outer ward would have been workshops, granaries and stables. Nearby **Bodelwyddan Castle** is a Victorian mansion, but the interest here is the contents: Victorian furniture from London's Victoria and Albert Museum and sculptures from the Royal Academy complement 200 period works of art from the National Portrait Gallery.

In a superlative setting between the Conwy Estuary and Snowdonia's foothills, **Conwy** is one of the best-preserved medieval fortified towns in Britain. Its **castle ★★★** (Cadw) with eight massive towers erupting from the rock, is the best-looking of all Edward I's creations; it was built by James of St. George, Master of the King's Works in Wales. The town is an example of a *bastide* (a concept stolen from France), laid out and walled in conjunction with the castle. Within the walls, dotted with 21 towers and three gateways, you will find the medieval merchants' lodgings of Aberconwy House

*The old town of
Caernarfon is
protected within
its town walls –
the castle walls
form one side and
the castle itself
sits with its feet
in the waters of
the Seiont and the
Menai Straits*

ISLANDS OFF THE PEMBROKE-SHIRE COAST

**Skomer and
Skokholm are
home to puffins,
guillemots, storm
petrels and manx
shearwaters, and
can be visited
from Martin's
Haven.**

**A Breton saint
named Justinian
lived on Ramsey
Island back in the
6th century; it is
now the habitat of
sea birds and
seals. Boats leave
from Whitesands
Bay and the
harbor at St.
Justinians where
the saint was
buried.**

**Boats from
Tenby frequently
make the short
hop to Caldey
Island. A
community of
Cistercian monks
live here, who
make chocolate,
yogurt and
perfume to sell to
visitors. Only men
can tour the
modern monastery
itself ∎**

(NT) and the Elizabethan townhouse of Plas Mawr.

Bodnant Garden (NT), south across the banks of the River Conwy, is the most attractive in Wales, consisting of terraced gardens which are linked by pergolas above a wonderful pinetum and wild garden.

Back on the coast, **Penrhyn Castle** (NT), near Bangor, was built by Thomas Hopper between 1820 and 1845 to look like a medieval castle. The furnishings are opulent and ostentatious.

Caernarfon Castle (Cadw) ★★★ was modeled on fortresses at Constantinople. A report in 1296 tells of 400 skilled masons at work, with 1,000 unskilled laborers to assist, and 30 boats and 160 wagons to keep the builders supplied. Edward's eldest son was born here and became Prince of Wales, and Prince Charles was invested here in 1969. Like Conwy, the town is enclosed in walls contemporary with the castle.

★★★ PEMBROKESHIRE *152A1-2* COAST NATIONAL PARK PEMBROKESHIRE

The only British national park focused almost exclusively on the coast lies in the far-flung south-west corner of Wales. The impressive cliffs alternate with secluded coves and big sandy beaches, good for swimming, though the waters are chilly.

You need to leave the car to get a true feel for the park, which is best known for its 186-mile Pembrokeshire Coast Path.

The North Coast

From Cardigan down to St. David's Head is the wilder, more dramatic and rugged part of the coast, with few resorts or sandy beaches. The lower part of **Fishguard** is still an old fishing village, the location for the 1971 movie of *Under Milk Wood* starring Richard Burton and Elizabeth Taylor. **Strumble Head** has a rugged grandeur, while little lanes to its west lead to pretty villages such as **Trevine**, **Porthgain** and **Aber-Eiddy**.

The national park also takes a bite out of the inland countryside east of Fishguard. The treeless expanse of grass and heather of the **Preseli Hills** (Mynydd Preseli) may well have been from where the bluestone rock used in the construction of Stonehenge (see p.78) came. The hills have their own prehistoric sites, such as the 5,500-year-old burial chamber of **Pentre Ifan** and the Bronze Age cairn at **Foel Eryr** peak.

DRIVE

UP THE WYE, AROUND THE BRECON BEACONS AND DOWN THE USK

172 miles (allow 2/3 days)

This tour takes in the wooded Wye Valley and part of the Brecon Beacons with a feast of Norman castles, strongholds of barons whom William the Conqueror pitted against the troublesome Welsh. Many of them are now in ruins, but still worth a visit.

From Chepstow, drive north for 16 miles on the A466 to Monmouth.

1 Monmouth, Monmouthshire

The Norman castle where Henry V was born has gone from this market town, but the king is remembered in **Agincourt Square**. Flanked by 17th- and 18th-century buildings, it holds a statue of C.S. Rolls, of Rolls Royce, who died in a flying accident. The medieval **bridge** is fortified. Just east of town, climb Kymin Hill, topped by a **Naval Temple**, for lovely valley views.

NAVAL CONNECTIONS
Along with several fine, old inns, Monmouth has a museum housing a quality collection of Nelson relics. These include his fighting sword and models of his ships.

Nelson himself visited the town in 1802, before his heroic death in 1805 at the Battle of Trafalgar ■

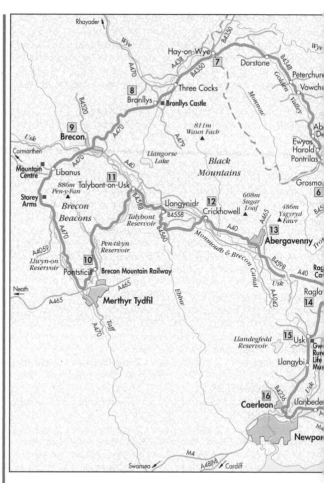

Take the A4136, then the B4228 past Staunton, and left along B4432 to Symonds Yat.

2 Symonds Yat, Herefordshire

At Symonds Yat, a viewpoint commands a magnificent view over the River Wye.

Continue north, turning right onto the B4227 to Goodrich.

3 Goodrich, Herefordshire

The red sandstone **Goodrich Castle** (EH) was ruined by a pounding during the Civil War.

Cross the River Wye and take the B4228 on to Ross-on-Wye.

4 Ross-on-Wye, Herefordshire

This attractive town has interesting old streets, a market place notable for its arcaded, 17th-century **market house**, a fine **church** with a 208-foot spire, and Tudor **almshouses**.

Leave on the A49, then the B4521 Abergavenny road to Skenfrith.

5 Skenfrith, Monmouthshire

Skenfrith Castle, one of three castles built by Hubert de Burgh in the 13th century (the others are Grosmont, see below, and White, west along the B4521), still has its moat and remnants of curtain walls around a partially preserved keep. The **village** has a charming little church and a mill.

Continue on the B4521 for a short distance, then turn north on the B4347 to Grosmont.

6 Grosmont, Monmouthshire

Grosmont's impressive ruins have a rare, cylindrical 14th-century chimney. The village **church** has an effigy of a knight.

Follow the B4347, then the B4348 through the Golden Valley and on to Hay-on-Wye.

7 Hay-on-Wye, Powys

This beguiling little town on the edge of the Brecon Beacons National Park is a center for the secondhand book trade.

Every year the town holds a literature festival.

Head southwest for 8 miles along the B4350 and A438 to Bronllys.

THE WELSH LANGUAGE

Roughly one in five (or 500,000) inhabitants of Wales can speak Welsh, which is the first language of many people, particularly in the northwest.

Welsh is broadcast on the television channel S4C and on BBC Radio Cymru; it can be read on bilingual road signs and place names, and is taught in schools.

In the latter half of the last century, however, the Welsh language was judged immoral and backward by English education commissioners, and pupils who spoke it were often forced to wear wooden boards around their necks bearing the words "Welsh Not."

No one expects foreigners to be able to speak Welsh, but if you learn just a few words of greeting you'll make many more friends ■

8 Bronllys, Powys

The scenery at Bronllys is dominated by the Black Mountains and the Brecon Beacons. During troubled times, women and children hid in the tower of the 12th-century church. Bronllys Castle is ½ mile along the A479.

Take the A438, the A470 and the B4602 to Brecon.

9 Brecon, Powys

See p.157

Continue south along the A470. Just before Merthyr Tydfil, take unclassified roads north to Pontsticill.

10 Pontsticill, Powys

Forest walks and boating on the Pen-twyn and Pontsticill reservoirs, and a vintage steam train on the Brecon Mountain Railway are popular.

Take small roads through the hills to Talybont-on-Usk.

11 Talybont-on-Usk, Powys

The Monmouth and Brecon Canal was built to carry coal and iron ore. It reopened in 1970 and now offers rented narrowboats and walking along the towpaths.

Follow the B4558 to Llangynidr, then the B4560 to Crickhowell.

12 Crickhowell, Powys

Alisby Castle was sacked by Owain Glyndwr. The 17th-century bridge has 12 arches on one side, 13 on the other.

Take the A40 for 7 miles to Abergavenny.

13 Abergavenny, Monmouthshire

This is a major center for exploring the Brecon Beacons.

Welsh love spoons were carved by lovers to denote betrothal in much the same way that engagement rings are given today

The town has a busy **market**, a **castle** and St. Mary's Church with ancient tombs and effigies.

Take the A40 to Raglan.

14 Raglan, Monmouthshire

Raglan Castle (Cadw) was one of the most elaborate of medieval Welsh castles and much stands intact: battlements, towers, courts, and a carved coat of arms.

Begun in 1435, it was enlarged in the 1460s and then again in Elizabethan times by a great hall and long gallery.

Follow the road south to Usk.

15 Usk, Monmouthshire

Built on the Roman ruins of *Burrium*, Usk has two main attractions: the old **church** with a beautiful screen, and the **Gwent Rural Life Museum** with domestic farm interiors and early agricultural implements.

Cross the river and continue along unclassified roads for 8 miles to Caerleon.

16 Caerleon, Newport

Caerleon Roman Fortress has an impressive grass amphi-theater, and well-preserved baths; finds are displayed at the Legionary Museum.

Take the B4236, then join the A48 for Penhow.

17 Penhow, Newport

Penhow Castle is a 12th-century fortified manor. Three miles east, Roman walls surround **Caerwent**, which was once the important Roman civilian town of *Venta Silurium*. The village church has smaller and more fascinating relics of the period.

Continue straight along the A48 for 8 miles to Chepstow.

The West Coast

St. Brides Bay has good sandy beaches at Newgale, Druidston and Broad Haven, a boating center at **Solva**, and the picturesque fishing village, **Little Haven.**

Marloes Peninsula has fine sandstone cliffs, good beaches and views of the islands from Wooltack Point.

The main attraction here is **St. David's Peninsula**, much of it owned by the National Trust, and **Whitesands Bay**, which has one of the loveliest beaches in Wales. **St. David's ★ ★ ★**, nominally the smallest city in Britain, is really just a village. Saint David, patron saint of Wales, founded a monastery here in the 6th century which had become a bishopric by Norman times. The cathedral, tucked away in a valley, is reached from the village by steps called "the 39 Articles." The nave roof, made of 15th-century Irish oak, is the aesthetic highlight, while the spiritual impetus rests with Saint David's shrine.

The South Coast

The northern limits of the Norman influence in Wales stopped around the middle of St. Bride's Bay on a boundary known as the Landsker. The oil refinery of **Milford Haven** is unattractive, but **Pembroke** is a one-street town whose fine, 12th-century castle, with a circular 100-foot keep, stands with cliffs on three sides. **Carew Castle** is next to both a tidal mill and a Celtic cross.

The coastline excels around **St. Govan's Head** with its hermitage chapel on a rocky ledge and remarkable rock formations. **Bosherston** has 80 acres of interconnecting lily ponds. **Tenby**, with four sandy beaches, is the most popular resort in the region, a combination of narrow, cobbled streets within the walls of its old town and of pastel-shaded Regency and Georgian houses overlooking the harbor. A Tudor scientist named Robert Recorde, who invented the "equals" (=) sign, was born here.

The Cathedral of St. David, the patron saint of Wales, nestles in a protective hollow hidden from the view of possible marauding Vikings

WALES

★★★ PORTMEIRION   *153C4*
GWYNEDD

An Italianate village on the coast of Wales: is it possible? Portmeirion is the most charming place in the Principality. It was begun in 1925 by architect Clough Williams-Ellis, who called it "a lighthearted live exhibition of architecture, decor and landscaping." His intention was to prove that buildings could actually enhance an already beautiful landscape. Towers, spires, turrets, domes, campaniles, triumphal arches, murals and weatherboard cottages make up this joyous fantasy, in a thickly wooded setting on the edge of a big sandy bay. It is familiar to many who haven't even been here from the cult TV series *The Prisoner*.

Many of the cottages offer first-rate accommodations as part of the Portmeirion Hotel.

Snowdonia National Park in North Wales is the most attractive part of the Principality, with mountains reaching their peak in Snowdon itself at 3,560 feet

★★ POWIS CASTLE   *153D4*
POWYS

Powis Castle (NT) differs from other medieval Welsh fortresses in that it never fell into ruin.

Though built in the 13th century, its architectural history spans seven centuries. Not only does the house contain an expected gamut of fine furniture, tapestries and paintings, but it also holds a glittering collection of Indian treasures acquired by Clive of India, founder of British India. The house's hanging gardens are the only formal gardens in Britain still in their 17th-century form.

SNOWDONIA   *153C4*
NATIONAL PARK, GWYNEDD

The national park occupies almost the whole of the northwestern corner of Wales.

Of the mountainous districts of England and Wales, Snowdonia's grandeur and variety of scenery is

rivaled only by the Lake District (see p.176). You'll find not only jagged peaks, but also glaciated valleys and lakes, moorland and tracts of coniferous forest. The 3,560-foot Snowdon is the highest mountain in England and Wales, yet it, like other peaks in the park, can be easily climbed. For the more sedate, there are good scenic drives, several narrow-gauge railways to ride, and mines from the once-thriving slate quarrying business to visit.

Snowdon and the North

Naturally, Snowdon ★ ★ ★ is the most popular mountain to climb, with a café at the top to provide refreshment. If you don't feel like walking, the rack and pinion Snowdon Mountain Railway ascends from Llanberis (you could walk back down!).

To get a feel for the range, which includes the Carneddau

mountains just to the north, drive from Betws-y-Coed down the Llanberis Pass on the A4086, then back along the A5 from Bethesda to Capel Curig.

The Victorian mountain resort of riverside Betws-y-Coed is a good base for exploring the area, although it is separated from the mountains proper. Just outside town are the Swallow Falls. Further west, Llanberis is worth visiting not only for Snowdon ascents but also for its Welsh Slate Museum, an evocative semi-abandoned slate quarry with turn-of-the-century machines operated by skilled artisans. Also of interest is Power of Wales, which offers underground tours of the largest pumped storage power station in Europe. Above ground, the Pen-y-gwryd Hotel at Nant Gwynant justifies at least a lunch stop; it was Sir Edmund Hillary and Sherpa Tensing's base camp as they trained for their conquest of Mount Everest.

The village of Beddgelert is another contender for best base in the region. Guided tours of Sygun Copper Mine, just outside, take you through winding tunnels and into large chambers. To the east, the mining town of Blaenau Ffestiniog is not pretty, and its surrounding hills are covered with discarded slate. But there's plenty of interest here in Llechwedd Slate Caverns, where a tramway takes you deep underground, through huge caverns and past an underground lake, into a Victorian slate miner's world. There's also the Gloddfa Ganol Slate Mine (with walking visits). Both of the above also have demonstrations of slate splitting and cutting.

The former slate-bearing Ffestiniog Railway, the most famous of the North Wales lines, runs from Blaenau Ffestiniog all the way down to the coast at

WALKS

SNOWDONIA NATIONAL PARK

The mountain to climb is of course Snowdon.

There are half a dozen established routes: the least interesting, but easiest, follows the mountain railroad.

The Horseshoe Route is the most demanding, while the Miners' Track and the Pyg Track, from the top of the Llanberis Pass, fall somewhere in between.

The nature trail around Llyn Idwal has dramatic scenery. There are lovely, fairly untaxing walks near Cader Idris: around the Cregennan Lakes; the old railroad track along the Mawddach Estuary; and the Precipice Walk above the estuary.

Take note that Snowdonia's mountains may look tame, but they should be approached with respect and care; changes in the weather can be sudden and dramatic ■

OWAIN GLYNDWR

In any historic exploration of Wales, the name Owain Glyndwr crops up a lot.

He was wronged in a land dispute with the English Lord Grey of Ruthin, and in 1400 declared himself Prince of Wales. He waged war against Henry IV, and ended up in control of most of Wales. In 1404 he was proclaimed King of Wales, and though he suffered defeats, he was never captured, and his legend and status lives on today ■

Porthmadog. The drive back to Betws-y-Coed passes **Dolwyddelan Castle**, a brooding native Welsh stronghold.

Cader Idris and the South

In the southern half of the park, lonesome whitewashed farms are more common than brightly colored windbreakers worn by walkers. The dominant feature is the great **Cader Idris** mountain, which isn't too tough to climb. **Dolgellau**, surrounded by walks of every level of difficulty and the only town in the park, is the obvious base. Good scenic driving routes radiate from the town: south to Machynlleth, west to Barmouth, east to Mallwyd, north of Ffestiniog and northeast to Bala. **Bala** sits on Wales' largest lake, with another narrow-gauge railway along its shore.

The only compulsive sight here is another of Edward I's fortresses, **Harlech Castle** (Cadw). Once at the sea's edge, it now sits ½ mile inland, dramatically sited on a high crag; it was captured by Owain Glyndwr in 1404.

THE VALLEYS   *153C1*
RHONDDA CYNON TAFF and CAERPHILLY

The traditional industrial heartland of Wales lies in the deep valleys below the Brecon Beacons, from Pontypool in the east to Llanelli in the west. Workers came here at the end of the 18th century to extract iron ore, then in their droves in the 19th and early 20th centuries to dig for coal, living in closely-knit towns of row upon row of terraced houses.

But time has changed the landscape; country parks cover many of the slag heaps now, as all but one of the underground pits have ceased operating. Some have become gritty tourist attractions, with the ex-miners leading the tours. Such is the Big

Pit Mining Museum at Blaenavon ★ ★ ★, where, supplied with a safety helmet, lamp and "self rescuer," you descend 300 feet in a cage down the mine shaft to underground roadways and the coal faces. On the surface, the workshops and pithead baths are open to the public. There are guided tours around the **Blaenavon Ironworks** (Cadw), whose furnaces date from the 18th century.

In the early 1920s, some 180,000 people toiled in the Rhondda Valley, once the blackened symbol of industrial Wales. The last pit closed in 1986. The **Rhondda Heritage Park** evokes the days of a working pit with great intensity through a dramatic underground tour, and in the pithead buildings of the Lewis Merthyr Colliery.

★★ WYE VALLEY   *153D2*
MONMOUTHSHIRE

The River Wye. as it descends into the Severn Estuary, defines the border between England and Wales. The thickly wooded slopes of this sandstone gorge are at their loveliest in fall, and have been a beauty spot for 200 years, evoked by Wordsworth in *Lines Composed a Few Miles Above Tintern Abbey*.

Tintern Abbey (Cadw) ★ ★ ★, painted by J.M.W. Turner, is an irresistible attraction. The shell of the Cistercian monastery's church, still with tracery in its glassless windows, sits next to remnants of monastic quarters.

The driving tour on p.162 covers the sights north of Tintern. South of Tintern, **Chepstow's** mighty Norman castle is one of the most impressive. It stands high above the Wye with four courtyards, a keep, gatehouse and towers; its size summarizes the importance English kings placed on subjugating the Welsh.

THE NORTH OF ENGLAND

Encompassing England's extremes
of rurality and urbanization, the
North of England features five
national parks, including the Peak
District in Derbyshire and the
Yorkshire Dales in North Yorkshire,
along with pristine historic cities
like York in North Yorkshire,
Durham and Chester in Cheshire

CALENDAR OF EVENTS

FEBRUARY –
Viking Festival, York.
Begins with a grand
fireworks display and
includes a longships
race, Viking feasts
and folk dancing,
ending with a torchlit
procession.

MARCH OR
APRIL – Bacup
Nutters Dance,
Bacup, near
Rochdale. On Easter
Saturday the town
band plays for the
Britannia Coconut
Dancers who clatter
their way along the
streets in outlandish
costume.

EARLY APRIL –
The Grand National,
Aintree, near
Liverpool. The
world's most famous
steeplechase. First
raced in 1839.

MAY TO JUNE –
Isle of Man T.T.
Races. The island's
famous motorcycle
festival is raced on
the public highways
and is one of the
most exciting in
the world ■

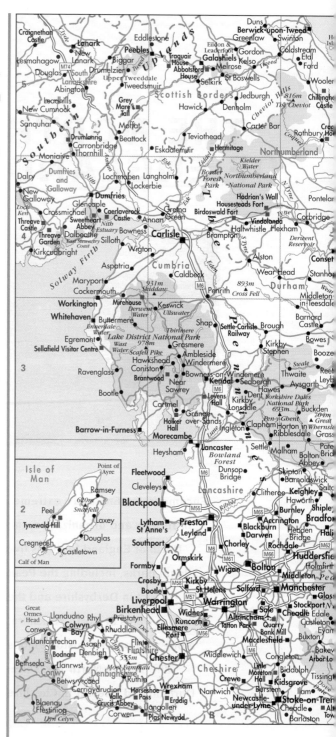

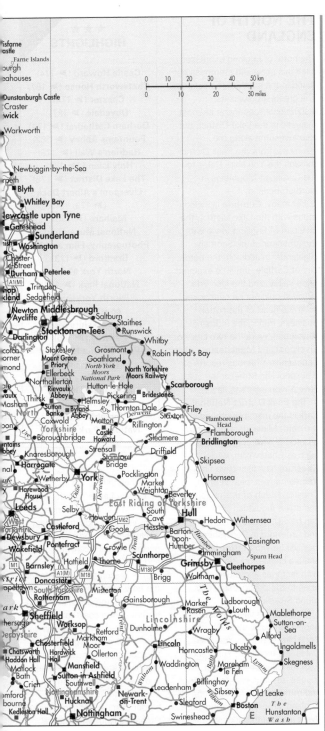

Map labels (reading the map):

Lindisfarne Castle, Farne Islands, Bamburgh, Seahouses, Dunstanburgh Castle, Craster, Alnwick, Warkworth, Newbiggin-by-the-Sea, Morpeth, Blyth, Whitley Bay, Newcastle upon Tyne, Gateshead, Sunderland, Washington, Chester-le-Street, Durham, Peterlee, Bishop Auckland, Trimdon, Sedgefield, Newton Aycliffe, Middlesbrough, Saltburn, Staithes, Runswick, Darlington, Stockton-on-Tees, Whitby, Scotch Corner, Richmond, Stokesley, Grosmont, Robin Hood's Bay, Mount Grace Priory, Goathland, Ellerbeck, North York Moors National Park, North Yorkshire Moors Railway, Northallerton, Rievaulx Abbey, Hutton-le-Hole, Scarborough, Swaledale, Thirsk, Helmsley, Pickering, Bridestones, Masham, Sutton Bank, Byland Abbey, Thornton Dale, Filey, North Yorkshire, Coxwold, Malton, Staxton, Ripon, Boroughbridge, Castle Howard, Rillington, Flamborough Head, Pennines, Knaresborough, Strensall, Sledmere, Flamborough, Bridlington, Abbey, Stamford Bridge, Driffield, Skipsea, Harrogate, Wetherby, York, Pocklington, Hornsea, Harewood House, Market Weighton, Beverley, Leeds, Selby, East Riding of Yorkshire, South Cave, Hull, West Yorkshire, Castleford, Howden, Hessle, Hedon, Withernsea, Dewsbury, Pontefract, Goole, Barton-upon-Humber, Easington, Wakefield, Crowle, Thorne, Scunthorpe, Immingham, Spurn Head, Barnsley, Hatfield, Brigg, Grimsby, Cleethorpes, District, Doncaster, M180, Waltham, Chapeltown, South Yorkshire, Misterton, Gainsborough, Market Rasen, Ludborough, Louth, Mablethorpe, Park, Rotherham, The Wolds, Sutton-on-Sea, Sheffield, Worksop, Retford, Dunholme, Wragby, Alford, Ingoldmells, Hathersage, Lincolnshire, Derbyshire, Chesterfield, Markham Moor, Ollerton, Lincoln, Horncastle, Ulceby, Skegness, Chatsworth, Hardwick Hall, Mansfield, Waddington, Mareham le Fen, Haddon Hall, Matlock Bath, Crich, Sutton in Ashfield, Southwell, Billinghay, Sibsey, Old Leake, Cromford, Ashbourne, Nottinghamshire, Newark-on-Trent, Leadenham, The Wash, Kedleston Hall, Hucknall, Sleaford, Boston, Hunstanton, Nottingham, Swineshead

Scale: 0 10 20 30 40 50 km / 0 10 20 30 miles

CALENDAR OF EVENTS

LATE JUNE –
The Hoppings, Newcastle. Visitors can enjoy the fun of the largest traveling fair in Europe. Includes the Lord Mayor's Parade procession.

JULY – The Cumberland Show, Carlisle. A venerable event that dates back to the 1830s with all the fun of a traditional county show and more!

SEPTEMBER and OCTOBER –
Blackpool Illuminations. Close to 500,000 light bulbs go on every night as the famous illuminations decorate the whole parade and Blackpool Tower.

NOVEMBER –
Huddersfield Contemporary Music Festival. Held over 10 days, the festival has established itself as one of the leading international arenas for new music ■

WALKING IN THE NATIONAL PARKS

With five national parks in the north of Britain, there is a superlative range of walks at all levels to be enjoyed.

In any of the more remote parts of the parks (especially in the Lake District, where more rescues are made than anywhere else in Britain) pay heed to the weather, dress properly, and equip yourself with a large-scale Ordnance Survey map ■

THE NORTH OF ENGLAND

The north of England expresses itself in a scale and sternness not found in the south of the country. The greatest draw is its inspirational scenery, at its most majestic in the Lake District, but also awesome along the Pennines, from the Peak District through the Yorkshire Dales to the Cumbrian Mountains in Northumberland.

For many, **Cumbria** is synonymous with the Lake District, the only part of England to vie with the grandeur of the Scottish Highlands. In addition, the border city of **Carlisle**, the little-explored Lune Valley, and the lush Eden Valley should not be overlooked.

At the heart of the cotton business, during the Industrial Revolution, were the two cities of **Liverpool** and **Manchester**, while Lancashire's famous resorts of Blackpool and Morecambe still have a working-class flavor.

The **Peak District National Park** is the main playground in the north Midlands. **Derbyshire** has some jawdropping mansions such as Chatsworth, while **Cheshire** has distinctive timber-framed houses, best seen in Chester. Much of this region was and still is industrial: cotton mills can be visited at Styal in Cheshire and Cromford in Derbyshire. Derbyshire and **Staffordshire** share a china-producing heritage, with factories and museums open to the public, especially round Stoke-on-Trent.

Yorkshire is vast and its people famously blunt. North Yorkshire offers the Yorkshire Dales and the North York Moors, with ruined abbeys on both fringes. Ancient streets, buildings and museums make **York** one of England's most compelling cities. West and South Yorkshire are largely industrial, the charms of its cities – **Leeds**, Bradford and Sheffield – largely dependent on their Victorian industrial legacy.

Northumberland and the northeast was a coal-producing and ship-building area, the former reason that accounts for the now economically depressed urban area from Middlesbrough further up the coast to beyond Newcastle-upon-Tyne in Tyne and Wear. There are large tracts of fine countryside, notably Northumberland National Park and the Northumberland coast. Top attractions include the border castles, Hadrian's Wall and Durham's Norman cathedral.

★★ BEVERLEY 171D2
EAST RIDING OF YORKSHIRE

A diversion into the flat Humberside landscape is well rewarded by this old-fashioned market town of cobbled streets and pleasing Georgian buildings. Soaring **Beverley Minster**, big enough to be a cathedral, holds a treasure trove of medieval art and craft, particularly in the beautiful Percy Tomb, the 68 exquisitely carved misericords, the stained glass in the east window, and the west front.

St. Mary's Church is almost as lovely; its chancel ceiling features a unique 15th-century painting of 40 English kings, while its wealth of stone carvings include a rabbit thought to have inspired the white rabbit in *Alice in Wonderland*.

BLACKPOOL 170B2
LANCASHIRE

Candy floss and donkey rides on the beach, fish and chips and "Kiss Me Quick" hats, nightclubs and fairgrounds, guest houses run by matronly landladies – the North's top seaside resort is unashamedly unpretentious and brash. More famous than its 7 miles of sandy beaches and its three piers are the landmark **Blackpool Tower**, modeled on the Eiffel Tower in Paris; **Blackpool Pleasure Beach** with 140 rides and entertainments including a dozen rollercoasters; and, in September and October, the glittering light show of the Blackpool Illuminations.

BRADFORD 170C2
WEST YORKSHIRE

The prosperity of sprawling, industrial Bradford peaked in Victorian times as the city became the world capital for making worsted; it is still the foremost wool centre in Britain.

Locations which provide various evocations of the city's past include the **City Hall**, the Wool Exchange, the **Industrial Museum** in a former spinning mill, and, above all, the factory village at **Saltaire** north of the city, built by the enlightened industrialist Titus Salt to free his workforce of Bradford's smog. Its vast mill displays a large collection of impressive works by the Bradford-born artist, David Hockney.

The city's top attraction, the **National Museum of Photography, Film and Television ★★★** (both free and extremely popular with children), ignores its heritage altogether. As well as a lively history of all kinds of media, there are hands-on exhibits galore (make your own TV show, for example), and there is a giant IMAX theater next door.

★★ CALDERDALE 170C2
WEST YORKSHIRE

A drive along the A646 through Calderdale, from Halifax to Burnley, not only gives a flavor of the Pennines, with bleak moorland above the drystone-walled valley, but also takes in appealing mill towns.

The well-preserved industrial town of **Halifax** is little visited. Its greatest treasure is Piece Hall, a magnificent former cloth market surrounding a great courtyard, now brought to life by a general market. Close by at **Calderdale Industrial Museum** you can see textile machinery at work and learn about the origins of toffee and "cat's eyes," both of which were invented here.

Hebden Bridge is a mill town turned smart commuter base. Walks along the Rochdale Canal pass back-to-back cottages and old mills, and you can climb up to **Heptonstall**, a captivating village with a cobbled square and the oldest Methodist chapel in the world in regular use.

ISLE OF MAN

This self-governing part of the British Isles (but not part of the U.K.), 33 miles long and 13 miles wide, is situated in the middle of the Irish Sea.

It has its own laws and parliament (the world's oldest), it issues its own currency, has its own Celtic language (now rarely heard) and tailless cats, called, like its residents, Manx.

Steam railroads and electric streetcars add to a sense of dislocation. The Victorian resort of Douglas may be past its prime – offshore banking is the big business now – but along the southwest coast you will find picturesque ports, sandy beaches and glen-cut cliffs.

Be sure to go up to Snaefell, the island's highest point, and to visit the folk museum village of Cregneish.

Ferries visit the island from Heysham, Fleetwood and Liverpool, or there are flights available from the mainland ■

WALK

DURHAM

Start at Market Place, go down Silver Street to Framwellgate Bridge, and cross. Bear left into South Street for views of the cathedral. Take the path down to Prebends' Bridge, where Turner painted the lovely cathedral vista. Cross the bridge and climb the cobbled South Bailey with Georgian facades. Next, turn left into The College, the medieval and Georgian cathedral close. A passage from the far side of The College allows you to zigzag down the slope to the small archeological museum in a picturesque riverside mill. You could continue along the riverbank back to Framwellgate Bridge ■

★ CARLISLE, CUMBRIA *170B4*

During its long, warring history, the Scots both attacked and held Carlisle, Cumbria's chief town. The Norman **castle** (EH), re-fortified by Henry VIII, was the main English bastion in the northwest against the Scots; there are splendid views from the keep and poignant graffiti by those incarcerated below.

The excellent **Tullie House Museum** elaborates on the city's past, with a particularly good Roman collection – Carlisle was the main Roman base at the western end of Hadrian's Wall (see p.176). The small, red-stone **cathedral**, founded in 1122, has outstanding stained glass in its east window, and fine capitals and a painted ceiling in its choir.

★★★ CASTLE HOWARD *170D3*
NORTH YORKSHIRE

The fame of this colossal baroque palace has reached the living rooms of homes round the globe thanks to the TV series *Brideshead Revisited*.

The grandeur of the parkland, with lakes, a colonnaded mausoleum and temple, provides a fitting backdrop to the house. The young Sir John Vanbrugh is generally accepted as master designer for the house, though the extent of assistance from the well-established architect Nicholas Hawksmoor is much debated. The centrepiece of the building is the 70-foot Great Hall, with pillars, arches, murals and statuary. There are notable picture and costume collections.

★★★ CHESTER, CHESHIRE *170B1*

The Romans built an important military base called Dewa on a bend of the River Dee in AD 79. **The Dewa Roman Experience**, an imaginative reconstruction of a Roman galley and a street, and a serious look at on-going

archeological work, provides a good introduction to Roman Chester. The city's most evocative Roman sight is a complete underfloor heating system, across the street beneath a café.

The wide-ranging **Grosvenor Museum** excels in its Roman displays. A tour of the city in the company of a Roman centurion, dressed in body armor and helmet, takes you onto the **city walls**, and passes the remains of the largest Roman **amphitheater** unearthed in Britain.

Though Roman in origin, the **city walls** are largely medieval: you can walk their 2-mile length via towers and gates. Along the city's four main streets run **The Rows**, a striking two-tiered arrangement of stores with a covered mall, fronted by lofty, black and white timbered facades. Nose around the superb stores (Watergate Street is packed with antiques) and you'll find vaulted crypts and galleries with painted plasterwork.

Chester's **cathedral** has 14th-century, delicately carved choir stalls and misericords. Children will enjoy **Chester Zoo**, a couple of miles from the city center.

DURHAM *171C4*
COUNTY DURHAM

Durham is one of England's most memorable small cities – primarily for its enormous cathedral. The country's finest piece of ecclesi-astical Norman architecture erupts out of thickly wooded banks on a bend of the River Wear. Largely traffic-free lanes around the peninsula, riverside paths and, in summer, river cruises and rowing boats for rent, add to the city's appeal.

The first church on the site of the present day **cathedral ★★★** was erected in 995 to house the coffin of Saint Cuthbert, taken from Holy Island (see p.184) to avoid its desecration by Danish raiders. The bulk of the present church was built between 1093 and 1133, in unadulterated Norman style, most tangible in the nave's colossal pillars still incized with chevron patterns.

The church's size was made possible by the ground-breaking use of rib vaulting and pointed arches. At one end of the nave, Saint Cuthbert's tomb was such a popular place of pilgrimage that more room was needed, resulting in the Chapel of the Nine Altars, in Early English style. The 8th-century historian, the Venerable Bede, lies in the Galilee Chapel at the other end of the nave. The cathedral precincts include the **Monk's Dormitory**, an enormous barn-like room with a museum of Saxon carved crosses, and the **treasury**, displaying remarkable fragments of Saint Cuthbert's coffin and relics of the saint, as well as the original 12th-century Sanctuary Knocker and ancient, scrolled books.

For hundreds of years Durham was the headquarters for a quasiregal state, called a *palatinate*. Its governors, prince bishops, lived in the **castle**, divided from the cathedral by Palace Green, whose surrounding buildings were once the administrative offices for the palatinate. These buildings, like the castle, are now part of Durham University, the third oldest and most prestigious in England after Oxford and Cambridge. Fascinating tours of the castle include the medieval Great Hall and the shadowy Norman Chapel.

There are extensive collections in the **Oriental Museum** but much more fun is the vast **North of England Open-Air Museum** at Beamish, halfway between Durham and Newcastle-upon-Tyne. Life a hundred years ago is re-created in superb detail through reconstructed buildings, which include a pub, store, residential terrace, railroad station, farm and colliery.

The superb bulk of Norman Durham Cathedral was built in a spectacular position above the River Wear. It dominates the view from the water, the town, the railroad and the countryside for miles around

THE BRONTËS

The Brontë sisters are each remembered primarily for one novel apiece: Charlotte (1816–55) for *Jane Eyre,* **Emily (1818–48) for** *Wuthering Heights* **and Anne (1820–49) for** *Agnes Grey.*

They lived with their father, Reverend Patrick Brontë, in the parsonage at Haworth, along with their brother Branwell, who took to drink and drugs.

Soon after the sisters were published under the pseudonyms of Currer, Ellis and Acton Bell, Branwell died of tuberculosis, as did Emily three months later and Anne the following year. The last of the remarkable trio, Charlotte, died during pregnancy in 1855 ∎

★★★ HADRIAN'S WALL 170B4
NORTHUMBERLAND

The surviving sections of this 1,900-year-old, 73-mile fortification, running across the top of England from the Tyne to the Solway Firth, is the most impressive legacy of Roman rule in Britain. Marking the northern boundary of the Roman empire, it was masterminded by the Emperor Hadrian and begun in AD 122. Built of stone and turf, it was manned by up to 20,000 troops who lived in small forts (or milecastles) every Roman mile, and in larger forts every 7 miles.

The southern area of Northumberland National Park has the finest surviving parts of the wall, and walking along the the crest of Whin Sill crags around Houseteads Fort is very popular. There is a summer bus service which uses the road running parallel to the wall. From west to east, don't miss the well-preserved **Birdoswald Fort** (EH); the **Roman Army Museum** at Carvoran; **Vindolanda Fort** (EH), where a section of the wall has been reconstructed and there is a superb museum; **Houseteads Fort** (EH/NT), the most complete fort on the wall, with hospitals and latrines; the excavated cavalry fort of **Chesters** (EH); and **Corbridge Roman Site** (EH), the garrison town of *Corstopitum.*

Hexham, on the banks of the River Tyne, makes an attractive base for exploring the area. Its abbey, founded in the 7th century by Saint Wilfrid, has a little-altered Saxon crypt and bishop's throne.

★★ HARROGATE and 171C2
HAREWOOD HOUSE
NORTH YORKSHIRE

Antique shops, tearooms and colorful gardens distinguish the genteel spa town of **Harrogate.**

It is an important conference center, and its wealth of facilities make it a good Yorkshire touring base. You can taste the waters at the Royal Pump Room, and enjoy the 60 acres of Harlow Carr Botanical Gardens.

Harewood House, 6 miles south, is one of the finest mansions in England. It is essentially Palladian in style, with rooms in a lighter neoclassical style, typical of the architect Robert Adam. Thomas Chippendale was commissioned to make the furniture, and "Capability" Brown landscaped the grounds, which have lakeside walks, and a bird aviary for over 150 species.

★ HAWORTH 170C2
WEST YORKSHIRE

In summer, literary pilgrims on the Brontë trail overrun this dour Yorkshire village. The sisters' home is now the **Brontë Parsonage Museum,** full of mementoes of the gifted and tragic family. Emily and Charlotte are buried in the churchyard. Various landmarks reached on foot over the open moorland are possible models for places in the Brontë books, most famously Top Withens as *Wuthering Heights.*

★★★ THE LAKE 170A3
DISTRICT NATIONAL PARK
CUMBRIA

The Lake District has England's finest mountain scenery, with over 60 summits, called "fells," of over 2,500 feet. Beneath the peaks lie lush stone-walled pastures and the lakes themselves, either glinting in the sunlight or moody and ruffled in the frequent rainstorms.

Scooped out by Ice Age glaciers, the lakes are known as "waters" or "meres." Spring and fall are the best times to visit: in summer, roads and villages are packed with vacationers and the lovely country-house hotels can be full.

For over two hundred years tourists have been coming here:

the resident William Wordsworth complained bitterly about it. Now the "Lake Poets," Wordsworth, Samuel Taylor Coleridge, Robert Southey, and Thomas de Quincey add to the area's appeal, as well as Arthur Ransome (who set his *Swallows and Amazons* here), and Beatrix Potter. At any time of year you can find invigorating upland air: this is absolutely fantastic walking country (see p.178).

The Southern Lakes   *170B3*
The most crowded part of the region has a gentle, farmed and forested landscape and a concentration of literary sights.

Windermere is best enjoyed from a steamer that plies the 10½ miles from Ambleside via Bowness to Lakeside. In contrast to its tranquil, wooded western side, the eastern shore is developed, especially round the resorts of **Bowness** and **Windermere** town, where B&Bs and guest houses are plentiful. **Brockhole National Park Visitor Centre**, near Ambleside, gives an excellent introduction to the area, and the **Windermere Steamboat Museum** has a lovely array of Victorian and Edwardian vessels. **Hawkshead** is a conspicuously attractive village, free of traffic

but rarely of tourists. There is a gallery of Beatrix Potter's original illustrations for her story books. She wrote many of them at the old farmhouse of Hill Top (NT) in **Near Sawrey**, a village she described as being "as nearly perfect a little place as I ever lived in."

Grizedale Forest, to the south, is a large tract of woodland, with paths passing modern sculpture through to the shores of **Coniston Water**, where the National Trust's steam yacht *Gondola* puffs along its 5-mile length. Donald Campbell died on the lake trying to break the world waterspeed record in 1967. On Coniston's east shore, looking across to the fell known as the "Old Man of Coniston," is **Brantwood**, home to critic and philosopher John Ruskin. It is full of the eminent Victorian's mementoes. North of Ambleside at the top of Windermere lies the heart of Wordsworth Country, in the village of **Grasmere** and the footpaths round Grasmere and Rydal Water. To the west you can make a lovely circular drive along glacial **Langdale Valley**, with the serious climbing country of the Langdale Pikes at its end.

Grasmere Island can be reached by rowing boat, or enjoyed from the vantage point of the surrounding fells

WILLIAM WORDSWORTH
The poet was born in Wordsworth House (NT), in Cockermouth in 1770.

He went to school in Hawkshead and between 1799 and 1808 he lived at Dove Cottage, Grasmere, which is open to the public.

In 1813 he and his family moved to Rydal Mount, where he died in 1850. You can still see the lakes through his eyes by purchasing his own *Guide to the Lakes* ∎

THE NORTH OF ENGLAND

WALKS

THE LAKE DISTRICT

The Lake District has some of the best walking in Britain. Most fells are accessible to the average walker, but Langdale Pikes, Scafell Pike, Scafell and Great Gable offer more serious fell walks with departure points from the head of the Langdale Valley, Wasdale Head, Eskdale and Borrowdale.

Helvellyn is the most frequently climbed, from Thirlmere, or with more difficulty and interest from Glenridding. Skiddaw and the Old Man of Coniston are the easiest to climb.

Flat walks follow the shores of Grasmere and Rydal Water, Buttermere, Loweswater and Ennerdale Water.

On Derwent Water and Ullswater you can start with a lake cruise, and return on foot ■

The Northern Lakes   170B3

This area is grander than the southern lakes and more accessible than the western lakes. The A591 road up from Ambleside passes the sinuous reservoir of Thirlmere and lofty Helvellyn. Keswick commands an exceptionally beautiful setting; its lake, island-studded Derwent Water, is stunning. On its eastern side, Castlerigg Stone Circle is a dramatically-sited prehistoric place. On the western shores the woodland Lingholm Gardens dazzle in early summer.

Utterly romantic Borrowdale is one of the most scenic lakeland valleys; a varied drive takes you past woodlands and the road to Seathwaite, the wettest place in England, over bleak Honister Pass and beside Buttermere and Crummock Water, with majestic fells on all sides. Head on for Mirehouse, often visited by Tennyson, near the banks of Bassenthwaite Lake.

Many believe serpentine Ullswater to be the most spectacular lake, pastoral at one end, craggy at the other. On its slopes at Gowbarrow Wordsworth saw his daffodils ("I wandered lonely as a cloud" ...), near to which are the much-visited waterfalls of Aira Force. Treat yourself to English tea (reserve ahead) at the famous Sharrow Bay Hotel (see p.297).

The Western Lakes   170A3

Here you'll find the most desolate, untamed part of the region, bereft of towns and offering stupendous drives and walks. Confident drivers should take the road over the alarmingly steep Hardknott Pass (where there are the remains of a Roman fort) on to verdant Eskdale, or turn down delightful Dunnerdale. Eskdale can also be explored on a narrow gauge railroad from Boot to attractive Ravenglass, the

park's only coastal village of any significance. Grim mountains and scree slopes hem in Wast Water, England's deepest lake; the cul-de-sac road continues to Wasdale Head, a base for the ascents to Scafell and Scafell Pike, the highest in England at 3,210 feet. For more accessible escapism head for Ennerdale Water, surrounded by a lakeside track that is walkable in about two hours.

Beyond the National Park   170B3

Some interesting sights cluster in The Lake District's southeastern approaches, and along the Cumbrian coast.

You could happily fill a few wet hours in Kendal, known both as the "Auld Grey Town" and for its energizing (and very sweet) mint cake. Visit the Georgian Abbot Hall for its art gallery and engrossing Museum of Lakeland Life and Industry.

Nearby Sizergh Castle (NT) has a 14th-century defensive tower, 15th-century great hall, and Elizabethan oak carvings and paneling, while Elizabethan Levens Hall, close by, has fun topiary gardens. Moving west, Cartmel's fine parish church was the centerpiece of a grand medieval priory. Outside the village, there is fine furniture and woodcarving, and a motor museum at Holker Hall. The sedate resort of Grange-over-Sands commands fine views of the vast sands of Morecambe Bay. Near industrial Barrow-in-Furness stand the red sandstone remains of Furness Abbey (EH).

Up the coast a visitor center does a public relations exercise at Sellafield nuclear reprocessing plant, while Whitehaven, a coal port during the 17th-century and later laid out in a Georgian grid, gives an insight into early industrial England.

THE NORTH OF ENGLAND

LANCASTER 170B2
LANCASHIRE

During the 18th century, Lancaster was England's chief trading port with the Americas. The town has many elegant Georgian houses; the Customs House is now a maritime museum. The castle has a medieval gatehouse, keep and tower, much altered in the 18th century. The nearby medieval priory church has lovely oak stalls. For a traditional dose of the English seaside head for Morecambe, with sand, family entertainment and illuminations.

LEEDS 171C2
WEST YORKSHIRE

The city center holds a flamboyant variety of Victorian architecture, in ornate shopping malls and proud public buildings such as the Corn Exchange and Town Hall. The City Art Gallery excels in its Victorian and 20th-century British art (notably sculpture by Henry Moore), while Armley Mills Museum and Thwaite Mills recall the city's industrial heritage.

★★ LIVERPOOL 170B1
MERSEYSIDE

Blighted by urban decay after decades of economic decline, Liverpool may not sound like an appealing place to visit, yet the resilient Liverpudlians (or "Scousers"), the twin modern cathedrals, the first-rate art galleries and score of museums, the musical and maritime heritage, make this one of England's most engrossing cities.

During the 19th century, Liverpool supplanted Bristol as the major west coast seaport, trading with the Americas and transporting millions of migrants. Take the ferry across the River Mersey to appreciate the trio of grand Edwardian buildings at Pier Head; on top of the clocktowers of the Royal Liver Building stand the city symbols, the "liver" birds. The brick warehouses of Albert Dock ★ ★ ★ have been overhauled into a smart shopping and museum complex. Here you'll find the Museum of Liverpool Life, covering everything from local riots to the city's football (soccer) teams (you can tour Anfield, the ground of Liverpool Football Club); the Merseyside Maritime Museum, with a fascinating display on emigration and slavery; the Beatles Story (see opposite); and the Tate Gallery Liverpool, sharing modern art with its parent gallery, the London Tate (see p.48).

For more fine art, seek out the Walker Art Gallery on William Brown Street. It is strong on early Italian and Flemish work, and represents pretty much the full gamut of British artists. Across the way stands St. George's Hall, one of the country's finest neoclassical buildings and tone-setter for the surrounding, undeniably impressive cityscape.

The neo-Gothic Anglican cathedral, the largest of its denomination in the world, and biggest church in England, is the masterpiece of Sir Giles Gilbert Scott. Begun in 1904, it was finished three-quarters of a century later. The Roman Catholic cathedral, more agressively modernist in style, is nicknamed "Paddy's Wigwam" because of its tent-like structure. Sir Edwin Lutyen's original design proved too costly, so only the crypt is his.

For a utopian vision of industrial Britain visit the model garden village of Port Sunlight on the Wirral peninsula. Built by the philanthropist William Hesketh Lever in 1887 to house his soap factory workers, the village takes its name from Sunlight Soap. A heritage center tells the story.

THE BEATLES

Liverpool's most famous sons are remembered in a sight-and-sound experience of the Swinging Sixties, in the Beatles Story at Albert Dock, complete with a psychedelic scene and a walk-through Yellow Submarine.

The "Fab Four" first appeared in the Cavern Club on Mathew Street in January, 1961. Gone now, its site is covered by the Cavern Walks Shopping Centre, where you can hunt down Beatles' souvenirs.

An evocative statue of Eleanor Rigby sits on a bench around the corner on Stanley Street. You can take a "Ticket to Ride" on the Beatles Magical Mystery Tour coach, which leaves from Albert Dock to take in Strawberry Fields and Penny Lane ■

DRIVE

A TOUR ROUND THE DALES

153 miles (allow 2 days)

The tour follows the edge of the Yorkshire Dales via market towns and ruined castles. It then ventures through the heart of the national park and visits Fountains Abbey and Ripon, with its cathedral and Hornblower or "Wakeman" who sounded a horn to let residents know that his night watch had begun.

FARNE ISLANDS

Lying just off the Northumbrian coast and reached April to October by cruises from Seahouses, these 28 tiny, rocky islands, owned by the National Trust, owe their fame to seabirds, a colony of gray seals, and a saint.

As many as 17 species of seabird such as puffins, kittiwakes and eider ducks nest here from May to July (the best time to visit).

Only two islands can be visited: Staple, and Inner Farne, where Saint Cuthbert died in 687, and in whose memory there is a chapel ■

Leave Ripon on the A6108 for 10 miles to Masham.

1 Masham, North Yorkshire

Once an important market town, as signified by its vast square, Masham (pronounced "Mass'm") is now known for its brewery (tours available) which produces the rich Old Peculier beer. Five miles further along the A6108, you can visit the beautifully tended riverside ruins of 12th-century Jervaulx Abbey.

Follow the A6108 for 8 miles to Middleham.

2 Middleham, North Yorkshire

In his childhood days, Richard III lived in Middleham's ruined but impressive castle (EH). The view from the keep is of the wild moorland around Wensleydale. The town is a racehorse breeding and training center.

Continue north on the A6108 for a further 2 miles to Leyburn.

3 Leyburn, North Yorkshire

This busy Wensleydale center has a strong working agricultural

flavor and is mainly Georgian in appearance. Above the market place there is a lovely view of the dale from The Shawl, a grassy terrace on a limestone scar.

Keep on the A6108 to Richmond.

4 Richmond, North Yorkshire

Lording it high above the River Swale at the eastern gateway to Swaledale, Richmond is one of the north's loveliest towns, dominated by a massive Norman castle (EH), with a splendid keep and curtain walls. On the grand cobbled marketplace stands the **Theatre Royal**, an outstandingly well-preserved example of Georgian architecture, as well as the Green Howard's Museum, a former church that serves as a repository of military memorabilia for a famous Yorkshire regiment. Nearby is a good collection of local bygones in the Richmondshire Museum. A mile-long riverside walk brings you to the remains of **Easby Abbey**.

Take the B6274 to the junction with the A66 and turn left to Greta Bridge. After crossing the River Greta turn right onto unclassified roads to Barnard Castle.

5 Barnard Castle, Durham

The highlight here is not in fact the ruined castle by the River Tees, from which the town has taken its name, but the **Bowes Museum**. This remarkable collection of paintings, porcelain, furniture, jewelry and glass put together by 19th-century coal magnate John Bowes and his wife, is housed in a surprising imitation French château.

The picturesque ruins of **Egglestone Abbey** stand on a bend of the River Tees 1 mile south off the B6277, and **Bowes,**

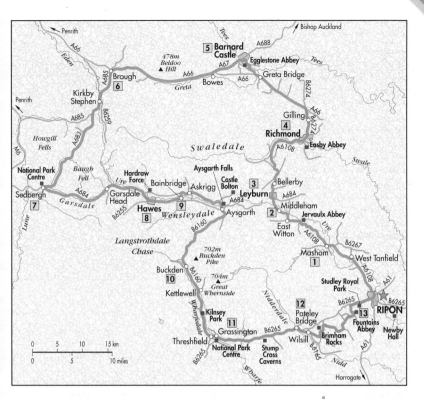

southwest along the A67, has another ruined castle set on Roman earthworks. Charles Dickens based Dotheboys Hall of *Nicholas Nickleby* fame on the village's boarding school.

> *Take the A67 to Bowes, then follow the A66 west along the line of an old Roman route to Brough.*

6 Brough, Cumbria

The striking remains of the castle at the lonely settlement of Brough also stand on a Roman site. The fortress was built by William II and restored in the 17th century by Lady Anne Clifford, who carried out repairs on several buildings in the dales area.

> *Take the A685 to Kirkby Stephen, then the A683 to Sedbergh.*

7 Sedbergh, Cumbria

Surrounded by lofty fells, this small market town makes a good center for some arduous fell walking. In 1525, long before it had become a prosperous knitting center, its well-known school, now a private boarding school, was established. The drive east along the A684 up narrow, green high-sided **Garsdale** passes through laconically-named The Street, the valley's only community.

> *Continue east along the A684 to Hawes.*

8 Hawes, North Yorkshire

At the sheep and cattle marketing center of **Hawes**, you can learn about the history behind the making of Wensleydale cheese at the local museum and purchase the soft and creamy product in a

CASTLE OF "THE BUTCHER"
Brough Castle was built in the 12th and 13th centuries to replace a stronghold destroyed by the Scots.

It was the home of the 13th Baron Clifford (1435-61) who was known as "The Butcher" due to his cruelty during the Wars of the Roses ■

L.S. LOWRY
(1887-1976)

Some critics regard Lowry's paintings of "matchstick" figures against a soulless landscape of smoking chimneys and factories more as interesting social comment than high art. Whatever the case, they memorably pit the inconsequential individual against the sheer force of industrialization.

The artist lived all his life in and around Manchester, painting in his free time while working as a rent collector until he retired in 1952.

His studio has been re-created at Manchester's City Art Gallery (also with a fabulous Pre-Raphaelite collection), and many of his works can be seen at the Salford Museum and Art Gallery in Salford ■

number of shops. With a 90-foot drop, nearby **Hardraw Force** is the highest waterfall in England.

Take the A684 for a further 4 miles to Bainbridge.

9 Bainbridge, North Yorkshire

The characterful, pretty village of **Bainbridge** is set round its green. **Askrigg**, a little downstream, rests at the heart of "Herriot country" where scenes from the English TV series *All Creatures Great and Small*, based on books by ex-veterinary surgeon James Herriot (a pseudonym), were filmed. Of the many waterfalls in the area, **Aysgarth Force**, where the River Ure tumbles over terraces for over a mile, is the best known. A couple of miles northeast, Mary, Queen of Scots was imprisoned at 14th-century **Castle Bolton** in the 1560s.

From Bainbridge, cross the River Ure and turn left, continuing on unclassified roads, then at Aysgarth take the B6160 to Buckden.

10 Buckden, North Yorkshire

Tiny villages scattered along Wharfedale, such as Buckden and **Kettlewell** make good starting points for walks. Downriver, **Kilnsey Crag's** radical overhang attracts rockclimbers, while **Kilnsey Park** is a visitor center with a fish theme.

Follow the B6160 south and turn left at Threshfield onto the B6265 into Grassington.

11 Grassington, North Yorkshire

The principal tourist center for Wharfedale is a pretty place of cobbled alleys and tea shops. East along the B6265 are

impressive underground caverns at **Stump Cross**.

Continue along the B6265 to Pateley Bridge.

12 Pateley Bridge, North Yorkshire

Nidderdale's lively market and tourist center has a fine local museum in an old Victorian workhouse, with replica stores and displays on life in the Dales. There is also a photogenic ruined church. East of town off the B6265 lies **Brimham Rocks**, an area of pillars and rocks which have been eroded into fantastic shapes by the elements.

Leave by the B6265 turning right after 1 mile onto the B6165. At Wilsill turn left and follow unclassified roads past Brimham Rocks to Fountains Abbey.

13 Fountains Abbey ★ ★ ★, North Yorkshire

Yorkshire's, and arguably England's, finest abbey ruins (NT) date from the 1130s, when Fountains became the Cistercian's richest monastery in the country, holding farm lands across much of the North of England. The scale of the extant buildings – such as the dormitory, refectory and infirmary – bear out its former importance.

Fountains Hall was built in the early 17th century with stone plundered from the abbey, and all around lies sumptuous **Studley Royal** estate, a park of artificial lakes and classical temples created by a former chancellor of the exchequer in the 18th century. Don't miss the mock-medieval St. Mary's Church, designed by the famous Victorian architect William Burges.

Return to the B6265 for the journey back to Ripon.

MACCLESFIELD 170C1
CHESHIRE

Macclesfield was the center of the English silk industry, employing 10,000 workers in 1820. The **Silk Museum and Heritage Centre** follows the history of the process, while at **Paradise Mill,** where the last handloom closed down in 1981, you can see old Jacquard looms.

★ MANCHESTER 170B1
GREATER MANCHESTER

Nicknamed "Cottonopolis" for its status in the textile industry during the Industrial Revolution, Manchester was a cramped, dirty city. There is now a sense of civic pride in the city's Metrolink tram system, its spruced-up Victorian buildings, such as the Free Trade Hall, the Town Hall and the Royal Exchange, and in its soccer teams "Man City" and "Man United." By the end of the 1980s the city had a new nickname, "Madchester," for being at the cutting edge of the youth scene, with its music, clubs and large student population.

In a revived area called Castlefield, a **Roman fort** has been partially reconstructed (the Roman name for Manchester was *Mancunium*, and the locals are known as Mancunians). The top attractions in Castlefield are the **Museum of Science and Industry,** with working machines and hands-on exhibits on air and space, electricity, textiles, printing and photography; and the **Granada Studios Tour.** Granada is a successful independent TV company; you can explore the set of the soap *Coronation Street*, the Baker Street movie set, and take a backstage tour.

Eleven miles south of Manchester's center at Styal, the Georgian cotton mill **Quarry Bank Mill** (NT) is water-powered and has been completely restored.

★ NEWCASTLE-UPON- 171C4
TYNE, TYNE AND WEAR

For a long time a great coal-producing center and worldleader in shipbuilding and engineering, Newcastle-upon-Tyne has suffered in the post-industrial age. First impressions are not promising, yet the city has a distinctive, austere beauty, while its heavily accented citizens, called "Geordies," seem to have a permanent twinkle in their eye.

Six great bridges span the River Tyne, the earliest a double-decker road and rail bridge constructed in the 1840s by Robert Stephenson; below, the **Quayside** has Bessie Surtees House (EH). The city took its name from the "new castle" built in 1080; a later **Norman keep** can still be seen. The Victorian city center is best seen on **Grey Street** and **Eldon Square. Laing Art Gallery** exhibits British artists from the 18th century, and the **Museum of Antiquities** is where you can gen up on Hadrian's Wall.

The Tyne Bridge seems remarkably high, but this is because it spans the river which was home to some of the finest shipbuilding yards in the country and trading ships needed to pass below to reach wharves beyond the bridge

THE NORTH OF ENGLAND

WALKS

NORTHUMBER-
LAND
NATIONAL
PARK

The northernmost section of the Pennine Way crosses this national park from Hadrian's Wall (see p.176) to the Scottish border.

The Cheviot Hills have the most challenging terrain (with few clear paths), around summits like Windy Gyle and The Cheviot.

For some gentler walking you should focus on Coquetdale and Breamish Valley ∎

TWEEDMOUTH

In July, the traditional Salmon Feast is held at Tweedmouth, and the Salmon Queen is crowned. The custom was revived in 1945 and includes a carnival ∎

THE NORTHUMBERLAND COAST   170C5

England's most northerly town, **Berwick-upon-Tweed**, has alternated between English and Scottish rule more than a dozen times. Within the impressive Elizabethan walls stand original barracks, now a regimental museum and art gallery, while three bridges straddle the salmon-rich River Tweed.

The famous Christian center of Holy Island ★★★, or Lindisfarne, can be reached at low tide by a causeway. Saint Aidan came from the Scottish island of Iona (see p.231) to establish a monastery here in 635; its fame spread both through the dazzlingly illustrated *Lindisfarne Gospels* (in the British Museum, see p.26) and Saint Cuthbert, who became bishop in 685. The present priory ruins (EH) are of a medieval Benedictine building. The 16th-century castle (NT) was converted into a private house by Sir Edwin Lutyens in 1903. You will see plenty of birdlife if you take a coastal walk round the island's flat sandy shore.

Bamburgh Castle is dramatic with its gray Norman keep standing on a crag above the sea. The interior, revamped by Lord Armstrong at the end of the last century, has fine armory and porcelain. A short walk along the coast from the kipper capital of Craster, **Dunstanburgh Castle** (EH) is the largest of the county's ruined strongholds. **Alnwick Castle** is a different proposition: its rooms are in Italian Renaissance style with old masters and a collection of Meissen china, while its grounds were landscaped by "Capability" Brown. Medieval **Warkworth Castle** (EH), in a winding loop of the River Coquet, was the setting for three scenes from Shakespeare's *Henry IV*.

★★ NORTHUMBERLAND NATIONAL PARK   170B4

Few visitors explore this lonely national park between the grassy Cheviot Hills on the Scottish border and Hadrian's Wall. With one main road running through it, this is the least populated national park; only 2,500 inhabitants in 400 square miles. Walking along the old sheep drovers' tracks in the rugged north is a major attraction, along with Hadrian's Wall (see p.176).

In the midst of **Border Forest Park** is **Kielder Water**, good for sailing, canoeing and fishing; a 12-mile forest drive starts at the northern end.

To the north, you can reach the moors along a dead-end road through **Coquetdale**. Near **Rothbury**, an attractive market town, stands **Cragside House** (NT), built by the Victorian industrialist Lord Armstrong. He converted 900 acres of rough moorland into a vast park, laying out 40 miles of paths. The house, the first to be lit by hydro-electricity, is an ostentatious monument to the Victorian age.

Continuing north, **Breamish Valley** is good for walking or picnicking. In the grounds of **Chillingham Castle** are wild white cattle, the nearest modern equivalent to prehistoric oxen. Between the park and Berwick lie two villages, both with craft workshops: the model estate village of **Ford**, and thatched **Etal**, with a ruined 14th-century castle.

★★★ NORTH YORK MOORS NATIONAL PARK   171D3
NORTH YORKSHIRE

The classic landscape of the North York Moors is a purple carpet of heather on open moorland, but other images include: green dales, villages of stone cottages, ruined abbeys, woods, and a spectacular coast.

The Western Fringes

Coxwold is a pretty village with golden stone cottages behind broad green verges. In Shandy Hall the 18th-century novelist Laurence Sterne wrote *The Life and Opinions of Tristram Shandy*. Close by, **Byland Abbey** (EH) once had the country's largest Cistercian priory church; its west front is a reminder of its former glory. The inland cliff of **Sutton Bank** has fine views. The market town of **Helmsley** has grand houses round its market square, the remains of a 12th-century castle (EH) and **Duncombe Park**, a Palladian mansion with landscaped gardens.

In a picturesque wooded stretch of Rye Dale, **Rievaulx Abbey** (pronounced "Reevo") (EH) ★★★ is a magnificent ruin. Founded in 1132, it was the first of the great Cistercian houses in Yorkshire, and has been decaying since 1538 when it was closed down.

The Heart of the Moors

Farndale has a marvelous display of wild daffodils in spring. **Rosedale**, once a thriving iron district, is just as pretty. At a crossroads on the moors stand **Young Ralph**, the park's symbol, and **Old Ralph**, two examples of medieval waymarkers. **Hutton-le-Hole** has a folk museum with a medieval longhouse and an Elizabethan manor. The busy town of **Pickering**, known as the "Gateway to the Moors," has a lot to offer: a good local museum, a ruined "motte and bailey" castle (EH), 15th-century wall paintings in its church, and the **North Yorkshire Moors Railway** ★★★ (see panel p.186). There are spectacular waterfalls near Goathland, such as Mallyan Spout. At **Wade's Causeway**, southwest of Goathland, you can walk along 1¼ miles of Roman road with flagstones and gutters still intact. **Esk Dale** has a string of unspoilt villages and is met by Westerdale and Great Fryup Dale.

The Eastern Moors

Extensive Forestry Commission plantations make this the least appealing part of the park. Yet there is a pleasant 9-mile drive through **Dalby Forest**, while **Bridestones Nature Reserve** has several strange weathered rock formations.

Above the abbey runs Rievaulx Terrace (NT), a beautiful landscaped garden with mock Greek temples

WALKS

THE NORTH YORK MOORS

A highlight of the park is the 93-mile Cleveland Way from Helmsley round the top of the moor, then down the beautiful coast to Scarborough.

The valleys of Rye Dale, Farndale and Rosedale are all rewarding to explore on foot, and the North Yorkshire Moors Railway will transport you into some of the park's best road-free scenery ■

The picturesque harbor at Whitby, with its fishing boats and pastel-colored houses backed by the abbey on the hill, was first captured on film by early photographer Frank Sutcliffe

THE NORTH YORKSHIRE MOORS RAILWAY

Moorsrail is the park's top attraction. It was one of the world's first railroads, built in 1835 when horses pulled the carriages. Now steam and diesel trains do the job for the 18-mile trip along Newton Dale from Pickering to Grosmont.

The stops at Levisham, Newton Dale Halt and Goathland offer majestic walks ■

★★★ NORTH YORKSHIRE COAST   *171D3*

Cottages pile on top of each other in a glorious jumble round the tiny harbor of **Staithes. Runswick Bay**, also a fishing village, is more orderly with red-roofed, white-washed, cliff-clinging cottages above a fine, sandy beach.

A Norwegian whalebone arch reminds you that **Whitby** was once an important whaling center; now interest lies in the old town on the east side of the River Esk, with antique stores, and jewelers selling the gemstone jet. On Grape Lane is the **Captain Cook Memorial Museum** in the house where he lived during his apprenticeship. A flight of 199 steps climbs to the remains of Whitby Abbey (EH), founded in AD 657; one of its monks, the herdsman Caedmon, composed the *Song of Creation*, the earliest known poem in English. The adjacent churchyard was the setting for the opening scene in Bram Stoker's *Dracula*.

In a precarious cliff-top site with steep flights of steps and narrow passages, **Robin Hood's Bay** is yet another lovely fishing village. Though associations with the famous outlaw are tenuous, smuggling stories are readily authenticated. Low tide reveals vast sands, rock-pools and fossils.

Scarborough has for hundreds of years been a port, a salubrious spa town and Yorkshire's top fun-loving seaside resort, with two big sandy beaches and presently a variety of amusement parks. On a headland between the beaches sits an impressive, brooding, 12th-century castle (EH).

★★★ PEAK DISTRICT   *170C1* NATIONAL PARK, DERBYSHIRE/ WEST YORKSHIRE

In 1932 a mass trespass on the Peak District's moors was the initial step to the foundation of the first of Britain's national parks (designated in 1951). Squashed in a triangle between Derby, Sheffield and Manchester, the park suffers from overcrowding perhaps more than any other: avoid it on summer weekends and public holidays. It really comprises two parks in one: White Peak and, in an upside down U around it, Dark Peak.

White Peak has a softer, more rounded landscape, with fields hemmed by stone walls and verdant dales. **Dark Peak**, formed out of sandstone rock known as millstone grit, is wild, largely uninhabited and treeless, with heather moorland on the slopes and a peat desert at its top – accessible only to well-prepared walkers and climbers.

White Peak

In the far south, beautiful Dovedale ★★★, the best known of the peak's valleys, can only be explored on foot. The Manifold Valley is only marginally less lovely and much less crowded; Ilam is its handsome estate village. Nearby Tissington has a Norman church, Jacobean manor and ducks on the pond. At Bakewell, the only town actually within the park, bakeries sell world-famous bakewell puddings (don't refer to them as tarts).

Don't miss either of the two superb stately homes on its doorstep. Haddon Hall, a medieval manor house with muralled chapel, galleried banqueting hall, great chamber and so forth, has been added to in every century from the 1100s to the 1600s.

Chatsworth House ★★★, home of the dukes of Devonshire, is without doubt one of England's grandest stately homes, with tapestries, Louis XIV furniture and fine art in baroque state rooms, and galleries devoted to sketches and sculpture. The stunning grounds, designed by Brown and Joseph Paxton, include a 260-foot fountain and a remarkable cascade.

Just south of Bakewell, Lathkill Dale offers a lovely wooded riverside walk, as does Monsal Dale from the famous Monsal Head viewpoint and viaduct near Little Longstone. The village of Eyam achieved a fame it would rather not have had. In 1665, the plague arrived from London in an infected box of clothes. Led by their rector, the villagers cut themselves off from the outside world to stop the disease from spreading: five out of six of all the inhabitants died.

The faded Regency spa town of Matlock Bath has an alpine feel, sitting in a deep gorge from which cable cars climb up to the Heights of Abraham above. The town has a good museum on local mining, and Temple Mine can be explored. The National Tramway Museum at Crich and the early industrial village of Cromford, where you can visit the first water-powered cotton-spinning mill by Richard Arkwright in 1771, are both interesting.

Buxton, just outside the park's western limits, is the region's largest and most gracious town. A spa since Roman times, at the end of the 18th century the 5th Duke of Devonshire tried to create a Bath (see p.55) of the north, commissioning the building of the Palladian-style Crescent, thermal baths, pump room, pavilion and opera house .

Castleton is the park's cave exploring center. Around the village, five limestone caverns are open to the public. Peak Cavern, at the base of the hill on top of which stands Peveril Castle (EH) commanding lovely views, has a vast entrance. Blue John Cavern specializes in the crystalline fluorspar called "Blue John." More Blue John can be seen in Treak Cliff Cavern, along with fine stalactites. In Speedwell Cavern an underground boat trip follows a tunnel which formed part of a lead mine, while a visit into Bagshawe Cavern is geared towards those with an even greater sense of adventure.

Dark Peak

You can get a feel for the bleakness of Dark Peak by whizzing through it on the A57 from Glossop to Sheffield. For deeper exploration, head from Edale gorges up onto the crags and uplands around the bogland of Kinder Scout, the highest point. The gritstone edges of Stanage and Curbar, east of Hathersage, and Eyam provide dramatic tops.

WALKS

THE PEAK DISTRICT

Dark Peak is primarily strenuous walking territory. The Pennine Way begins at Edale in a sharp ascent to the massive boglands of Kinder Scout.

Easier rambles can be found in the forest round Derwent Reservoirs and on the eastern and western ridges, for example along Stanage Edge and The Roaches.

In White Peak, walks hug the valley bottoms, sometimes following the route of disused railroad tracks such as the Monsal Trail.

Other extremely popular walking areas include Dovedale, the Manifold Valley and Lathkill Dale ■

ALTON TOWERS

Twelve miles east of Stoke-on-Trent lies Britain's most famous theme park.

Against the backdrop of the gaunt shell of the house of the 15th Earl of Shrewsbury, set in 500 acres of beautiful parkland, are over 125 rides, including rollercoasters such as the "Corkscrew," the "Dragon," the "Alton Beast," and the world's first vertical drop rollercoaster, "The Oblivion," which drops 60 meters and has a G-Force of 4.5 ■

WELL DRESSING

During the Middle Ages in Tissington, well dressing began as a way of saying thanks for pure water. The practice, virtually unique to the Peak District, can now be seen during the summer months in dozens of the area's villages. Natural elements like petals, stones and leaves inlaid into a clay frame make a large, colorful biblical scene over the well ■

SHEFFIELD *171C1*
SOUTH YORKSHIRE

Since the Middle Ages, Sheffield has been a producer of English cutlery, and by the 19th century it was the country's foremost steel town. This large, hectic conurbation has exceptional art galleries, the most enjoyable of which is the **Ruskin Gallery**, a collection put together by 19th-century art critic John Ruskin to educate the local working class. The best industrial sights are the **Sheffield Industrial Museum** at Kelham Island, where cutlery craftsmen and machinery can be seen, and the atmospheric 18th-century scythe factory of **Abbeydale Industrial Hamlet**.

★ STOKE-ON-TRENT *170C1*
(THE POTTERIES) STAFFORDSHIRE

If names like Wedgwood, Minton and Royal Doulton set your pulse racing, then you'll enjoy a trip to this sprawling industrial and residential conurbation made up of six individual towns. The museums and factories (called "potbanks") are scattered but well signposted; alternatively, take the "China Link" bus service from Stoke station. The tourist information center at Hanley (tel. 01782 284600) has good maps.

Gladstone Pottery Museum at Longton is a good starting point; craftspeople give demonstrations of traditional methods of pottery making at this preserved 19th-century potbank with distinctive bottle-shaped kilns. At the **City Museum and Art Gallery** in Hanley is an extensive collection of English pottery and porcelain.

As for the factories, visit **Wedgwood** at Barlaston, **Royal Doulton** at Burslem and **Spode** at Stoke: all have shops, museums and factory tours. In the **Chatterley Whitfield Mining**

Museum at Tunstall there are steam-driven machines on the surface, and guided tours take visitors below ground.

Nine miles north of Stoke in Cheshire visit the thickly patterned, timber-framed moated manor house of **Little Moreton Hall** (NT), built in the 15th century.

★★★ YORK *171D2*
NORTH YORKSHIRE

Until the Industrial Revolution, York was the north of England's most important city – as *Eboracum* in Roman times, as *Jorvik*, capital of a Viking kingdom in the 9th century (York is a corruption of *Jorvik),* as a Norman stronghold with two castles, and as an increasingly rich city from the fruits of the wool trade in the Middle Ages. Buildings and a cornucopia of museums bring to life every significant period of the city's history.

Consider taking a walking tour to explore the narrow old streets close to the minster, such as The Shambles, where butchers once plied their trade. Despite its history and popularity, street entertainers, bistros and a student population have ensured that York has not become just a stuffy showpiece.

Top Sights & Museums in York
★★★ Cathedral. This masterpiece of Gothic architecture is the largest medieval church in Britain, famed for its medieval stained glass – the west window containing the oldest display in the country, the giant east window holding the largest single expanse in the world. But don't overlook the magnificent choir screen, the Chapter House and the undercroft, where you can see giant concrete foundations inserted for support in the 1960s and the walls of a Roman headquarters.

Take a walk along the top of York's city walls for a superb view of York Minster

★★★ **The Walls**. You can walk along the top of the city's medieval walls for much of their 2¾-mile length. The most interesting stretch, with superb views of the minster, runs from Monk Bar to Bootham Bar (bar being the word used to describe a gateway).

★★★ **Castle Museum**, Eye of York. Victorian York is recaptured in a lifesize reconstructed cobbled street, with subsequent and preceding centuries re-created in rooms with a wonderful array of bygones. You can also visit the cell where highwayman Dick Turpin was held.

★★ **Jorvik Viking Centre**, Coppergate. York's top attraction involves traveling back in time through the history of York to a Viking age brought to life with the aid of sound effects and smells. There are also excavated objects to peruse.

★★ **National Railway Museum**, Leeman Road. Quite simply, here you'll find the finest collection of rolling stock in the country, including the world's fastest steam engine and royal carriages.

Other Sights and Museums in York

ARC, St. Saviourgate. The Archaeology Resource Centre allows you to play at being an archeologist.

★ **Clifford's Tower** (EH), Tower Street. There are panoramic city views from the top of this 13th-century tower.

Fairfax House, Castlegate. This lovely Georgian house has a fine collection of period furnishings and art bequeathed by local chocolate magnate Noel Terry.

★ **Merchant Adventurers' Hall**, Fossgate. This medieval timber-framed building was built by the city's wealthiest guild.

★ **Museum of Automata**, Tower Street. Everything from mechanical toys to robots, with plenty of hands on activity.

Treasurer's House (NT), Chapter House Street. Until the 1500s this was the home of the minster's treasurers.

★ **Yorkshire Museum**, Museum Gardens. The museum's archeological sections provide a good introduction to the city's complex history.

SETTLE-CARLISLE RAILWAY

The 71-mile railroad trip up and over the dales and through the Eden Valley stakes a fair claim to be the most scenic in England – particularly the stretch from Settle to Kirkby Stephen.

With a host of viaducts, bridges and deep tunnels, it also stands as a triumph of Victorian engineering ■

THE NORTH OF ENGLAND

WALKS

THE YORKSHIRE DALES

Five long-distance footpaths traverse the Yorkshire Dales National Park, including the best of the Pennine Way (from west of Skipton to Tan Hill Inn on the park's northern boundary) and the Dales Way (up Wharfedale and on to Sedbergh).

You could, of course, just tackle a portion of their lengths. Every dale has fine, easily manageable walks. The park's greatest walking challenge is the circuit round the Three Peaks.

The most popular walks are concentrated round Malham Cove, the spectacular gorge of Ingleton Glen with its many waterfalls, and round Hardraw Force and Aysgarth Falls ■

★★★ YORKSHIRE DALES NATIONAL PARK
170C3

NORTH YORKSHIRE/CUMBRIA

Covering some 700 square miles, the Yorkshire Dales National Park takes its name from the many river valleys (or dales) that cut through the bleak upland moors. Lonesome farms sit on the slopes and compact villages near gushing rivers and waterfalls. The scenery is best appreciated by walkers, but roads along the dales allow for excellent driving tours (see p.180).

Wharfedale. At the edge of the national park as the River Wharfe passes a beautifully sited ruined priory near **Bolton Abbey**, Wharfedale is pastoral. A little upstream the river charges through a narrow channel in **Strid Wood**. Beyond the pretty village of **Burnsall** the valley is lined with the white scars distinctive of limestone uplands.

Grassington is the major tourist center; smaller, hardier settlements like **Arncliffe**, **Kettlewell**, **Buckden** and **Hubberholme** (with a particularly lovely church) cater more for those who like to walk.

Airedale. In the uppermost reaches of the valley around **Malham ★★★** is the dales' most extraordinary scenery, a landscape of limestone cliffs, crags and scars. A 4-mile walking trail (details from the information center) takes you up **Malham Cove**, a 300-foot cliff with a cracked "pavement" on top. Beyond lies the moorland lake of **Malham Tarn**, and to the east the forbidding craggy gorge of **Gordale Scar**. The market town of **Skipton** is the southern gateway to the park, its impressive castle rebuilt after the Civil War.

Ribblesdale. The grand scenery of three famous peaks – Ingleborough, Whernside and Pen-y-ghent – dominates the

valley; the challenging Three Peaks trek leaves from **Horton in Ribblesdale**. Ingleborough Cave and **Gaping Gill** pothole are more easily reached from Clapham and **White Scar Cave**, where the guided tour follows an underground river, from Ingleton.

Dentdale, in Cumbria, though confusingly within the Yorkshire Dales National Park, has **Dent**, with whitewashed cottages on cobbled streets.

Nidderdale. That Nidderdale lies outside the national park is no reflection on its beauty. Beyond the town of **Pateley Bridge** (see p.182) the scenery is breathtaking; near the dale's top is **How Stean Gorge**, and a road with superb views continues the route from Lofthouse on to Masham.

Wensleydale. The gentlest and most pastoral of the dales, follows the River Ure from Hawes to Ripon, well outside the national park boundary.

Swaledale ★★★. The most northerly and least visited of Yorkshire's major dales is wooded in its lower stretch between Richmond (see p.180) and Reeth, while stone walls and barns, abandoned lead mines and black-faced Swaledale sheep inhabit the sinuous upper valley. Peaceful **Reeth** has a museum on the region's mining and sheep farming. Turn right at Reeth into the northernmost dale of **Arkengarthdale**, which passes through strange-sounding hamlets like Booze and Whaw on its course up to remote **Tan Hill Inn**, England's highest pub. The road continues back to Swaledale, a neat circular drive. Near Thwaite, a diversion south takes you to the **Buttertubs Pass**, named for a group of potholes near the top of the pass where villagers would hang their butter to keep it cool as they rested on the journey to market.

THE SCOTTISH LOWLANDS

All the characteristics of Scotland –
from the whisky to the Scottish
dialect, from bagpipe music to
tartans – are found northwards from
the Border. Yet the Lowlands have
their own heritage, quite distinct
from the Highlands

CALENDAR OF EVENTS

MARCH 1 – Whuppity Scoorie, Lanark, South Lanarkshire. A custom thought to help drive away winter, in which children charge around the church hitting each other with paper balls!

APRIL – Golf Week, St. Andrews, Fife. An organized week providing a golfing vacation with professional tuition and a chance to play on the historic course.

END MAY – Perth Arts Festival. Held over 12 days, this is one of the best and liveliest of its kind in Scotland. Centers around classical music, drama and the visual arts.

JUNE – Beltane Festival, Peebles, Borders. This is one of the area's common-riding celebrations. During the ceremony the Beltane Queen is crowned ■

THE SCOTTISH LOWLANDS

The Lowlands is an inappropriate name. Much of the area is far from low. To the east, the A1 follows the coast to avoid the hill mass of the Lammermuirs. The A697 meets the frontier at the River Tweed, crossing it by the handsome bridge at Coldstream. The M6 from the south becomes the A74 and, beyond Gretna Green, climbs to its highest point

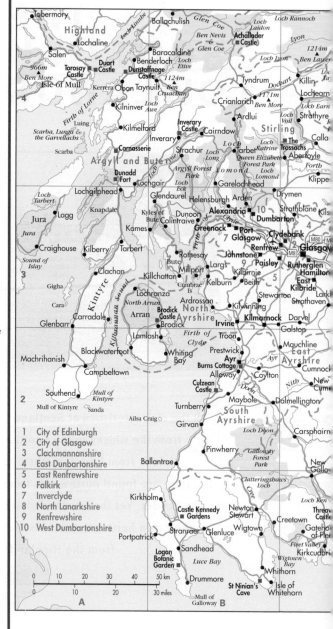

1 City of Edinburgh
2 City of Glasgow
3 Clackmannanshire
4 East Dunbartonshire
5 East Renfrewshire
6 Falkirk
7 Inverclyde
8 North Lanarkshire
9 Renfrewshire
10 West Dumbartonshire

by Beattock amid the windswept, humped hills from which springs the River Clyde.

Beyond Carter Bar on the A68 the traveler is challenged by the rolling uplands, the essential **Border country**: waves of blue hills which so often witnessed the pennants and pikes of raiding armies. These were disputed lands in the long and drawn out medieval brawl between Scotland and England. The Border towns are sturdy places, their abbeys

CALENDAR OF EVENTS

AUGUST –
Marymass Festival, Irvine, North Ayrshire. Held since the beautiful Mary, Queen of Scots visited the town in 1563 due to the lasting impression she made. It includes the crowning of the Marymass Queen and horse races.
Edinburgh Festival. Edinburgh is packed out for three weeks at this, the most important and successful event of its kind. Innovative performances in comedy and the arts take place all over the city.

OCTOBER – Border
Festival, The Borders. Aims to increase awareness of the area's heritage in towns and villages throughout the region.

NEW YEAR'S
EVE – Hogmanay, George Square, Glasgow. Revelers come to see the old year out and the new year in with joined hands and the singing of *Auld Lang Syne* ■

THE BIG HILLS OF THE LOWLANDS

Checking out where the highest hills are is a good way of finding scenic areas in the Lowlands.

You will find the highest "Lowland" hill, The Merrick (2,766 feet) near beautiful Glen Trool in the Galloway Forest Park in the southwest.

The next highest, Broad Law (2,754 feet), lies between Moffat and Peebles in the Borders – in a wild stretch of hill country which also has the Grey Mare's Tail Waterfall, off the A708 going north from Moffat, as well as White Coomb (2,696 feet), another strenuous walk.

Certainly, for typical Scottish hill scenery, you do not have to go to the Highlands ■

still ruined reminders of English raiders in the mid-16th century. Towns like Jedburgh, Kelso or Melrose have a strong sense of community and are fiercely proud of their heritage.

Yet many tourists pass them by, racing on to the cities of the Central belt. The same happens to Galloway, an attractive area to the west of the main A74. From the south-facing coastline of the Solway Firth, mixed woodlands and farms run up to big, dark hills. Pastel-painted houses in little towns overlook wide main streets – lots of space for the old weekly produce markets.

Traverse Galloway's forested slopes by the river valleys to reach Ayrshire. Here is the country of Robert Burns, wall-to-wall golf courses in old-established coastal resorts which had their heyday when the Scottish city folk came for their summer beach vacations.

Edinburgh and Glasgow are at least 2 hours' drive from the Border. Scotland's two largest cities offer contrasting experiences. Edinburgh is all about grand skylines and sweeping theatrical backdrops – after all, nowhere else in Scotland has a grand castle and mini-mountain (Arthur's Seat) looming only minutes from the main shopping streets. Edinburgh people are reserved – some would say almost smug. They think they live in the finest city in the world.

Glasgow is warmer, in the sense of making the visitor feel at home. The locals are more "upfront" and friendlier. The city equals Edinburgh in terms of its visitor attractions and culture, while outstripping it in shopping choice and probably in nightlife as well. As an old mercantile and commercial center, Glasgow has some of the finest Victorian architecture in Britain.

Both these cities lie in the Central belt, the narrow waist or corridor of Scotland. From both cities you can see the Highlands. From Edinburgh you can also see the patterned fields of Fife, across the Firth of Forth. Visit northeast Fife – truly Lowland – for the finest golf courses in the world and plenty of pastel-painted fishing villages with character.

On the whole, Lowland Scotland offers plenty of interest without having to resort to tartan!

The ancient seat of the Scottish kings, Edinburgh Castle perches protectively high above the city, with almost sheer cliffs below on three sides

WALK

OLD EDINBURGH

For a different angle on the Old Town, start from the Castle Esplanade, then walk downhill to the traffic circle at the Lawnmarket.

Look for a short, narrow street going off to the right. This is Upper Bow. Incredibly, it was the main route to the castle. Go down the steps at the far end to Victoria Street which becomes West Bow at the lower end, opening on to the Grassmarket. Cross over. About halfway along, on the south side, look for a set of steps, The Vennel. Go up as far as a stretch of 17th-century town defences, Telfer's Wall, and look back for a fine profile of the castle ■

★★★ EDINBURGH   *193D3*

The capital of Scotland grew from the huddle of houses that once stood high on a steep-sided rocky hill in the shadow of a castle. Now right in today's city center, the Castle Rock is at the head of a long ramp sloping away eastwards. The Royal Mile was built along it, leading down like a backbone from the castle to the Palace of Holyroodhouse at its lower end. The Royal Mile is the axis around which the Old Town of Edinburgh still revolves.

By the 18th century, the tall tenements and narrow streets had become overcrowded and dirty. The city authorities then planned and built a New Town to the north with wide streets, grand neoclassical, columned facades and warm, gold sandstone. Today the Old and the New towns give Edinburgh its unique appearance.

Edinburgh is a hopelessly romantic place. Stand on **Princes Street** and look east to a grand gesture on the skyline – the handsome columns of the National Monument. They are like a chunk of a Greek temple on Calton Hill. Turn southeast to view the cliff line of Salisbury Crags and Arthur's Seat. Turn again and the rock walls and sturdy ramparts of the Castle fill the view southwards. Then observe the street scene at the Gothic sky-rocket of the Scott Monument, the flying spire of the High Kirk of St. Giles, the honey stonework of the classically inspired National Gallery, the fairy-tale towers of Ramsay Gardens next to the castle – and it is self-evident that Edinburgh is a city with a style all its own.

First-time visitors usually start with **Edinburgh Castle**, which welcomes around one million people every year. There is plenty to see, though with the military still present on the Rock, not every building is open to inspection. After enjoying rampart views, take in the oldest building in Edinburgh, 11th-century **St. Margaret's Chapel**, high on the ramparts. Then visit the atmospheric vaults, in one of

WILLIAM PLAYFAIR and EDINBURGH

William Playfair was responsible for some of Edinburgh's finest architecture: the classical design of the National Gallery, completed in 1857, is acknowledged as among the best in Edinburgh.

He is less happily associated with the National Monument – the columnated facade on Calton Hill. It was started in 1822 as a copy of the Parthenon and a tribute to the dead of the Napoleonic Wars, but money ran out in 1829 and it was never finished.

It is known as "Scotland's Disgrace," but it does have a certain appeal in its present state ■

which is the famous 15th-century cannon, **Mons Meg**. Also visit the Scottish United Services Museum and the Scottish National War Memorial (a very emotional place) beside the Palace and Great Hall. The biggest highlight is probably the Honours of Scotland Exhibition, where you can see the surprisingly battered Scottish crown, the oldest in Europe.

Beyond the Castle there is a wide choice of things to do on the **Royal Mile**. These range from serious museums, for example, the Writers' Museum in Lady Stairs House, to the Museum of Childhood. There are historic buildings like Gladstone's Land, a unique 16th-century survivor, and novelties which include the **Scotch Whisky Heritage Centre**, with its hi-tech, slow motion ride in cut-away mock whiskey barrels through the story of Scotland's national tipple.

Eventually, after many digressions down closes (alleyways) running off the main street, as well as an excursion along Victoria Street and into the Grassmarket for shopping, you should arrive at the gates of the **Palace of Holyroodhouse**. This is still the official residence of the royal family when they visit Scotland (though they seem to prefer Balmoral Castle – see p.225). It closes when a member of the royal family comes to stay. The palace started life as a guest house of the adjacent and now ruined abbey. Today, after a history which includes fire, murder, renewal, decay and final restoration, it houses portraits, tapestries and fine furniture from the royal collections.

Other major attractions within easy reach of the Royal Mile include the **Royal Museum of Scotland** in Chambers Street, traditional in the breadth of its

collections housed in spacious, soaring Victorian columned halls (with a grand new extension under construction). The **National Gallery of Scotland**, in the Mound, houses some of the best old masters to be found outside London, plus a good selection of impressionists and, naturally, some fine Scottish paintings. North of Princes Street, the **Scottish National Portrait Gallery**, adjacent to the Museum of Antiquities, has a large collection of paintings, drawings, prints and sculpture.

The essence of the **New Town** can be seen in the north facade of **Charlotte Square**, a chunk of neoclassicism said to be Europe's finest piece of civic architecture. At No. 7, you can visit **The Georgian House** (NTS), furnished in the period of the end of the 18th century when it was the height of fashion to move to the grand and spacious new houses springing up during Edinburgh's "Golden Age."

The city also has a number of places of interest a little further afield. The **Royal Botanic Garden** is well worth viewing and with extensive exhibits under glass makes a good all-weather excursion. (You could walk from Princes Street.) Or climb **Arthur's Seat** for an overview, take a trip to Craigmillar Castle or Lauriston Castle on the outskirts (the latter has the ritzier location). A little further out are the houses and parks of Dalmeny and 17th- to 18th-century Hopetoun, where you can see the treasures of some of Scotland's old families.

Cross the Forth Bridge for **Deep Sea World** at North Queensferry. This spectacular marine show includes a 120-yard perspex tunnel allowing close-ups of spectacular fish. Or visit **Rosslyn Chapel** by Roslin in Midlothian. Here you can enjoy fine 15th-century stone carving, including the wonderfully ornate **Prentice Pillar;** there are also fine woodland walks and views to the Pentland Hills. If you have transport, you could combine this with a trip up the chairlift at the **Hillend Ski Centre**, which takes you high up the Pentlands for outstanding city views.

As for the timing of your Edinburgh visit, be warned: the **Edinburgh International Festival**, which brings other festivals, plus the Fringe and the Military Tattoo in its wake, means the city is packed with visitors. If you avoid this annual cultural overkill in late August to early September, there will be a greater choice of accommodations and less crowding in restaurants and bars, on the streets and at the sights.

Edinburgh is a vibrant and entertaining city, offering a unique dimension on the Scottish experience. The views from the city of the East Lothian countryside from the top of Calton Hill, the patterned fields of Fife glimpsed from the windy corners of George Street in New Town, or even the hint of the Highlands from the castle ramparts, will remind you there is plenty more to Scotland.

★★★ GLASGOW   *192C3*

In terms of its interest and relevance to visitors to Scotland, Glasgow has well and truly arrived. Not so long ago it stood in the shadow of Edinburgh, its sophisticated neighbor in the east. Now, the native Glaswegian friendliness and pride in the city has been allied with a bold series of initiatives to create a post-industrial city which boasts outstanding Victorian architecture ("Britain's finest Victorian city" is an often quoted description), unrivaled cultural and artistic

displays in museums and galleries, the best shopping in Scotland and an overall air of confidence and excitement that many prefer to Edinburgh. Make no mistake Glasgow has spent time, effort and money capturing the attention of visitors, by building on the successes of its Garden Festival, the accolade of European City of Culture in 1990, and more recently the City of Architecture award.

Glasgow started out as a religious center – it still boasts Scotland's finest medieval cathedral – but soon developed into a mercantile and trading port. Eventually it made fortunes trading with the Americas (hence Virginia and Jamaica Street in downtown Glasgow today). American Independence severely damaged this trade, and the city turned to local reserves of coal and ironstone to create a new industrial base. It became the second city of the British Empire, the "Workshop of the Western World" during the 19th century.

Glasgow's demise mirrored the nation's decline as a manufacturing power. However, Glasgow has been reborn, and tourism now plays a very important role.

The city certainly isn't perfect and, like Edinburgh, still has problem areas in the outer suburbs, and downtown, where plans for new buildings have not yet come to fruition. But if you like the sheer bustle of city life and the entertainment, culture, shopping, and eating and drinking choices which it offers, then put Glasgow on your itinerary. After all, transportation links are so good you can always make a day trip to Edinburgh – just an hour away.

Finding your way in Glasgow's city center is very straightforward, thanks to a basic grid pattern of streets. **George**

ROBERT BURNS

Robert Burns (1759–96) should have lived and died anonymously as just another Ayrshire farmer. Instead, he is Scotland's best-known poet, celebrated by Scots at home and abroad on January 25, his birthday.

Though he was lionized as the "plowman poet," he was well educated, and from 1787 he contributed to Johnson's Scots Musical Museum, researching, improving, polishing and indeed creating many of the songs still widely sung in Scotland today.

His poems, first published in the 1786 Poems, Chiefly in the Scottish Dialect, brought him fame, but little fortune. Worn out by poor health, he died in Dumfries ∎

Square, minutes from Queen Street (train) Station is a good starting point. The Square is bounded on its east side by the City Chambers, Victorian design at its most exuberant, with ornate marbled interiors.

To the southeast lies the Merchant City, so called because many of the buildings date from the great days of trade. Some have connections in particular with the Tobacco Lords, a coterie of powerful merchants who made fortunes through the Americas trade. Today the Merchant City is an area of small and exclusive stores – look for the Italian Centre, for example, with its designer labels seen nowhere else in Britain outside London.

West and south of George Square are the main shopping streets, notably along Buchanan Street and Argyle Street. Princes Square is a covered mall off Buchanan Street with a sophisticated and exciting modern design. St. Enoch Centre, likewise covered, is off Argyle Street – the stores here are bigger, but less exclusive.

Away from the stores, historical Glasgow centers around the area near the Cathedral and the old High Street – the original settlement before commercial developments pulled the city westwards. Beside the Cathedral is the newish St. Mungo's Museum, a curious, eclectic collection of the emblems of rites of passage across the world which takes the broadest interpretation of religion. Dali's painting of Christ of St. John of the Cross hangs close to, for example, Shiva as Nataraja, the Lord of the Dance, while · upstairs are found Australian aboriginal paintings.

Opposite the museum is the oldest building in Glasgow. Provand's Lordship dates from

1471 and contains period rooms with appropriately creaky furniture and a friendly ghost, according to one attendant.

In the opposite direction, west of the city center, there is another cluster of cultural attractions, starting with the Art Gallery and Museum at Kelvingrove. Its setting is high Victorian in a warm, red stone, its echoing halls containing one of the finest civic art collections in Britain, as well as a broad range of exhibits in silver, glass and porcelain. There is also a wide selection of archeological and ethnographic material displayed.

After this major museum, cross the street for the Glasgow Museum of Transport, with its historic steam locomotives, cars and ship models, as well as a re-created Glasgow street of the 1930s. Alternatively, walk north through leafy Kelvingrove Park for a few minutes to the Hunterian Museum and Art Gallery – more historic material in the museum section (opened in 1807, it is Scotland's oldest) with, in a separate building, another major art collection. The last is very strong on the impressionists and has several Scottish works, including some by the architect Charles Rennie Mackintosh, featuring paintings, plans and a reconstructed house interior.

The Burrell Collection is another of Glasgow's highlights. Amassed by the millionaire shipping magnate Sir William Burrell, a collector with eclectic tastes, his wide-ranging horde of objets d'art (about 8,000 separate items) was donated to the city. You will find everything from Roman glassware to French impressionism here in a custom-built airy setting in Pollok Park.

Although it presents a vivid contrast to the high art of the other museums, the People's

Palace is also very worthwhile. This handsome Victorian building in Glasgow Green, east of the High Street, tells the story of the ordinary folk of Glasgow. It touches on politics by way of radical weavers, votes for women and "Red Clydeside." All in all, it is a fascinating portrait of city folk in the recent past. At the back are the Winter Gardens, where you can have a refreshing cup of tea amid the waving palm fronds of this all-weather glasshouse.

Yet another glimpse of Glasgow in the recent past can be found at the Tenement House (NTS), where a Glasgow tenement has been preserved intact as a slice of everyday life. A relative of the tenement's owner (who lived there all her life) inherited the property and realized that she had acquired a time capsule, as the owner had never once "modernized" her home or its contents.

Just as the People's Palace and the Tenement House are antidotes to high art and grand collections, so the Barras, Glasgow's fleamarket (open at weekends) is a down-to-earth contrast to high-fashion designer stores. It is great fun to stroll through, with always the possibility of a bargain or a genuine antique turning up. It is exciting, fascinating, and as full of the unexpected as Glasgow itself.

Glasgow also offers great nightlife – just ask your hotel receptionist or behind the bar. They are sure to be Glaswegians and enthusiastic about their revitalized city.

★ AYR 192B2

This is a major center and resort town on the Clyde coast. Close to the birthplace of Scotland's most famous poet, Robert Burns, it is also a center of the Burns Trail and Burns industry.

The town center, in and around the High Street, offers quite a good choice of stores, with many of the main streets traffic-free. The Kyle Centre is the largest covered shopping mall. Note that parking near the center involves buying a ticket from a nearby store, which should be displayed on your windshield.

George Square is the heart of Glasgow, and the starting point for any walking tour of the city center

SCOTLAND'S OTHER FAMOUS POET

William McGonagall, the Scottish doggerel poet (1825–1902), always said he was commanded by an inner voice and was immune to criticism. His verse soon met with acclaim. His eulogy to the Tay Bridge was one occasion when his talents were brought to bear:

Beautiful
Railway bridge
of the Silvery
Tay!
I hope that God
will protect all
passengers
By night and
day,
And that no
accident will
befall them
while crossing
The Bridge of
the Silvery Tay
For that would
be most awful
to be seen
Near by Dundee
and the
Magdalen
Green ∎

Everyone who comes to Ayr inevitably follows the signs for **Burns Cottage and Museum**, the birthplace of Scotland's national bard (see p.198), at nearby Alloway. The presentation is of very high quality, with headphones giving individual commentary within the dark little cottage, authentically restored, while the adjacent museum, with its unique artifacts and papers, gives an insight into the hardships of Burns' early farming career.

Altogether, this makes a good introduction to other places associated with Burns. These include, the **Tam o' Shanter Experience** (a multi-media presentation) to the south and the adjacent Brig o' Doon which, along with the Auld Kirk of Alloway, feature in Burns' poem *Tam o' Shanter*. These are overlooked by the **Burns Monument and Gardens**.

Formerly an important resort town for traditional beach vacations, Ayr has plenty of pubs and restaurants as well as evening entertainments, including the town's own theater company, Borderline, and the Gaiety and the Civic theaters. Families are also well catered for with such nearby attractions as **Wonderwest World** to the south of the town, which is Scotland's largest theme park. **Ayr Farm Park** is also of interest to young children, as is **Belleisle Park** within the town. Both have plenty of livestock. The wooded grounds of **Rozelle Park** conceal the Maclaurin Art Gallery with changing exhibitions of contemporary art, and a pleasant tearoom.

★ BIGGAR 193D3

This market town is equidistant from both Edinburgh and Glasgow and has retained a vigorous personality. It has an interesting church, a puppet theater and also offers worthwhile window-shopping along its wide, main street.

However, it is chiefly noted for its museums. These include the **Gladstone Court Museum**, assembled by the active locals and featuring street scenes and plenty of nostalgic artifacts. There is also the **Greenhill Covenanters House**, where you can find out more about the Covenanters who took part in the complex and bloody religious wars which racked 17th-century Scotland.

On a lighter note, Biggar is also home to the unique **Biggar Gasworks Museum** (HS), a preserved town gasworks, where you can revel in gassy odors.

CLYDE COAST 192B2-B3

If golf is your game, then the Clyde Coast offers plenty of choice, particularly on either side of Ayr, where Troon to the north and Turnberry to the south are towns associated with the British Open. Away from these coastal links, the landscapes are bright green with permanent pasture (Ayrshire is famous for its dairy cattle) giving way to hill country in places scarred by now defunct industries such as coal mining and steelworks.

Largs to the north offers a Viking experience in its new **Vikingar**, the Viking Heritage Centre. (The Norsemen's power and influence on the western seaboard was severely dented in 1263 when they lost the Battle of Largs here.)

Down the road is **Kelburn Country Centre**, which gives an insight into life on a grand Scottish estate. **Kelburn Castle** is the centuries-old home of the earls of Glasgow, who, if the displays in the visitor center can be believed, seem to have been singularly unsuccessful in retaining their store of wealth over the years. You can also enjoy gardens, country walks, period displays, a museum, plus "The Secret Forest," a slightly scary adventure walkway cut into the deep woods.

Another highlight on the coast is **Culzean Castle** (NTS). Built on a site associated with the Kennedys from the 14th century, Culzean Castle was the creation of the Scottish architect, Robert Adam, and completed in 1792. Today, the elegant castle and 560 acres of grounds are part of a country park in the hands of the conservation body, the National Trust for Scotland. Among Culzean's many features is the apartment in the castle given by the Scottish people in grateful thanks to General Dwight D. Eisenhower in 1946.

Further south along an increasingly wild coastline is the resort and fishing port of Girvan. In the interior between Girvan and Ballantrae is a network of off-the-beaten-track roads well worth exploring, especially along the valley of the River Stinchar (pronounced "*stin-shar*"), where the scenery of woodland, farm, moor and ruined castle is reminiscent of a romantic Victorian oil painting of mainland Scotland.

CLYDE ISLANDS   192B3

The islands in the Firth of Clyde include, in order of size, Ailsa Craig, the Cumbraes, Bute and Arran. Of these, **Ailsa Craig** is a granite lump in the Outer Firth, which is home to thousands of breeding gannets. It also rejoices in the name of "Paddy's Milestone," from its conspicuous position on the old sea route from Glasgow to Ireland.

The **Cumbraes** are two little islands reached from Largs. Millport, the main town, is a traditional resort. The island of **Bute ★** is a bit larger, still with the air of a traditional seaside

vacation about it, almost pleasantly time warped – though the local tourist authorities have tried to change that. It offers a fascinating castle in the main town of **Rothesay**, as well as fine walking in pleasantly rural surroundings, with views of the sea and a horizon filled with hills. You could take in Bute on a tour from Glasgow, crossing the Firth of Clyde at Wemyss Bay, then leaving the island again at Colintraive, a 5-minute trip, to reach more attractive scenery in Cowal.

The largest Clyde island is **Arran ★★**. It has for long been a part of the tourist scene and is still a focus for Glaswegians escaping the city. The impressive skyline with the granite ridge of **Goat Fell** and its companion hills have attracted generations of geologists, walkers and climbers. At lower levels, **Brodick Castle and Country Park** (NTS) is another big attraction. The castle is the former seat of the dukes of Hamilton and is filled with fine furniture, paintings, silver and sport trophies. The gardens and parkland are famed for their rhododendrons, in bloom from spring until well into the summer.

There is a road right around the coast that is well worth following to discover out-of-the-way spots such as the ancient standing stones on **Machrie Moor**, and the tiny coastal settlements with their crafts and other local businesses. Arran is sometimes described as "Scotland in miniature" because of its attractive scenery. It could also be included in any western seaboard tour by hopping across on the ferry from Ardrossan on the Ayrshire coast to Brodick and then, continuing west, taking the summer-only ferry from Lochranza in the north of the island to Claonaig to rejoin the mainland on the Mull of Kintyre.

WALK

ST. NINIAN'S CAVE

This is a beach walk to an early Christian site associated with Saint Ninian.

To reach the start, go due south from Whithorn. Off the A747, take a minor road, signed Physgill. Walk a short way down a country lane until a signed path goes right into a shallow wooded valley. The valley deepens as it nears the coast, and the path ends on a pebbly beach. Go right again and follow the beach until St. Ninian's Cave comes into view, cut into the coastal cliff.

Note the religious symbols cut into the walls and surrounding rocks by generations of pilgrims.

Return by the outward route ∎

AROUND DUMFRIES

Approaching Dumfries from the east, take the coastal B725 road. You will pass the Brow Well. This odd little rock-cut pool was visited by Robert Burns because it was famous for its mineral properties. The poet was unwell with rheumatic fever and probably bacterial endocarditis, and he had been advised to try swimming in the sea. He died back home in Dumfries within three days of his visit to Brow.

Closer to Dumfries along the B725 lie the ruins of moated Caerlaverock Castle, a unique triangular design created by an unknown builder during the late 13th century ■

★ COLDSTREAM   *193E3*

Travel north on the A697 and Coldstream is the first place you come to in Scotland. It is associated with the army regiment the **Coldstream Guards**, as the local museum will inform you. As well as being a handsome little place, busy going about its own rural business, Coldstream offers an insight into country life at **The Hirsel**, just to the north of town. This is the estate of Lord Home of the Hirsel, the title currently held by the son of the late Sir Alec Douglas Home, a former British prime minister. As well as country walks (popular with birdwatchers) by loch, woods and fields, there is a visitor center and craft complex in a converted farm building.

★ DUMFRIES   *193C1*

Gateway to and largest town in Galloway, Dumfries is known as "the Queen of the South" (a relative term, north of the border). Built in attractive, red sandstone, quarried locally, Dumfries has a good shopping center and also makes the most of its Robert Burns connections.

These include Burns' local pub, the **Globe Inn**, which still survives; **Burns' House Museum**, where he spent the last three years of his short life, now containing many letters, papers and other artifacts associated with the poet; the **Burns Mausoleum**, where the poet is buried; and the **Robert Burns Centre** by the banks of the River Nith. This explores the Dumfries connection in detail, as he was an exciseman (collector of excise taxes) here after the failure of his farming efforts.

★★ DUNBAR   *193E3*

The little east-coast town of Dunbar boasts Scotland's best sunshine records – as long as the *haar* (sea mist) stays offshore.

A small resort that grew from a port, evidence of its early prosperity can be seen in elegant, handsome Georgian town houses. Dunbar was also a strategic place of defense, overlooking the main coastal route to Edinburgh. (The Scots' armies were defeated here more than once.) The shattered fragments of the town's castle,

Most people come to Dumfries for its connections with Robert Burns, but the town itself is attractive, with the elegant 15th-century Old Bridge crossing the River Nith

now home to nesting kittiwakes, still perch above the harbor.

With plenty of atmosphere and historic places of interest, Dunbar also makes a good excursion from Edinburgh, taking in North Berwick, another attractive little coastal resort, along the way.

DUNDEE 192D4

Dundee has an industrial background in textile processing (mostly jute), and is also associated with making jam and, formerly, whaling. It has made the leap to "post-industrial city" much less convincingly than Glasgow, but it proudly bills itself as "City of Discovery," a reference to the RRS (Royal Research Ship) *Discovery*, berthed here as a floating visitor attraction. Built using the local experience of constructing rugged whaling vessels, this was the ship used by Captain Scott, who perished on his way back from the South Pole. Nearby is the 1824 frigate *Unicorn*, the oldest British Navy ship afloat.

Within the city are the McManus Galleries, the main museum and civic art collection,

and the Barrack Street Museum. Its most famous exhibit was eulogized as *The Great Tay Whale* by the doggerel poet William McGonagall (see p.200). The Glens of Angus are within easy reach.

★ DUNFERMLINE 193D3

Find time for this workaday town within minutes of the highway and the Forth Bridge. Beneath its business-like exterior are some interesting aspects. This was the old capital of Scotland during the time of King Malcolm Canmore in the 11th century. Then, under the influence of King Malcolm's saintly wife Margaret, Dunfermline became a religious center. Some of the finest Scoto-Norman architecture throughout Scotland can be seen in the Dunfermline Abbey complex.

Later, Dunfermline's fortunes were bound up with the production of damask linen – a tale told in the local museum. Then in 1835, the wife of a poor weaver in the town gave birth to a boy, Andrew Carnegie. The family emigrated to the United States when Andrew was 12 years old. Carnegie's industrial career later made him the embodiment of both great wealth and philanthropy. A fascinating museum is found at the back of the cottage where he was born. Elsewhere in the town is a Carnegie Hall, Carnegie Library, Carnegie Centre (with wonderfully ornate Turkish baths!) and also the Pittencrieff Park. As a boy, Carnegie was forbidden to enter these formerly private grounds. Perhaps in revenge, once he became a millionaire, he bought the estate and presented it to the town to be enjoyed by all. It is well worth strolling around Dunfermline – a typical Scottish Lowland town without pretensions.

DAMASK AT DUNFERMLINE
Dunfermline is particularly associated with the production of damask linen.

This technique was brought to Edinburgh originally by Huguenot master weavers, who set up business there before the end of the 18th century. They used a secret process which made attractive patterns on plain linen cloth.

Dunfermline weaver James Blake masqueraded as a witless laborer, got himself a job cleaning the Huguenot looms and memorized the process. The industrial spy then built his own loom in Dunfermline, laying the foundation for the damask linen industry there ■

The attractive, old harborside houses of Pittenweem in Fife welcome home the fishermen who still brave the worst weather the North Sea can throw at them

A RIDE TO HERMITAGE

The approach to Hawick from the south on the A7 is picturesque, but an alternative is to take the B6399 via Newcastleton and visit Hermitage Castle. It is a grim ruin in the looming Border hills with interesting historical associations.

The castle is linked with Mary, Queen of Scots, who rode 50 miles there and back in a day from Jedburgh to visit the wounded Earl of Bothwell.

Another tale of this 14th-century fortress is of the wicked Lord Soulis. He was such a cruel despot that the locals eventually revolted, wrapped him in lead and boiled him to death in a cauldron. Enjoy your visit! ∎

★★★ EAST NEUK OF FIFE   *193D4*

The East Neuk (pronounced "nyook") does not appear on maps. It means the east corner of Fife and is characterized by an air of neatness and order in the fields and farms, and a well-scrubbed sparkle to the coastal villages. It seems both a million miles from any contact with the old industrial Scotland and also from the tartan of the Highlands.

Its main attractions mostly lie by the coast, especially in the salty ambiance of places like St. Monans and Pittenweem, still actively pursuing fishing, as well as Anstruther. This attractive coastal community is the setting for the Scottish Fisheries Museum which explores the long struggle of the eastern seaboard communities to earn a living from the sea.

Crail, furthest east, is very attractive. It has what must be the most often photographed harbor in Scotland. The village's handsome town house, with its bell cast in 1520 and inscribed in

Dutch, is a reminder of east coast Scotland's old trading links with the Low Countries across the North Sea. The architecture, with its crow-stepped gables, is also Dutch influenced.

However, if you tire of admiring the white-painted old cottages and exploring the little alleyways (the *sea wynds*), then take a trip inland to Kellie Castle (NTS) behind Pittenweem. This dates from the 14th century, though it was heavily restored in late Victorian times. As well as ornate plasterwork on the castle, there's a fine, walled garden worked on organic principles.

HAWICK   *193D2*

Hawick is the largest of the Border towns and an important textile center, without being over-picturesque. It is worth a trip to buy woolen goods and to dip into the town's museum in Winton Lodge in the middle of a pleasant park. Here you'll find plenty of background on the development of textiles and other local and more war-like traditions.

★ HELENSBURGH and LOCH LOMOND   *192B3*

Helensburgh is sometimes described as a "museum of villas," though this prosperous place on the shores of the Clyde estuary is certainly not a museum. The villas in question are the large houses built by successful businessmen in Glasgow's commercial heyday.

The most famous is **Hill House** (NTS). Open to view, it was designed by Charles Rennie Mackintosh for the publisher Walter Blackie in 1904. It shows Mackintosh's innovative style and attention to detail.

Over the hill from Helensburgh lies Scotland's other famous body of water: **Loch Lomond**. Famed in song, the "bonnie banks" are certainly attractive (especially the east shore, which is much less busy) and have the advantage of being easily accessible. Boat trips go from several places around the loch, including Luss, Balmaha and Balloch. Climb Duncryne Hill, behind Gartocharn at the southern end of the loch, for one of the finest views in Scotland, with Loch Lomond winding its way into the northern hills.

Or sample the West Highland Way on foot beyond Rowardennan, where the public road ends on the east side of the loch, to enjoy the oak woods and mountain views.

★ JEDBURGH   *193E2*

Another textile town where, it is said, tweed was invented, Jedburgh (pronounced "Jedbruh") was for a long time on the receiving end of Border disputes. The excellent visitor center at **Jedburgh Abbey** (HS) is a starting point for discovering the heyday of the four great Border abbeys (Jedburgh, Melrose, Kelso and Dryburgh).

But Jedburgh is not lacking in other historical attractions. The Castle Jail Museum is housed in a former "model" Victorian prison, while **Mary Queen of Scots House** is a fortified house associated with Scotland's tragic queen. In fact, because of Jedburgh's strategic position on the road to Scotland, it is associated with many historical figures from Bonnie Prince Charlie to William Wordsworth.

★★ KELSO   *193E3*

Perhaps the most handsome of the Border towns, though with the most ruined **abbey** (HS), Kelso's attractiveness partly lies in its broad central square, with attractive town houses. Nearby is the fragment of abbey, while across from this is **Turret House**, the local museum which tells the story of Kelso as a market town.

Stately homes in easy reach are **Floors Castle**, described as the largest inhabited house in Scotland, and **Mellerstain House**, with exquisite decorative plaster works by the architects William Adam and his son Robert.

WHITHORN PILGRIMAGE

Whithorn and its priory was a place of pilgrimage for centuries, notably for the Stewart monarchs.

The old pilgrim road which crossed the Galloway moors and uplands is paralleled by today's A712 road between Newton Stewart and New Galloway as it passes through the Galloway Forest Park.

The picturesque road is known as the "Queen's Way," recalling Mary, Queen of Scots, and has a number of circular touring options. Alternatively, it can be used as a meandering route west to avoid the A75 ■

KILMARNOCK *192B3*

A large and workaday town in Ayrshire, Kilmarnock is often bypassed on the way between the Ayrshire golfing resorts and Glasgow. However, it offers a particularly interesting castle in pleasant grounds.

Dean Castle and Country Park is a museum run by the local authority. It contains an interesting collection of European armor, historic musical instruments, and a number of Robert Burns artifacts. Dean Castle was the ancestral home of the Boyds and consists of a 14th-century keep (castle fortress), dungeon and battlements and a (slightly later) small palace block. Though much of it has been restored, the pervading original atmosphere is still impressive.

★★★ KIRKCUDBRIGHT *192C1*

No matter which route is chosen westbound between Dumfries and Kirkcudbright, the trip through the pleasantly rolling and rich Galloway countryside is rewarding. Within easy reach of Kirkcudbright, one of the most pleasing of the southwestern towns, there are plenty of places of interest.

Arbigland Gardens, by the coast, offers sheltered walks and wooded glades, as well as a curious connection with John Paul Jones. Born in a cottage in the grounds, he eventually became the founder of the United States Navy.

Threave Garden (NTS), by the town of Castle Douglas, makes another worthwhile excursion, which is easily combined with a visit to the grim tower of 14th-century Threave Castle, another stronghold of the Black Douglas, set on an island in the River Dee.

Closer to Kirkcudbright lies **Dundrennan Abbey** (HS), founded by the Cistercians in 1142, picturesquely ruined and associated with Mary, Queen of Scots, who spent her last night in Scotland there.

West of the town, at Gatehouse-of-Fleet, itself an attractive place, you will find the **Mill on the Fleet**, a former bobbin mill, which tells the story of Gatehouse-of-Fleet, set up as a spinning community. (A "bobbin" is the reel onto which the cotton is wound.)

As for Kirkcudbright itself, its substantial pastel-painted houses are set in quiet streets ideal for leisurely strolls. Visit the antiques stores and the gallery by the harbor, as well as **Broughton House** (NTS), home of the artist Edward Hornel of the famed "Glasgow School." Kirkcudbright has attracted many other artists over the past years.

The 16th-century **Maclellan's Castle** (HS) is a ruined turreted mansion set right in the center of town – and a contrast to the elegant 18th-century Georgian work that contributes to the town's pleasing appearance.

LINLITHGOW *193C3*

This town, in the busy central corridor between Edinburgh and Glasgow is chiefly noted for **Linlithgow Palace** (HS). This once magnificent royal palace, birthplace of Mary, Queen of Scots, was burned down during the last Jacobite uprising in 1746. Today its cold and echoing halls only hint of past glories.

Next door to the palace is **St. Michael's Church**, the largest surviving pre-Reformation Church in Scotland. The 16th-century upheaval of the Reformation and the establishment of the Protestant faith unfortunately took its toll on many highly decorated Scottish Catholic churches – which were usually wrecked by zealots.

Also nearby is **Bo'ness**, with an interesting museum exhibiting local pottery, and the terminus of the re-created **Bo'ness and Kinneil Railway**, running steam-hauled services on this evocation of a long-lost typical branch line.

community, founded by Saint Ninian in the 5th century (ahead of the more famous Saint Columba and the island of Iona). The results of an extensive archeological investigation on the site, overlooked by the ruins of a

★★★ THE MACHARS   *192B1*

Wanderers in the west of Galloway seeking byways may stumble upon The Machars, which rest in a green triangle south of the Galloway moors. Though the surrounding scenery is neither high nor spectacular, the coastline has a wild feel, while inland woods mingle with rolling pastures, where black and white cows wade through deep, green grass.

Take the road down towards the tip of the triangle and at **Whithorn** you arrive at the true birthplace of Christianity in Scotland. This is marked by **Whithorn Visitor Centre**, only yards away from the site of Scotland's earliest religious

12th-century **priory** (HS), are portrayed in the visitor center.

There is a separate priory museum and a great walk to **St. Ninian's Cave**, along the pebbly shore, about 5 miles to the southwest (see walk p.201).

Newton Stewart, to the north, is The Machars' gateway town. It is also the nearest town to the **Galloway Forest Park**, around Glen Trool, further north.

Follow signs off the main A714 and you eventually reach countryside that looks every bit as rugged as the famous Trossachs (see p.243), with loch and wooded hillslopes and high, gray hills. Yet you are in Galloway – nowhere near the Highlands of northern Scotland.

Linlithgow Palace is now an echoing ruin, but this was once the magnificent home of Scottish royalty – Mary, Queen of Scots, was born here in 1542

DRIVE

EAST LOTHIAN AND THE BORDERS

148 miles (allow 2 days)

Edinburgh is the starting point for this tour, which heads first towards East Lothian, with its good sunshine record and low rainfall. On the way, Edinburgh's eastern suburbs include Portobello, which once had resort pretensions, as suggested by its promenade and sandy beaches, and then Musselburgh, where there is one of the oldest golf links in Scotland.

THE BASS ROCK

The core of a volcano, the Bass Rock rears out of the Firth of Forth and is conspicuous in local coastal views.

With around 14,000 nest sites, the Rock also has the third largest "gannetry" in the world. The scientific name of the Northern Gannet, *Sula bassana*, recalls the bird's connection with the site.

The Bass also has a variety of historical and literary associations, featuring as a prison in Robert Louis Stevenson's *Catriona*.

Boat trips go to the Bass from North Berwick ∎

Take the B1348 at the east end of Musselburgh by the race course.

Beyond **Musselburgh**, note the giant beam engine of the Scottish Mining Museum's display at Prestongrange. A little further is the site of the Battle of Prestonpans, where the Jacobites routed an unready government army under General Cope in 1745.

The B1348 becomes the A198 at Longniddry and continues towards Gullane.

1 Gullane, East Lothian

On the way to Gullane, the A198 continues through the attractive little settlement of Aberlady, with its nature reserve supporting large populations of wading birds. Gullane is a prosperous little golfing resort, with a golden beach and sand dunes running past the British Open Championship venue of Muirfield. To the east lies Dirleton with its country-style village green over which looms 13th-century Dirleton

Castle. A signpost leads to the attractive beach at Yellowcraigs.

Continue on the A198 to reach North Berwick.

2 North Berwick, East Lothian

A small, seaside golf resort with North Berwick West course only minutes from the main street; this is a golfing venue of great antiquity and the essence of a traditional Scottish coastal links. North Berwick also offers great views from the top of the Berwick Law as well as endless sandy beaches.

Continue on the A198 and turn left at a signposted minor road for Tantallon Castle.

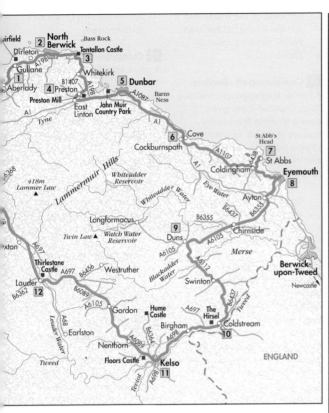

TANTALLON CASTLE

This great headland castle is associated with the powerful Douglas family, who were also earls of Angus, and took part in many of Scotland's power struggles.

In a conflict with King James V, the forces of Archibald, 6th Earl of Angus, were besieged in Tantallon in 1528. The King's cannon failed to make any impression after 20 days.

On hearing the siege was lifted, Archibald made his way to his castle, and sallying out with his men, captured the retreating train of artillery.

However, the Crown gained Tantallon when Archibald retired into exile in England in the following year ∎

3 Tantallon Castle

The A198 runs high above the sea with excellent views of the Bass Rock, then swings sharply south, with the red wall of Tantallon Castle on the skyline. With seacliffs 100 feet high on three sides, Tantallon is essentially a fortified headland. Past historic Whitekirk, one entrance to the John Muir Country Park is signposted (left), offering beach and woodland walks.

Return to the A198 and continue south. Turn right at the B1407 to enter Preston.

4 Preston Mill, East Lothian

About a mile along the B1407, the attractive red roof of Preston Mill can be seen. This 18th-century meal mill is a historic survivor of a once common rural feature, the kiln. This one is a curious cross between a Dutch type and an English oast house. It is a few minutes' stroll south to Phantassie Doocot (NTS), a beehive-type home for pigeons.

Continue east on the B1047, then turn left on to the B1377. Turn left to rejoin the A1. Take A1087 at the traffic circle for Dunbar.

5 Dunbar, East Lothian

A slightly faded but still attractive resort with some fine Georgian architecture, Dunbar shows its layers of history in its fragmentary castle, its two harbors (the first associated with Oliver Cromwell) and its handsome 17th-century town house with steeple.

EYEMOUTH MUSEUM

Friday, October 14, 1881 was a disaster for many east coast fishing communities.

A total of 129 men were lost at sea on that day, with Eyemouth suffering the highest individual toll.

So great was the wind and so sudden its onslaught while the fleet was at sea that nothing could be done for the crews of the fishing vessels.

On land, an Eyemouth local saw "the strange spectacle of trees being bodily lifted out of the earth, and carried along with the wind in upright positions, as if they were aeriel creatures with powers of propulsion."

Eyemouth Museum tells the sad story ■

Continue on the A1087 and join the A1 east of the town. Follow this for 8 miles to Cockburnspath.

6 Cockburnspath, Borders

A former staging post in coaching days, Cockburnspath gives access to some fine coastal scenery, (follow a footpath shorewards to Cove), and it is also the eastern terminus of the Southern Upland Way.

Continue on the A1 and turn left at the A1107. At Coldingham, turn left at the B6438 for St. Abbs.

7 St. Abbs, Borders

There are fine coastal views from an unclassified road going left by woodland 3 miles from the A1. Continue through Coldingham to St. Abbs, which has a voluntary marine reserve, popular with divers, as well as a nature reserve by the lighthouse.

Rejoin the A1107, turning left for Eyemouth.

8 Eyemouth, Borders

An active fishing port with regular fish markets, the community's seafaring links are explored in the local museum. It also records the storm of 1881 that cost 129 local fishermen their lives.

Follow the B6355 south west, crossing the A1 and joining the A6105 at Chirnside for Duns.

9 Duns, Borders

An attractive little market town on the southern edge of the Lammermuirs, Duns is worth srolling around. The town is associated with the medieval scholar Duns Scotus, as well as the Scottish racing driver, the late Jim Clark.

Follow the A6112 south to Coldstream.

10 Coldstream, Borders

Another attractive community on the border. Visit the museum and The Hirsel (see p.202).

Leave by the A697, then turn left at the A698 for Kelso.

11 Kelso, Borders

This handsome Borders town has a large central square. Floors Castle, Turret House Museum and Kelso Abbey are some of the places to see close to the town.

Take the A6089 through Gordon, and go left on the A697. Turn left along the B6362 to Lauder.

12 Lauder, Borders

Divert north on the B6364 for a view of the Borders from the battlements of Hume Castle, 6 miles north of Kelso. Lauder, with its ancient tolbooth, has an interesting parish church dated 1673. Sixteenth-century Thirlestane Castle is near the town.

Leave Lauder on the A68 towards Edinburgh. Crichton Castle is signposted on the left near Pathhead.

13 Crichton Castle, Midlothian

Associated with the earls of Bothwell, this 14th- to 16th-century castle looms over the Lothian countryside. Note the castle's unique diamond-faceted stonework on the facade of the north range. On the way into Edinburgh the road passes close to Edinburgh Butterfly World near Dalkeith and the Scottish Mining Museum at Newtongrange.

Take the B6367 to Pathhead; turn left and follow the A68 to return to Edinburgh.

★★★ MELROSE *193D2*

Though not a large place, Melrose packs a lot of sights and has a good choice of eating places and accommodations as a bonus.

Its most conspicuous feature is its handsome **abbey** (HS), originally founded in 1136. Amid the ruins, some lavish ornamentation still survives: carved into the walls are fruit and foliage and numerous little figures, even a pig playing the bagpipes high on the walls. It is well worth taking the time to have a look around.

Melrose Motor Museum and **Priorwood Gardens** (NTS), next door to the abbey, are two other attractions.

The town is overlooked by the three-peaked silhouette of the **Eildon Hills**. This distinctive landmark was chosen by the Romans as a navigating aid to their largest camp in Scotland, at Newstead, close to Melrose, which they called *Trimontium* (Latin for "triple peaks"). Though practically nothing can be seen above ground here, the story is told in the **Trimontium Exhibition** within Melrose by way of models, displays and artifacts excavated from the camp.

In the surrounding countryside are other features well worth including on any tour. Sir Walter Scott is inescapable hereabouts, not only at **Abbotsford**, his family home (see Selkirk p.216), but also in his association with **Smailholm Tower** (HS), a 16th-century fortified tower, about 8 miles east of Melrose. Sir Walter's grandfather farmed nearby. There are breathtaking views over the blue waves of Border Hills from the top.

On the way, you can take in **Scott's View**, a panoramic view over the curving River Tweed with the Eildon Hills as a backdrop – another reminder that high-grade Scottish landscapes

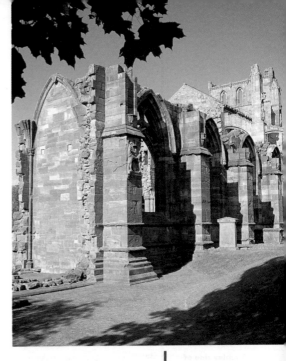

are certainly not confined simply to the Highlands.

Dryburgh Abbey (HS) is only a little further – the most peacefully secluded of the Border abbeys, with its tree-girded riverside setting. Sir Walter is buried here. In the other direction, if quality woolens are on your shopping list, then visit **Galashiels**, and in particular the Peter Anderson Woollen Mill.

★ MOFFAT *193D2*

If the traffic on the A/M74, the main artery through the Southern Uplands, begins to get to you, then break your trip at Moffat. If you want a scenic route to Edinburgh, you'll leave the busy highway here anyway.

Moffat was a minor spa town during the 18th century, though its main trade was as a small market center for the (sheep) farmers around. Today it serves travelers with a variety of craft items and woolen goods, as well as cafés and hotels.

At the head of the valley in which Moffat lies, you can see

The ruins of Melrose Abbey, founded in 1136, may look gaunt and empty, but there is still some elaborate stone carving to be found

TRIMONTIUM

The Roman fort at Trimontium, near Melrose, was abandoned as a permanent base around AD 185.

At its peak, including a garrison of 1,000 troops, there may have been anything between 2–5,000 people here. The site was discovered while railway navvies were excavating a cutting for the Waverley Route in 1855 ■

NEIDPATH CASTLE

In order to visit this impressive tower, you could go by car, but another option is to walk upstream from the handsome Tweed Bridge in Peebles.

Stay on the Peebles side of the river and go through a public park. The path then narrows, passing through a small pinewood, close to the river to emerge within sight of Neidpath, high on the bank.

You could return the same way, or as an alternative, continue past, as far as a former railroad viaduct (the tracks have gone). Cross the river here and return to Peebles by the opposite bank, which also has a path ■

the **Devil's Beef Tub** (the main A701 passes above it). This steep-sided amphitheater, actually a glaciation feature, was used for hiding stolen cattle in past, more lawless days.

Alternatively, take the A708 north to Edinburgh via Peebles and you pass the **Grey Mare's Tail** (NTS), a waterfall also created by grinding glaciers, which carved out the "hanging valley" over which the fall hurtles.

★★★ NEW LANARK   193C3

The south of Scotland is full of scenic surprises. The River Clyde rises in the Border hills and wanders northwards, gathering subsidiary streams. As it approaches the town of Lanark, it tires of its gravelly meanderings and throws itself over rocky shelves and into a wooded gorge, attaining a force that aroused the interest of mill entrepreneurs in the early days of the Industrial Revolution.

This is New Lanark. By the end of the 18th century, it was Scotland's single largest industrial enterprise, founded by a Glasgow entrepreneur, David Dale, as a model industrial village. Conditions for the workers were good for its day, with housing and education provided.

It attracted many dispossessed Highlanders who otherwise would have emigrated. Robert Owen, Dale's son-in-law and manager of New Lanark, used it as a proving ground for his egalitarian and cooperative theories known as "Owenism." Later, Owen tried to set up a similar development at New Harmony, Illinois. The spinning venture and other activities gradually petered out, but New Lanark has been saved and populated again. Today, looming among the tall trees and rushing river in this sylvan valley, you will

see mill buildings and tenements, stone built and mellowed by time. The story of the venture is told in a well-equipped **visitor center** within one of the mill buildings.

For an industrial community, the setting remains unspoiled and there are walks upstream to see fine waterfalls, including the famous Falls of Clyde, visited by many famous British painters over the years. Above the valley stands the much older town of Lanark, a market center with a good range of stores along its main street.

★★ NORTH BERWICK   193D3

If Edinburgh gets too crowded, then head for the East Lothian coast. Standing below prosperous farmlands and the dark line of the Lammermuir Hills, the Lothian seacoast has not only lots of golf courses, but some very wild stretches of dune and golden sand and a few small resorts, of which North Berwick is one.

Westwards the sands roll out to Yellowcraigs, where the offshore island of **Fidra** is said to have been the inspiration for *Treasure Island*, Robert Louis Stevenson's famous adventure story. However, a more tangible connection includes scenes from the same author's *Catriona*, the sequel to *Kidnapped*, which evokes a vivid portrayal of the tangy, seagull-haunted dunes and the sand.

The **Bass Rock** is also offshore, and conspicuous to the east of North Berwick, a great domed rock rising from the Firth where gannets occupy 14,000 nest sites (see p.208). The Atlantic or northern gannet's scientific name, *Sula bassana*, refers to the Bass Rock. Boat trips go out from North Berwick to the Rock.

Like the Bass Rock, the **Berwick Law** behind the resort is a volcanic plug – a hard core of rock which was once the inside of a volcano. The top of this distinctive triangle offers a great view of the whole coastline and right across the Firth to Fife.

Also east of North Berwick you'll see the impressive fortified wall of **Tantallon Castle** (HS), a 14th-century Douglas stronghold guarding a rocky headland. Pace the battlements and investigate the nooks and passageways of this time-worn fortress – you'll certainly feel the atmosphere.

Inland, hidden in the grainfields and gentle wooded countryside, you can also track down the Museum of Flight. This is an outstation of the Royal Scottish Museum and is on a former airfield at East Fortune. It features many historic aircraft and displays material on the airship R34 which flew from this very field to New York in 1919.

★★★ PEEBLES 193D3

This attractive little town is set in the rolling Borders hills by the banks of the River Tweed. It has a comfortable, well-to-do air, serving a rural hinterland of prosperous farms and substantial properties. It is also within an easy day's trip from Edinburgh (and Glasgow), which may partly explain why it is usually a bustling place. The shops are also very varied – good for antiques, jewelry and books.

The town was the birthplace of William and Robert Chambers, who were the founders of the Edinburgh publishing company formerly associated with dictionaries and encyclopedias. The Chambers never forgot their home town, endowing it with the impressive town center municipal buildings which today house the library and museum.

And to prove that Scotland has museums on just about every subject, Peebles is also home to the **Cornice Museum of Ornamental Plasterwork**, where you can see how the ornate plastering of Scotland's grand buildings was achieved. You can even try out the process for yourself – materials and protective clothing will be provided!

Neidpath Castle stands a mile upstream on the River Tweed, and can be reached by the main road west or, more pleasantly, by a riverside walk. This medieval and impressively authentic looking L-plan tower house was adapted to the more peaceful times of the 17th century, then fell into decay in the 19th century, and has now been partly restored by the present owners.

The massive solidity of medieval Neidpath Castle is to be found in a fine situation on the banks of the River Tweed – parts are still in ruins, but it is being restored

★★★ ST. ABBS *193E3*

There are many facets to Scotland. One, which is sometimes overlooked in the tourism promoters' desire to convey tartan-bedecked Highland life, is the country's wild coastline. When exploring the eastern borders, perhaps on the way to or from Edinburgh, it is worth stopping off at the tiny coastal village of **St. Abbs**. You might not be able to park within the village itself, partly because of limited space and partly because of the popularity of the area with scuba-diving enthusiasts. But if you head to the signposted **St. Abbs Head Nature Reserve** and park at Northfield Farm, which is also the visitor center, you can then walk to the lighthouse and see some extremely impressive cliff scenery with enormous seabird colonies and wide-ranging views.

For another viewpoint on this area's seagoing connection, visit the little port of **Eyemouth**, only a mile or two to the southeast. Here, there is still an active fishery, as well as the Eyemouth Museum, which tells the story of the hard struggle against the sea endured by generations of the town's fishermen.

★★★ ST. ANDREWS *193D4*

Nowhere else in Scotland is quite like St. Andrews. Not only does it have the essence of an eastern seaboard town with its gray spires and salty air, but it is an ancient settlement which was once the religious center of Scotland, as well as the home of Scotland's oldest university.

Look across the roofs of the Borders fishing port of St. Abbs to the tiny harbor, a popular starting point for scuba-diving trips. Its impressive walls hold back the worst of the North Sea waves

Yet despite these attractions, the main reason why so many visitors want to see the place is that St. Andrews is the historic home of the game of **golf**.

According to legend, Saint Rule, a Greek monk, was shipwrecked here. At the time, he was carrying relics of Saint Andrew, one of the Disciples, and so the cult of Saint Andrew was established. **St. Andrew's Cathedral** (HS) was founded in 1160. Natural disasters of fire and storm damaged its fabric before the destructive zeal of the 16th-century Reformers ended its role as a religious center. Today this poignant tale is explained by an interesting museum situated on the grounds.

But St. Andrew's Cathedral is not the oldest building in the

town. This distinction goes to the adjacent **St. Rule's Tower**, tentatively dated as early 12th century. Climb to the top for a view of the town which makes plain the still surviving medieval street plan of three roads running parallel to each other.

St. Andrews' **town gate** in South Street also provides valuable insight to the historical evolution of the town. The only gate or port in Scotland still in use, the West Port is a reminder of the times when all Scottish towns (or "burghs") were protected by walls and guarded ports.

At the other end of South Street are the **Pends**, arched passageways originally leading to the priory adjacent to the cathedral grounds. This is typical St. Andrews; ancient walling standing amid the buzz and clatter of modern-day traffic. The buildings of the **university** (founded in 1411) are integrated into the fabric of the town and add to its characteristic air.

St. Andrews Castle (HS) stands on the edge of the sea with an informative visitor center to tell its story. The castle is associated with the Reformer John Knox, whose party was besieged and captured here. As well as an awesome bottle dungeon (bottle-shaped to deter escape), the ruined fortress features a mine and counter mine. The mine, actually a tunnel, was made by the attackers during a siege in 1546–7. The work of their sappers (engineers) was to no avail, however, as a counter mine was extended from the castle to break into the attackers' mine. Marks made by the axes can still be seen after more than 400 years. This little underground excursion, though well lit, isn't for the claustrophobic.

DRAMA AT ST. ANDREWS CASTLE

St. Andrews Castle played a key role in the troubled times of the Reformation in Scotland, when the new Protestant faith challenged the established Catholic order.

The castle was at the time the home of the powerful Cardinal David Beaton. In 1546, he ordered the rounding up of George Wishart, a courageous, if dogmatic proponent of the new Protestantism. Wishart was strangled and burned before the castle, while Cardinal Beaton looked on.

Three months later, the castle fell to the Protestant reformers, who entered by a ruse, pretending to be masons working on the fortifications. Beaton was murdered and his body hung from the wallhead for all to see ■

THE COMMON RIDINGS

If you visit the museum at Halliwell's House in Selkirk, upstairs you can watch a video that will tell you much about the Common Ridings.

These events, which are peculiar to the Borders, are held annually and mostly relate to old customs concerning the maintenance of town lands and their protection. (It is no coincidence that these annual rallies are held in an area which was disputed and raided for hundreds of years.)

The Common Ridings are also a great celebration of horsemanship, with Selkirk claiming its Riding to be the largest mounted gathering to be held anywhere in Europe ■

For those tired of the historic sites, there is the **Sea Life Centre** with its wide-ranging displays of British native marine species, plus two local museums: the **Museum of St. Andrews Preservation Trust**, covering mostly the commercial life in the town, and the **St. Andrews Museum** with displays on the story of the town.

On the way round all these places, you might want to pause to shop – the town is extremely well endowed with quality stores selling antiques, rugs, gifts, woolens and *haute couture* clothing. Perhaps they exist to cater for "golf widows" whose husbands are lost somewhere on the shrine of St. Andrews' Old Course!

★★ SELKIRK 193D2

Hilly little Selkirk is a typical Borders town with mills by the river, substantial houses and little streets. The story of the town and its traditions, especially the annual Common Riding ceremony, is told at **Halliwell's House** up an alleyway off the main square. Once it was the local store of an ironmonger (a dealer in iron and hardware), but now it is the town museum, with the preserved ironmonger's store on the ground floor. The tourist information center is here as well.

Sir Walter Scott was the Sheriff in Selkirk for 30 years, and his former **courthouse** is open to the public. Close at hand is the main Sir Walter Scott connection: **Abbotsford**, the grand home he gradually built and filled with historical artifacts. Sometimes the house close to the River Tweed is described as "a series of Scottish quotations set in stone," as it reflects so many native building styles, and displays so many slices of history. His small desk is made with

wood from a Spanish Armada shipwreck, the library ceiling is copied from Rosslyn Chapel, and a showcase contains Napoleon I's brooch, found in his coach after the defeat at Waterloo. From a lock of Bonnie Prince Charlie's hair to the keys of Lochleven Castle, the story of Scotland is here. Find time to look around this unique house, where Sir Walter's presence haunts every room.

STRANRAER 192B1

The ferry port of Stranraer lies on the road to Ireland and is not, at first sight, the most picturesque of Scottish towns. Nevertheless, it has a museum and a visitor center at the **Castle of St. John**, a 16th-century tower house and former prison in the town center.

Within easy reach are a good range of other attractions. These include the splendid **Castle Kennedy Gardens** to the west, built by the 2nd Earl of Stairs who used the troops he was commanding to hew out the landscape features on a grand scale. In the other direction, on the coast east of Stranraer, you can take a trip to **Portpatrick**, formerly a port for ferries to Ireland, and now a pleasant little community. This is also the unlikely setting for **Little Wheels**, a center with model railroads, toys, dolls and transportation items to amuse the children.

For garden lovers, there is **Logan Botanic Garden** further down the hammerhead of the Rinns of Galloway. This is an outstation of Edinburgh's Royal Botanic Garden. It is located here because this is one of the mildest parts of Scotland, mollycoddled by the warming influence of the North Atlantic Drift (or Gulf Stream). The mild conditions are appreciated by tree ferns, palms and other New World species.

THE SCOTTISH HIGHLANDS

Once considered wild and remote,
the Scottish Highlands are now
valued by today's visitors for their
majestic landscapes and
their solitude

0 10 20 30 40 50 km
0 10 20 30 miles

5

Cape Wrath Faraid Head
Sandwood Bay Durness
Smoo Cove Bett
Butt of Lewis Port of Ness
Pentla
Tongu
927m
Ben Hope
Scourie
Arnol Black House Barvas Tolsta
Point of Stoer Altnaharra
Western Isles
Breasclete **Callanish**
Miavaig Stornoway
Drumbeg Unapool
Lochinver 998m
Ben More Loch
Inverpolly Nature Reserve Assynt Cho
Shin
Balallan Isle of Lewis
Summer Isles La
Elphin
Falls of Shin
Scarp **4**
Hushinish **Ullapool** Inv
South Lewis, Harris & North Uist **Tarbert** Shiant Islands Laide Ardgay
Scalpay **Inverewe Gardens**
Pabbay Harris Braemore Invergor
Rodel Gairloch **Corrieshalloch Gorge** 1045m
North Uist Duntulm 1109m Ben Wyvis
Tigharry **Hosta** Lochmaddy **Museum of Island Life** Loch Maree Sgurr Mòr Dingwall
Barpa Langass **The Quiraing** Kinlochewe
Uig Staffin Wester Ross Contin Fort
Benbecula Gramsdale **Dunvegan Castle** **Old Man of Storr** Lower Diabaig Liathach 1024m Achnasheen Muir of Ord
Creagorry Skeabost Loch Torridon Torridon **Inverness**
South Uist Dunvegan Portree Shieldaig Strathcarron Cannich
Raasay Bealach-na-Ba Stromeferry Drumnadrochit Inverfari
3 Sligachan Sconser Kyle of Lochalsh Loch
Lochboisdale Isle of Skye Cuillin Hills **Loch Coruisk** Kyleakin **Eilean Donan Castle** Invermoriston Mbor
1009m Sgurr Alasdair Shiel Bridge Highland Loch Ness
Kilbride Elgol 101m Invergarry Fort Augustus
Barra Canna **Armadale Castle & Clan Donald Centre** Isleornsay Knoydart Newtonm
Kisimul Kinloch Ardvasar Loch Quoich Glen Garry Laggan
Castlebay Rhum Morar Mallaig Dalwhinnie
Sandray Eigg Arisaig Loch Arkaig Spean Bridge
Mingulay The Small Isles Glenfinnan Corpach **Fort William** Loch Ericht
Berneray Muck Kinlocheil 1343m Glen
Ben Nevis Nevis
Castle Tioram Salen Ardgour Glencoe G Rannoch Station Kinl
Kilchoan **Castle Mingary** Strontian Ballachulish Glen **Achallader Castle** Rann
Coll Arinagour Loch Linnhe Goe Ben La
2 Tobermory Barcaldine Tyndrum Lochearnhe
Tiree Scarinish Loch na Keal, Isle of Mull Lochaline **Duart Castle** Crianlarich
Craignure **Torosay Castle** **Dunstaffnage Castle** Ardlui Strat
Staffa 966m Ben More Oban Taynuilt **Inveraray Castle** Callar
Fingal's Cave Isle of Mull Kilninver Ardlui The
Iona **Abbey** Kilmelford Loch Awe Stirling Trossachs
Fionnphort Aberfo
1 **Carnasserie** Strachur Tarbet
City of Edinburgh Scarba **Dunadd Fort** Argyll and Bute Loch Lomond Klip
City of Glasgow Colonsay Lochgilphead Loch Eck Garelochhead Drymen
Clackmannanshire Oronsay Glendaruel Helensburgh
East Ayrshire Loch Tarbert Knapdale Dunoon Alexandria **Dumbarton**
East Dunbartonshire Port Askaig Jura Lagg Kames 12
East Renfrewshire Rothesay Greenock **Glasg**
Falkirk Craighouse Tarbert Bute 8 11
Inverclyde Kilberry Clachan Largs Paisley Hamilt
Midlothian Islay Gigha Killchattan Millport East
North Lanarkshire Bowmore Lochranza Cumbraes Kilbrid
Renfrewshire Portnahaven Kintyre North Ayrshire Kilmarnock
West Dumbartonshire Mull of Oa Ardbeg Cara Ardrossan 4
West Lothian Carradale Arran **Brodick Castle**

A B C

1 City of Edinburgh
2 City of Glasgow
3 Clackmannanshire
4 East Ayrshire
5 East Dunbartonshire
6 East Renfrewshire
7 Falkirk
8 Inverclyde
9 Midlothian
10 North Lanarkshire
11 Renfrewshire
12 West Dumbartonshire
13 West Lothian

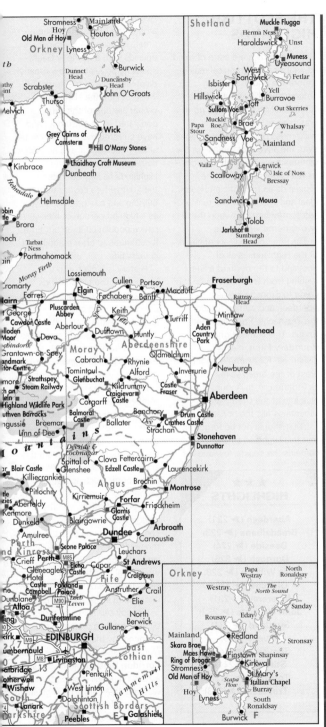

CALENDAR OF EVENTS

**JANUARY 11 –
Burning of the
Clavie**, Burghead,
Moray. The burning
Clavie (part of a
whiskey barrel) is
carried through the
streets by Clavie
King and his men.

**MARCH OR
APRIL – Inverness
Folk Festival.** Taking
place over Easter
weekend, this
festival helps
preserve an
important part of the
Gaelic folk tradition.

**LAST SATURDAY
IN MAY – Atholl
Highlanders Parade**,
Blair Castle, Blair
Atholl. The Duke of
Atholl formally
inspects his troops.
They make a colorful
sight.

**JULY – Highland
Games**, Inveraray.
You can enjoy
watching the tossing
of the caber,
throwing the
hammer, and the
piping and highland
dancing
competitions.

**SEPTEMBER –
Ben Nevis Hill Race**,
Fort William. This
involves a grueling
scramble
up and down
Britain's
highest peak ■

TOURISM IN THE HIGHLANDS

Some maintain that the Highlands became popular as a tourist destination after the publication of Sir Walter Scott's verse narrative *The Lady of the Lake* in 1810. Certainly, this put the Trossachs – the most accessible bit of the Highlands – on the map.

But the Romantic Movement, with its adventurous tourists, painters and poets seeking out new views and picturesque Highland scenes, was well under way years before it.

For example, in 1794 a Callander minister recorded that the Highland countryside around was "often visited by persons of taste, who are desirous of seeing nature in her rudest and unpolished state" ■

THE SCOTTISH HIGHLANDS

The Highlands are a state of mind as well as a geographical reality. Before the end of the 18th century and the growth of the Romantic Movement, the north was seen as a primitive wilderness populated by savages. With the advent of the cult of the picturesque – still with us today – travelers began to view the Highlands as romantic and heroic, ideal and unspoiled. The reality lies somewhere between these two extreme viewpoints.

The strict geological definition of the Highlands is all of Scotland to the north of a line running from Helensburgh on the Clyde to Stonehaven near Aberdeen and cutting through the Trossachs, Perthshire and Angus. This is the **Highland Boundary Fault**, clearly discerned, for example, to the west of the broad valley known as Strathmore, in Angus. The long blue line of the Grampian Mountains fills the horizon.

Yet it should not be forgotten that this Highland area also contains the coastal lowlands of

---

★ ★ ★
HIGHLIGHTS

Angus, Aberdeenshire and all around the Moray Firth. The "real" Highlands – marginal uplands with a formerly Gaelic-speaking population now greatly dispersed – lie to the north and west. In fact, the Highlands proper are one of the least populated parts of Europe, and have suffered more than their fair share of ecological and economic damage. Yet, despite the Highlands having lost most of their native tree cover through burning and overgrazing, as well as a high proportion of their native population in recent times, it continues to offer magnificent countryside.

History is woven into the landscape. The old *shielings* formerly used as shelters for the clan women and children, who looked after the cattle on their summer grazings, still survive as tumbled ruins in many a high mountain recess known as a *corrie*. They are reminders of a way of life long vanished. The planned settlements of places like **Ullapool** or **Tobermory** represent 18th-century government efforts to secure employment in disadvantaged areas. The small coastal villages of the north, such as **Bettyhill** in Sutherland, represent the efforts of all-powerful 19th-century landowners to displace whole communities in an effort to make money from unproductive landholdings. The clearances, in which Highland farmers lost their lands to flocks of sheep, are now interpreted as ethnic cleansing.

Nobody can fail to be moved by the brooding presence of **Glencoe**, by the shattered pinnacles and rock terraces of the **Torridon Hills**, or by the sunsets across the small isles on the western seaboard. The Highlands certainly offer their romantic, hauntingly beautiful moments.

★★★ ABERDEEN 219F3

No other Scottish city is like Aberdeen, with its remarkable granite character. Bold blocks of gray granite buildings, silver when the sun shines, lend distinction to this northern place. Granite may be austere, but the city is softened by an emphasis on flowers. Not only in parks, but in many other public spaces – even along the inner grounds of the ring road – roses brighten the view in high summer. Aberdeen regularly wins floral awards.

Aberdeen is also the oil capital of Britain. Before the end of the 1970s, it had the air of a large and comfortably well off market town. Then the black gold began to flow and new buildings, accents, attitudes, goods in stores and newcomers changed the look and sound of the place. Peripheral towns expanded, industrial parks on the outskirts filled up with strange looking pipes and tubes, drill bits and gantries. Aberdeen still looks like this today. It offers a good range of places to see within the old core of the city and makes a good base for exploring the hinterland with its castles, coastline, whiskey distilleries and royal connections.

Downtown Aberdeen's main street is **Union Street**, with the oldest part of the city at the sea end, known as the **Castlegate**. Here you will see a handsome tolbooth or town house, and one of the finest mercat (market) crosses in Scotland, both indicating the heart of an old Scottish burgh.

Down towards the harbor, Aberdeen's **Maritime Museum** on the Shiprow is housed within Provost Ross's House of 1593. (A provost is the Scottish equivalent of mayor.) Another historic survivor is **Provost Skene's House**, around the corner from Castlegate, off Broad Street. As well as painted ceilings and interesting artifacts from the 16th century, there is a pleasant little café. Opposite, in Broad Street, is the extraordinary facade of **Marischal College**, completed in 1903 as the second largest granite building in the world (only El Escorial in Madrid is larger). Within the university portals, Marischal Museum exhibits a wide-ranging ethnographic collection.

Marischal College, Aberdeen, with its massive tower, pinnacles and spires, is built of the granite that was used in many of the buildings of this northern city

Aberdeen Art Gallery is also within easy walking distance, past the bland modern shopping of the Bon-Accord and St. Nicholas centers, and is a peaceful haven close to the shopping streets. It has a good

ABERDEEN'S SENTIMENTAL SONG

Aberdeen's name turns up in the song *The Northern Lights of Old Aberdeen*. However, downtown Aberdeen is not the place to see this night sky phenomenon. In these northerly locations, you have a much better chance out in the darker hinterland! ■

Castle Menzies at Aberfeldy on Tayside lies in a sheltered position below a wooded hillside

selection of work from the 18th century to the moderns, some of it taking a Scottish theme, plus a few surprises (look out for the watercolors of William Blake and sculpture by Epstein).

Aside from these downtown places, Aberdeen offers other places of interest in **Old Aberdeen**, mainly gathered around the precincts of **King's College**. (Aberdeen grew up around the Dee estuary, while Old Aberdeen lies near the mouth of the River Don.) In Old Aberdeen, as well as a visitor center on the university campus at King's (founded 1494), there is **St. Machar Cathedral**, dating mainly from the 15th century. However, the Brig o'Balgownie is oldest of all – 1320. It spans the River Don at the far side of Seaton Park, overlooked by St. Machar's. It is a sobering thought to stand on a bridge which was already nearly two centuries old when Christopher Columbus first made contact with the New World.

The **Winter Gardens** in Duthie Park, by the River Dee, is a great place to go on a chilly winter day, and there are various attractions aimed at **children**, such as the Satrosphere, a hands-on scientific discovery center, the Beach Leisure Complex, or even the amusement park, the largest in Scotland, also to be found on Beach Boulevard.

★★ ABERFELDY 219D2

Lying 9 miles west of the main A9, Aberfeldy is sometimes bypassed by visitors going north, although it is well worth the digression. The stores are small and friendly. It has a **distillery** and a **water mill** to visit, among other attractions.

Other places nearby include 16th-century Z-shaped **Castle Menzies** on the Weem Road to the west. This is reached by way of the handsome bridge built by General Wade in 1733 over the River Tay, another famous salmon river.

BLACK ISLE 218D4

The Black Isle lacks some of the drama of the northern Highlands, but is an intriguing chunk of landscape, especially the eastern shore along the Moray Firth, with its little villages of Avoch, a former fishing community, and Fortrose, with a ruined cathedral. The chief interest lies at the tip.

Cromarty is a charming Scottish town. Though isolated by geography, it is full of interesting buildings and has seen its fortune rise and fall as a coastal trading and fishing port. The Cromarty courthouse is a good starting point for a short tour on foot. This handsome 1773 building, with its animated figures and tableaux in a courtroom scene, tells the story of Cromarty. Start a personal tape tour of the town from here. Cromarty was also the birthplace of the geologist and theologian Hugh Miller and the cottage where he was born is now a museum (NTS).

★ BLAIRGOWRIE 219E2

Blairgowrie, on the edge of the Highlands, is a town without pretensions. It prospered from the growth of water-powered mills on the banks of the impressively rushing River Ericht. After the mills closed, it became a center for the growing of soft fruits.

If planning a trip to this area over the high pass of Glenshee you will pass Blairgowrie. Stop off to track down the antiques store and the café in the converted granary, and take a peek into Keathbank Mill. With a happy disregard for thematic logic, this former mill on the edge of town is a visitor center and café which combines industrial archeology with a heraldry workshop on a very large scale and also an impressive "0"-gauge model railroad. Railroad enthusiasts will

be interested to know that this is a model of the Norton Fitzwarren junction of Britain's Great Western Railway.

★★★ BREADALBANE 219D2

Breadalbane is not a place you will see signposted. Yet it is a name of great antiquity, meaning the central portion of Highland Perthshire stretching roughly from Aberfeldy right through to Tyndrum. The name is derived from Gaelic *braghaid*, meaning the upper part, and *Alban*, meaning Scotland, hence the uplands – the very heart – of Scotland. This was the country of the Campbells, the Macnabs and Macgregors. It is a land of ribbon lochs, river valleys and high hills.

Tyndrum, at its western edge, is little more than a gathering of hotels, which has been reinvigorated by the discovery of gold in the nearby hills. It lies on an important road junction, as well as on the official long-distance footpath, the West Highland Way.

Crianlarich is also on an intersection, of a railroad junction as well as a road junction. If you enjoy mountain botany, walking, climbing, tracing ancient Scottish history, or just simply being in Highland scenery, then these are good bases, though perhaps the most picturesque settlement is Killin at the west end of Loch Tay. It has an almost alpine flavor, especially when the snow comes to the Ben Lawers range. The Breadalbane Folklore Centre is here (beside the picturesque Falls of Dochart) portraying the local legends, inlcuding the still revered healing stones of Saint Fillan, as well as fairy tales and clan warfare. From anywhere in this area, there are plenty of circular touring options. The western seaboard is within reach, as are the Trossachs (see p.243) and centers such as Perth (see p.234).

WADE'S BRIDGE AT ABERFELDY

The military road builder General Wade built many fine bridges in Scotland, and none so grand as his work at Aberfeldy.

However, it was not to everyone's taste. Dorothy Wordsworth with her brother William, the English Romantic poet, toured Scotland in 1803. She described how they "crossed the Tay by a bridge of ambitious and ugly architecture."

General Wade and his successor General Caulfield improved roads between the 1715 Jacobite Rebellion and the rebellion of 1745 as part of the government's policy of garrisoning the Highlands. The roads were needed to move troops around ■

THE SCOTTISH HIGHLANDS

THE CRIEFF CATTLE TRADE

The Crieff "tryst" or cattle market was an important affair in the days when the Highland black cattle were walked from their pastures in various parts of Scotland to an annual fall fair.

Throughout the north, there was a network of "drove roads" used by the cattle drovers. These old paths through the glens flowed together like tributaries of a river and converged on major markets such as Crieff. Cattle were fattened in the Highland summer, then taken south.

The town of Falkirk superseded Crieff in the trade's latter days, which finally ended with the coming of the railroads which could move livestock more quickly ∎

BUCHAN   219E/F3

The tip of northeast Scotland is Kinnaird Head at Fraserburgh, marking the turning point into the great bite of the Moray Firth. Buchan spreads out in an arc to the southwest. Spare and austere farmlands spread over low rolling hills. The coast has some of the finest beaches and cliffs to be found anywhere in Britain. The local communities are strong and vigorous.

The largest coastal towns of **Peterhead** and **Fraserburgh** are not picturesque. Both have busy and interesting harbors: Peterhead is the largest white fish landing port in Europe, while Fraserburgh has an excellent beach. On the Moray Firth shore, **Macduff** is another fishing community by the mouth of the River Deveron. **Banff** is on the opposite shore, with some architectural surprises in the form of fine Georgian town houses, saved from the redevelopers. Banff also boasts **Duff House**, a grand mansion designed by William Adam, now a newly-opened outstation of the National Gallery of Scotland.

If you want a beach or a clifftop walk to yourself, then choose anywhere between Banff and Peterhead. If agricultural history is of interest, then stop off at **Aden** (pronounced "aa-din") **Country Park**, 10 miles inland from Peterhead. An excellent exhibition deals with the development of farming here and the struggle to take in fields from the moors and mosses. This vivid presentation is entitled *Weel Vrocht Grun* – Scottish for "well-worked ground."

With its granite towns and villages, and its genuine sense of community, as well as a peerless coastline, Buchan is worth exploring for an alternative view of the Scots who live in the north.

★★ CRIEFF   193C4

Rural Perthshire on the Highland edge is cozy and picturesque. Little towns like Crieff, built on the slope of a hill, reflect this sense of well-to-do respectability. Crieff was once an important cattle town where the beasts from the Highlands were sold for southern markets. Then it became a spa and small resort.

Aside from the shopping possibilities, down by the River Earn you will find a cluster of other attractions: a pottery, a paperweight producer and a crystal glassware factory, where you can watch perspiring workers blow and shape molten glass.

Finally, if you still have not managed to solve your gift problems, then take a trip just north of Crieff to the **Glenturret Distillery**, where you can take a tour and a dram – and a look around in the store. There is an excellent heritage center and exhibition here as well.

★★★ DEESIDE   219E3

The River Dee rises in the heart of the Cairngorms and reaches the sea at Aberdeen. It has a good road beside it for more than 60 miles of the trip. It is famous for game fishing and has connections with royalty through **Balmoral Castle**.

In its lower reaches, the Dee flows through rolling wooded and farming country. **Drum** and **Crathes castles** (both NTS) lie in the broad valley and both are worth visiting, especially Crathes, with its fine gardens. The nearby town of **Banchory**, with its handsome, pink granite buildings, is a small resort popular with Aberdeen folk out for the day.

There is more to do and see at well-to-do **Ballater** further up the valley. This little town is close to the royals' castle at Balmoral and many of the Ballater stores are

BALMORAL CASTLE

If you decide to visit Balmoral Castle, the British royals' vacation home on Deeside, then remember that it is a private residence which only opens it grounds and ballroom.

The latter usually houses a painting exhibition from the royal family's extensive private collections. Don't expect to see anything of the rest of the rooms.

Check opening days in advance – usually May, June and July daily except Sunday.

Out of these months, Balmoral is transformed from a visitors' attraction into a high-security playground for the royals and heads of state ■

suppliers, sporting "By Royal Appointment" signs and coats of arms. Ballater offers a worthwhile excursion down **Glen Muick** to the southwest for a fine cross-section of Highland scenery and a near-guarantee of seeing red deer – or at least hearing them roar in the rutting (mating) season, in the fall, when the great antlered stags do battle.

With the woods thickening and the hills closing in, the road leads past Balmoral Castle and the nearby **Royal Lochnagar Distillery** ("By Royal Appointment," naturally), which has a visitor center attached.

At Braemar, the main road turns south to avoid the hills ahead. The village of **Braemar** is the setting for the most famous of the Highland Gatherings, held annually in September. (Highland Games are unique blends of sporting prowess, music and dancing.) The story of the origins of the Gathering at Braemar is told in the Braemar Highland Heritage Centre.

There is a scenic road west as far as the **Linn of Dee**, a picturesque spot below the larches, where the river is confined by water-smoothed rocks.

If you want to walk, seek out the **Devil's Punchbowl** (also known as the Earl of Mar's Punchbowl) on Quoich Water, or the **Colonel's Bed**, a hidden rocky shelf in a gorge in Glen Ey near Inverey, west of Braemar – and yes, a colonel did once sleep there. There are always plenty of legendary stories to discover in the area.

The maturing cellars of the Glenfiddich Distillery at Dufftown have a unique atmosphere which comes from the scent of the whiskey, and the sheer amount and size of the barrels, numbered and dated, lying in the dim light and working towards the day when they can be tasted

★★★ DORNOCH 219D4

One of the most handsome towns in the Highlands, with its pleasing yellow sandstone houses, Dornoch is sometimes called the "St. Andrews of the north" because of its superb **golf** course. The town's skyline is dominated by the spire of Dornoch **Cathedral** which, though much altered over the centuries, dates originally from the 13th century. The former town jail is now a craft center with exhibitions.

As well as miles of beach, dunes and challenging golf, Dornoch is also within easy reach of places of interest such as Dunrobin Castle at Golspie.

★ DUFFTOWN 219E3

The local industry is instantly identifiable, either by a plume of steam or a sweet, grainy scent hanging in the air – Dufftown has a lot of **whiskey distilleries**.

The most famous is **Glenfiddich**, who pioneered the policy of opening the doors to let visitors see what goes on inside these odd buildings.

Above the distillery are the foursquare ruins of ancient **Balvenie Castle** (HS) which gives its name to a local malt whiskey. Down the hill is **Mortlach Church**, an ancient religious site, said to be founded in AD 566. Look for the leper's squint in the church wall – lepers were allowed to come and look in, though they were not allowed in the church.

"Modern" Dufftown dates only from 1817 – a planned town, built by the local landowner – the wide streets and regular layout are typical of northeast Scotland's planned or improved settlements.

★ DUNBLANE 219D1

Sometimes overlooked because of its proximity to Stirling, just off the A9, Dunblane is a quiet place, which originally grew up around its cathedral. In March 1996, tragedy struck Dunblane. The community was devastated when many of their children were massacred by a gun man at the local primary school.

The seat of the local bishop, Dunblane **Cathedral** dates from the 13th century, but followed

the common pattern of destruction and restoration – for example, the nave was roofless for three centuries until 1893.

For military history, drive west to the village of Doune. **Doune Castle** (HS) is Scotland's best-preserved medieval castle, and has often been used as a movie set. This formidable square of buildings represents a 14th-century state of the art security system – note the separate stair-way to each main hall and the emergency exit from the Duke's bedroom. Life was far from secure in medieval Scotland, especially if you were the Duke of Albany, Robert Stewart, and your job was the Scottish Regent, a caretaker king.

★ DUNKELD 219D2

As the main A9 swings down towards the River Tay, you will notice the hills and woods closing in – you are now entering the real Highlands. Dunkeld, just off the road, has picturesque houses and a cathedral, founded in the 12th century and damaged in the Reformation three centuries later. The nave remains roofless; the choir is restored and in use.

Down the road from Dunkeld is the likewise small community of **Birnam**, a name associated with Shakespeare's *Macbeth*, where Birnam Wood marches to signal the doom of Macbeth himself.

On the west side of the A9 is a sign to **The Hermitage** (NTS), where a nephew of the 2nd Duke of Atholl (whose descendant still owns country in the vicinity) built a pleasure ground in the wooded valley of the River Braan. The Hermitage Folly dates from 1753 and consists of a belvedere (basically a circular shelter) overlooking a waterfall. Once it even boasted a mirrored interior which was designed to give the impression of water pouring into the structure from all directions.

DURNESS 218C5

Durness is noted for its fine coastal and mountain scenery, notably at **Faraid Head** and also the famous **Smoo Cave**, a huge cavern formed in the limestone seacliff. The village is a good base for discovering the lonely landscapes around Cape Wrath. To reach the northwestern tip means a ferry crossing of the Kyle of Durness, then a trip by minibus.

★ ELGIN 219E4

Elgin is the largest town in the district of Moray, a commercial and administrative center serving the whiskey country around the River Spey, and the personnel of the nearby air bases. It has been rebuilt many times over the centuries. However, its original central street, now filled with a large church (the "muckle kirk"), as well as the series of alleyways leading off, can still be made out. Look for the arcading dating from the 18th century, which still fronts a few stores.

You will find the handsome ruins of **Elgin Cathedral** (HS) northwest of the main street. "The Lantern of the North," as it was known, was founded in 1224 and burned down in 1390 by the notorious Wolf of Badenoch. This local villain was the fourth son of King Robert II. He was excommunicated by a local bishop for deserting his wife and causing disorder. In revenge, he wrecked the cathedral. Though rebuilt, the cathedral was damaged again during the Reformation. Much stonework was pillaged and used elsewhere, though the structure was taken into the care of the nation in 1825.

Elgin Museum features local dinosaurs, unique to the area; creatures that were only 2 feet high and hopped. There is also a good display on local history.

THE BATTLE OF KILLIECRANKIE

The Jacobites (from the Latin *Jacobus* meaning "James") were supporters of the exiled King James VII of the House of Stewart.

The Battle of Killiecrankie in 1689 was the first attempt by the Jacobites to restore the Stewarts to the throne. At Killiecrankie they won the day, after government forces were unable to withstand the charge of the Highland clans.

However, the Jacobite leader John Graham of Claverhouse, Viscount Dundee, was killed by a stray bullet in his hour of victory. Without Bonnie Dundee's charismatic leadership, the rebellion soon fizzled out ■

THE MASSACRE OF GLENCOE

In 1691, the government ordered all clan chiefs to take an oath of allegiance before January 1, 1692.

Most fell into line, but a chieftain of the Macdonalds of Glencoe, Alisdair Macdonald, called Maclain, was late for the rendez-vous with the local sheriff-deputy. This was excuse enough for the forces of law. Campbell militia (clansmen on the government side) entered the glen, asked for lodging with the clan, which they were granted freely. Several days later, acting on orders from high authority, they turned on their hosts, but bungled the slaughter so that several Mac-donalds escaped into the snow.

In all 36 died, and it was this breaking of a hospitality code – "murder under trust" – that shocked Scotland. The king had blood on his hands ■

★★★ FORT WILLIAM 218C2 and THE ROAD TO THE ISLES

Because of its strategic position, it is almost impossible to avoid Fort William. It was first fortified in 1690, though practically all traces of a fort have now gone. The town has lots of stores of all kinds and in the summer, bustles with activity.

The **West Highland Museum** features a lot of Jacobite material, including a tartan suit said to have belonged to Bonnie Prince Charlie. The summit of Britain's highest mountain, **Ben Nevis** (4,406 feet), lies within 4 miles of the main street, although the main peak cannot be seen from Fort William itself, as it lies beyond a looming shoulder of the mountain. There are fine views of it from the A830 to Mallaig.

This route is sometimes called the **Road to the Isles**, though strictly speaking this name belongs to an old cattle-droving route to the north. The **Glenfinnan Monument** is a popular stopping-off point en route. The monument and visitor center here mark the spot where Bonnie Prince Charlie first set foot on the Scottish mainland in 1745 at the start of his rash escapade to return a Stewart king to the British throne. The road beyond begins to offer superb views of the seas and across to the Inner Hebrides.

Mallaig, at the terminus of both road and railroad, has a fishing and aquarium exhibition, Mallaig Marine World.

Another touring option west of Fort William takes in a pictures-que loop through the area known as Moidart. Just one highlight in this area of very high scenic value is **Castle Tioram**, 14th-century seat of the Macdonalds of Clan Ranald, burned in 1715 and now an atmospheric ruin on a tiny islet inaccessible at high tide.

★★ GAIRLOCH 218C4

On a sparsely populated sea-board, Gairloch is a very important center, though really only a small coastal village. It offers plenty of accommodations, as well as a Heritage Museum, golf, a sandy beach and a choice of local walks and excursions.

One of these is to visit **Inverewe Gardens** (NTS), 6 miles further north. Here a barren headland was transformed from 1862 onwards into a magnificent garden, which takes advantage of the mild air of the North Atlantic Drift to grow a range of exotic plants – though the gardeners here take pains to point out that sub-tropical is not a word they use. Inverewe is a gardening pilgrimage well worth making and is colorful for much of the year.

★★★ GLENCOE 218C2

Scene of the infamous massacre of the Macdonalds by their guests, the Campbells, in 1692, Glencoe is probably the most famous glen in Scotland.

It allows some of the finest hills in the central Highlands to be viewed with no effort from the main road running the length of the glen. The vista takes in **Buchaille Etive Mor** ("the great shepherd of Etive"), the mountain guarding the eastern approaches to the glen, as well as the **Three Sisters**, the three long spurs running off Bidean nam Bian, the highest peak in Argyll. Matching these south side features is the long wall of the **Aonach Eagach** ridge enclosing Glencoe to the north. This is a most spectacular ridge-walk – but no place for the faint-hearted, the unfit or the novice. If you fit into any of these categories, stay in the valley and enjoy the brooding atmosphere of the glen which is so evocative of that ancient treachery.

GREAT GLEN *218C3*

Millions of years ago, the top half of Scotland slipped 60 miles along a fault line. Today, it is along that fault line, the Great Glen Fault, that we can travel 60 miles from east to west by water, thanks to the engineering genius of **Thomas Telford**, who linked the lochs within the glen with the Caledonian Canal of 1803–22. The busy A82 also follows the glen, parallel with the canal.

This route passes by **Spean Bridge**, where the famous Commando Memorial recalls the World War II exploits of the various army units who used the rugged hills around here as a training ground.

Further up the glen at **Fort Augustus**, you can see canal life up close, with the workings of a set of canal locks in the center of the village. Fort Augustus is at the south end of the most famous stretch of water in Scotland – **Loch Ness**, the largest loch in Scotland in terms of volume and the second

deepest (after Loch Morar) at over 800 feet, with dark brown water colored by the peat on the hills around. All this is certainly large enough to support the **Loch Ness Monster** industry – a spread of visitor centers and exhibitions concentrated in Drumnadrochit, halfway up the west side of the loch. The fabled beast's frequency of appearance is in directly inverse proportion to the number of cameras trained on the loch. The cynic's view is that this frequency of appearance is probably related to the number of calm, warm days during the summer, when the large body of water creates mirages, and odd gusts of wind from the hills ruffle the water.

You may prefer the east side of the loch, which is wilder and more peaceful, with superb views from the top of the B862 (another of the area's former military roads) or from Inverfarigaig nearby, which has a pleasant forest walk with a good panoramic view over the loch.

Ben Nevis, at 4,406 feet, is Britain's highest mountain, and yet it is within 4 miles of the main street of Fort William. There are several routes to the top, of varying degrees of difficulty. On the north face is the only patch of snow in Britain that has never been known to melt, even in the hottest summer

HELMSDALE   *219D4*

Beyond Inverness, the main A9 stays close to the coast on its way north. Helmsdale is a kind of frontier on this trip. Beyond it the great moors of **Caithness** roll to the sea, with the road hugging the slopes of rugged headlands. This is the Ord of Caithness.

Before that, however, you can learn much about the area by calling at the **Timespan Heritage Centre** in Helmsdale itself. This touches on many aspects of the local area from prehistoric times to the Highland Clearances and the Kildonan Gold Rush of 1869.

Further along the coast is another cluster of places to visit, centered on the coastal community of **Dunbeath**. There is a heritage center housed in the old school just off the old main road (Dunbeath is bypassed on the A9). This is well worth visiting for the insight into the lives of the locals past and present, as well as the workings of the estates, and a reminder of the future – a display on the oil industry.

A little to the north you will find the **Lhaidhay Croft Museum**, a typical "longhouse," or croft, with house, stable and cowshed in a long line. A friendly curator and an eerie feeling that the owners have just stepped out for a moment give this place an authentic atmosphere.

The **Clan Gunn Heritage Centre** is also nearby.

INNER HEBRIDES   *218B3*

Lying between the peninsula of Kintyre and the island of Skye, the Inner Hebridean islands vary in size. At one end of the scale are the Small Isles, reached from Mallaig or Arisaig.

Muck, **Eigg** and **Canna** represent one extreme of island life – rugged little chips of land on the western horizon. Their neighbor, **Rum**, was once the hideaway of a egocentric, wealthy English industrialist, George Bullough. Now it is a nature reserve where studies of red deer are carried out.

Coll★ and **Tiree**★, which can be reached from Oban, are other examples of out-of-the-way islands. Tiree is flat, so the Atlantic clouds sail straight over, giving the place more than its share of sunshine.

Tobermory, at the northern end of the island of Mull in the Inner Hebrides, is a busy little port with fishing boats and ferries to the mainland, as well as hotels with lively bars and traditional music

Colonsay ★★ is a favorite with many voyagers. Varied habitats of moor, pasture, beach, cliff and woodland give the landscape interest for such a small island. There is an woodland garden at Kiloran House and a ruined priory on Colonsay's neighbor Oronsay, accessible on foot at low tide.

Islay and mountainous Jura are larger. Islay is involved with distilling and farming and has more of a sense of a purposeful community than many of the other islands. A typical Islay malt whiskey is heavy and complex with peaty overtones – try a 16-year-old Lagavulin for a real island experience! Islay also has plenty of wildlife and good beaches. Its neighbor, Jura, by contrast, is sadly depopulated: a series of estates with empty moors, woods and a single road which peters out at the north end of the island. This means you will have to walk if you want to see the outside of Barnhill, where George Orwell wrote the then futuristic novel *1984*.

Mull ★★ is another island that has seen great changes and a widespread dispersal of its native people. It has spectacular coastal scenery on the west side of the island. The restored Duart Castle, seat of the Clan Maclean, is worth a visit, though if time is short you'll find Torosay Castle more entertaining, with its sense of a lived-in family home, as well as its pleasant gardens with their Italian statuary. You can even reach Torosay by rail as a narrow gauge railroad runs from the Craignure pier, where the ferry arrives, to within a short distance of the house itself.

Many visitors make the pilgrimage across Mull to visit tiny Iona, where Saint Columba from Ireland spread the Christian gospel throughout much of the north and west.

★★★ INVERARAY 218C2
Designed by the 3rd Duke of Argyll in 1743, handsome Inveraray offers plenty for visitors, including the present duke's own seat at nearby Inveraray Castle.

Inveraray Jail, one of the handsome Georgian buildings in the town, is now a living museum. The former county prison and courthouse has been converted to show what life was like for prisoners in the 19th century. As well as a tableau in the courtroom, there is an authentically clad warder and prisoner to tell you all about life inside. (After the wax model figures in the tableau, the real-life talking figure can be somewhat startling!)

South of the town, the Auchindrain Old Highland Township is a unique, surviving example of a communal tenancy farm. Many of the old buildings have now been restored, and a visitor center, portrays the rural life of the 18th century through its exhibitions.

THE KILDALTON CROSS
Take time out from the birdwatching, the beaches or the whiskey tasting which Islay offers to journey east along the dead end road at the south end of the island and you will find Kildalton Cross.

This is a tall, ringed cross carved from a single slab of rock. On the shaft and arms are depicted biblical scenes. It is a spectacular piece of workmanship, the more remarkable because it dates from the second half of the 8th century.

The cross has been identified as being of the Iona style, just one of five schools of stone carving flourishing in the West Highlands during medieval times ■

THE SCOTTISH HIGHLANDS

INVERNESS

Though Inverness is not filled with ancient picturesque buildings, this route helps you get your bearings.

From the pedestrian area on High Street, with the spire of Tolbooth Steeple ahead of you, go up Castle Wynd past Inverness Town House, to reach the (mock) castle and the statue of Flora Macdonald. Look for the steps leading down on the other side to the River Ness.

Go down the riverside on Bank Street as far as Fraser Street, on which is situated Abertarff House (NTS), one of the town's oldest buildings.

Afterwards, return to the main shopping area via Church Street, noting the fine Market Arcade ■

INVERNESS *218D3*

Like Fort William at the other end of the Great Glen, Inverness is on the main route north (though the A9 now bypasses it). The "capital of the Highlands" is a booming town with major stores and all the conveniences of a major center. It is without any historical ambience – even its castle is a Victorian replica, serving as a courthouse. As well as catering for all kinds of practical needs from books and maps to gifts, it is a good base for exploring.

Culloden Moor nearby is where the last battle was fought on British soil in 1746 between the Jacobites and the British. Today there is an excellent visitor center on the site.

Further on is the extraordinary **Fort George**, the largest surviving military fortification in Europe and the Hanoverian government's response in the aftermath of Culloden.

Cawdor Castle is also within easy reach of Inverness. Home to the earls of Cawdor for more than 600 years, its venerable, dusty ambience is relieved by entertaining explanatory notes in each room.

★★★ JOHN O'GROATS *219E5*

Is it worth driving all the way up the A9 to reach this famous northerly point? Definitely yes, if you like big, open skies, and if you also take in the naturally-formed columns of rocks known as "sea stacks" off Duncansby to the east of John O'Groats; park near the lighthouse. John O'Groats itself is little more than souvenir and craft stores.

The most northerly point of the mainland is really **Dunnet Head**, west of John O'Groats. Take a look at **Mary Ann's Cottage**, where a local lady's house has been taken over by history enthusiasts. Also in the vicinity is

the **Northlands Viking Centre**, where you are reminded of the influence of those Scandinavian warriors in settling this coast a thousand years ago.

The two main towns here are **Thurso** and **Wick**. The Heritage Centre at Wick tells the story of the town's involvement in the herring fishing industry.

KIRRIEMUIR *219E2*

"Kirrie" is attractive, authentic, and home to friendly people. It is wonderful to leave the main road to Aberdeen and track down this community. It is famous for connections with J.M. Barrie, creator of Peter Pan. The house of his birth (NTS) is open to view.

Kirriemuir is also gateway to the **Angus glens**. If you really want a taste of solitude, then drive up Glen Isla or Glen Clova. In the other direction is **Glamis Castle**, closely asscociated with the present royal family, and the **Angus Folk Museum** (NTS), a row of cottages now converted into a thoroughly sanitized portrait of rural life in the past.

★★ OBAN *218C2*

Oban is built around a sheltered bay. It is both ferry port and tourist center, a dual role which it has performed since the Highlands were first opened up and the railroad came here in 1880. There are plenty of accommodations, a paperweight factory, a distillery, audio-visual displays and summer shows.

McCaig's Folly is prominent above the harbor. It was built by a local banker as a family memorial. Both the folly and Pulpit Hill make excellent viewing points. There is a good choice of **cruising** excursions – Loch Etive is spectacular – as well as a choice of routes by road. Exploring north will take you across the Connel Bridge to the **Sea Life Centre** at Barcaldine.

McCaig's Folly occupies a commanding position above the handsome town and harbor of Oban

TACTICS OF CULLODEN

Culloden was the final showdown in the civil war. The rebels numbered only about 6,000 men from a potential Highland fighting force of 30,000.

However, the fury of a Highland charge was feared by regular infantrymen. The infantryman's bayonet thrust in close fighting was turned aside by the Highlander's leather *targe* (shield) held on his left arm. The Highlander then closed in with his broadsword and *dirk* (short knife). The infantrymen learned to thrust diagonally at the opponent on his right, away from the *targe* towards the enemy's unprotected side. This worked so long as the infantryman's comrade on his left performed the same maneuver at the same time as him! ■

★★ ORKNEY ISLANDS   *219E5*

The green isles of Orkney have a Viking heritage and more prehistoric sites than anywhere else in Britain. The main town, **Kirkwall**, has a number of fine buildings. These include St. Magnus Cathedral (HS), founded by Jarl Rognvald in 1137, still used as a church, and displaying some of Scotland's finest Norman architecture.

Among the prehistoric sites out in the countryside, **Maes Howe** is a huge burial chamber dating from around 2500 BC, later robbed by the Vikings who left some classy graffiti, including the famous design of the Maes Howe dragon.

The **Ring of Brogar** is Orkney's best-known stone circle, with 36 stones surviving from around 60, and there are other mounds and standing stones adding to the mystery of these grand but completely fathomless monoliths.

Skara Brae is yet another unforgettable prehistoric site. In an ancient settlement only rediscovered in 1850, 5,000-year-old stone dressers, beds and cupboards have survived as fittings to the snug circular dwellings, older than the Pyramids of Egypt.

Orkney also has spectacular **bird** and **seal colonies**, plus a more recent heritage as a watering station for polar expeditions and as a naval base – Scapa Flow, which was the main anchorage of the Grand Fleet in both world wars and is recalled in an exhibit at Lyness on Hoy. The east side of Scapa Flow is protected by islands linked by causeways, On tiny **Lambholm** is the remarkable Italian Chapel built by Italian POWs during World War II out of scrap material.

THE FALLS OF BRUAR

The Falls of Bruar are another scenic spot north of Blair Castle. They are accessible from the old A9 and are also within the extensive lands of the dukes of Atholl (135,000 acres of Highland Perthshire valued at some $350 million).

Robert Burns visited here on his Highland tour and suggested to the duke that he might plant more trees to increase the beauty around the falls. The suggestion was taken up and the Falls of Bruar today are noted for their mature woods.

A fairly steep walk uphill to a bridge gives visitors a commanding view of the falls and, perhaps more importantly, makes for a pleasant break from the traffic on the A9 ∎

★★ PERTH   *219D2*

In recent years Perth has become a very desirable place to live, and has seen a net gain in population.

For the visitor, the town has plenty to offer. In its grid of streets, mostly completed in the early 19th century, there is a handsome legacy of impressive buildings as well as plenty of quality stores.

It has a theater, civic museum and art gallery, as well as a military museum at **Balhousie Castle** telling the story of the famous Scottish regiment, the Black Watch. On the edge of town you can find one of the finest of Scotland's small gardens at **Branklyn Garden**, or go a little further out to the **Fairways Heavy Horse Centre**, where you can see working Clydesdale horses in action.

Scone Palace is one of Scotland's grandest stately homes, and as seen today mainly belongs to the early years of the 19th century. It has magnificent collections of porcelain, furniture, ivories, 18th-century clocks and 16th-century needlework, as well as a coffee shop, restaurant, gift stores, playground and fine gardens to explore.

★ PITLOCHRY   *219D2*

Pitlochry is the classic Scottish inland resort town. Queen Victoria's doctor, staying nearby, recommended the wholesome air. Consequently, the well-to-do built large mansions in this previously quiet weaving village.

The arrival of the Perth to Inverness railroad in 1863 accelerated the growth of the fledgling resort, and Pitlochry developed a popularity it has ˙ retained ever since.

The **Hydro-Electric Visitor Centre** in the town overlooks Loch Faskally and has an exhibit on the complex Tummel Valley hydro-electric plan. Another feature of the town is the **Pitlochry Festival Theatre**, showing an easily digestible program right through the main summer season.

To the north is **Killiecrankie** (NTS), not just a very scenic river gorge with woodlands and steep rocks, but a dramatic battle site. A visitor center tells the story of both the battle and the gorge itself, with superb walks among the tall pines and larches.

Combine a trip here with a visit to the Duke of Atholl's **Blair Castle**, the very essence of a grand Scottish fortress, stuffed with weapons and fine furniture – and a dramatic history as well. Blair was the last castle in Scotland to be besieged.

★★★ SHETLAND   *219F5*

Any notion of Scotland as only a land of tartan and Highland dancers will end after 14 hours' steaming by boat due north from Aberdeen (though you can fly). Either way you arrive in the far-flung archipelago of Shetland, a grouping of islands which have nothing to do with Gaelic culture, but have, instead, a strong Scandinavian heritage.

Nowhere in Shetland is more than 5 miles from the sea. It is a place of ever-changing sea-scapes, of vast cliffs thronged with seabirds and fingers of salt water stretching inland.

The sea has brought voyagers since Viking times, giving the main town, **Lerwick**, a cosmo-politan air. Lerwick was founded in the 17th century by Dutch fishermen, and its lanes, flag-stoned streets and harborfront buildings are full of atmosphere.

Over the hill is the old capital of **Scalloway**, complete with a forbidding, 17th-century castle built by the cruel despot Earl Patrick Stewart.

Other places to see on **Mainland** (the main island) include the fascinating **Jarlshof** (HS) on the southern tip. Here, archeologists have unearthed layer upon layer of settlement from the Bronze Age to medieval times. On the way down, call at the **Shetland Croft House Museum**, a preserved small-scale farm, where rural life on the land is vividly brought alive.

On Mainland you will also encounter the mystery of the **brochs**. These are a northern specialty: dry-walled circular towers (like upturned flowerpots in profile) built close to the sea and obviously for defensive purposes. They are perhaps 2,500 years old, and nobody is absolutely certain who built them. There is a well-preserved one,

Clickhimin Broch (HS), just outside Lerwick, while the very finest one is to be found on the outer island of Mousa.

Shetland's other main islands include **Yell** and – perhaps more interesting – **Unst**, especially as you can go there and boast you have seen the most northerly Scottish castle (Muness), the most northerly post office, at Haroldswick, or the most northerly lighthouse at the delightfully named Muckle Flugga. To see this last place, you must walk to Herma Ness, a nature reserve on the very tip. Do not try to do all of this on a day trip from Lerwick – find accommodation on Unst. Since you have come all this way, it is worth making the most of this very different aspect of Scotland.

SCAPA FLOW AND THE GERMAN FLEET

At the end of World War I the German High Seas Fleet was interned at the British naval base at Scapa Flow (see also p.233).

The German naval officers made secret arrangements to ensure their fleet would not be used by the British against them. The result was the simultaneous scuttling of the German Fleet on a mid-summer day in 1919.

In doing so, they created a massive amount of scrap metal which was salvaged for years afterwards.

However, not all the ships were raised, and the hulks still lying on the seabed contribute to what is rated as Britain's best amateur diving site ■

Jarlshof is a very ancient settlement dating to prehistoric times. It has been extensively excavated and is now preserved with grassy banks and viewing platforms

DRIVE

HIGHLANDS CASTLE TRAIL

137 miles (allow 2 days)

Located away from the turbulent mainstream of the warring past, many castles survive intact.

This tour takes in some of the finest examples, and shows the sheer variety of the surrounding countryside, which ranges from high hill pass to wooded river valley.

VARIATIONS ON THE CASTLE THEME

Aberdeenshire has a variety of castle architecture.

This ranges from early *mottes* (see p.14), to later immense structures, the great castles of enclosure closely related to mainstream European traditions of which Kildrummy by the River Don is an example.

Later still are the ornate castles built by successful merchants and entrepreneurs like William Forbes' Craigievar Castle (1626). However, this castle has been so popular that it has had to close to visitors, following damage to its ornate ceilings ■

Leave Aberdeen by the A90 south, then take a left at the Stonehaven slip/access road.

1 **Stonehaven, Aberdeenshire**
Many towns close to Aberdeen have become "dormitories," but Stonehaven has retained its character as well as some interesting stores. Originally a fishing settlement, it was extended in 1795 by a local laird who built a grid of wide streets around a square a little way from the old harbor. This plan survives today. Visit the 16th-century harborside **Tolbooth**, now the local museum. To the south lies **Dunnottar Castle**, a 14th-century stronghold on a dramatic headland. Watch out for the worn steps of this complex of buildings ringed by cliffs. The Scottish crown jewels were hidden here during the Commonwealth Wars of the 17th century.

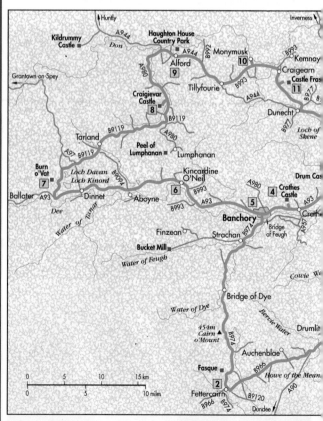

Leave by the A957, turn right and rejoin the divided highway A90, continuing south for 7 miles to the B966, then turn right to Fettercairn.

2 Fettercairn, Aberdeenshire

The center of this peaceful little place on the edge of the hills is dominated by a grand Gothic arch commemorating a visit by Queen Victoria in 1861. **Fettercairn Distillery** runs a tour and an audio-visual presentation on one of Scotland's oldest distilleries.

To the north is the faded grandeur of **Fasque House**, home of the descendants of William Gladstone, Queen Victoria's prime minister. Further on, the road climbs to the Cairn

o' **Mount**, an old pass into Deeside. It offers spectacular views over Angus and down to the sea.

Leave by the B974 north. Once over the Cairn o' Mount, turn right at Strachan to reach Banchory. Go right on the main A93, then follow signs (left) for Drum Castle 26 miles on.

3 Drum Castle, Aberdeenshire

The original part of Drum Castle (NTS), its large square tower, dates from the 13th century, with a 17th-century Jacobean mansion house adjacent. There is much of interest inside, while the building itself stands in a fragment of the ancient Caledonian Forest, Scotland's native tree cover, known as the "Old Wood of Drum."

Return to the A93, turn right, then follow signs for Crathes Castle 6 miles away.

4 Crathes Castle (NTS), Aberdeenshire

This is one of Aberdeenshire's very finest castles, with exceptional interior decoration, notably its painted ceilings. As a further bonus, the gardens are also of the very highest caliber, set within topiary yew hedges.

Return on the A93 for 3 miles to Banchory.

5 Banchory, Aberdeenshire

An attractive little town of characteristic pink granite, often busy with day visitors from Aberdeen. The nearby **Brig o'Feugh** (Bridge of Feugh) is a popular place to watch salmon leaping the rapids of the River Feugh during their migrations upriver to spawn.

Follow the A93 west to Kincardine O'Neil.

THE CAIRN O' MOUNT

The Cairn o' Mount recalls the name The Mounth, from the Gaelic *monadh,* **meaning moorland and mountain.**

The Mounth name survives as part of the names of other ancient routes through this mountain barrier which sits to the south of Royal Deeside and is crossed by only a few other roads today.

The Cairn part refers to the giant heap of stones at the highest point, by a parking lot with an annotated panorama board. This cairn goes back to about 2000 BC, with its skyline shape doubtless altered by the endless generations of travelers who have passed this way ∎

THE STONE OF DESTINY

The Stone of Destiny, or the Stone of Scone, was the crowning seat of Scottish monarchs until stolen by King Edward of England in 1297.

It can be seen today in Westminster Abbey in London, although in July 1996 it was decided that it should be returned to Scotland, either to St. Margaret's Chapel in Edinburgh Castle, or St. Giles Cathedral in Glasgow. At the time of writing, it was not known when this would take place.

Controversy has always surrounded the Stone. Some Scots believe it is a fake, while some historians think the real Stone was hidden before Edward's arrival, and only found again in the early 19th century.

It then either vanished again or remains hidden, awaiting Scotland's independence. Whatever the truth, the Stone remains a powerful symbol of nationalist sentiment among many Scots ■

6 Kincardine O'Neil, Aberdeenshire

This is one of Deeside's earliest settlements, a formerly important crossing place of the River Dee and a resting place for travelers coming off the high passes to the south. The ruined church was founded in 1233 for this purpose and has a 14th-century doorway.

Continue on the A93. Turn right on the B9119. Burn o' Vat parking lot is on the left.

7 Burn O' Vat, Aberdeenshire

The birch and pinewood here has a circular path, with boards underfoot and steps, so that most can reach the point on the Vat Burn where it tumbles through a rocky hollow formed by glaciers about 12,000 years ago. This out-of-the-way cleft was formerly used to hide stolen cattle.

There is also a fine view over the nearby lochs Davan and Kinnord, two "kettleholes" formed by melting iceblocks. The whole area is a **nature reserve** and there are a variety of other walks in the woods starting from the east side of the A97.

Continue on the B9119; go left at the A980.

8 Craigievar Castle (NTS), Aberdeenshire

This picturesque castle, off the B980, can be seen from outside only at present.

Continue on the A980 then bear right on the A944 for Alford.

9 Alford, Aberdeenshire

At Alford (pronounced "aa-furd") is the **Grampian Transport Museum**, with the *Craigievar Express* – a steam-driven road vehicle of 1895, built by the local mailman. **Haughton Country Park** is nearby, where people come to picnic and ride the narrow-gauge railroad. There is an interesting excursion along the A944 to the magnificent ruin of 13th-century **Kildrummy Castle**, built to a shield-shaped plan and the center of dramatic tales involving both English invaders and Jacobite rebels. Below is **Kildrummy Castle Garden**, built in the quarry which supplied the stone for the castle.

From Alford, take the A944 towards Aberdeen. Turn left on the B993, and left again on an unclassified road for Monymusk.

10 Monymusk, Aberdeenshire

This typical estate village, with its attractive terraced cottages, was built for his farmworkers by the laird, Sir Archibald Grant, who also planted 50 million trees on his land. Monymusk was also a very ancient settlement, a religious community of Irish origin predating the late 12th-century St. Mary's Church by centuries.

Return to the B993, continue east and turn right on a minor road for Craigearn, then right again for Castle Fraser.

11 Castle Fraser, Aberdeenshire

Castle Fraser (NTS) is another magnificent example of the native flowering of castle building in this part of Scotland. Gradually developed from the mid-15th century to the early 19th century, this is a truly impresssive castle with fine towers and turrets. It also has an attractive, warm, walled garden.

Turn left after leaving the castle grounds on an unclassified road. Go right on the B977 and left on the A944 (at Dunecht) for Aberdeen.

★★★ SKYE, ISLE OF 218B3

The Isle of Skye exerts a magnetic pull on visitors. It is a byword for spectacularly craggy mountains. Thus it is forgiven its relentlessly wet climate, which is inevitable as the big hill masses get in the way of the prevailing Atlantic weather fronts moving out of the southwest.

The new bridge linking Skye with the mainland may do little for the immediate scenery of the Kyle of Lochalsh, the strait between, but should make it even more popular with visitors.

As generations have done before them, they will come to gaze on the rocky spires of the **Cuillins** from Sligachan (on the main road to Portree, the largest town), or take the narrow road to Elgol to see the other side of the Cuillins across Loch Scavaig. This vista has inspired writers such as Sir Walter Scott and artists of the caliber of J.M.W. Turner.

In addition to the Cuillins, Skye has plenty of other scenic wonders, thanks to its complex geology of overlapping ancient **lava flows**. At one point, the **Quiraing**, they have slipped steadily but infinitesimally over the ages to create a weird landscape of pinnacles and dislodged rock-tables.

Away from topographic curiosities, **Dunvegan Castle**, seat of the chief of the Clan Macleod, is also on many visitors' itineraries. As there have been Macleods here for seven centuries, there is plenty of historic material to see, including the famous **Fairy Flag**, which all clansfolk believe will save them just once more if waved in time of need or battle.

Back in Portree, find time to visit the **Skye Heritage Centre**, which tells the story of the island from the crofters' point of view, which makes a change from the heroic clan tales! The **Skye Museum of Island Life** is based on a former croft and has plenty of rural artifacts, which add a touch of realism.

Incurable romantics can always visit Flora Macdonald's grave. She helped Bonnie Prince Charlie avoid capture while on the run after the Battle of Culloden.

The Cuillins, as seen from Sligachan, still snowbound, make for rugged and demanding climbing country

KILT ROCK

The geology of Skye is inescapable.

A parking lot on the A855 by Ellishader in Trotternish marks Kilt Rock. Here, the sea cliff is composed of vertically jointed dolerite. Erosion has resulted in a curious pleated effect, like a kilt.

There is a safe viewing area, fenced off, by the cliff edge ■

The view from the Cairngorms towards Loch Morlich and Aviemore show the almost uniform, rounded heights and hollows created by glaciers in the last Ice Age

THE ARCTIC IN SCOTLAND

The Cairngorms is the collective name for the high plateau to the south of Aviemore and which have four of the five highest mountains in Scotland.

The highest areas are Arctic tundra unique in Britain. The area is a battleground for conservationists versus ski resort developers ■

★★★ SPEYSIDE   *219D3*

The valley of the River Spey runs from the Grampians in a north-easterly direction down to the Moray Firth. It is often marked on maps as Strathspey (from the Gaelic *strath*, which means "a broad valley"), while the local tourism authorities have anglicized it to "Spey Valley" (which has, understandably, upset the purists). Whatever it is called, it is a beautiful stretch of countryside, leading from the estuary, with its seal-haunted beach, to the headwaters in the lonely hills many miles away and known as the *Monadliath*, (Gaelic for "the gray moors").

In between lie handsome towns like **Fochabers**, near the coast, with its plethora of antiques stores and an excellent local history display, and **Aberlour**, another neat little place built from sturdy granite and well worth a stroll along its main street. Further upstream, beyond Grantown-on-Spey among the old pinewoods, the great mass of the **Cairngorms** looms. There are ospreys to spot by Loch Garten, a

preserved steam railroad nearby at Boat of Garten, and all the commercial developments of the winter ski center of **Aviemore,** with its modern and rather brutal concrete high-rise architecture which can be something of a shock if you are expecting a picturesque Highland village.

Further west, the Spey's character changes, moving sluggishly and spreading into a reedy loch used by waterfowl (there is a nature reserve here, at Loch Insh). The river passes close by **Kingussie**, where you should take in the **Highland Folk Museum** for its illuminating picture of primitive Highland life in times gone by.

At nearby **Newtonmore**, the **Clan Macpherson Museum** contains many relics associated with the clan, and tells the tale of Ewen Macpherson of Cluny, who after the Battle of Culloden took refuge in a hideout high on the slopes of Ben Alder, called "Cluny's Cage."

Thereafter, the Spey leaves the main road, though you can follow it into remote country on a small single-track road which goes for 17 miles as far as **Garvamore Bridge**, a military bridge built by General Wade in 1735.

★★★ STIRLING 219D1

Stirling is one of the most exciting of Scottish towns and it has played a key role in Scotland's history. It was for centuries a strategic crossroad controlling movement between the Lowlands and the Highlands. Whoever commanded Stirling Castle (HS) controlled Scotland. Therefore the **Battle of Bannockburn**, which secured Scotland's liberty from the English for almost four centuries, was fought within sight of the castle walls in 1314. An informative visitor center (NTS) on the site tells the full story.

Most visitors make their way to the **castle** which dominates the town's skyline from its high rock. The fine Renaissance work in the former royal court of the Stewart monarchs has had some of its former splendors restored and it is well worth taking a tour.

There is a good exhibition and display within the castle as well as in the **Royal Burgh of Stirling Visitor Centre** on the Esplanade just outside the castle walls. The views from the Esplanade and the ramparts are magnificent, taking in much of the lower valley of the River Forth, Scotland's central corridor, as well as long views to the distant Highlands, notably the high peaks beyond Loch Lomond.

The **old town** of Stirling nestles below the Esplanade with High Street, the mercat cross and Tolbooth all adding to the ambience. Several historic buildings have survived, including the magnificent Kirk of the Holy Rude (1456). You can have a cup of coffee at Darnley's House at the foot of the High Street – said to be the place where Lord Darnley, Mary, Queen of Scots' somewhat sulky and unco-operative husband, used to prefer to stay when his wife had business in the castle!

Further down, the later Victorian developments start, with plenty of **shopping** opportunities including excellent antique books and prints, outdoor wear and jewelry. In the center of Stirling is the **Thistle Centre**, a modern shopping mall. A walk down the hill is like going straight from a medieval scene through the centuries to the present day.

Stirling also has a good art gallery and museum, the **Smith Art Gallery**. It is along the road from the tourist information center (which has an impressive section of the old town wall just opposite). For another good view of Stirling, make your way to the **National Wallace Monument**. This high tower on a crag was built by the Victorians in a fit of patriotic nostalgia in celebration of the first of Scotland's freedom fighters, William Wallace. You will meet Wallace himself (or at least an eerie hi-tech "talking head") within his battle tent, and there are other audio-visuals and displays telling his story.

After the steep walk to the tower you may need to take time out at the little café – and you will definitely need some refreshment if you climb the dizzying spiral stairs right to the top of the tower for views over the valley and the landscaped parklands of the modern university below.

Stirling makes its history come alive with a **summer program** of costume drama both in the streets and in the castle. With *ceilidhs* (Scottish musical evenings) and pipe bands galore, Stirling can be a memorable experience for a visitor who takes time to look.

Looking across Upper Loch Torridon towards Beinn Alligin there are some spectacular views. But this is also otter country, so sit quietly and keep your eyes open

TOMINTOUL   219E3

This is the highest village in the Highlands, at 1,160 feet, and it sits on a windy plateau within a ring of hills. The Duke of Gordon planned and built the settlement around 1776. It has its own stores and a museum as well, and makes a good base for exploring the sometimes overlooked corner between the better-known valley of the River Spey to the north and Royal Deeside to the south.

The A939 which takes you there is a former military road snaking over the brown heathery domes of the Grampians and passing the lonely tower of 16th-century **Corgarff Castle** on the way. Many tales are associated with this lonely spot, including its burning and later re-fortification for use by government troops who formerly spent much time hunting for illegal whiskey stills. The road to Tomintoul still leads on to Scotland's finest whiskey country today.

★★★ TORRIDON   218C3

If you are in Inverness and want to see some authentic western landscapes instead of a busy town, just keep driving for about an hour and you will eventually reach Glen Torridon.

If the Trossachs (see p.243) represent romantic grandeur, the Torridon hills represent something much wilder and on a larger scale. A mecca for Scottish hillwalkers and climbers, the ancient red sandstone, with its topping of pale quartzite, is sculptured and split into rock terraces and cliffs. The mountains of **Beinn Alligin**, furthest west,

Liathach, like an upturned boat, and the long-toothed ridge of **Beinn Eighe** loom over the single-track road running through the glen. You will either love these elemental, naked rock forms, or want to scurry back to the relative softness of the Moray Firth coast.

Among other places, there are accommodations at tiny Kinlochewe at the east end of the glen, or at Shieldaig, spread along a crescent of bay. If time permits, explore the north side of **Loch Torridon**, switchbacking as far as Diabaig, which clings to the side of a steep slope overlooking the loch.

★★★ TROSSACHS and CALLANDER   218D1

As the Romantic Movement in art and poetry grew, there came a change in attitude to wild landscapes. While the 18th century had found such places brutal and vulgar, the new travelers attached a romance and grandeur to all things natural. Besides, the Highlanders had been "tamed" after the last uprising half a century before. Almost within sight of the burgeoning cities of Edinburgh and Glasgow there was a cluster of hills where wooded slopes were reflected in beautiful lochs. The prospect was pleasing and wild – but not too wild. Just into the Highlands and no more, the Trossachs caught the mood of the age. They still remain synonomous with fine, green Scottish scenery of the kind which decorates souvenir boxes of shortbread.

You can set the Trossachs in their historic context by starting at the **Rob Roy and Trossachs Visitor Centre** in **Callander**. Within a few minutes of Stirling, this tourist town is the Trossachs' main gateway. The visitor center in a former church on the main street introduces the local folk hero, Rob Roy, a kind of Robin Hood in a kilt (except he was real) and describes Rob's life of cattle rustling and skirmishing with Lowland law from his base in the secret places of the Trossachs. Both the daring deeds of Rob Roy Macgregor and the beauties of the Trossachs were made even more popular by the writings of Sir Walter Scott. The town itself has cafés and wool stores galore.

Afterwards head west (stopping for a steamboat trip on Loch Katrine if time permits) to enjoy the view from the highest point on the **Duke's Road** (the main A821) over the forests and hills, before dropping down to the village of Aberfoyle, where the Scottish Wool Centre might further delay you.

WALKS

CALLANDER CRAGS

From Callander's busy main street, take the path into the woods beside the tennis courts. Climb up until the path goes right and emerges on a rocky edge. The route continues to the highest point of Callander Crags. Here you can see as far as the Pentland Hills. Continue in an easterly direction, watching your step as you cross the rocky slabs, to descend to the tarred road.

Go right, back down the glen. You will see a parking lot in the trees. Go left here for the Bracklinn Falls, a picturesque waterfall. Return to the parking lot, then go downhill through the woods, emerging back on the main street in Callander ■

WALK

NOSS

For a memorable day watching Shetland's bird-life, catch the ferry from Lerwick to Bressay.

It's about 2 miles by road to the next ferry crossing which takes you to Noss, a National Nature Reserve with an information center.

Walk east, then follow the southern shore of Noss over rising ground, following the perimeter of the island. Eventually you come to an awesome view of the Noup of Noss, with vast cliffs and colonies of seabirds. Be very careful here! The cliffs are high and they overhang in places.

Continue your anti-clockwise circuit of the island, descending gradually until you are back to the ferry port ■

★★ ULLAPOOL   218C4

The British Fisheries Society was founded in 1786 with the specific aim of exploiting the rich resources offshore and bringing prosperity to the marginal agricultural land of the west.

The herring of **Loch Broom**, a large fjord-like inlet, prompted the society to build Ullapool as a fishing port. Today, the wide streets and grid plan of this small northwest Highland town are still plain to see. Though the herring came and went, there is still a fishing connection, most apparent when the Russian *klondykers*, or factory ships, are in the bay. Otherwise, Ullapool caters for visitors with its museums, gift shops and fine pottery. Because Ullapool is linked with Stornoway in Lewis by ferry, the town also has a good range of accom-modations, and some excellent fish restaurants.

It is also a good base for excursions to the ancient eroded mountains to the north around the **Inverpolly Nature Reserve**. If exploring this wild area, note that the coastal loop road also leads to **Lochinver**, an attractive northwestern fishing port on a rugged coastline.

WESTERN ISLES   218B4

The Western Isles (or Outer Hebrides) lie in a long line from the Isle of Lewis down to Barra. They are the heartland of the Gaelic language and are noted for their distinctive culture and way of life. On Lewis, the old Sabbatarianism is still very strong – so do not expect anything to be open on a Sunday. The folk here are friendly and proud and such customs should be respected.

Keep in mind that **Lewis** and **Harris** are one island. Lewis is noted for beaches, standing stones and other prehistoric sites. Most of the settlement is on the

coast. Inland Lewis is mostly rolling empty moor whose black peat is cut, stacked, dried and used for fuel.

Visit the **Standing Stones of Callanish** (HS) – a cross-shaped setting of stones which have stood in the wind, magnificently atmospheric, for about 5,000 years. You should also see the Black House at Arnol on the west coast. This is a preserved typical dwelling of the recent past – black because of the peat smoke which finds its way out through a hole in the roof, blackening furniture and inhabitants.

Harris ★★ is mountainous, empty and has arguably the very best beaches in Scotland (if a little on the chilly side). In Harris the sense of scant population is very strong – this is the edge of Europe in many ways, with a long history of clearance and depopu-lation, and every so often a scheme emerges to revitalize the local economy. The latest, now abandoned, was to remove a whole mountain near the south-ern tip of the island to create a superquarry in order to build highways in far-off England. Many of the protesting voices were not native born, but settlers escaping the rat-race of the cities. They now fear that the islands' unspoil-ed solitude will be lost for ever.

Further down the island chain lie **Benbecula** and the **Uists**, linked together by causeways. Long sandy shores face the Atlantic (nearest western neighbor: Newfoundland, Canada) with white crofts facing out over the *machair*, a rich shell sand bound together with grass and wild flowers.

The chain of islands trails away southwards toward **Barra**, where Kisimul Castle, stronghold of the Macneils, stands in Castle Bay, and beyond to other tiny Hebridean outposts.

NORTHERN IRELAND

One Irish writer perfectly sums up
Northern Ireland as "a place apart."
This often beautiful and politically,
historically and religiously
fascinating region of the island
of Ireland is very much Irish in
character yet, for the foreseeable
future, part of the United Kingdom

CALENDAR OF EVENTS

MAY – Belfast Civic Festival and Lord Mayor's Show. Concerts, competitions and parades are in abundance during the second and third week of May.

JUNE 2-5 – Guinness Canal Festival, Newry. A floats and bathtubs race on the canal, followed by celebrations.

JULY 1 – Northern Ireland Game and Country Fair, Shane's Castle, Antrim. Crowds gather to watch this field sports event covering all aspects of country life and sport.

AUGUST – SUMMER BANK HOLIDAY. The "Ould Lammas Fair," Ballycastle, Causeway Coast. Ireland's oldest country fair ■

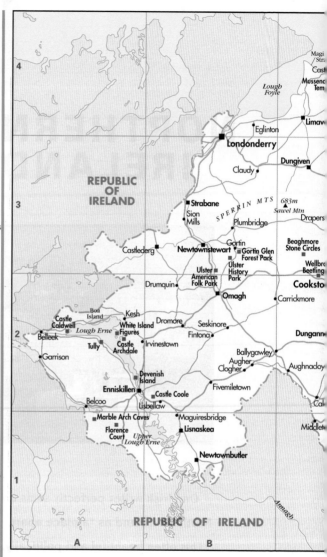

NORTHERN IRELAND

The Troubles – the euphemistic word commonly used to describe the province's political unrest – seemed to be coming to an end when, at midnight on August 31, 1994, the IRA (Irish Republican Army) announced a ceasefire in its campaign of violence; in January, 1995, British troops stopped patroling the streets in daylight hours, but in 1996 several bomb explosions in the U.K. put an end to the ceasefire.

Another ceasefire was agreed in July 1997, and the peace process was re-established when voters in both Northern Ireland and the Republic overwhelmingly supported the April 1998 peace agreement, and in June 1998 the Northern Ireland Assembly was

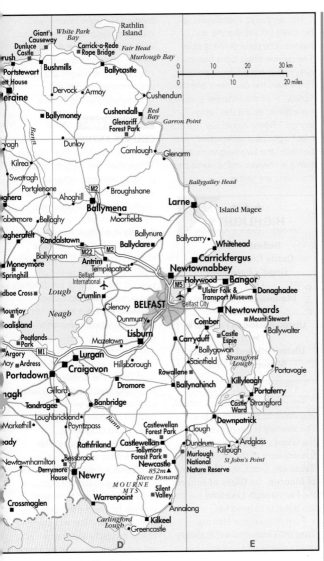

CALENDAR OF EVENTS

SEPTEMBER
18-22 – That Elusive Irish Ancestor, Armagh and Omagh. Family history conference with lectures, workshops, and tours of the Ulster countryside.

SEPTEMBER 29– OCTOBER 1 – Irish Bird-Watching and Wildlife Fair, Lough Neagh Discovery Centre, Oxford Island.

OCTOBER 1-3 – Banks of the Foyle Festival, Londonderry. Literature, dance, theater and comedy along with folk, classical, rock and cathedral music.

NOVEMBER – Belfast Festival, Queen's University, Belfast. This is one of Europe's top arts festivals and is a major attraction ■

elected. This was once again threatened in August 1998 when the so-called "Real IRA", a splinter group opposed to Northern Ireland peace, were responsible for a bomb explosion in Omagh.

Security forces are still evident in Northern Ireland, and you will still have to pass through checkpoints at the border with the Republic, but this should not deter you from visiting. Even before the ceasefire Northern Ireland was one of the safer places to take a vacation, with low levels of street crime. Added to this is the warmth of welcome you will receive: locals are very eager to disabuse you of the province's tarnished image, and are exuberant with thanks for your being broadminded enough to visit them.

ORANGEMEN AND HIBERNIANS

All around Northern Ireland Orangemen parade on July 12 to commemorate the victory of Protestant William III (of Orange) over Catholic James II at the Battle of the Boyne in 1690.

While there have been parades through Catholic areas, they are usually peaceful affairs (although there was considerable unrest at the 1995 and 1996 marches).

Dressed traditionally in orange sashes and bowler hats, the Orangemen march to the deafening sound of drums, pipes and flutes under the flag of a particular Orange Lodge and the Union Jack.

On August 15 the Catholics have their day as the Ancient Order of Hibernians march to different tunes dressed in sashes of green (the symbolic color of Ireland) ∎

Not only in its friendliness is Northern Ireland like the rest of Ireland. The pace of life is slow. The cuisine often lacks finesse, but comes in mammoth portions. In the bars the Guinness and the "crack" – as the repartee is called – are great, as are the "sing-alongs." Some would say that the most significant differences between the two neighbors are that it is cheaper in the north and the roads are better.

★★★ HIGHLIGHTS

Belfast (▶ 248)
Castle Coole (▶ 255)
Giant's Causeway (▶ 252)
Mountains of Mourne (▶ 255)
Ulster-American Folk Park (▶ 256)
Ulster Folk and Transport Museum (▶ 256)

For what other reasons should you come to Northern Ireland? The scenery is the prime allure – the Giant's Causeway, one of the wonders of the world on the Causeway Coast, the Mountains of Mourne, the Glens of Antrim, the Fermanagh Lakeland are the top districts to head for.

Furthermore, the National Trust (NT) manages a remarkably large collection of properties in the province, including a number of fine Palladian stately homes. There are also a few first-rate open-air museums which bring to life Ulster's history, including its close ties with the United States of America.

If you wish, it is easy to turn your back on the Troubles as a tourist by avoiding the main cities and areas like South Armagh. Yet to get even a superficial under-standing of the complexities of

modern Northern Ireland, you must visit fascinating Derry and especially the capital Belfast, where, immediately outside the city centers, the signs of poverty and sectarian enmity are unfortunately all too evident.

★★★ BELFAST   247D2

COUNTY ANTRIM

In the capital of Northern Ireland, "Protestant and Catholic ghettoes grind against each other like angry millstones, turning out an endless harvest of death and injury." Thus began a feature on the city in a British newspaper in 1993. Times, of course, have changed since then, but first-time visitors who came to the city even at the height of the Troubles and avoided the depressed enclaves (which is easy to do if you wish) would commonly express surprise at the normality and seeming prosperity of the city. Heavy economic subsidies have made the largely pedestrianized center surprisingly pristine for a city with such a scarred reputation, and a vast investment program is regenerating the docks. The Golden Mile may not live up to its glamorous name, but you will find a concentration of places to eat and drink along here good enough to rival most regional cities in Britain. The arts scene – opera, concerts and drama – is upbeat too, invigorated by a large student population.

Belfast is a product of the Victorian industrial age. Ship-building, engineering, linen and rope-making flourished here, and the decline of these industries has led to massive unemploy-ment and working-class poverty. The city's most enduring peaceful symbols are the two great yellow Harland and Wolff dockyard cranes, nicknamed Samson and Goliath, while numerous haughty

Victorian buildings fill the city center. **City Hall**, on Donegall Square, is the most impressive structure, topped by handsome copper domes, with elaborate stucco and a staircase of three types of Italian marble inside.

Guided tours (Wednesday mornings only) also visit the council chamber where Unionists sit face to face with rival SDLP (Socialist Democratic Labour Party) and Sínn Fein councilors. The handsome **Linen Hall Library**, also on the square, makes a peaceful sanctum.

Victorian churches which deserve to be sought out include Roman Catholic **St. Malachy's**, on Alfred Street, for its over-the-top interior, and **Sinclair Seamen's Church**, in dockland, for its nautical theme – the pulpit is made from a ship's prow and the organ bears port and starboard navigation lights.

But Belfast's most widely enjoyed piece of Victoriana must be the **Crown Liquor Saloon** on Great Victoria Street opposite the often bombed multistoried Europa Hotel. Here you can eat Guinness and Strangford oysters in the privacy of your own paneled "snug" amid a riot of color and ornamentation of scrolled lions, griffins and leaf-patterned pillars. From the pub the Golden Mile heads south down Great Victoria Street to **Queen's University** and the extensive, wide-ranging **Ulster Museum**. It includes everything from fine art to a dinosaur gallery, but its strength lies in its study of the history of the province and city, as well as in its antiquities such as treasures from the *Girona*, a ship from the Spanish Armada which was wrecked off the north coast.

Those with something of an intrepid disposition should venture into **West Belfast**, the city's poverty-stricken sectarian heartland. The best way to visit is by taxi: the driver might furnish you with lots of local color (i.e. who was killed where). For trips into the **Catholic Falls** go to the Republican taxi stand at Castle Street; to venture into Protestant

SOME BELFAST ADVICE

"There is a story that when incoming jets throttle back for the approach to Belfast's Aldergrove Airport, the pilots tell their passengers to put their watches back to local time – 1690." Quoted by Russell Miller, *Sunday Times*, April 27, 1980 ∎

The elaborate Victorian City Hall on Belfast's Donegall Square has guided tours of its impressive and extravagant interior

NORTHERN IRELAND

THE ULSTER WAY

The Ulster Way forms a 560-mile circular footpath around the whole of the province.

It sticks pretty close to the coast for most of the time, cuts across the Mountains of Mourne, heads up to Lough Neagh, out to western County Fermanagh and returns to the north coast by way of the Sperrin Mountains.

Parts of the walk are well signposted, but others are not.

The Northern Ireland Tourist Board publishes an excellent leaflet which details circular walks based on the best sections of the long-distance footpath ■

Shankill go to the Loyalist taxi stand at Castle Street.

Republican flags and lamp-posts painted white, yellow and green mark the **Falls Road**. You could buy your own flag from the Sínn Fein office along with Republican calendars and book-lets of Irish resistance songs. Look out for street murals, their high-quality artwork at odds with messages of hate and images of masked gunmen. Some of the best can be seen on the edge of the Ballymurphy Estate.

The **Peace Line**, sometimes palisade metal fencing, some-times a wall, slinks between the Falls and Shankill, in places cutting terraced streets in two. On its northern side the curb-stones are painted red, white and blue and a few Union Jacks fly, while a set of Loyalist murals can be seen on Percy Street just off the **Shankill Road**.

ANTRIM, GLENS OF COUNTY ANTRIM   247D3

The Antrim Coast Road clings to the water's edge from Larne around to Ballycastle, skirting the mouths of nine valleys, or glens, as it passes through a number of sleepy villages. At each, a winding lane ascends a wooded valley and onto moorland and stone-walled fields.

The Gaelic-named glens have translations: the first two, Glenarm and Glencloy, mean "glen of the army" and "glen of the hedges," for example. **Glenarriff** (the plowman's glen), described by William Thackeray as a "mini-Switzerland," is the most visited. Flat bottomed and wide where it meets the sea, it becomes flanked by high, steep, rocky ridges higher up as it narrows to a "V" and reaches a forest park with waterfalls.

Glen Ballyemon (the glen of Eamon's Town), **Glenaan** (the

glen of rush lights) and **Glencorp** (the glen of the slaughter) all meet to rush down to **Cushen-dall**, "capital of the glens," which is distinguished by its Curfew or Garrison Tower. At the bottom of **Glendun** (the brown glen), the National Trust owns the pretty village of Cushendun, its whitewashed cottages designed and built by Clough Williams-Ellis of Portmeirion fame (see p.166).

Murlough Bay is bewitchingly beautiful and remote. Back lanes take you through lime green hillsides covered in windbent trees and rocky outcrops where sheep play King of the Castle to a ridiculously isolated cottage at the edge of the sea. In the past, local Protestants would row across the channel from here to the visible Mull of Kintyre in Scotland for church on Sundays.

★★ ARMAGH and AROUND, COUNTY ARMAGH   246C2

The city of Armagh is, surprisingly, the ecclesiastical capital of all Ireland since Saint Patrick (see p.252) chose it as his main church in AD 445. Rival cathedrals, both dedicated to Saint Patrick, crown two of Armagh's seven small hills.

Brian Ború, a warrior king who evicted the Vikings from Ireland, is buried in the Gothic **Protestant Cathedral**. Mosaics and a painted, vaulted ceiling make the 19th-century **Catholic cathedral** remarkably lavish. A spread of fine Georgian architecture dignifies the streets below, best seen around the green sward of **The Mall**, once the city's racecourse, and now a tranquil park and cricket ground.

The buildings here include the comprehensive Armagh County Museum and the Regimental Museum of the Royal Irish Fusiliers. Don't overlook the nearby 18th-century **Observatory**

WALKS

AROUND THE GIANT'S CAUSEWAY

This is the most exciting place to walk in Northern Ireland. The shorter of two circular walks takes you up the cliff, above the Giant's Causeway, from where a great view of the columns clearly show in fact three causeways, the largest looking like a crocodile's snout.

A longer, 5-mile trek takes you around several stunning bays before doubling back across the cliff tops.

Chambers of gray vertical basalt columns seem to be superimposed into the ochre cliff-sides. Many of the rocks' weird shapes have been given names, such as the Chimney Tops, the King and his Nobles, and the Organ ∎

and the **Planetarium** with its computerized star shows and mock-ups of space craft.

Between Armagh and Loch Neagh are two interesting National Trust properties. **Ardress House**, 5 miles east of Moy, is a 17th-century gentleman farmer's residence with some fine plasterwork inside. **Argory**, 4 miles northeast of Moy, neoclassical in style, has a wealth of fascinating contents left virtually untouched since the turn of the century. Its grounds contain a pretty sundial garden. At **Peatlands Park**, near the southern shore of Loch Neagh, you can discover a protected portion of Ireland's famous bogland. The park's virgin bogs, low wooded hills and small lakes can be toured on a narrow-gauge railroad, and turf-cutting demonstrations are laid on.

★ CARRICKFERGUS 247E3
COUNTY ANTRIM

One of the best preserved Anglo-Norman castles in Ireland dominates this small seaside town. Standing on a basalt promontory on the shore, in its long history it has seen action against the Scots, the local Irish, the French and John Paul Jones, founder of the American Navy. It hosts medieval fairs in the summer months.

William of Orange landed here in 1690, and you can seek out sights related to the Protestant pretender around the town. Just east of town at Boneybefore, an 18th-century cottage with a re-created interior acts as the **Andrew Jackson Centre**: the family of the 7th American President lived in the village before emigrating in 1765.

CAUSEWAY COAST 247C4
COUNTY ANTRIM/ COUNTY LONDONDERRY

Northern Ireland's north coast has something for everyone: the Giant's Causeway (possibly the most remarkable natural sight in the U.K., and Ireland's only World Heritage Site), impressive cliffs, beaches, and the cheerful resorts of Portstewart and Portrush.

In **Ballycastle** a modern sculpture commemorates

SAINT PATRICK

The patron saint of Ireland was born on the west coast of Britain.

He worked as a shepherd on Slemish Mountain in County Antrim before training in France as a missionary. He returned to Ireland around AD 432 and then spent 30 years founding churches.

Places in Northern Ireland commonly associated with him are: Antrim, where he established his diocese; Downpatrick, where he is buried; and sites on the Lecale Peninsula southwest of Downpatrick such as Struell Wells, Saul and Slieve Patrick.

On St. Patrick's Day the Irish national emblem, the shamrock, is widely worn. By tradition, it was used by Saint Patrick to illustrate the Trinity ∎

Marconi's first wireless transmission to **Rathlin Island** in 1898. When the weather allows, you can take a boat across to the island, home to thousands of seabirds and some 100 humans. A cave is said to be where Robert the Bruce, hiding from the English, was inspired to greater things by a spider attempting to climb a wall.

Back on the mainland, tourists with nerve can cross the 60-foot **Carrick-a-rede Rope Bridge** from April to September as it sways over a rocky cleft. It was originally hung to enable salmon fishermen to reach their nets.

The scientific explanation for the **Giant's Causeway ★★★**, a promontory of 40,000 closely-packed multi-sided basalt columns, is that it was formed after a volcanic eruption about 55 million years ago. Molten basalt poured out above the chalky rockbed and formed hexagonal columns as it cooled and contracted. Myth has it that the giant Finn MacCool built it as a road to cross to Scotland – a similar but smaller causeway is visible on the island of Staffa. For once, the fairy tale theory seems equally plausible. It is difficult to imagine how something that looks so geometrically exact can be natural. You can follow MacCool's first steps by climbing on to the spine of the causeway, and walking over the columns as they turn from brown to black and disappear under the spume.

The causeway has evoked numerous eulogies over the decades, though some travelers have been less than impressed. "Mon dieu! I have traveled 150 miles to see that!" said the novelist William Makepeace Thackeray in 1842. Now that it is a feature in every Wonders of the World book, the causeway sometimes fails to live up to

expectations. Photographs of it also tend to distort its size. In reality, it is dwarfed by the surrounding towering cliffs. A minibus takes you down to the causeway from the National Trust's visitor center, but the cliffs make this great walking territory (see p.251).

After such exposure to the elements, the best prescription is a "hot Bush." **Bushmills**, just down the road, has the oldest licensed whiskey distillery in the world. It first received its license in 1608, though distilling has taken place here since at least the 13th century. To earn your free dram you have to tour the distillery. If you turn on the charm, you might get a shot of all three types – the malt, Black Bush and regular Bushmills.

Further west, **Dunluce Castle** makes it on to almost as many brochure covers as the Cause-way, thanks to its jagged 13th-century ruins perched on the cliff edge. Beyond Coleraine at Castlerock, **Hezlett House** (NT) is a thatched cottage dating from 1690 with curved floor to ceiling roof timbers (cruck trusses). In the Downhill Estate (NT), neo-classical **Mussenden Temple**, based on the temple of Vesta at Tivoli, stands alone right on the edge of the cliff. Amazingly, it used to be a library. Its inspiration was the "eighteenth-century desire to contrast a sublime and romantic situation with a logical and civilized building."

Stretching west for 6 miles across to the mouth of Lough Foyle, dune-backed **Magilligan Strand** is said to be Ireland's longest beach.

COOKSTOWN and AROUND, COUNTY TYRONE 246C2
Cookstown is now just a typical mid-Ulster farming town, but it used to be an important

linen-making center. A few miles west, the final process in linen manufacture of beetling, or polishing, flax fibers was carried out at **Wellbrook Beetling Mill** (NT), whose machines are still in working order.

The lovely house of **Springhill** (NT), northeast of Cookstown, dates from the 17th century, when a military family from Ayrshire in Scotland moved here. One of the outbuildings houses a costume museum.

★★ DERRY   *246B3*
COUNTY LONDONDERRY

Often called the "Cockpit of The Troubles," even the name of this city is contested. Now that so much of the Protestant population has left the city, locals tend to call it by its original title, Derry, while British organizations like the BBC doggedly refer to it by its formal title of Londonderry (the prefix London was added in the 17th century). A local disc-jockey solved the dilemma by using the name Stroke City.

A seminal event of the Troubles known as "Bloody Sunday" occurred in Derry on January 30, 1972, when British troops shot dead 13 Catholics during a civil rights march. It took place in the Bogside district, once a notorious Republican no-go area. A memorial commemorates the dead near an enormous sign that has for long brazenly announced: "You are now entering Free Derry." Meanwhile, in the poor Protestant Fountain area, murals read "No Surrender" and chicken wire covers tenement windows.

Yet despite being a microcosm of Northern Ireland in its poverty and threatened violence, in its resilience, optimism, humor and *joie de vivre*, Derry is charming. Half of its 90,000 inhabitants are under 25. At its huge, joyful

Halloween celebrations, some choose to dress up as soldiers, Ian Paisley or Gerry Adams.

In terms of conventional sightseeing, the city's top attraction is its 17th-century **walls**, some of the most complete in Europe. At Shipquay Gate stand five of the cannon from the 1689 siege (see panel). The nearby **Tower Museum** gives a first-rate introduction to the city's history, including details on the considerable significance of its port as an emigration point for America. The city center within the walls contains old-fashioned shops and bars, as well as the spruce Derry Craft Village where you can buy crystal, linen T-towels and other local products.

The 17th-century Protestant **St. Columb's Cathedral** holds relics of the siege and Cecil Alexander, who wrote the famous hymn that begins, "There is a green hill far away/without a city wall" inspired by Derry's setting.

★ DOWNPATRICK   *247E1*
COUNTY DOWN

A granite boulder in Downpatrick's Protestant **cathedral** graveyard marks the accepted site of Saint Patrick's bones. The Regency cathedral is notable for its box pews. Pass the many Georgian buildings along English Street down from the hilltop cathedral to the former jail. Saint Patrick's story is told in the gatehouse of the **St. Patrick Heritage Centre**, while the rest is the **Down County Museum**, which includes old prison cells refurbished to recreate conditions the prisoners experienced.

Rowallane (NT), northwest of Downpatrick, near Saintfield, is a magnificent garden which has been built over *drumlins* (mounds left by glacial action); it is renowned for its colorful display of azaleas and rhododendrons.

WALKS

LOUGH ERNE AND AROUND
County Fermanagh has fine walks in the Marble Arch Nature Reserve (next to the caves), a lovely limestone gorge that is coated with bluebells in spring, and in woodland on the shores of Lower Lough Erne in Castle Archdale Country Park and Castle Caldwell Forest Park ■

"NO SURRENDER"
When Catholic troops loyal to King James II came to Derry in 1688, 13 apprentices locked the city gates against them.

The citizens declared allegiance to the Protestant King William III, and the longest siege in British history followed, lasting 105 days. A quarter of the city's 30,000 population died, and people ate cats, dogs and rats. A crimson flag was flown bearing the words "No Surrender," still a rallying cry for Protestant Unionists ■

NORTHERN IRELAND

MOUNTAINS OF MOURNE

Tollymore Forest Park has attractive walks enlivened by picturesque cascades, and the Silent Valley has paths to follow.

For something a bit more demanding, Slieve Donard is best climbed from Bloody Bridge, south of Newcastle on the A2.

From Donard Park, you can follow the River Glen up to the Brandy Pad, a smuggling track which winds its way through the mountains via Hare's Gap, where semi-precious stones have been mined ■

LOUGH ERNE and AROUND COUNTY FERMANAGH *246A2*

Wooded hills encompass Lough Erne, the largest lake in County Fermanagh's lovely lakeland. In addition, 154 islands, many wooded, some rich with Celtic and Christian ruins, dot its waters. Pretty lakeside roads skirt the whole of Lower Lough Erne. In summer, cruises leave from Enniskillen, the county town between the upper and lower loughs, motor boats can be rented and trips can be made out to the islands from various points on the lake. Fishing is big business here too, with the tourist authorities eager to promote record catches.

The Lakeland Visitor Centre in **Enniskillen** provides information on the region. While the town has been on the receiving end of much violence during the Troubles – 11 people were killed and 61 injured in an IRA bomb attack on a Remembrance Day ceremony in 1987 – the island site is attractive and it makes an obvious base. Sightseeing focuses on the castle and its turreted watergate, which house the Fermanagh Heritage Centre and a regimental museum.

On Lower Lough Erne, **Devenish Island** has extensive monastic remains dating from the 12th century, including a fine round tower. On **White Island** you can see a remarkable series of eight carved stone figures. In a Christian burial ground on **Boa Island** (bridged to the mainland) you will find a two-faced Janus figure, a Celtic idol. Lakeside **Castle Archdale Country Park** and **Castle Caldwell Forest Park** both offer pleasant woodland walks. The border with the Republic of Ireland slices through the tiny village of **Belleek**, known for its delicate "basket weave" pottery; visit the shop and museum, and tour the factory.

Away from the lake, the **Marble Arch Caves**, 10 miles southwest of Enniskillen, have very impressive geological formations; part of the tour involves crossing an underground lake by boat. The nearby Palladian house of **Florence Court** (NT), the seat of the earls of

The Mountains of Mourne, County Down, in the southeast, provide fine walking country

Enniskillen, has superb plasterwork on the staircase and in the dining room. The Florence Court Yew stands in the forest park.

Set in landscaped parkland, **Castle Coole** (NT) ★ ★ ★, 1½ miles southeast of Enniskillen, is billed as the grandest Palladian mansion in Ireland. Designed by James Wyatt, top British architect of his day, it was completed in 1798. Period furniture vies for attention with more magnificent plasterwork and other exquisite architectural details throughout the house; the State Bedroom, beautifully restored, was prepared for a visit from King George IV.

★ ★ ★ MOUNTAINS OF MOURNE, COUNTY DOWN   247D1

Northern Ireland's grandest scenery sweeps around in a great arc of granite mountains between Dundrum Bay and Carlingford Lough, a patchwork of tiny sheepcropped fields with drystone walls lying below the peaks.

As well as being popular for rock climbing, this area can only be properly enjoyed on foot, but a scenic route, the B27, does pass through the range via the Spelga Pass and Dam.

The main recreation area is the **Silent Valley** with reservoirs and dams, and superb mountain panoramas. There are trails, a visitor center and a shuttle bus up the valley (no cars are allowed). A local feature is the 22-mile circuit of the drystone Mourne Wall which starts and finishes at the valley. The gently rising 2,796-foot **Slieve Donard** (the highest in the range and in Northern Ireland) rewards climbers with a hermit cell and stupendous views from the top.

The best base for the Mourne area is the resort of Newcastle, "Where the Mountains o' Mourne sweep down to the sea." Worth exploring are: **Murlough National Nature Reserve** on Dundrum Bay, with guided walks to the dunes; **Castlewellan Forest Park**, set round a baronial castle, with an arboretum; and **Tollymore Forest Park**, with lovely woodland trails. The coast road south leads to the fishing harbor of **Annalong**, where a 19th-century corn mill produces flour. The ruins of an Anglo-Norman castle protrude into Carlingford Lough at Greencastle.

STRABANE   246B3
COUNTY TYRONE

This border town was an important printing center in the 18th and 19th centuries. John Dunlap, printer of the original American Declaration of Independence and of America's first daily newspaper, the *Pennsylvania Packet*, learned his trade at **Gray's Printing Press** (NT), as did James Wilson, grandfather of the American President Woodrow Wilson. The whitewashed and thatched Wilson family home, 2 miles southeast at Dergalt, is open to the public.

THE AMERICAN CONNECTION

Most emigrants from Ireland to America left in the mid-19th century after the famine – mainly Roman Catholics from the south. Some 250,000 Presbyterian Ulster Scots had already left in the 18th century.

From their descendants came several American presidents: the ancestral homes of Andrew Jackson and Woodrow Wilson can be visited (see p.251 and p.255); others include Ulysses S. Grant from Aughnacloy in County Tyrone, and Theodore Roosevelt from Larne, County Antrim.

To trace Ulster ancestry, begin at the General Register Office, Oxford House, 49 Chichester Street, Belfast BT1 4HL; tel: 01232 252000 ∎

NORTHERN IRELAND

SPERRIN MOUNTAINS

At the edge of the Sperrin Mountains, Gortin Glen Forest Park offers trails through conifer forest and along mountain streams.

Sika deer can be seen on the way ■

A BRIEF GUIDE TO NORTHERN IRELAND'S POLITICS

Unionists or Loyalists wish Northern Ireland to continue as part of the U.K. They are mostly Protestant. The Reverend Ian Paisley is leader of the Democratic Unionist Party (DUP).

Republicans, or Nationalists want a united Ireland. They are usually Catholic. They include John Hume, leader of the Social Democratic and Labour Party (SDLP), which is committed to peaceful change, and Gerry Adams, leader of Sínn Fein, the political wing of the IRA (Irish Republican Army) ■

★★ STRANGFORD LOUGH 247E2 COUNTY DOWN

Roads skirt the western shore of the landlocked sea inlet of Strangford Lough and the breezy coast of the Ards Peninsula. The island-studded lough is an important wildlife habitat: two-thirds of the world's Brent geese winter here, and there are large numbers of common seals.

To observe the birdlife, go to **Castle Espie** on the western shore. The marine life is described at the aquarium at **Portaferry**, while the National Trust has a wildlife exhibition and wildfowl collection at the 700-acre country estate of **Castle Ward** and lays on summertime boat trips (note that a car ferry links Portaferry to Strangford). Castle Ward (NT) itself is a most peculiar 18th-century mansion, partly classical in style, and partly Gothic. A Palladian temple and 17th-century tower house are in the fine grounds.

Mount Stewart (NT), on the lake's northeastern shore, was the home of the important 19th-century statesman Viscount Castlereagh. Its reputation lies not so much in the richly decorated interior of the early 19th-century house as in its gardens, host to imaginative parterres, topiary and rare and tender plants. The banqueting hall, the Temple of the Winds, erected for the 1st Marquis of Londonderry in 1783, copies a famous Athenian building.

★★★ ULSTER-AMERICAN 246B3 FOLK PARK, COUNTY TYRONE

The Mellon family is responsible for this theme park, which has grown up around the cottage where Thomas Mellon was born in 1813. After emigrating to Pennsylvania, Thomas became a millionaire. His son, the chief architect of Pittsburgh, went on

to become one of the richest men in the world.

Costumed locals demonstrate traditional crafts, cooking griddle cakes over peat fires and spinning wool, in a re-created 18th-century Ulster village with a smithy and a weaver's cottage. In the **Emigration Gallery** you relive the dreadful conditions of a trans-atlantic voyage on a replica ship.

★★★ ULSTER FOLK 247E2 AND TRANSPORT MUSEUM COUNTY DOWN

You could spend a day at this vast open-air attraction. Domestic, communal, commercial and industrial buildings – urban terraces, one-room cottages, a farmhouse, a flax mill, and a church – have been painstakingly recorded, dismantled and reassembled. Each has period furnishings and in summer you can watch demonstrations of spinning, weaving and thatching.

Across the main road, the **Transport Museum** has horse-drawn carts, steam rollers, railroad rolling stock, airplanes and the singularly unsuccessful locally built De Lorean sports car.

★ ULSTER HISTORY 246B3 PARK and AROUND COUNTY TYRONE

The park offers a history of settlements in Ireland. Full-scale replicas of buildings – neolithic huts, *crannog* (artificial island) dwellings, and a Norman motte and bailey castle – tell the story.

The attraction sits at the edge of the Sperrin Mountains, a tract of moorland where the sheep outnumber the people. A scenic drive passes through adjacent **Gortin Glen Forest Park**, giving good views of the mountains. Gold is occasionally found in the hills: at the **Sperrin Heritage Centre**, Cranagh, 7 miles east of Plumbridge, you can pan for gold.

TRAVEL
FACTS

All you need to know to make
your trip as comfortable as
possible; how to get around,
what to take, where to go for
entertainment and even how to
trace your ancestors

TRAVEL FACTS

CONTENTS

BEFORE YOU GO

AIRLINES

The following are a selection of airlines with frequent flights from the U.S. to Britain.
• **American**: (800) 433 7300 – Direct flights from Boston, Dallas (Fort Worth), Los Angeles, Miami, Nashville, New York, Philadelphia or Raleigh (Durham) to Manchester, Glasgow, London Heathrow or London Gatwick.
• **British Airways**: (800)-AIRWAYS – Direct flights from Baltimore, Boston, Chicago, Charlotte, Dallas, Denver, Detroit, Los Angeles, Miami, New York, Philadelphia, Pittsburgh, San Francisco. Some arrive at London Heathrow or Gatwick; others go to Glasgow or Manchester.
• **Continental**: (800) 231 0856 – Flights from New York, Houston, Denver and other cities to London Gatwick.
• **Delta**: (800) 241 4141 – Flights from hundreds of U.S. departure points to London Gatwick or Manchester.
• **TWA**: (800) 892 4141 – Direct flights go from St. Louis to London Gatwick, but within the U.S., TWA operate numerous connecting flights linking other cities with St. Louis.
• **United**: (800) 241 6522 – Main flights are from New York, Newark, Los Angeles, San Francisco, Seattle and Washington D.C. to London Heathrow.
• **Virgin Atlantic**: (800) 862 8621 – Flights from Boston, Miami and Orlando to London Gatwick; and New York, Los Angeles and San Francisco to London Heathrow.

ARRIVING
By air

London has four main airports: Heathrow and Gatwick handle most international flights; Stansted and London City sometimes take on the overflow of international flights (mostly from other points in Europe). Luton is also near enough to London to be considered another possibility (if you are flying into Britain from elsewhere in Europe) and want to be near the capital.
• **Heathrow** (tel. 0181 759 4321) is the international airport closest to the center of London (15 miles west). There are direct links to the Piccadilly line of the underground or subway train (also known as the "tube"). The buses **Airbus A1** or **A2** also connect Heathrow with various stops within central London. A taxi to west London will cost as little as £17; going further into central London will cost about £30–£35.
• **Gatwick** (27 miles south; tel. 01293 535353) has a direct link by British Rail train (the Gatwick Express, 24-hour service) to London's Victoria Station. The Flightline 777 bus connects with London Victoria Coach Station. Because Gatwick is relatively far away, a taxi to central London will be roughly £45.

If you want to check on your departure time from either Heathrow or Gatwick before you make your way back to the airport, call the airport direct for flight details.
• **London City** (in London's Docklands area, 10 miles east; tel. 0171 646 0000) links with British Rail or the Docklands Light Railway via shuttle buses. A taxi into central London should cost around £20.
• **Stansted** (37 miles northeast of central London; tel. 01279 680500) links with British Rail (the Stansted Express) and National Express bus service. A taxi into London will cost about £38.
• **Luton** (30 miles northwest of Central London; tel. 01582 405100) links with British Rail and Flightlink bus 757, also Jet Link for other London airports. A taxi to London will cost at least £70.

Other major U.K. airports and their links to city centers:
• **Manchester International** (10 miles south; tel. 0161 489 3000): British Rail and National Express bus service; a taxi should cost around £12.
• **Belfast International**, Crumlin (18 miles northwest of Belfast, Northern Ireland; tel. 01849 422888): buses; a taxi should cost around £21.
• **Birmingham International** (8 miles southeast; tel. 0121 767 7145): British Rail; a taxi should cost around £11.
• **Edinburgh** (7 miles west; tel. 0131 344 3136): buses; a taxi should cost around £15.
• **Glasgow** (9 miles west; tel. 0141 887 1111): buses, a taxi should cost around £14. (Also see *Getting Around* on p.268.)

By bus from elsewhere in Europe

Bus/ferry, bus/hovercraft or bus/catamaran combinations are the least expensive way to get across the Channel and into Britain (see also *By boat* opposite).

• **National Express** (operating in the U.S. as British Travel International, PO Box 299, Elkton, Virginia, 22827; tel. (800) 327 6097. U.K. address 4 Vicarage Road, Edgbaston, Birmingham B15 3ES) is Britain's leading bus (short-distance) and coach (long-haul) service. For times and fares, credit card reservations and disabled passenger assistance in English call 0990 808080.

For more information on bus services between Britain and the rest of Europe, and to find out about discounts for students and senior citizens, contact:

• **Eurolines**: 0171 730 8235
• **InterEurope Travel**: 0171 630 5188.

By train

• **The International Rail Centre** at London Victoria Station (tel. 0171 834 2345) can tell you about getting by train from Amsterdam, Brussels, Paris and other European cities to London and points beyond. There are also train/ferry, train/hovercraft and train/catamaran combinations (also see *By boat* opposite).

The jewel in the crown of train travel between the Continent and Britain is the **Eurostar** train, which travels through the "Chunnel" (the tunnel under the English Channel between France and England). Eurostar trains run between Paris (Gare du Nord) and London (Waterloo); there are also services from Lille (France) and Brussels (Belgium) to London. Children under 4 travel free; the fare for children aged 4–11 is 20 percent less than the adult fare. There are also special reductions for wheelchair passengers or people who are blind and any person accompanying them. For more information contact your travel agent or The Rail Shop; tel: 0990 300003 or Eurostar, Waterloo International Terminal; tel: 0345 881881.

If you wish to take your car **Le Shuttle** will transport you and your car by train through the Channel Tunnel from Folkestone (England) to Calais (France). No reservation is required; simply turn up or call 0990 353535 for more information.

By boat

Ferries take foot passengers as well as cars. Companies connecting European ports with British ones by ferry, hovercraft and catamaran include:

• **Brittany Ferries** (tel. 0990 360360): Caen (France)–Portsmouth; Cherbourg or St. Malo (France)–Poole; Roscoff (France)–Plymouth; St. Malo (France)–Portsmouth; Santander (Spain)–Plymouth or Portsmouth
• **Color Line** (tel. 0191 296 1313): Bergen, Stavanger and Haugesund (Norway)–Newcastle
• **Hoverspeed** (tel. 01304 240241 for reservations or 01304 240101 for inquiries): Boulogne (France)–Folkestone; Calais (France)–Dover
• **North Sea** (tel. 01482 377177): Zeebrugge (Belgium)–Hull; Rotterdam (Netherlands)–Hull
• **P&O European Ferries** (tel. 0990 980980): Calais (France)–Dover; Cherbourg (France)–Portsmouth; Le Havre (France)–Portsmouth; Zeebrugge (Belgium)–Felixstowe; Bilbao (Spain)–Portsmouth
• **Hover Speed** (tel. 01843 595522): Calais (France)–Dover; Boulogne (France)–Folkestone; Ostend (Belgium)–Dover.
• **Scandinavian Seaways** (tel. 01255 240240): Hamburg (Germany), Esbjerg (Denmark), and Gothenburg (Sweden)–Harwich and Newcastle; Amsterdam (Holland)–Newcastle
• **Stena Line** (tel. 0990 707070): Calais (France)–Dover; Cherbourg (France)–Southampton; Dieppe (France)–Newhaven; Hook of Holland (Netherlands)–Harwich; Dun Loaghaire for Dublin (Republic of Ireland)–Holyhead (Wales); Rosslare (Republic of Ireland)–Fishguard (Wales).

Shipping your car

There are a number of companies that can ship your car over if you are going to be in Britain for a while and it would be more economical to have your own car sent over than to rent one:

• **Allstate International** (J.F.K. offices), 177, 150th Avenue, Jamaica, NY 11434; tel. 718/244 6712, fax 718/656 5139. Also offices near Newark Airport, in Baltimore,

Boston, Chicago, Dallas, Miami, Los
Angeles, Philadelphia and San Francisco.
• **International Sea and Air Shipping**, 6
Connarty Court, East Brunswick, NJ 08816;
tel. 908/390 0322. Also offices in Los
Angeles and London; tel. 0181 965 3344.

Cruise lines

• **Cunard** (Suite 400, 6100 Blue Lagoon
Drive, Miami, 33126 tel. 305/463 3000; U.K.:
01703 716500) is the premiere cruise line,
with four ships that make regular trips
across the Atlantic. The *Queen Elizabeth II*
makes regular crossings between April and
December, connecting Baltimore, Boston
and New York City with Southampton,
England. Other ships stop at several ports of
call before crossing the Atlantic. For more
details, the travel section of the Sunday
papers or the *Yellow Pages* can fill you in on
other cruise lines that sail to Britain.

CLIMATE and WHEN TO GO

Contrary to popular belief, it is not always
raining in Britain! Generally, the British
climate is mild, if unpredictable. Different
parts of Britain fare better than others. The
far northwest of Scotland is warmer than
you might imagine since it gets the benefit
not only of breezes from the Gulf Stream,
but also nights that stay light until nearly
midnight.

   Summer offers the best weather (dry
and reasonably hot), but even then the
evenings can be pretty cool. Keep in mind
that it is also the busiest time of year, with
foreign and British vacationers fighting for
every inch of space at resorts, and prices for
accommodations at their highest.

   In spring, though there may be some
rain, the countryside is at its most beautiful
with colorful flowers such as daffodils, tulips
and bluebells everywhere; any visitor who
wants to take full advantage of England's
green and pleasant landscape should try to
come at this time.

   Fall can be the best time to visit the
Yorkshire Moors, Peaks and Dales, as well
as the Scottish Highlands. The Lake District
gets a lot of rain, though June can be an
exception to this rule.

   Winter nights tend to be damp and chilly
rather than really freezing, with little snow
(at least until January or February), but

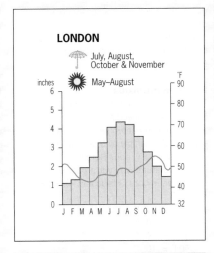

LONDON

July, August,
October & November

May–August

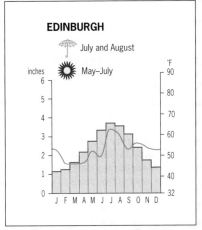

EDINBURGH

July and August

May–July

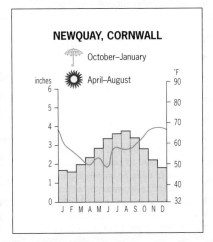

NEWQUAY, CORNWALL

October–January

April–August

during the day there is a surprising amount of sunshine – and even if the weather is dismal, this time of year sees theater, opera, ballet, concert and movie seasons in full swing.

Fahrenheit/Celsius

To convert Celsius into Fahrenheit: multiply by 9, divide by 5, and add 32.

To convert Fahrenheit into Celsius: subtract 32, multiply by 5, and divide by 9.

Sounds easy, huh? Here are a few of the temperatures you will probably encounter, in both Celsius and Fahrenheit:

0 F =	-18° C
32 F =	0° C
40 F =	4° C
50 F =	10° C
60 F =	16° C
70 F =	21° C
80 F =	26° C

CUSTOMS and QUARANTINE

• **If you are a U.S. citizen visiting Britain, you may bring in** (duty-free):
200 cigarettes or 100 cigarillos or 50 cigars or 250 grams of tobacco; 2 liters of table wine and 1 liter of alcohol over 22 percent volume (most spirits) or 2 liters of alcohol under 22 percent volume (fortified or sparkling wine); 60 ml of perfume and 250 ml of toilet water; other goods to a value of £136 ($200).

For further information, contact H.M. Customs and Excise, New King's Beam House, 22 Upper Ground, London SE1 9PJ; tel: 0171 865 3000, for *A Guide for Travellers*.

• **If you are traveling to Britain directly from another EU (European Union) country**, there is no limit on the importation of tax-paid goods purchased within the EU. However, guidance levels as suggested by Customs are:
800 cigarettes and 400 cigarillos and 200 cigars and 1 kg of tobacco;
90 liters of table wine and 10 liters of alcohol over 22 percent volume and 20 liters of alcohol under 22 percent volume;
110 liters of beer; an unlimited amount of perfume and toilet water; other goods un-limited but up to a value of £71 ($106) if duty-free. Alcohol and tobacco limits apply to travelers 17 years or over. You cannot bring fresh meats, plants, vegetables, controled drugs, firearms or ammunition into Britain.

There are no currency restrictions.

• **When departing Britain, you may bring home to the U.S.:** up to $400 worth of foreign goods duty-free, as long as they have been out of the U.S. for at least 48 hours. Each member of a family is entitled to this amount, no matter what age. For the next $1,000 worth of goods, a flat 10 percent is charged as duty; above $1,400, duties vary depending on the merchandise.

• **Travelers over 21 may bring home** 200 cigarettes or 50 cigars or 250 grams of tobacco; 1 liter of alcohol or table wine.

There is no duty on works of art or antiques that are more than 100 years old. You can mail goods home first, but they must not be worth more than $50 and may not consist of liquor, tobacco or perfume. For more information, write or call the U.S. Customs Service (1301 Constitution Avenue, Washington DC 20229; tel. 202/927 6724) and ask for their booklet, *Know Before You Go*.

If you leave Britain to return home from another EU country, you may bring in the same amounts of tobacco, alcohol and perfume (see above).

Quarantine regulations

No animals of any kind are allowed into Britain without first having to go into quarantine for six months.

TRAVELERS with DISABILITIES

Britain prides itself on being progressive in setting the pace for Europe to accommodate people with disabilities. Its National Accessible Standard is a rating given to hotels, restaurants and places of interest based upon their accessibility to wheelchair-users, people who are blind, people who are deaf and other people with disabilities. Tourist agencies have leaflets on the accessibility of local attractions, transport-ation, hotels, restaurants and public restrooms.

Many movie theaters and theaters across Britain have loop systems for the hard of hearing. For more information on travelers with disabilities, see *Travel*

Agencies on p.266, *Public Transportation* on p.270, and *Tourist Information* on pp.266 and 282.

Useful publications

• **AA Guide for the Disabled Traveller**
(available from the Automobile Association and bookstores).

• **Accessible Holidays in the British Isles**
(Hobsons; updated yearly). Available direct from the Holiday Care Service (see opposite), a registered charity offering information, advice and support for people with disabilities and their carers.

• **Holidays in the British Isles – A Guide for Disabled People** (available from R.A.D.A.R., see opposite).

• **Disability Now** – a magazine for people with disabilities – available at newsagents throughout Britain.

• **Artsline in London** (tel. 0171 388 2227) – these are the people to call for information about accessibility to various art and entertainment venues in and around the capital.

In addition, the telephone directory for your area (your hotel should have one, and failing that, the nearest library) includes a section on **Arts Access** – a guide for people with disabilities to local venues (movie theaters, theaters, museums and galleries, sports and leisure venues), rating each according to various criteria, such as whether the entrance is accessible, if there are special restroom facilities, an elevator on the premises, whether wheelchairs are available on loan, and parking.

While still in the U.S., you may want to contact one of the following organizations to help you plan your trip:

• **Mobility International U.S.A.**, Box 3551, Eugene, Oregon 97403; tel. (voice and TDD) 541/343 1284

• **Society for the Advancement of the Handicapped (S.A.T.H.)**, 347 5th Avenue, Suite 610, New York, NY 10016; tel. 212/447 7284

• **Travelin' Talk**, Box 3534, Clarksville, TN 37043; tel. 931/552 6670. This organization can put you in touch with people who have disabilities in the part of Britain – or anywhere worldwide – that you are visiting, so that they can give you the benefit of their experience of traveling with a disability.

Organizations for the disabled in Britain are:

• **Disability Action** (2 Annadale Avenue, Belfast BT7 3JH, Northern Ireland; tel. 01232 491011

• **Holiday Care Service**, 2nd Floor, Imperial Buildings, Victoria Road, Horley, Surrey RH6 7PZ; tel. 01293 774535 (011-44-1293-774 535 if calling from the U.S.)

• **Royal Association for Disability and Rehabilitation (R.A.D.A.R.)**, 12 City Forum, 250 City Road, EC1V 8AF; tel: 0171 250 3222

• **Royal National Institute for the Blind (R.N.I.B.)**: 0171 388 1266

• **Royal National Institute for the Deaf (R.N.I.D.)**: 0171 296 8000

• **The Automobile Association (AA)**
operate a Disabled Drivers' Helpline; (0800) 262050 (toll free U.K only).

DRIVING
Breakdown
Several companies offer international breakdown services to members of affiliated organizations, including:

• **The Automobile Association (AA – same as AAA in the U.S.)**: (0800) 887766 for breakdowns (toll free U.K. only) or 01256 20123 for general information

• **Royal Automobile Club (RAC)**: (0800) 828282 (members only) for breakdowns (toll free U.K only) or 0990 722722 for information.

Driver's license and age required to drive in Britain
An American driver's license is valid in Britain. It is useful also to have an International Driver's License as another piece of ID. If you want an International Driver's License, you must get it while you are still in the U.S. (see your local AAA office).

The legal age to drive in Britain is 17 years or over.

Car rental details
You must be over 21 (in some cases over 25) but not over 70 (in some cases 75), and have been driving for at least a year, to rent a car. Most of the major rental companies have offices at British airports, principal railroad stations, as well as in all big cities.

Car rental companies with offices in the U.S. and Britain include:
- **Alamo**: (800) 327 9633 (U.S.); 0870 6006655 (U.K.)
- **Avis**: (800) 331 2112 (U.S.); 0990 900500 (U.K.)
- **Budget**: (800) 527 0700 (U.S.); (0800) 181181 (U.K., toll-free)
- **Hertz**: (800) 654 3001 (U.S.); 0990 996699 (U.K.)

Other rental companies in Britain include:
- **Europcar**: 0345 222525
- **National Car Hire**: 0990 365365
- **Thrifty**: 01494 442110

All these companies offer nationwide emergency coverage, one-way rentals and other options.

It may cost more to rent an automatic, as most cars in Britain are manual (stick shift). Keep in mind that if you decide to drive a manual the stick shift will have to be manoeuvred with your *left* hand!

Insurance

You only need third-party insurance in Britain; if you are driving your own car, this means that you only have to take out comprehensive insurance to cover the duration of your trip. You can get a "Green Card" (international insurance certificate) from your usual auto insurance representative. Rental companies normally include insurance in their fees, but it is always worth checking.

ELECTRICITY
- **Voltage = 240 volts (50 cycles AC)**.

All sockets in Britain have three holes, so you will need a three-(square) pronged adapter for any appliances, such as a travel iron or hairdryer, that you bring with you from the States. You will also need a converter to reduce the voltage that goes into the appliance from 240 to 110 (U.S. voltage).

For further information, particularly regarding larger appliances such as laptop computers, you can obtain a free booklet entitled *Foreign Electricity Is No Deep Secret*, from the adapter/converter manufacturer Frazus, Murtha Industrial Park, Box 142, Beacon Falls, Connecticut 06403; tel. 203/723 6664. Include a stamped self-addressed envelope.

HEALTH
Medical insurance before you go

The International Association for Medical Assistance to Travelers (I.A.M.A.T.) can offer invaluable help, as it can provide you with a list of approved doctors and clinics within Britain or anywhere else in the world. For a free list, write or call I.A.M.A.T., 417 Center Street, Lewiston, NY 14092; tel. 716/754 4883.

Other companies that specialize in helping you once you are abroad in the event that you need your medical records sent over, must be brought back to the U.S. quickly, or for financial help if you need special or emergency medical treatment are:
- **International S.O.S. Assistance**, Box 11568, Philadelphia, Pennsylvania 19116; tel. 215/244 1500
- **Travel Assistance International**, 1133 15th Street NW, Suite 400, Washington DC 20005; tel. 202/331 1596.

Vaccinations

You do not need any vaccinations before visiting Britain, but depending on how much you are going to be roughing it, it would be wise to have a mini first-aid kit with you, made up of band-aids, vitamins, aspirin, antacid tablets and the like. If you need any special prescription medicines (and even if you think you have brought enough along), get your doctor to write you a prescription (using the drug's generic rather than U.S. brand name) to take with you. Similarly, if you wear glasses or contact lenses, you should really take a spare pair (or at least their prescription) with you.

INSURANCE

You, your belongings, and your vacation should all be adequately insured. Most travel agencies, tour operators and insurers offer special health-and-accident, flight, trip-cancellation and luggage insurance, or comprehensive insurance packages that cover most or all of these contingencies. Some helpful addresses are:
- **AAA**, see your local club or write 1000 AAA Drive, M/S 42, Heathrow, FL 32746; tel. (800) 336 4357.
- **Access America Inc.**, P.O. Box 11188, Richmond, VA 23230; tel. 804/285 3300.

PASSPORTS and VISAS

All U.S. citizens must have a valid 10-year (or 5-year if under 16) passport to enter Britain. If you do not already have one, you must apply in person to one of the 13 U.S. Passport Offices. Some local county courthouses, state and probate courts, and local post offices also accept passport applications. In addition to a completed application form (Form DSP-11), you have to bring with you proof of citizenship (birth certificate – the original, with raised seal – or naturalization papers); proof of ID (driver's license, employee ID card or anything with your photo and signature on it); two identical, recent photographs of yourself, full face, measuring 2 x 2 inches square (black and white or color); and the application fee (currently $65).

If you want to renew a passport that has expired or is about to expire, you can renew it by mail. You need to send: your old passport; Form DSP-82; two identical photographs; and a check or money order to the value of $65.

You should allow at least four weeks for your passport to arrive in the mail, although most passport offices do their best to get your application processed within 10 days.

For more information, call the National Passport Center; tel: 603/334 0500.

U.S. citizens do not need a visa to enter Britain, so long as they do not intend to stay for more than six months.

PUBLIC HOLIDAYS
For 1999

• **England and Wales**: January 1 (New Year's Day); April 2 and 5 (Good Friday and Easter Monday); May 3 (May Day – usually the first Monday in May); May 26 (Spring public holiday – usually the last Monday in May); August 30 (Summer public holiday – usually the last Monday in August); December 25 and 26 (Christmas Day and Boxing Day).

• **Northern Ireland** as for England and Wales, but also St. Patrick's Day (March 17) and July 12 (Orangeman's Day).

• **Scotland**: January 1 and 2; Good Friday (but not Easter Monday); May 3 (public holiday); May 31 (Spring public holiday); August 2 (Summer public holiday – usually the first Monday in August); December 25 and 26. Please note that if New Year's Day or Christmas or Boxing Day falls on a Saturday (or Sunday), then the following Monday (and Tuesday) will also be given as a holiday.

Other festivals (stores and banks will be open when these fall on working days)

February 14 – St. Valentine's Day when loved ones exchange gifts and greetings cards.

March 1 – St. David's Day in Wales

March 31 – Mother's Day or "Mothering Sunday," the last Sunday in March

April 23 – St. George's Day in England

June 16 – Father's Day, the third Sunday in June

October 31 – All Hallows' Eve or Halloween – the "trick or treat" ordeal is rapidly spreading to Britain

November 5 – Guy Fawkes' or Bonfire Night commemorating the failed attempt of "traitor" Guy Fawkes to blow up the Houses of Parliament in 1605 – celebrated with fireworks, firecrackers, and potatoes baked over an open bonfire

November 10 – Remembrance Sunday, known in the U.S. as Armistice Day, is commemorated in Britain on the Sunday nearest to November 11

November 30 – St. Andrew's Day, patron saint of Scotland.

TIME

There is only one time zone for all of Britain.

England is actually home to the standard of time-keeping, Greenwich Mean Time (GMT), the gauge by which all other time zones are calculated.

Eastern Standard Time is 5 hours behind GMT, which means that when it is 12 noon in London it is 7 a.m. in New York (Eastern Standard Time).

As you travel west you fall more hours behind GMT, so that at 12 noon in London it will be 6 a.m. in Chicago (Central Time is 6 hours behind GMT), 5 a.m. in Denver (Mountain Time is 7 hours behind GMT), and 4 a.m. in Los Angeles (Pacific Time is 8 hours behind GMT).

TRAVEL FACTS

Clocks go back on the last Sunday in October, just as they do in the U.S.; they go forward, however, nearly four weeks earlier than they do in the U.S., on the last Sunday of March rather than the end of April. Thus during these weeks British Summer Time (BST) is actually 6 hours ahead of Eastern Standard Time.

TOURIST INFORMATION OFFICES

• **The British Tourist Authority (B.T.A.)** has offices in the following U.S. cities: **New York** – 7th Floor, 551 Fifth Avenue, New York, NY 1076-0799; tel. 212/986 2200 or 1-800 Go 2 Britain; and **Chicago** – John Hancock Center, Suite 1510, 625 N. Michigan Avenue, Chicago, IL 60611, (personal callers only); tel. (800) 462 2728

Other tour operators that can help you plan your trip
• **American Express Vacations**, 110 E. Broward Blvd, Fort Lauderdale, FL 33301, tel. 954/565 9481.
• **Globus and Cosmos Tourama**, 5301 S. Federal Circle, Littleton, CO 80123; tel. (800) 221 0090
• **Maupintour**, 1515 St. Andrew's Drive, Lawrence, KS 66047; tel. 785/843 1211 or (800) 255 4266
• **Trafalgar**, 11 E. 26th Street, New York, NY 10010; tel. 212/689 8977 or (800) 854 0103.

TRAVEL AGENCIES
Once you are in Britain there is an abundance of travel agencies which can help you plan your trip within England, Scotland, Wales and Northern Ireland.

Among those with an international reputation is the **Automobile Association** (AA; known as AAA in the States): not just for travelers with cars, the AA also publish several series of travel guides, can provide you with useful maps, atlases, and town plans, and can help you if you feel like touring the rest of Europe. Most of these publications are available direct from the AA and good bookstores. They also have a 24-hour help line, which is open to non-members as well; tel. 0990 500600.

Every city and town center also has a branch of at least one of the following major agencies:

• **American Express Travel Services** (central office, tel. 0171 828 7411)
• **A.T. Mays** (H.O., tel: 01294 462199)
• **Thomas Cook** (0171 499 4000)
• **Thomson** (0171 387 9321)
Students or other young travelers may like to try one of the following:
• **Student Travel Association (S.T.A.)**, 86 Old Brompton, London SW7; tel. 0171 361 6161 (also branches at 117 Euston Road, London NW1 and in Cambridge and Manchester)
• **Campus Travel** (52 Grosvenor Gardens, London SW1W 0AG; tel. 0171 730 8111)
• **InterEurope Travel** (83 Buckingham Palace Road, SWIW 00J; tel. 0171 630 5188).

For people with disabilities, the above travel agents have been recommended for staff dedication and efficiency when dealing with the special needs of travelers with disabilities (see also *Travelers With Disabilities* on p.262).

WHAT TO TAKE
Clothing
The choice of what clothes to bring with you depends of course on what time of the year and where you are going, but even if your trip is planned for the summer months, it is wise to pack a warm jacket and one or two sweaters, as the evenings can be chilly, and the further north you go the colder it is likely to get.

If you are visiting in winter, you will certainly need a heavy coat; if it is

CLOTHING CONVERSION CHART
Men's clothes
U.K.	36	38	40	42	44	46	48
U.S.	36	38	40	42	44	46	48

Women's clothes
U.K.	8	10	12	14	16	18	20	22
U.S.	4	6	8	10	12	14	16	18

Men's shoes
U.K.	7	7½	8	8½	9	9½	10
U.S.	8	8½	9	9½	10	10½	11

Women's shoes
U.K.	3	4	4½	5	5½	6	6½	7	7½	8
U.S.	5	5½	6	6½	7	7½	8	8½	9	9

waterproof so much the better. Alternatively, you could always pack a small folding umbrella.

Be sure to bring some sturdy shoes – even if you only plan to see London, you will find yourself doing a lot of walking – as well as one pair of more formal footwear. Jeans are acceptable in most establishments (even the theater), so long as they do not look too weather-beaten or torn, though some night-clubs and restaurants do still stipulate "no jeans." It is a good idea to have more formal attire (jacket and tie; dress or skirt and blouse) with you, so that you are ready for any eventuality.

It is always best to pack light, particularly if you are going to be traveling around a lot by train or bus when even the smallest suitcase or backpack can soon seem like it weighs a ton.

Electronic equipment

If you bring any electronic equipment (for example, a hairdryer or travel iron) do not forget to bring an adapter and converter to compensate for the change in voltage (see *Electricity* on p.264).

Battery-powered personal stereos, radios and televisions do not present a problem, since the batteries sold in Britain are the same voltage and type as those sold in the U.S. If you are bringing an expensive camera or camcorder with you, it is a good idea to register it with U.S. Customs at the airport before you depart – otherwise they might think you bought it overseas, and try to charge you duty on it when you return!

Luggage

Airlines allow you to check in two pieces of luggage – the allowance is that no piece can be bigger than 62 inches (length plus height plus width) or weigh more than 70 pounds.

In addition to this you are allowed one piece of carry-on luggage, which should be small enough (maximum size 45 inches all around) to fit comfortably under the seat in front of you (carry-on luggage should never be stored in the overhead racks).

If you are going to be flying from Britain to other European destinations, the weight allowance for checked-in luggage is 44 pounds in total.

Remember to pack in your carry-on bag at least one change of clothes and some toiletries (soap, toothbrush and toothpaste, shampoo, deodorant). That way, if the rest of your luggage somehow gets sent to Moscow instead of Glasgow, you will at least be able to have something to change into. Along the same lines, never pack money, travelers' checks or other valuables in the luggage that you check on board the plane.

Recommended reading

If you want to try to get some background on Britain and the British, you might want to read one or more of these books:

The English World (edited by Robert Blake), *The English Companion* (Godfrey Smith) and *Notes From a Small Island* by Bill Bryson are good places to start; Paul Theroux's *The Kingdom by the Sea*, one transplanted American's acerbic impressions of Britain as he traveled around its coasts (on foot and by train and bus) in the summer of 1982. It is, in spite of its harshness, an insightful and interesting read.

Suggested classics would have to include the novels of the Brontë sisters, Jane Austen, Thomas Hardy, Anthony Trollope, Robert Louis Stevenson, and Charles Dickens – each evoking particular landscapes, social mores and lifestyles of Britain's past and with certain resonances for modern times.

Daphne du Maurier's novels are mainly set on the moorland and coasts of the Cornwall she loved (*Rebecca*, *Frenchman's Creek* and *Jamaica Inn*, for example), and her *Vanishing Cornwall* is a fine testament to the spirit and history of Cornwall.

More contemporary works of fiction are *London Fields* (Martin Amis); *What a Carve Up!* (Jonathan Coe); *The Good Apprentice* (Iris Murdoch).

Mystery fans who also want a touch of comedy need look no further than Dorothy L. Sayers' Lord Peter Wimsey stories; along the same lines, the Jeeves and Wooster stories by P.G. Wodehouse or the Mapp books by E.E. Benson all take a sharply humorous look at English eccentricities. More modern social comedy can be found in the writings of Tom Sharpe, David Lodge, Tom Stoppard, and Alan Bennett.

GETTING AROUND

CYCLING

Much of the English countryside is ideal for cycling, although you must be sure that you are in good shape and that you have your route planned carefully.

Certain regions are better for cycling than others, such as Norfolk and Lincolnshire, which are famed for their even (dare we say flat?) landscape. Many city centers have cycle lanes, but as always it is advisable to be a very confident cyclist before attempting to navigate your way through London's rush-hour traffic. Oxford and Cambridge have very good provisions for cyclists, as traditionally students and professors alike get around by bicycle in these famous university towns .

You can take a bicycle on most rail services (it will be stored in the luggage compartment) for around £3 on most trips, free on services in southeast England. However, make sure in advance that there is a luggage compartment on your train.

The Cyclists Touring Club (C.T.C), Cotterel House, 69 Meadrow, Godalming, Surrey GU7 3HS provides maps, information and a list of places in Britain that rent bicycles; they can also help you plan itineraries and routes. There is a fee for membership; contact them on 01483 417217 to find out more.

The magazine *Cycle Tours and Campains*, (available in newsagents) will provide useful tips on areas and cities in Britain that are particularly hospitable to cyclists. Consult the *Yellow Pages* for whichever city or town you are in for the names of local bicycle shops and outlets that rent bicycles and can undertake repairs.

DRIVING DETAILS
Accidents

If you are involved in an accident, you should do the following: put on your hazard lights to warn any other drivers to keep clear of the scene; exchange names, addresses, insurance details, and make of car and license plate numbers with any other driver(s) involved; if there are any witnesses, get their names and addresses too; get as much evidence of the accident as possible –

if you have a camera or camcorder, record visual evidence of any damage done.

If anyone has been hurt, get to a phone as quickly as possible to call either the police, ambulance, fire (dial **999** to be connected with any of these emergency services) or with a breakdown company if your car has been disabled – there are emergency telephones at mile intervals on all highways. You must fill in an accident report and get others involved to sign it if possible. Never sign anything that confers responsibility for the accident on you.

Get in touch with your insurance agent as soon as possible, to file a claim form.

How to be a local driver

The most obvious difference about driving in Britain is that you must keep to the left-hand side of the road, and that, if you have rented a car, the steering wheel will be on the right. You can only pass on the right.

Superhighways (motorways) are signposted with an "M" number (for instance, the M1 motorway is the main route directly north out of London; the M40 heads northwest to the Midlands; the M4 heads directly west; and the M20 southeast to the Channel ports.

Smaller **highways** (two lanes, known in Britain as "dual carriageways") are classed as "A" roads on a map. These carry less heavy freight vehicles but are also less direct.

The more minor roads, "B" roads, are in fact the historic lanes and byways of Britain, offering some spectacular scenery, but also much slower going.

Traffic circles (roundabouts) can sometimes be confusing for drivers, but they are signposted well in advance and once you get the hang of them they are fairly easy to navigate. The basic rule is always give way to traffic already on the roundabout, coming from your right.

Pedestrian crossings take a number of different forms in Britain. When approaching a "zebra" crossing (so-called because of the white stripes across the black tarmac) you must stop if there are any pedestrians about to or in the act of crossing the street.

A "pelican" crossing is similar to a zebra crossing except that there are also traffic lights – if they are showing red or yellow, you must stop.

If you have any questions about Britain's Highway Code, telephone the AA's information line (for members of the AA): 0990 500600.

Age required to drive
(see *Driving* on p.263)

Breakdown (see *Driving* on p.263)

Drinking and driving penalties
As in the U.S., driving while under the influence of alcohol is taken very seriously. If you are caught driving whilst suspected of being above the legal limit of alcohol (80mg/liter), you will be offered a breathalyzer test. If you refuse, you will be required to go to the police station for a blood test. If you comply and are found to be over the limit, you will be subject either to a hefty fine and/or possible imprisonment and/or a ban from driving, depending on how much over the limit you are.

Fines
Fines are imposed for a variety of violations, including illegal parking (see below), speeding, driving without a license, driving dangerously, failing to stop at a halt sign or traffic light, driving without insurance, failure to report an accident, failure to stop after an accident and driving whilst under the influence of alcohol or drugs.

Fuel
Gas (petrol) is considerably more expensive in Britain than it is in the United States. It is sold by the liter: leaded as 4-star (97-octane) while there are two grades of unleaded, Super (98-octane) and Premium (95-octane). Diesel fuel for cars is also available in most service stations.

Insurance (see p.264)

Parking
A double yellow line near the curb means that you cannot park there at any time. A single yellow line means you can only park there in the evenings and on Sundays. In London, "Red routes," with a complete ban on parking, are marked with red lines at the side of the road. If you park illegally you may be given a Fixed Penalty Notice (fine) or the car may be wheelclamped; you will have to wait several hours before it is un-clamped, and there will be a fine. Parking lots (car parks) are marked with the sign "P"; rates vary. In some areas, a machine distributes the ticket allowing you to park in a parking lot for any time between 1 to 8 hours. You may pay on exit or at a machine in the parking bays.

Rental (see *Driving* on p.263)

Road signs
The international road signs used in Britain will be familiar to any driver. If in any doubt, you can pick up a copy of the *Highway Code* at any newsagent or bookstore.

Safety belts (seatbelts)
It is British law that safety belts must be worn in the front seats at all times, and in the back seats if the car is fitted with them. Children under 12 are not allowed to ride in the front passenger seat.

Speed limits
The speed limit within a city center or built-up area is 30 mph. On dual carriageways and motorways the limit is 70 mph; on other roads it is 60 mph.

Tolls
Tolls are charged on the following:
• **England**: Batheaston Bridge (Bath), Clifton Bridge (Bristol), Dartford Bridge and Tunnel (London), Dunham Bridge (Lincoln), Humber Bridge (Hull), Itchen Bridge (Southampton), Mersey Tunnel (Liverpool), Severn Bridge (southwest England–South Wales), Tamar Bridge (Devon–Cornwall), Tyne Tunnel (Newcastle), Whitchurch Bridge (Whitchurch), Whitney-on-Wye Bridge (Hereford-Hay-on-Wye)
• **Scotland**: Erskine Bridge (Glasgow), Forth Bridge (Edinburgh), Tay Bridge (Dundee); Skye Bridge (Kyle of Lochalsh)
• **Wales**: Cleddau Bridge (Pembroke), Penrhyndeudraeth Bridge (Porthmadog).

HITCH-HIKING
Hitching is reasonably safe in Britain, but anyone – particularly a woman alone – may still be taking a risk. If you are determined to travel around Britain this way, be sure to

take the following precautions. Once you are in the vehicle, keep your door unlocked and your luggage at hand. Never accept a ride in the back of a two-door car. If you feel unsure of the driver or the direction you are going in – or for any other reason – do not make a big fuss just ask to be let out immediately.

When waiting for a ride stand where drivers can stop safely and get back on the road safely. The best places are before the entrance to a motorway (it is illegal to thumb a lift on the motorway itself), or by a paved shoulder.

• The **London Tourist Information Centre** at Victoria (see p.283) publishes a list of suggested routes to take for hitch-hikers. It is difficult to get lifts out of London, but easier once you are in smaller cities such as Oxford or Cambridge. If you are heading out of London, it is best to get the subway or a bus to an outer suburb (Hendon is a good choice because this is where the M1 motorway to the north begins) and try your luck there.

MAPS

General maps for all of Britain or for a particular region are published by the AA. Michelin's maps are also comprehensive.

Within a given city, your best bet are the exhaustive A–Z maps published by the A–Z Map Company. Ordnance Survey maps are wonderfully detailed and are essential if you are planning to do any serious hiking (see Walking on p.272) or are interested in out-of-the-way footpaths and historical sites. They come in several different scales and special editions are available for regions such as Dartmoor and the Lake District.

All the above maps are available at train stations, bookstores and newsagents throughout Britain.

ORGANIZED TOURS

There are many specialized tours available, which can be arranged either before you go or once you are in Britain. Whether your tastes run to the Yorkshire Moors of the Brontë sisters, stately homes, Wordsworth's Lake District, the castles (or distilleries!) of the Scottish Highlands, Welsh rock-climbing or English Civil War battlegrounds, your travel agent or the local

tourist information centre in Britain (see p.282) will be able to help you.

The British Trust for Conservation Volunteers (B.T.C.V.) offers the slightly unusual but good-for-the-soul opportunity to spend, for instance, a few weeks clearing a Nottinghamshire coppice, trimming a Wiltshire hedgerow or restoring derelict mine engine houses in Cornwall. To find out more, contact the B.T.C.V. at Maidencroft Farm, Higher Wick, Glastonbury, Somerset, BA6 8J4; tel: 01458 835292.

London's magazine *Time Out*, available from newsagents, lists all the guided London walks available (on themes such as Sherlock Holmes, London, Legal London and Cockney London) in any given week – there are often two or three a day to choose from.

PUBLIC TRANSPORTATION
Air

British Airways and a number of small, regional airlines fly routes within Britain. Although comparatively expensive (compared to train or coach travel), they can cover some of the longer distances in Britain (for example, between London and Inverness) quickly and efficiently.

Selected regional airlines are:
• **Air U.K.**: 0345 666777
• **British Airways**: 0345 222111
• **British Midland**: 0345 554554
• **Caledonian Airways**: 01293 535353/ 01865 758400.

Regional airports include:
• **Cardiff (Wales)**: 01446 711111
• **Bristol**: 01275 474444
• **East Midlands**: 01332 852852
• **Exeter**: 01392 367433
• **Leeds/Bradford**: 0113 250 9696
• **Liverpool**: 0151 486 8877
• **Newcastle-upon-Tyne**: 0191 286 0966
• **Plymouth**: 01752 772752
Scotland has numerous small airfields as well as major airports at Glasgow, Edinburgh and Aberdeen (see p.259).

Canals

England has a large network of canals, dating from the Industrial Revolution, that run through the heart of Britain – you can travel by canal into the center of London! Canal boat vacations are very popular with the British, and you may like to try one yourself. The tourist offices in different regions of Britain will be able to put you in touch with local rental companies who can provide you with a canal boat, maps, itineraries and lists of stores, restaurants and attractions along the way.

Buses and coaches

• **National Express**, 4 Vicarage Road, Edgbaston, Birmingham B15 3ES; tel. 0990 808080 is Britain's main operator of short-haul (bus) and long-haul (coach) services. The Tourist Trail Pass provides you with unlimited travel, with 3 different time spans, on National Express routes in England, Scotland, and Wales.

• **Scottish Citylink** (tel: 0990-505050) run services in Scotland. There are four levels of travel to choose from: 3 days in a period of 3 consecutive days, 5 days out of 10, 8 days out of 16 and 15 days out of 30. There is also the Discount Coach Card offering a 30 percent discount on fares; it is available to young people, students and senior citizens and is valid for up to one year. For more information, contact your travel agent or the British Tourist Authority (see Information Tourist Offices p.282).

Each city or town will also have its own network of local services. Other useful numbers are:

• **Transpak**: 0171 833 4472
• **Oxford Bus Company**: 01865 711312

There are regional, young person, student and senior citizen discount tickets available.

Taxis

Taxis in Britain usually take one of two forms: black cabs that can hold up to five people and lots of luggage, and smaller "mini-cab" services.

Black cabs have meters; **mini-cabs** usually offer set prices depending on how far you are going – sometimes mini-cabs will let you share with another occupant if one of you can be dropped off somewhere en route. Make sure with all mini-cabs that you settle on a price beforehand. Even if the cab is metered any driver should be able to give you an estimated price, subject always

of course to traffic fluctuations. If you cannot get the driver to give you an approximate idea of the charge beforehand, find another.

Black cabs are often equipped with special "lifts" to make them more accessible to people with disabilities. Another option for those with disabilities is the "dial-a-ride" systems that exist nationwide.

The number for central London is 0171 482 2325; the *Yellow Pages* can help you locate regional dial-a-ride programs wherever you may be in Britain.

Train

The recently privatized rail service operates a dense network of trains throughout Britain. InterCity trains connect the larger cities, using high-speed (InterCity 125) trains. London is included in the regional service known as Network SouthEast.

There are two classes of travel: first and standard (economy). First-class cars are more luxurious, and their price (some 50 percent higher) reflects this.

If you think you are going to travel around a lot while you are in Britain, it is worth getting a **BritRail Pass**. There are four types available, each valid for 4, 8, 15 or 22 days or for one month of unlimited travel in England, Scotland, and Wales. You can get either a First Class, Standard, Senior Citizen (over 60) or Youth (under 26) Pass.

In addition, there is the **BritRail Flexipass** (valid for any 4, 8 or 15 days in a period of one month).

The **London Extra Pass** offers unlimited travel on 3 or 4 days out of 8, or 7 days out of 15, on all trains in southeast England, in addition to travel on London's underground and buses. You must purchase these passes before you leave the U.S.

They are available from most travel agencies and from BritRail Travel's International Offices by rail or phone from 1500 Broadway, New York, NY 10036; tel. 212/382 3737 and (800) 677 8585, or in person from the British Travel Shop, 551 Fifth Avenue, New York City.

Once in Britain, there are a number of Rail Rover (passes) to choose from, allowing you unlimited travel within a specified region of Britain. They are good value for one or two weeks.

The ScotRail Rover provides unlimited travel in Scotland for 4 out of 8 days, 8 consecutive days, or 12 out of 15 days. In addition, there are Area Rovers for specified regions of Scotland for rail travel on 3 out of 7 or 4 out of 8 days.

Contact National Rail Enquiries for details.

London's British Rail stations

• **Charing Cross, Liverpool Street, Victoria and Waterloo**: 0171 928 5100 (services to East Anglia, the southeast, and southern England)
• **Euston, Marylebone and St. Pancras**: 0171 387 7070 (services to the west Midlands, east Midlands, the northwest, north Wales and Scotland via the west coast)
• **King's Cross**: 0171 278 2477 (services to West Yorkshire, the northeast of England and eastern Scotland)
• **Paddington**: 0171 262 6767 (services to west and southwest England, the south Midlands and south Wales).

British Rail also has a "Disabled Travel Arrangements" unit to handle any queries or complaints you might have: 0171 922 6061 (Charing Cross); 0171 922 6482 (Euston); 0171 922 4904 (King's Cross); 0171 922 6793 (Paddington); 0171 922 6466 (St. Pancras) and 0171 922 4500 (Waterloo).

Numbers for other major British Rail stations

Birmingham New Street/York/Cardiff/Edinburgh/Glasgow: 0345 484950; Belfast: 01232 899411.
The National Rail inquiries line is open 24 hours a day for timetable information.

London underground and bus

The London underground (known as the "tube") covers London comprehensively, with more than 250 stations and 11 lines (Bakerloo, Central, Circle, District, East London, Hammersmith & City, Jubilee, Metropolitan, Northern, Piccadilly and Victoria). An extension to the Jubilee line is due to be finished by 1999, this will add 11 more stations. The Docklands Light Railway also links up with some underground (subway) stations.

All the lines are color-coded, and there are maps posted on every platform and in every station entrance to help you get around. Connecting services are well signposted. The routes are divided into zones (Zone 1 is inner London), and fares depend on how many zones you cross. You buy tickets either from the ticket window or from a machine within the station entrance. For further information, contact London Transport (passenger information): 0171 222 1234.

London's **buses** take a bit more getting used to, but they can be more economical, and you get to see where you are rather than being underground in a tunnel. On most single- and double-decker buses you pay the driver as you get on; there are still some, however, on which you board and then pay the conductor. Again, the fare will depend on how far you are going.

The **One-Day Travelcard** gives you un-limited journeys on buses, and underground and British Rail trains within the zones specified, for one day of travel after 9.30 a.m. Monday to Friday, all day Saturday and Sunday.

The **Visitor Travelcard** offers similar benefits but is for 1, 2, 3, 4 or 7 days and in-cludes discount vouchers for top London sights. You must purchase this before you leave the U.S. from British Tourist Authority offices (see Tourist Offices p.266).

WALKING

Britain enjoys an extensive network of ancient short- and long-distance footpaths which reach across the whole country; these are particularly rewarding in the national parks where they cross some spectacular countryside.

If you plan to do any serious hiking, contact the following organizations for help:
• **The Ramblers' Association**, 1–5 Wandsworth Road, London SW8 2XX; tel. 0171 582 6878
• **Ramblers Holidays**, PO Box 43, Welwyn Garden City, Hertfordshire AL8 6PZ; tel. 01707 331133.

Remember, too, that you will need some very good maps (see *Maps* p.270).

DAY-TO-DAY

ACCOMMODATIONS
It is always wise to make reservations for accommodations in advance, either before you go or as soon as you get to a city or town where you would like to stay. Head for the local tourist information center who should be able to help you.

Hotels come in all shapes and sizes in Britain, from vast sprawling estates to tiny cottages with only a few rooms. To find out more, consult the AA *Hotel Guide*, which inspects 4,000 hotels in Britain and Ireland, and is available in the U.S. through AAA.

The British Tourist Authority also produces a brochure called *Britain: Stay At An Inn*, giving you the low-down on historic, picturesque coaching inns throughout England, Wales and Scotland.

There is a full list of recommended hotels in the Hotels and Restaurants section starting on p.285, along with an explanation of the diamond-rating system employed.

Bed-and-breakfast (B&B) establishments are usually a cheaper alternative, and may also suit travelers who want to get more of a feel for local life at the place where they are staying. As the name suggests, prices include a room and breakfast (served in a communal breakfast room at a fixed time in the morning). They are usually smaller establishments (often a farmhouse or private home with just a few rooms); in some cases you may be able to eat your evening meal here for an added charge. The AA *Bed and Breakfast Guide*, which inspects over 3,000 establishments (updated yearly) in Britain and Ireland, will tell you all you need to know.

Useful addresses
• **British Hotel Reservation Centre**, 10 Buckingham Palace Road, London SW1W 0QP; tel: 0171 828 2425, fax: 0171 828 6439. Hotel, B&B and hostel bookings.
• **The Independent Traveller**, Thorverton, Exeter EX5 5NT; tel. 01392 860807; specialize in self-catering accommodations.
• **Worldwide Bed and Breakfast Association**, P.O. Box 2070, London W12 80W; tel. 0181 742 9123.

Camping and caravanning There are a multitude of lovely **campgrounds** throughout Britain. Before you arrive, you should get an International Camping Carnet, which entitles you to discounts at many campgrounds. They are often combined with caravan (motor home or trailer) parks, another popular way of exploring the countryside. A helpful handbook is the AA *Camping and Caravanning Guide* (updated yearly).

Useful addresses
• **The Camping and Caravanning Club**, Greenfields House, Westwood Way, Coventry, West Midlands CV4 8JH; tel. 01203 694955
• **The Caravan Club**, East Grinstead House, London Road, East Grinstead, West Sussex RH19 1UA; tel. 01342 326944.

Renting a **holiday cottage** or **apartment** is how many people spend their vacations. These can take the form of an apartment, country house, trailer, or cottage – all are furnished, and the rates can be a significant saving over staying in a hotel or B&B. They are usually "self-catering" (that is, you have to do your own cooking, though all are equipped with kitchen appliances, such as refrigerators and ovens, and all the utensils, plates and cups you need).

Families with children or the more independent traveler can find this a very pleasant way of passing time in one part of the country. Lists of available properties can be obtained from the British Tourist Authority (see p.266).

House-swapping is an alternative particularly suited to families. All you do is register details of your home with an agency such as those listed below, then for a fee they can provide you with a list of possible homes in which you could stay in the country or region of your choice. It is then up to you to get in touch with the homeowner and work out a time that is mutually agreeable.
Some useful addresses are:
• **Home Interchange** – information available from the British Tourist Authority (see p.266)
• **Servas**, 11 John Street, Room 407, New York, NY 10038; tel. 212/267 0252.

During the summer and at other times when university students are not in residence, many British **universities** open their doors (and facilities) to visitors. This is another inexpensive option, and is well worth looking into:

• **British Universities Accommodation Consortium Ltd** (B.U.A.C.), P.O. Box 1146, University Park, Nottingham NG7 2RD; tel. 0115 950 4571
• **Connect Venues**, The Workstation, Sheffield S1 2BX; tel: 0114 249 3090.

Youth hostels

Hostelling International (formerly the International Youth Hostel Federation) provides another cheap and pleasant accommodation alternative. For the price of the membership fee you get an International Hostel Card which entitles you to stay at any of the thousands of HI hostels worldwide.

There are more than 400 **youth hostels** in Britain. Some are in beautiful old buildings, surrounded by spectacular countryside, others are closer to city life (and local amenities). Facilities can range from dormitory-style rooms to more private accommodations.

You need not be a certain age to stay in a youth hostel. There is a limit, however, on how long you can stay: four days in London (even if you change hostels) and three days elsewhere in Britain.

To find out more, contact:
• **Hostelling International**, 733 15th Street, NW, Washington DC 20005; tel. 202/783 6161 and (800) 444 6111
• **Youth Hostels Association (Y.H.A.) (England and Wales)**, Trevelyan House, 8 St. Stephen's Hill, St. Albans, Hertford- shire AL1 2DY; tel. 01727 844126
• **Scottish Youth Hostels Association (S.Y.H.A.)**, 7 Glebe Crescent, Stirling FK8 2JA; tel. 01786 451181
• **Youth Hostel Association of Northern Ireland (Y.H.A.N.I.)**, 22–23 Donegall Road, Belfast BT12 5JN; tel. 01232 324733.

CHILDREN

The British are becoming more and more aware of the potential money to be made from vacationing families, and there are more and more attractions that children (and adults!) will find interesting and fun.

Popular children's attractions

There are several excellent zoos and safari parks, including London Zoo, Edinburgh Zoo, Colchester Zoo and Blair Drummond Safari Park (Scotland). The English resorts of Blackpool, Scarborough and Poole also offer wonderful aquariums.

Theme parks are rapidly growing in number throughout Britain, the biggest and most popular ones include: Thorpe Park (Chertsey, Surrey); Alton Towers (Alton, Staffordshire); Legoland (Windsor, Berkshire); Chessington World of Adventure (Outer London); American Adventure (Ilkeston, Derbyshire).

Other popular children's attractions throughout Britain include: the Tower of London, Madame Tussaud's, the Natural History Museum, the Planetarium, the Science Museum (London); the Dinosaur Museum (Dorchester); Cheddar Caves (Cheddar); Severn Valley Railway (Bewdley); the Museum of Childhood (Beaumaris, Wales); Lightwater Valley Action Park (North Stainley, North Yorkshire); Edinburgh Butterfly Farm; the Aviemore Centre (Aviemore, Scotland); the Jorvik Centre (York).

Popular coastal resorts in England and Wales include those at Weston-super-Mare, Whitby, Great Yarmouth, Weymouth, Newquay, and Llandudno – all with special activities (donkey rides, amusement arcades, beaches, fun fairs) geared for children of all ages.

Help with the kids

Most airports and many of the larger stores, train stations and restaurants have mother- and-baby rooms and can offer you high- chairs, strollers and other paraphernalia to make everything a bit less of a hassle.

COMPLAINTS

If you have a complaint, the best policy is to go directly to the source.
• The **Trading Standards Office** deals with consumer complaints regarding goods bought in stores: 0181 356 5000

• Also check the *Yellow Pages* under "Consumer Organisations."

CRIME

A recent survey found that Britain has a low crime rate (particularly when compared with the U.S.), but ironically, the British perceive themselves as surrounded by ever-increasing dangers!

Basically, the standard rules apply:

• Try not to wave jewelry or cash around, particularly in big cities.

• Always keep your purse or wallet where it is easy for you to reach and difficult for a pickpocket to get hold of.

• Lock your car up carefully and keep valuables out of sight, and always try to look like you know where you are going, even if you are hopelessly lost!

• If possible, avoid going to isolated areas alone. Always walk in well-lit places, avoiding poorly lit parking lots, dark alleyways and tall shrubbery.

• If using an automatic teller machine (ATM), choose one in a well-lit area with plenty of foot traffic, such as one at a grocery store. Machines inside establishments are the safest to use.

• Separate money from your credit cards, and use credit cards and/or AAA traveler's checks as much as possible, leaving unneccessary valuable items or money behind.

CONVERSION CHART

miles	kilometers	mph	kph
1	1·6093	70	112
·6214	1	43	70

inches	centimeters		
·3937	1		
1	2.54		

feet	meters	yards	meters
1	·3048	1	·9144
3.2810	1	1.094	1

sq. feet	sq. meters	sq. meters	sq. yards
1	·0929	1	1.196

pounds	kilograms	ounces	grams
2·2	1	1	28·35
1	·4536	·0353	1

With these commonsense rules in mind, you should not have your vacation spoiled by theft or assault of any kind.

ETIQUETTE

The English have a reputation for being reserved. While this is a generalization, it has a basis in truth. You may have noticed the words "the English" in the previous sentence, not "the British." Britain is just that, a (not always smooth or happy) bringing together of four very different countries: England, Scotland, Wales, and Northern Ireland, each with its own history, literature, customs, and ethnic groups (although strictly speaking Britain is England, Scotland and Wales – the addition of Northern Ireland makes it the U.K.).

Don't refer to England if you mean all of Britain – or, worse still, speak of everywhere else in Britain as if it were a suburb of London. You will definitely step on toes if you mistakenly lump together this united kingdom of Scotsmen, Welshmen, Yorkshiremen, Mancunians (those from Manchester), Liverpudlians (those from Liverpool), etc., etc. – each with its own cultural heritage and pride – into one bundle. Imagine how insulted a Texan would be if a foreigner thought that New York *was* America, and you will get some idea of what we mean!

While some travelers find that people get more friendly as they travel north, this of course is another generalization, and depends on what you are used to (city-dwellers from the States will find nothing strange in the fact that no one will meet your eye on the crowded London subway). From the British point of view, Americans have a reputation for being a bit too loud, a bit too ostentatious and a bit too curious. This is not to say that the Brits are unfriendly – they just take more time to warm up! With a little practice you should be able to pick up on when to talk and when to listen. Body language (the English generally need more personal space around them than Americans) will also give clues as to how to act.

As a guest in Britain you will naturally want to follow the social rules – but having said this, don't feel you have to be something you are not: many Brits are charmed by Americans' comparative openness and frankness. And as is true anywhere else in the world, if you are friendly, most people will respond in kind.

GENEALOGY

Many visitors to Britain have ancestors who originally came from England, Scotland, Wales or Ireland. If you would like to combine your vacation with a bit of detective work by trying to trace your roots, here are some places that can be of help:
The Family Records Centre (1 Myddelton Street, London EC1R 1UW; tel.0151 471 4800) is where a copy of all birth, death and marriage records for England and Wales are kept. If you know your relative's date of birth, or where in Britain they were born (for anyone born before 1917), you can begin to uncover your family tree. You will need time, however, and considerable diligence and patience – each time you request to see a copy of a birth (or death, or marriage) certificate it has to be found for you and it costs £6 to personal callers (£15 by postal application). The Centre is closed on Sundays and public holidays.

Things are easier in **Scotland**, where you can search the computerized records at New Register House, Edinburgh, EH1 3YT; tel: 0131 334 0380, for £16 a day.

In **Northern Ireland** contact the General Register Office, Oxford House, 49 Chichester Street, Belfast BT1 4HL; tel: 01232 252000.

If you would rather have someone else do the hunting for you, the **Society of Genealogists** (14 Charterhouse Buildings, Gaswell Road, London EC1; tel. 0171 251 8799) can give you a list of reputable genealogists.

HEALTH MATTERS

Medical help is readily available throughout Britain. The National Health Service (NHS), which operates most clinics and hospitals, is free to U.K. and European Union citizens and residents. Private medical care is also widely available. If you need a doctor, dentist or other health professional, your hotel or the local *Yellow Pages* can point you in the right direction. The treatment offered by British medical professional (NHS or private) is uniformly excellent.

Drugstores

Boots is by far the largest (and oldest) chain of drugstores (also known in Britain as "chemists"), selling not only prescription and over-the-counter medications but also toiletries, health foods and drinks, foods for people with special dietary needs such as diabetics, camera film, disposable diapers and other baby products, and sunglasses. (See *Opening Hours* p.279.)

LANGUAGE

"Two great nations divided by a common language" could describe the linguistic gulf that separates the U.S. from Britain.

Here are some examples to help you:

American	British
elevator	**lift**
ATM	**cashpoint**
call collect	**reverse charge call**
phone booth	**call box**
call	**ring up**
(as in "to telephone")	
one-way ticket	**single**
round-trip ticket	**return**
suspenders	**braces**
pants	**trousers**
underwear	**pants**
pantyhose	**tights/stockings**
washcloth	**flannel**
parking lot	**car park**
French fries	**chips**
potato chips	**crisps**
cookies	**biscuits**
jelly	**jam**
Jell-O	**jelly**
turnips	**swedes**
zucchini	**courgettes**
eggplant	**aubergine**
candy	**sweets**
soft (hamburger) bun	**bap**
cotton candy	**candyfloss**
trunk (of a car)	**boot**
hood (of a car)	**bonnet**
gas	**petrol**
divided highway	**dual carriageway**
paved shoulder	**lay-by**
edge of road shoulder	**verge**
rotary/traffic circle	**roundabout**
truck	**lorry**
highway/freeway	**motorway**
underground	
pedestrian passage	**subway**

subway	**tube/underground**
sidewalk	**pavement**
street	**road**
trash or garbage can	**dust or rubbish bin**
first floor	**ground floor**
second floor	**first floor**
two weeks	**fortnight**
rent	**hire**
main street stores	**high street shops**
drugstore	**chemist**
liquor store	**off-licence**
check (in a restaurant)	**bill**
ball-point pen	**biro**
police officer	**bobby**
client, consumer	**punter**
line up/in line	**queue**
orchestra seats	**stalls**
14 lbs (weight)	**a stone**
restroom	**loo/toilet/W.C.**

MEDIA

Britain has a well-deserved reputation for excellent news reportage. The BBC (British Broadcasting Corporation) is the standard-bearer of this tradition, and transmits not just nationwide but also (in the form of its World Service radio programs) impartial analysis and pithy commentary to all corners of the globe. It is also well known for the quality of its documentaries and costume drama productions which are sold worldwide.

Television

Though it often comes as a shock to Americans, Britain also has only five television stations. Of these, the two BBC stations are similar to the U.S. "public broadcast" stations in that they are non-commercial – funded instead by the television license fee that every household with a television must pay yearly. The other three television stations (ITV, Channel 4, and Channel 5) are independent and funded by advertising.

The five stations are:
• **BBC 1**: featuring mostly light enter-tainment, children's programs, soap operas, blockbuster movies and news features
• **BBC 2**: offers serious drama, music, films, more avant-garde arts programs, in-depth news reportage and public affairs programs
• **ITV** (Independent Television): offers a mixture of made-for-tv movies, news,

children's programs, soap operas, and light entertainment. Different independent companies serve different regions within Britain, such as Granada (Greater Manchester), Carlton (London), HTV Wales, Yorkshire TV, Westcountry, and Scottish.
• **Channel 4**: Britain's youngest television station features more off-beat programs as well as news, public affairs, movies and arts programs, and several popular U.S. imports such as *Roseanne, Cheers* and *LA Law*.
• **Channel 5**: the newest British independent television station, showing a cross-section of programs including movies news, Australian soaps, wild-life documentaries, children's programs, sporting events (including major league baseball live), and chat shows hosted by well-known U.S. celebities.

This system of national programing is supplemented by local BBC and independent programs and stations. Satellite and cable stations have begun to make some inroads into the audience ratings; an ever-increasing number of companies serve up the usual mix including music, movies, classic television shows and international sporting events.

Radio

In Britain, the BBC has five major radio networks:
• **Radio 1** (also known as 1 FM; 97.6–99.8 MHz/FM): pop music and youth-oriented programs
• **Radio 2** (88–91 MHz/FM): mostly easy-listening music
• **Radio 3** (90.2–92.4 MHz/FM): classical music
• **Radio 4** (92.4–94.6 MHz/FM; 198 KHz/AM): news, drama, comedy, current affairs, arts programs
• **Radio 5 Live** (693 and 909 KHz/AM): rolling news and sport.

In addition there are hundreds of local, regional BBC affiliates that offer a mixture of music, discussion, and topics of local interest to cities and regions all over Britain.

There are also many independent radio stations, including:
• **Capital Radio** (95.8 MHz/FM): mostly popular music, aimed at a young audience
• **Classic FM** (100–102 MHz/FM): popular classical music

• **Virgin Radio** (105.8 FM and 1215 KHz/AM): rock music from the 1950s to the 1990s
• **Atlantic 252** (252 KHz/AM): similar to Virgin Radio

plus any number of regional independents.

Newspapers and magazines

British journalism is rigorously outspoken and discriminating. There are several national newspapers, usually divided up into what are called "tabloids" (more sensational, less "serious"), daily papers such as *The Sun*, the *Daily Star*, *The Mirror*, *The Express*, and the *Daily Mail*, and those known as "broadsheets" such as *The Guardian*, *The Times*, the *Daily Telegraph* and *The Independent*.

Most papers clearly have a bias towards left- or right-wing politics. All feature television and radio guides, information on the money markets, weather trends, and accounts of the worlds of entertainment, sports and politics. There are local papers for every British town, city and region.

There are literally hundreds of general and specialist magazines in Britain, with new ones hitting the shelves every year. Some names (such as *Vogue* and *GQ*) you will be familiar with, but the contents will be different for U.K. consumption.

A good magazine for any visitor to London is *Time Out*, a weekly guide to what is on in London's theaters, movie theaters, museums and clubs.

MONEY MATTERS

The British unit of currency is the **pound sterling**, more simply known as the pound (£), made up of 100 pence (p).

Pounds come in denominations of £5, £10, £20 and £50 bills or notes – Scotland also has £1 notes still in circulation – and there are also 1p, 2p, 5p, 10p, 20p, 50p, £1 and £2 coins (or "pieces").

Travelers' checks are welcome at most hotels, restaurants and stores, and can be cashed at most banks and *bureaux de change*. It is wise to get travelers' checks in pounds sterling, as you will not lose money every time you change them, and have a mix of large and small denominations.

American Express, Thomas Cook and most of the major banks will cash travelers'

checks provided you have some form of ID (such as your passport).

(For bank opening hours, see *Opening Hours* p.279.)

Credit cards (VISA, Mastercard, American Express) are widely accepted throughout Britain.

NIGHTLIFE AND ENTERTAINMENT

London may be in some respects Britain's entertainment capital, if only for the sheer number of its theaters, movie theaters and clubs, but every city (and even some smaller towns) has its share of night diversions.

The **theater** is alive and well, not just in London (although its hundreds of offerings are hard to beat), but in renowned regional theater companies throughout the land.

At the **movies**, you will find a predominance of U.S. imports, although the domestic product is getting more and more funding all the time. Most cities and larger towns will have at least one "cinema multiplex" catering to the needs of the local population.

In addition, nearly everywhere you go you will find **nightclubs** and venues for **opera, ballet, concerts, comedy, cabaret and galleries**. A glance through any local newspaper will give you the low-down on what is on that evening.

Pub life thrives, and a new regulation allowing children into pubs (many have a special family room) means that families can take advantage of this unique aspect of British life (see *Opening Hours* p.279). Pubs can be anything from tiny nooks with original oak beams and regulars who look like they have been there since 1606 to spanking new establishments attracting young crowds. In short, whatever your taste, there is a pub in Britain for you. Most try to preserve an atmosphere conducive to conversation and a good time for all. Many court trade by having quiz nights, karaoke nights or other group-oriented diversions.

Getting **tickets** for a show or event is usually fairly straightforward – as long as it is not the hottest ticket in town! If you think you may have trouble getting to a "must see," you can book tickets in advance through your travel agent or the British Tourist Authority (see Tourist Offices p.266). Once in Britain, you can get tickets either direct from the venue or by calling a ticketing service (listed in the *Yellow Pages* under "Ticket Agencies") and charging them to your credit card. Some hotels offer a reservation service, but their charges can be high.

There are two other options specifically for booking theater tickets:
In Leicester Square, the **Society of West End Theatres Half-Price Ticket Booth** (S.W.E.T.) has same-day tickets for many plays and shows available half price from 1–6:30 p.m. Monday to Saturday; noon–6:30 p.m. Sunday and matinée days (usually Thursday and Saturday). There is always a long line.

The **Tokenline** (tel. 0171 240 8800) sells theater tokens in denominations of £1, £5, £10 and £20 which can be exchanged at more than 125 theaters nationwide – there is no expiry date and you can get as many as you like. If you want to get some theater tokens before you leave the U.S., write to the Society of London Theatre, Bedford Chambers, The Piazza, Covent Garden, London WC2E 8HA.

(See *Spectator Sports* p.281.)

OPENING HOURS
Banks
Normal banking hours are 9.30 a.m.–3.30 p.m., although many of the major banks stay open until 4.30 or 5.30 p.m. at least a few days a week and may also be open on Saturday mornings until noon or 12.30 p.m.

Banks in Scotland and Northern Ireland usually close during the lunch hour (12 to 1 p.m.). In Northern Ireland banks do not open until 10 a.m.; in Scotland they usually stay open until 6 p.m. on Thursdays.

Stores
Stores are open between 9/9:30 a.m. and 5:30/6 p.m., although many stay open until 8 p.m. one day a week. Supermarkets are usually open until around 8 p.m. on weekdays. Newspaper stores are open from about 5:30 a.m. to 5 p.m., and on Sunday mornings until noon. Smaller grocery stores are often open long hours (8/9 a.m. to 10 p.m.), though the 24-hour store is still fairly rare in Britain. With the passing of recent new regulations, more stores and shopping malls are open on Sundays. Some stores and banks in smaller towns usually close early (12/1 p.m.) one day a week, often Wednesday or Thursday.

Post offices
Post offices are open from 9 a.m. to 5:30 p.m. weekdays and 9 a.m. to 12:30 p.m. on Saturdays. The main one in each city (see *Post Offices* p.280) may stay open later and post offices in rural areas are often closed on Wednesday afternoon.

Drugstores
Drugstores ("chemists" in Britain) are usually open from 9/9:30 a.m. to 5:30 p.m. Monday to Saturday; at least one in any city neighborhood or town will also stay open until 8/9 p.m. each evening and on Sundays for prescriptions and emergencies. There is always at least one drugstore open late (in larger cities even 24 hours); the local paper will usually tell you where this drugstore is and how late it will be open.

Pubs
Pubs are allowed to serve food and drink from 11 a.m. to 11 p.m. weekdays and noon to 10:30 p.m. on Sundays (England and Wales); 11 a.m. to 11 p.m. weekdays and 12:30 to 11 p.m. on Sundays (Scotland); 11:30 a.m. to 11 p.m. and 12:30 to 10 p.m. on Sundays (Northern Ireland).

Museums
Museums are usually open from 10 a.m. to 5/6 p.m. Monday to Saturday, and Sundays 2 to 5/6 p.m. Some stay open later one night a week (to 7/8 p.m.), but may also shut one day a week (Monday or Tuesday). Other places of interest usually follow this pattern.

PLACES OF WORSHIP
The Church of England and the Church of Scotland (what Americans would know as Episcopalian and Presbyterian churches) serve the predominant religion in Britain – Protestant. This is a multi-cultural nation, however, and its places of worship, even in the smaller cities and towns, reflects this. In short, if you are a practicing Protestant, Catholic, Jew, Muslim, Buddhist, Hindu, Greek or Russian Orthodox, you will be able to find a place of worship in Britain. Your hotel or the local *Yellow* or *White Pages* will be able to tell you of the nearest one.

POST OFFICES

• **London**: "London, Chief Post Office" is all anyone needs to get a letter to you from abroad. It will be kept at the *poste restante* desk at the Trafalgar Square post office, 24–28 William IV Street (*poste restante* address: Poste Restante, Trafalgar Square P.O., London WC2N 4DL; tel: 0171 930 9580; open 8 a.m.–8 p.m. Monday to Saturday (open 8:30 a.m. Friday).

You will need some form of ID, such as your passport or international driving license.

Other major cities

• **Edinburgh**: 8 St James Centre, EH1 3SR
• **Belfast**: 25 Castle Place, BT1 1BB
• **Cardiff**: The Hayes, 2–4 Hill Street, CF1 2ST
• **Cambridge**: 9–11 St. Andrew's Street, CB2 3AX
• **Glasgow**: 47 Vincent Street, G2 5QX
• **Manchester**: 26 Spring Gardens, M2 1AA
• **Oxford**: 102–4 St. Aldates, OX1 1ZY
• **Exeter**: Bedford Street, EX1 1AA
• **York**: 22 Lendal, YO1 1AA

For advice on postal services, call 0345 223344 (call charged at local rate).

An airmail postcard or letter sent from Britain will take anywhere between 4 and 10 days to arrive at its destination; it will probably take about the same length of time for any mail to reach you from outside Britain.

RESTROOMS

Public restrooms are plentiful in train and bus stations, shopping malls, and museums, and are generally maintained to a high standard. The exception to this may be those in parks or on the street, although even here every effort is made to keep them as welcoming as possible. Public restrooms on the street are usually free; some have attendants whom you can inform if there is no toilet paper or if a stall seems to be out of order for any reason. There is usually a small fee (about 20p) for using restrooms at main line railroad stations and for the aluminum booths that appear on the streets of London.

Men's and women's restrooms are distinguished by the now-familiar symbol for "man" (basic stick figure) and "woman" (basic stick figure in a skirt).

Sometimes there are separate facilities for people with disabilities (the sign is a simplified drawing of a person in a wheel-chair); there will be at least one stall equipped for people with disabilities (extra wide doors, and handles) in both the men's and women's restrooms.

Many restrooms also have a special "mother and baby" room or area for changing and feeding a baby. Unfortunately "father and baby rooms" are non-existent, although if this room is completely separate from both the men's and women's restrooms, fathers should have no qualms about taking their baby there if necessary.

SHOPPING

The British, like the Americans, love to shop, and you will find plenty of opportunities to spend your cash or use your credit card (although shopping hours are not as extensive as in the U.S.).

Different parts of Britain are traditionally associated with different **crafts** and **industries**. Sheffield produces some of the finest silverware and silver plate; Scotland and Wales great woolens; and the cities of the Midlands offer world-renowned Wedgwood, Royal Doulton and Royal Worcester china and pottery. Most cities and towns have neighborhoods that are known for antique stores, or bookstores, or jewelry.

London and other major cities have several shopping meccas; smaller cities will most likely have one **shopping mall** ("shopping precinct"), often pedestrianized (no cars allowed) in the city center, and a big mall on the outskirts of town.

Some city centers are better laid-out than others, and the fashion has moved from the anonymous mall to having more idiosyncratic groupings of craftstores, major name stores (John Lewis, Marks & Spencer, Debenhams) and food halls, along with clothes and shoe stores.

It is also worth striking out for the **markets**. Almost all cities and even towns and small villages have outdoor and sometimes indoor markets at least one day a week. Here you will be able to find genuine handicrafts and antiques, as well as freshly-baked bread and cakes, freshly-caught fish, woolens and hand-made goods. The British are not too enthusiastic about haggling, so though it is worth a try, if you meet resistance it is best to pay up or walk away. **Souvenirs** are not hard to come by – in fact, in some places (such as London's Oxford Street) they are hard to avoid! All the major tourist attractions and most train stations have a selection of postcards, books, chinaware, memorabilia, and foodstuffs – toffee candy, peppermint sticks ("rock"), teas etc. from which to choose. If you are visiting a very small or out-of-the-way place, the local post office is probably the best place to find something to rekindle memories after you are back home.

V.A.T. (Value Added Tax, levied on all services and most goods except for food and children's clothing) is currently 17.5 percent – it will already be added to any price you see displayed for an item. However, foreign visitors do not have to pay V.A.T. if they take advantage of the Retail Export Scheme (often called "Tax-Free Shopping").

When you pay (you must spend over £50 or £75 in one store, depending on the store), you should show proof that you are a U.S. citizen (or overseas resident) and ask for V.A.T. Form 407. Then hand in all the V.A.T. forms to British Customs when you leave the country. Your refund will be forwarded to you.

Some stores also participate in the Europe Tax-free Shopping (E.T.S.) system, for purchases of over £100. They will fill in a "Tax-free Cheque" showing how much of a refund you are entitled to. Once this has been stamped by customs, this check can be cashed at any E.T.S. payout point at ports, airports and train stations.

SPECTATOR SPORTS

The British love sports, particularly football (soccer), cricket, rugby, tennis, golf, racing, darts, snooker; and also, increasingly, ice hockey, basketball, and American football.
• **Soccer** is known as "the people's game." The season lasts from August until early May. The highlight is the FA (Football Association) Cup Final at London's Wembley Stadium around the middle of May.

England and Scotland have separate leagues (Welsh teams play in the English leagues); within each there are different ranks, or "divisions" from 1–4. The Premiere Division is made up of England's "major league" clubs. Although the game

has a reputation for violence and rioting among its spectators, the majority of Saturday afternoon games are real family events, with an atmosphere which should be experienced. If you thought the Brits were generally quiet, reserved or polite, you will witness quite the opposite when you become part of a crowd of fans!
• **Cricket** teams represent the different shires, or counties, of England rather than individual cities. Cricket rules are notoriously difficult to fathom, but overall the game is similar to baseball (particularly in the way some people find it slow, while enthusiasts think the intelligent strategy necessary, and the often brilliant plays, make it very exciting). The atmosphere is somewhat subdued compared to that of a football match, but there is passion none the less.
• **Rugby** has two major divisions: **Rugby Union** and **Rugby League**. Rugby Union teams have 15 players and Rugby League have 13 players, who are semi-professional. The game is somewhat like American football, and supporters are loud and vociferous when cheering their teams on.

In addition, football, rugby, cricket and other sports have national teams made up of the best players from England, Scotland, Wales and Northern Ireland respectively. In June 1996, England hosted the European Football Championship, held every 4 years. Plans are afoot to make a bid for the U.K. to host the soccer World Cup in 2006.
• **Tennis**: Wimbledon is justly famed as a major international event on the professional tennis circuit (last week of June and the first week in July). There are also smaller competitions throughout the year in Britain. Information about and coverage of sports events can be found in the daily press – usually the back pages. **Tickets** can be obtained at the venue, through a tourist agency, or by calling one of the ticket agencies listed in the local *Yellow Pages*. Here are a few for London (they can provide you with tickets to events outside London as well):
• **1st for Tickets**: tel. 0171 209 3412
• **Access Tix**: tel. 0171 821 6616
• **Dial-a-Ticket**: tel. 0171 930 8331
• **Premier Events**: tel. 0171 403 9555.
• **Ticketmaster**: tel. 0171 344 4444
• **Ticketron**: tel. 0171 724 4444; fax 0171 497 3000.

TELEPHONES

Public phones are plentiful in Britain, though sadly there are fewer of the old-fashioned red phone boxes than there used to be, most having been replaced by clear glass-and-steel boxes with a blue-and-red British Telecom (BT) symbol on all four sides.

Payphones can be found on the street, in train stations, hotels, the larger post offices and some stores. Most take 10p, 20p, 50p and £1 coins, though if you put a large coin in and do not use up the money you will not be refunded (for this reason having five 20p coins at hand to keep slotting in as necessary is wiser than sticking a £1 coin to make a local call).

Some call boxes take phonecards, they are distinctive for the green BT stripe on the outside. Phonecards can be bought in newsagents, post offices, the larger chains of stationery stores and anywhere that displays the phonecard sign; they come in denominations of 20, 40, 100 and 200 units of 10p each.

The most expensive time to make a call is between 8 a.m. and 6 p.m. The cheapest time is from 6 p.m. to 8 a.m. and at weekends. Having said that, there is a minimum standard charge of 10p if you are calling from a payphone.

Some useful information numbers are:
• **100** – for help making a call within Britain
• **155** – for help making an international call
• **192** – information for Britain, other than London (known as "directory enquiries")
• **142** – information for London
• **153** – international information

The code for calling the U.S. from anywhere in Britain is 001; you then just dial the area code and number you want to reach (for example, to make a call to Chicago you would dial 001-312/555 5555 – but don't forget they are 6 hours behind Britain, so calling after about 2 p.m. U.K. time would probably be best).

To send a telegram or telemessage overseas, dial (freephone) 190.

TIPPING

In a restaurant or hotel a service charge is normally included. Where it is not, you are expected to leave a tip of between 10 and 15 percent. Taxi drivers should also be tipped 10 to 15 percent, as should hairdressers. In pubs, the standard way to give the bartender a tip is to say "and one for yourself" when you are ordering a drink – people do not usually just leave a tip on the bar. You do not need to tip the bartender every time you order a drink, nor at all if you are only staying for one. You are not expected to tip theater or movie ushers or usherettes, nor elevator operators. A tip of 50–75p is usual for anyone who carries your luggage. Washroom attendants are usually tipped 10/20p.

TOURIST INFORMATION OFFICES
National offices
• **British Tourist Authority**, Thames Tower, Black's Road, London W6 9EL (written inquiries only)
• **British Travel Centre**, 12 Regent Street, Piccadilly Circus, London W1Y 4PQ (personal callers only)
• **Wales Tourist Board**, Dept. WM1, Davis Street, Cardiff CF1 2FU; tel. 01222 475226
• **Scottish Tourist Board**, 19 Cockspur Street, London SW1Y 5BL; tel. 0171 930 8661/2/3; 23 Ravelston Terrace, Edinburgh EH4 3EU; tel. 0131 332 2433 (postal and telephone inquiries only).
• **Northern Ireland Tourist Board**, 11 Berkeley Street, London W1X 5AD; tel. 0541 555250 (free); St. Anne's Court, 59 North Street, Belfast BT1 1NB; tel. 011232 246609; Tourist Information Centre, 8 Bishop Street, Derry BT48 6PW; tel. 01504 267284.

Regional offices
• **Bath**: Guildhall, High Street, Avon BA1 5AW; tel. 01225 462831
• **Birmingham**: Convention and Visitor Bureau, 2 City Arcade, West Midlands B2 4TX; tel. 0121 643 2514
• **Cambridge**: Wheeler Street, Cambridge-shire CB2 3QB; tel. 01223 322640
• **Cardiff**: P.O. Box 48, South Glamorgan CF1 2AX; tel. 01222 227281
• **Edinburgh**: Edinburgh and Scotland Information Centre, 3 Princes Street, Edinburgh EH2 2QP; tel. 0131 557 1700
• **Glasgow**: 35 St. Vincent Place, Strathclyde G1 2ER; tel. 0141 204 4400
• **Liverpool**: Merseyside Welcome Centre, Clayton Square Shopping Centre,

Merseyside L1 1QR; tel. 0151 709 3631
• **London Tourist Board and Convention Bureau**, 26 Grosvenor Gardens, Victoria, London SW1W 0DU; tel. 0171 730 3450
• **London Tourist Information Centre**, Victoria Station Forecourt; tel. 0171 730 3488
• **Manchester**: Manchester Visitor Centre, Town Hall Extension, Lloyd Street, Greater Manchester M60 2LA; tel. 0161 234 3157/8. Also at Manchester Airport, International Arrivals Hall, Terminal 1; tel. 0161 436 3344
• **Oxford**: Gloucester Green, Oxfordshire OX1 2DA; tel. 01865 726871
• **Plymouth**: Civic Centre, Royal Parade, Plymouth PL1 2EW; tel. 01752 264849
• **Stratford-upon-Avon**: Bridgefoot, Warwickshire CV37 6YY; tel. 01789 293127
• **West Country**: 60 St. David's Hill, Exeter, Devon EX4 4SY; tel. 01392 76351
• **York**: De Grey Rooms, Exhibition Square, North Yorkshire YO1 2HB; tel. 01904 621756.

The National Trust/English Heritage
The National Trust is a major landowner and charitable body formed in 1895 to safeguard Britain's places of historic interest and natural beauty. Property acquired is held on trust for the nation. It has hundreds of country houses, gardens and other places of interest open to the public.

English Heritage a government organization, owns hundreds of historic properties. Its sister organizations are Cadw (Welsh Historic Monuments) and Historic Scotland (HS). Properties include prehistoric and Roman remains, medieval castles and abbeys and some stately homes.

The Great British Heritage Pass offers unlimited free entry (except to the Tower of London where there's a 50 percent discount) to over 500 properties in membership of the National Trust, the National Trust for Scotland (NTS), English Heritage, Cadw, and Historic Scotland. It is valid for 7 days, 15 days or 1 month. Contact the British Travel Centre, 12 Regent Street, London W1Y 4PQ if you require any further information.

WATER
Water is safe to drink everywhere in Britain. The water from some regions (such as Buxton in North Yorkshire or the Scottish Highlands) is so pure that it is actually sold bottled. What comes out of the faucets ("taps" in Britain) in other regions may not be so perfect but it is still very safe to drink. If you ever harbor any doubts about water quality while in Britain, just phone the local water company (in the telephone book under "Water") and find out whether there is any cause for concern.

Both bottled carbonated and non-carbonated waters – domestic and foreign – are available in all supermarkets, most small grocery stores and most restaurants.

WATERSPORTS
Yacht racing developed as a sport as early as the 1600s in Britain with the Royal Thames Yacht Club being founded in 1775 – by contrast the New York Yacht Club wasn't set up until 1844. The great event of the yachting year in Britain is Cowes Week (first week in August), but every seaside town and harbor has its own regatta with rowing and sailing races.

Reservoirs, rivers, canals and lakes inland offer plenty of opportunity for getting afloat; there will be clubs and facilities for **waterskiing**, **windsurfing** (board sailing), **canoeing** and **dinghy sailing**. Inquire at the local tourist information offices for further details on what is available.

Most larger hotels have private **swimming** pools and the larger towns have public baths. Swimming in the sea in Britain can be chilly even in August and September when the waters have "officially" warmed up.

Scuba **diving** off the shores of the U.K. should only be undertaken with a qualified diving instructor as the currents are notoriously strong and weather conditions can be unpredictable, but wreck diving (particularly off the shores of the southwest counties) can be rewarding.

Angling is something of a national passion, both along the rivers and in the sea. Permits are required and seasons must be observed. The *Angling Times* is the bible.

Cornwall, and in particular Fistral Beach near Newquay, is the **surfing** capital of England, occasionally hosting international championships and producing homegrown winners on the Atlantic waves.

EMERGENCIES

EMBASSIES AND CONSULATES

• **London**: American Embassy, 24 Grosvenor Square; tel. 0171 499 9000
• **Edinburgh**: American Consulate General, 3 Regent Terrace; tel. 0131 556 8315
• **Belfast**: American Consulate General, Queens House, Queen Street; tel. 01232 328239.

EMERGENCY TELEPHONE NUMBERS

999 is the number to call in any emergency. This puts you through to an operator who can connect you to any of the following emergency services: **police, fire, ambulance, coast guard, mountain rescue or cave rescue.**

There is no charge for a 999 call from any private or public phone.

Other phone numbers you may need are:
• **Health Information Service** (calls are free and confidential): (0800) 665544
• **AIDS Helpline**: (0800) 567123
• **Victim Support**: 0171 735 9166
• **Time**: 123
• **Automobile Association** (car breakdowns): (0800) 887766 (members only)
• **Samaritans** 0345 909090

LOST PROPERTY

If you have lost something:
• **on the street** – inquire at the nearest police station
• **on a train** – inquire at the local station
• **in a taxi** – in London contact the Public Carriage Office, 15 Penton Street, London N1; tel. 0171 833 0996; elsewhere in Britain, contact the taxi company direct
• **on London Transport** (bus or tube) – inquire direct at the Lost Property Office, 200 Baker Street, London NW1 5RT, 9:30 a.m. to 2 p.m. Monday to Friday; tel: 0171 486 2496. You can pick up an inquiry form from any bus depot or tube station, and they will forward it to the relevant Lost Property Office.

Airports, bus stations and train stations usually have a desk or window where you can go to inquire about lost property or luggage that you may have inadvertently left behind.

Numbers for lost property and left luggage at London's British Rail stations are:
• **King's Cross**: 0171 922 9081
• **Liverpool Street**: 0171 922 9158
• **St. Pancras**: 0171 922 6478
• **Victoria**: 0171 922 9887
• **Waterloo (South-West Trains)**: 0171 922 6135
• **all other London stations** (lost property and left luggage): 0171 928 5151.

If you lose something in a museum, theater, other attraction or place of interest, just call them – if no one has yet turned it in, give them your name and a phone number where you can be reached, in case anyone does turn it in before you fly home.

MEDICAL CARE

In the event of a medical emergency, call **999** and ask for the ambulance service. They will give first aid and take you to the casualty department (emergency ward) of the nearest hospital.

In the more remote parts of the U.K., such as the Western Isles of Scotland and Cornwall, an emergency dash for hospital may involve a ride in a helicopter.

POLICE

The British police work from different constabularies or units throughout the country. They all wear the same dark blue uniforms, but their badges differ and will show clearly the name of the local branch of the force: such as "South Yorkshire Police" or "Isle of Man Constabulary."

Commonly known as "bobbies" (after Sir Robert Peel, Home Secretary when the Metropolitan Police Act was first passed in 1828, establishing a police force in London), the "cop" on the beat should be addressed as "Constable."

The initials P.C. or W.P.C. which you may see on their badges denote Police Constable and Woman Police Constable respectively. Those in higher ranks may be Inspectors, Detective Inspectors, Chief Inspectors and so on.

The police do not normally carry guns, (despite occasional speculation as to otherwise), only various styles of truncheon (a smaller version of a baseball bat) and two-way radio equipment to keep them in touch with their local police station.

HOTELS AND RESTAURANTS

A recommended guide to some of the
best places to stay and eat in Britain,
from a luxury hotel in London to a
country inn in the Lake District, and
from *foie gras* to fish and chips

ACCOMMODATIONS

Recommendations in this guide include some of the most comfortable, interesting and welcoming places to stay, in every corner of the country and to suit every pocket. They also cover every type of accommodation available.

AAA DIAMOND RATING

Diamond ratings are on a scale of one to five and range from simple accommodations to the most luxurious hotels. (Note: this rating has not been applied to inns, B&Bs and guest houses represented in the listings.)

Hotel and restaurant rating systems in Britain are based on criteria used by the AA in England. Due to cultural and social differences between Britain and the U.S./Canada, a direct point-by-point comparison cannot be made, but the diamond ratings do indicate the relative value of the establishment.

◆ **one-diamond hotels** are usually small, with simple but adequate furnishings and facilities. These hotels often have a more personal atmosphere than might be found in larger hotels.

◆◆ **two-diamond hotels** are generally small to medium sized. They usually have more facilities than one-diamond establishments, such as TVs and telephones in all rooms and at least half with en-suite (private) bath or shower.

◆◆◆ **three-diamond hotels** are usually medium sized, with more spacious rooms. They normally have a reception service as well as more formal restaurant and bar facilities. All rooms should have en-suite (private) bath or shower.

◆◆◆◆ **four-diamond hotels** are larger and more spacious. All rooms have en-suite bathrooms, and most hotels offer private suites as well. Porters, room service and a reception service are available. There is often a choice of restaurants. High standards of comfort and cuisine are expected.

◆◆◆◆◆ **five diamond** hotels denote luxury establishments offering the highest international standards in facilities, service and cuisine.

TYPES OF ACCOMMODATIONS

Inns (same as pubs)
Some of the most atmospheric places to stay in Britain, but rooms can be surprisingly expensive.

B&Bs (bed-and-breakfasts)
The cheapest accommodations in Britain, usually just a few rooms in someone's private home.

Guest houses
Guest houses come in all shapes and sizes. Sometimes they resemble B&Bs, other times they are more like small hotels. Many offer a (generally simple) evening meal.

Townhouses
More common in London in particular, town-houses are essentially mini luxury hotels that usually offer just a room and breakfast.

Hotels
Generally offer more facilities than B&Bs and guest houses, and most will have a restaurant. Standards vary greatly, from luxurious and very expensive hotels to those that are cheaper and more basic.

Country house hotels
Often beautiful mansions, with lovely grounds, and often serving *haute cuisine*; if your budget allows, country house hotels are where to go to really indulge yourself.

USEFUL TIPS

Where to stay

The Cotswolds and the Lake District probably have the greatest concentration of fine country-house-style accommodations in England. If your budget permits it, you can also stay in a succession of marvelous country houses on touring vacations of Wales and especially Scotland.

Reservations

Accommodations listed are the best around, so they fill up fast, particularly in popular vacation regions such as the Scottish Highlands, around national parks and in historic cities. Most hotels will hold accommodations on a credit card reservation. Many B&Bs and guest houses do not take credit cards, either trusting you to turn up or asking for a deposit or confirmation.

The AA in Britain operates a hotel booking service, available on the AA's website at www.theaa.co.uk, under hotel bookings.

Opening times

Many smaller establishments, especially in remote regions, close for the winter; check schedules before you make the trip.

Smoking

Many B&Bs and guest houses prohibit smoking; if you are a smoker, check in advance.

Bathroom facilities

Many B&Bs and guest houses offer rooms without en-suite (private) bathrooms. If you don't want to share, check before you book. Bathrooms sometimes come with just a bath or shower; if you have a preference, say so when you make your reservation.

Food

Hotel and B&B breakfasts are a British institution: a "fry-up," as they are aptly called, usually consists of fried eggs, bacon, mushrooms and even fried bread, plus grilled tomatoes, toast and sausages.

Some places also offer dishes like kippers (smoked fish) and porridge (traditionally a Scottish start to the day). After such a hearty breakfast, you can often save money by being able to forgo lunch!

Most hotels have a restaurant, but they vary greatly in quality of both cuisine and surroundings.

Costs

If you're traveling on your own, you may end up paying anything from half the cost of a double room to the full cost. In vacation areas, rates generally tend to be lower outside the summer season. In cities, some large partially business-oriented hotels lower their rates for the weekend. Breakfast is included in the rate except at some of the most expensive hotels. Hotels and B&Bs will often quote prices for accommodations with meals: "half-board" is the price including breakfast and an evening meal; "full-board" includes breakfast, lunch and dinner.

Taxes (V.A.T.) are almost always included. Many establishments will accept credit cards, although it is advisable to check when making reservations.

In this guide the following abbreviations are used for major credit cards:

AE = American Express
DI = Diners Club
MC = MasterCard
VI = Visa

The following price ranges apply for a twin or double room and breakfast for two in high season:

(£)   under £60
(££)   £60–100
(£££) over £100

LONDON

Belgravia

Halkin (£££) ◆◆◆◆
Halkin Street
SW1X 7DJ
Tel: 0171 333 1000
Fax: 0171 333 1100
*Small, fashion-conscious
hotel for the jetset. Italian
cuisine. 41 rooms. Satellite
TV. Air conditioning.
AE/DI/MC/VI*

The Lowndes (£££) ◆◆◆◆
21 Lowndes Street
SW1X 9ES
Tel: 0171 823 1234
Fax: 0171 235 1154
*Chic Belgravia hotel with a
high standard of accomoda-
tion and happy atmosphere.
All-day brasserie. Air condi-
tioning. Recent refurbish-
ment. 78 rooms. Satellite
TV. AE/DI/MC/VI*

Blackheath

Bardon Lodge Hotel (££)
◆◆◆
15–17 Stratheden Road
SE3 7TH
Tel: 0181 853 4051
Fax: 0181 858 7387
*Situated on the edge of a
pretty village, this small,
friendly hotel continues to
upgrade and improve facilities and service. A good
choice for upcoming
Millenium celebrations. 31
rooms. AE/MC/VI*

Bloomsbury

Academy (£££) ◆◆◆
17–21 Gower Street
WC1E 6HG
Tel: 0171 631 4115
Fax: 0171 636 6442
*Impressive Georgian hotel
with a restaurant offering
simple, but appetizing
dishes. 40 rooms. Satellite
TV. AE/DI/MC/VI*

Hotel Russell (£££) ◆◆◆◆
Russell Square
WC1B 5BE
Tel: 0171 837 6470
Fax: 0171 837 2857
*Popular hotel with plenty of
character. 329 rooms.
Satellite TV. AE/DI/MC/VI*

Finsbury Park

Mount View (£)
31 Mount View Road
N4 4SS
Tel: 0181 340 9222
Fax: 0181 342 8494
*Elegant Victorian guest
house, tastefully decorated,
which maintains period
features. Bedrooms have
original fireplaces and
stripped wood floors, with
Oriental rugs. Breakfasts
are hearty and feature vege-
tarian options. 6 rooms. No
restaurant. MC/VI*

Greenwich

The Pilot Inn
68 Riverway, SE10 0BE
Tel: 0181 858 5910
Fax: 0181 293 0371
*There is a warm and friendly
atmosphere at this popular
guest house situated close
to the river. Bedrooms are
furnished in modern style
and brightly decorated.
Reliable British food,
generous English breakfast.
7 rooms. AE/MC/VI*

Kensington

Comfort Inn (££) ◆◆
22–32 West Cromwell Road
SW5 9QJ
Tel: 0171 373 3300
Fax: 0171 835 2040
*Convenient to Earl's Court,
this bright, modern hotel is
well suited to both business
people and vacationers.
International cuisine.125
rooms. Satellite TV. Air
conditioning. AE/DI/MC/VI*

Copthorne Tara (£££) ◆◆◆◆
Scarsdale Place, off Wrights
Lane W8 5SR
Tel: 0171 937 7211
Fax 0171 937 7100
*Elegantly furnished rooms
with air conditioning, mini-
bars and satellite TV.
Several restaurants. 825
rooms. AE/DI/MC/VI*

**Forte Posthouse
Kensington** (£££) ◆◆◆
Wright's Lane
W8 5SP
Tel: 0171 937 8170
Fax: 0171 937 8289
*Bright, modern hotel close
to Kensington High Street.
Carvery and Italian bistro.
542 rooms. Satellite TV.
AE/DI/MC/VI*

**Hilton National London,
Olympia** (£££) ◆◆◆◆
380 Kensington High Street
W14 8NL
Tel: 0171 603 3333
Fax: 0171 603 4846
*Convenient to Earl's Court
Exhibition Centre and
Olympia. Modern and well
appointed. 405 rooms. Bar
and restaurant. Satellite TV.
Air conditioning.
AE/DI/MC/VI*

**Kensington Palace
Thistle** (£££) ◆◆◆◆
De Vere Gardens, W8 5AF
Tel: 0171 937 8121
Fax: 0171 937 2816
*A large, popular hotel close
to the Royal Albert Hall
offering a range of rooms,
all with modern facilities.
298 rooms. AE/DI/MC/VI*

Swiss House Hotel (££)
171 Old Brompton Road
SW5 0AN
Tel: 0171 373 2769 or 9383
Fax: 0171 373 4983
A warm welcome is assured

at this small, popular guest house. Bedrooms have en-suite facilities, with extras such as hair dryers and telephones. Continental buffet breakfast served in cozy dining room. 16 rooms. AE/DI/MC/VI

Knightsbridge
Basil Street (£££) ◆◆◆
Basil Street
SW3 1AH
Tel: 0171 581 3311
Fax: 0171 581 3693
Founded in 1910 and still family owned, this Edwardian hotel is an island of calm and a haven of English refinement in the middle of bustling Knights-bridge. 93 rooms. Bar and restaurant. AE/DI/MC/VI

Beaufort (£££) ◆◆◆◆
33 Beaufort Gardens
SW3 1PP
Tel: 0171 584 5252
Fax: 0171 589 2834
Everything is included at this swank townhouse. Expensive. 28 rooms. Satellite TV. Air conditioning. AE/DI/MC/VI

The Berkeley (£££) ◆◆◆◆◆
Wilton Place
SW1X 7RL
Tel: 0171 235 6000
Fax: 0171 235 4330
A traditional luxury hotel with outstanding facilities, the Berkeley has always been synonymous with the social life of Knightsbridge. Excellent restaurant. 157 rooms. Satellite TV. AE/DI/MC/VI

Capital (£££) ◆◆◆◆
Basil Street
SW3 1AT
Tel: 0171 589 5171
Fax: 0171 225 0011

A charming, small hotel with high-quality rooms, service and cuisine. 48 rooms, all with carefully designed furniture. AE/DI/MC/VI

Delmere Hotel (££) ◆◆
130 Sussex Gardens,
Hyde Park,
W2 1UB
Tel: 0171 706 3344
Fax: 0171 2262 1863
Smart, friendly staff are a big plus at this well-managed hotel. Bedrooms are well equipped and public rooms include a jazz-themed bar and very comfortable lounge. 38 rooms. AE/DI/MC/VI

Marylebone and Regent's Park
Hotel Ibis Euston (£) ◆◆
3 Cardington Street
NW1 2LW
Tel: 0171 388 7777
Fax: 0171 388 0001
A popular and busy hotel offering good-value budget accommodation. English and French cuisine. 300 rooms. Satellite TV. AE/DI/MC/VI

Sherlock Holmes Hotel (£££) ◆◆◆
108 Baker Street,
W1M 1LJ
Tel: 0171 486 6161
Fax: 0171 486 0884
Located on the street where the fictitious detective was based. Good quality and an interesting theme. 125 rooms. AE/DI/MC/VI

Mayfair
Athenaeum (£££) ◆◆◆◆
116 Piccadilly
W1V 0BJ
Tel: 0171 499 3464
Fax: 0171 493 1860
This hotel offers excellent standards in comfort and

luxury, including a health spa. À-la-carte restaurant. 156 rooms. Satellite TV. AE/DI/MC/VI

Claridge's (£££) ◆◆◆◆◆
Brook Street
W1A 2JQ
Tel: 0171 629 8860
Fax: 0171 499 2210
Frequented by royalty and celebrities. The best of quint-essential English luxury and tradition. Impressive service and food choice. 198 rooms. Satellite TV. AE/DI/MC/VI

Ritz (£££) ◆◆◆◆◆
150 Piccadilly
W1V 9DG
Tel: 0171 493 8181
Fax: 0171 493 2687
World-renowned hotel, popular with the rich and famous. Wonderful after-noon teas and elaborate cuisine. 131 rooms. Satellite TV. AE/DI/MC/VI

Notting Hill
Pembridge
Court (£££) ◆◆◆◆
34 Pembridge Gardens
W2 4DX
Tel: 0171 229 9977
Fax: 0171 727 4982
Unpretentious but smart townhouse hotel; relaxed wine-bar style restaurant. 20 rooms. Satellite TV. AE/DI/MC/VI

Victoria
Goring (£££) ◆◆◆◆
Beeston Place, Grosvenor Gardens, SW1W 0JW
Tel: 0171 396 9000
Fax: 0171 834 4393
Carefully understated and ultra traditional, this hotel has been in the family for three generations. 76 rooms. Satellite TV. AE/DI/MC/VI

West End
The Dorchester
(£££) ♦♦♦♦♦
Park Lane, W1A 2HJ
Tel: 0171 629 8888
Fax: 0171 409 0114
One of the most magnificent and glamorous hotels in the world. Three restaurants, including famous Oriental cuisine. 244 rooms. Satellite TV. Health club. AE/DI/MC/VI

Grosvenor House
(£££) ♦♦♦♦♦
Park Lane, W1A 3AA
Tel: 0171 499 6363
Fax: 0171 493 3341
Splendid hotel on a grand scale. Good food, good wine, lots of atmosphere. 454 bedrooms. Satellite TV. Health and fitness center. AE/DI/MC/VI

Le Meridien
Piccadilly (£££) ♦♦♦♦♦
21 Piccadilly, W1V 0BH
Tel: 0171 734 8000
Fax: 0171 437 3574
Close to Piccadilly Circus, this fine hotel has many attractions: tea in the Oak Lounge, a terrace garden for all-day meals and a health club. 266 rooms. Satellite TV. AE/DI/MC/VI

Regent Palace (£) ♦♦
Glasshouse Street,
Piccadilly, W1A 4BZ
Tel: 0171 734 7000
Fax: 0171 734 6435
Popular hotel recently renovated. Good value carvery and brasserie. 950 rooms. No smoking in restaurant. AE/DI/MC/VI

Rhodes Hotel (£)
195 Sussex Gardens
W2 2RJ
Tel: 0171 262 5617 or 0537

Fax: 0171 723 4504
Family-run guest house close to the West End. Comfortable accommodation in well-furnished bedrooms. Continental and English breakfast served in bright dining room. 18 rooms. No restaurant. MC/VI

Savoy (£££) ♦♦♦♦♦
Strand
WC2R 0EU
Tel: 0171 836 4343
Fax: 0171 240 6040
One of the world's top hotels: lovable traditions, Victorian grandeur, French and English cuisine. 207 rooms. Satellite TV. AE/DI/MC/VI

Westminster
Grosvenor
Thistle (£££) ♦♦♦♦
Buckingham Palace Road
SW1W 0SJ
Tel: 0171 834 9494
Fax: 0171 630 1978
Spacious hotel housed in an impressive Victorian building. A fine marble staircase leads up to comfortable bedrooms. 366 rooms. AE/DI/MC/VI

THE WEST COUNTRY

BRISTOL
Bristol
Berkeley Square (££) ♦♦♦
15 Berkeley Square
Clifton,
BS8 1HB
Tel: 0117 925 4000
Fax: 0117 925 2970
A good restaurant and trendy bar, with personal touches, set in an elegant and peaceful square. 41 rooms. Satellite TV. AE/DI/MC/VI

Henbury Lodge (£–££) ♦♦♦
Station Road
Henbury
BS10 7QQ
Tel: 0117 502615
Fax: 0117 509532
Small and family run with comfortable rooms. Convenient to the city center. 19 rooms. Restaurant. AE/DI/MC/VI

Mayfair Hotel (£)
5 Henleaze Road,
Westbury on Trym, BS9 4EX
Tel: 0117 962 2008
An elegant Victorian property, offering comfortable bedrooms and a relaxed and friendly atmosphere. Breakfast is served in an airy dining room. On-street parking. 9 rooms. No restaurant. MC

Swallow
Royal (£££) ♦♦♦♦
College Green, BS1 5TA
Tel: 0117 925 5100
Fax: 0117 925 1515
Housed in a fine old building. The Palm Court Ballroom is opulent. 242 rooms. Swimming pool, sports facilities. AE/DI/MC/VI

CORNWALL
Liskeard
(near Fowey/Plymouth)
Lord Eliot Hotel (£) ♦♦
Castle Street
PL14 3AU
Tel: 01579 342717
Fax: 01597 347593
This personally-run hotel close to the town center offers modest en-suite accommodation with modern facilities. Formal restaurant provides a pleasant setting for interesting, freshly prepared dishes. 15 rooms. AE/DI/MC/VI

Well House (£) ◆◆
St. Keyne
PL14 4RN
Tel: 01579 342001
Fax: 01579 343891
Gorgeous country house built by a tea planter. Excellent seafood and game. 9 rooms. Restaurant. AE/DI/MC/VI

Padstow (north coast)
Old Custom House
Inn (££) ◆◆◆
South Quay
PL28 8ED
Tel: 01841 532359
Fax: 01841 533372
An attractive period building overlooking the harbor. Pleasant rooms and public areas. Cream teas served in the conservatory. 27 rooms. Restaurant. AE/DI/MC/VI

Seafood Restaurant
(££–£££) ◆◆
Riverside
PL28 8BY
Tel: 01841 532485
Fax: 01841 532942
An outstanding and inventive seafood restaurant that also offers modern overnight accomodation in a waterside setting. 11 rooms. MC/VI

St. Ives
Hotel Rotorua (£) ◆
Trencorm Lane,
Carbis Bay, TR26 2TD
Tel: 01736 795419
Fax: 01736 795419
Modern hotel standing in well-tended gardens, close to Carbis Bay. Large, modern, well-equipped bedrooms. Outdoor heated pool, games room. Friendly service provided by attentive staff. 13 rooms. No credit cards.

Skidden House (£) ◆◆
Skidden Hill, TR26 2DU
Tel: 01736 796899
Fax: 01736 798619
Claims to be the oldest hotel in town. Centrally located on a narrow street. 7 charming rooms. Restaurant. AE/DI/MC/VI

DEVON
Barnstaple (north Devon)
Halmpstone Manor
(£££) ◆◆
Bishop's Tawton
EX32 0EA
Tel: 01271 830321
Fax: 01271 830826
A family-run manor house established in 1947. The atmosphere is relaxed and very friendly. Rooms individually furnished with nice touches. Excellent cuisine. 5 rooms. Restaurant. AE/DI/MC/VI

Chagford (Dartmoor)
Gidleigh Park (££–£££) ◆◆◆
TQ13 8HH
Tel: 01647 432367 or 432225
Fax: 01647 432574
Antiques and parkland galore in one of the country's plushest country-house hotels. 15 rooms. Restaurant. AE/DI/MC/VI

Dartmouth
Royal Castle (££–£££) ◆◆◆
11 The Quay, TQ6 9PS
Tel: 01803 833033
Fax: 01803 835445
A 17th-century waterside inn with character and style. 25 rooms. Satellite TV. Restaurant. AE/MC/VI

Exeter
Fairwinds Hotel (£) ◆◆
Kennford, EX6 7UD
Tel: 01392 832911
Fax: 01392 832911
Non-smoking hotel within easy reach of local towns. Small bar/lounge and restaurant serving a variety of interesting home-made dishes. Bedrooms are comfortable and suitable for both business people and vacationers. 7 rooms. MC/VI

Gulworthy (Dartmoor)
Horn of Plenty (££) ◆◆
Tavistock, PL19 8JD
Tel: 01822 832528
Fax: 01822 832528
Georgian restaurant with 7 bedrooms housed in a former coach house. AE/MC/VI

DORSET
Dorchester
Yalbury Cottage (££)
Lower Bockhampton
DT2 8PZ
Tel: 01305 262382
Fax: 01305 266412
Thatched cottage in Thomas Hardy country. Good set menu dinners and comfortable bedrooms. 8 rooms. Restaurant. MC/VI

Evershot
Summer Lodge
(£££ including dinner) ◆◆◆
DT2 0JR
Tel: 01935 83424
Fax: 01935 83005
Very pretty country house in a rural backwater with excellent Anglo-French cuisine. 17 rooms. Restaurant. AE/DI/MC/VI

Sturminster Newton
Plumber Manor (£££) ◆◆◆
Hazelbury Bryan Road
DT10 2AF
Tel: 01258 472507
Fax: 01258 473370
Jacobean country house. Delicious, hearty food

served in restaurant.
16 rooms. AE/DI/MC/VI

West Lulworth
Cromwell House (££) ◆◆
Lulworth Cove, BH20 5RJ
Tel: 01929 400253
Fax: 01929 400566
Small and cheerful hotel with lovely views across Lulworth Cove. 14 rooms. AE/MC/VI

SCILLY ISLES
Tresco
The Island (£££) ◆◆◆
TR24 0PU
Tel: 01720 422883
Fax: 01720 423008
Modern accommodation in a quiet location. Excellent dishes in a restaurant that has fine views. 40 rooms. AE/MC/VI

SOMERSET
Bath
Duke's (££) ◆◆
Great Pulteney Street
BA2 4DN
Tel: 01225 463512
Fax: 01225 483733
Housed in a Georgian building, good facilities and friendly welcome. 24 comfortable rooms. Bar and restaurant. AE/MC/VI

The Old Mill Hotel (££) ◆◆
Tollbridge Road, Batheaston
BA1 7DE
Tel: 01225 858476
Fax: 01225 852600
Originally a flour mill; the attractive hotel restaurant overlooks riverside gardens and the original waterwheel. Some bedrooms include four-poster beds. 26 rooms. AE/MC/VI

Priory (£££) ◆◆◆
Weston Road, BA1 2XT
Tel: 01225 331922

Fax: 01225 448276
Country-house hotel with a welcoming and relaxed atmosphere. Pretty rooms, all individually decorated. Fresh flowers and fruit combine with modern facilities. 29 rooms. Restaurant. AE/DI/MC/VI

Royal Crescent (£££) ◆◆◆◆
16 Royal Crescent
BA1 2LS
Tel: 01225 823333
Fax: 01225 339401
Pampering luxury at the city's most respected address; accomplished modern cuisine. 45 rooms. DI/MC/VI

Taunton
Falcon Hotel (£–££) ◆◆
Henlade, TA3 5DH
Tel: 01823 442502
Fax: 01823 442670
Brick-built Victorian house, set in a well-tended garden. Bedrooms vary in size and are equipped with modern comforts. Fixed-price and à-la-carte menus are served in the dining room; adjacent bar provides popular meeting place. 11 rooms. AE/DI/MC/VI

Wells
Swan (££) ◆◆◆
Sadler Street, BA5 2RX
Tel: 01749 678877
Fax: 01749 677647
Atmospheric old coaching inn facing the cathedral. 38 rooms. AE/DI/MC/VI

WILTSHIRE
Bradford on Avon
Woolley Grange (£££) ◆◆◆
Woolley Green
BA15 1TX
Tel: 01225) 864705
Fax: 01225 864059
Very welcoming family-run

hotel. Comfortable rooms with extras such as robes, flowers. 22 rooms. Restaurant. Pool, sports facilities. AE/DI/MC/VI

Lacock
At the Sign of the Angel (£)
6 Church Street, SN15 2LA
Tel: 01249 730230
Fax: 01249 730527
Inn dating from the 15th century in historic village of Lacock; traditional English fare. 9 rooms. AE/MC/VI

Salisbury
Milford Hall (££) ◆◆◆
206 Castle Street, SP1 3TE
Tel: 01722 417411
Fax: 01722 419444
Recently expanded Georgian mansion set in private grounds; imaginative menu. 35 rooms. Restaurant. AE/DI/MC/VI

SOUTH AND SOUTHEAST ENGLAND
BERKSHIRE
Windsor
The Castle (£££) ◆◆◆
High Street, SL4 1LJ
Tel: 01753 851011
Fax: 01753 830244
Georgian hotel with English atmosphere; central location opposite Windsor Castle. 104 rooms. Satellite TV. Restaurant. AE/DI/MC/VI

EAST SUSSEX
Hove
Imperial Hotel (££) ◆◆◆
First Avenue
BN3 2GU
Tel: 01273 777320
Fax: 01273 777310
Close to the waterfront, with good-quality modern bedrooms. Non-smoking lounge, informal bar and

stylish restaurant with a terrace. Friendly staff offer a good standard of service. 76 rooms. AE/DI/MC/VI

Hartfield (Weald)
Bolebroke Watermill (££)
Perry Hill
Edenbridge Road
TN7 4JP
Tel: 01892 770425
Romantic B&B in a delightful old mill and barn conversion. 5 rooms. AE/MC/VI

Rye
Jeake s House (£)
Mermaid Street
TN31 7ET
Tel: 01797 222828
Fax: 01797 222623
Stunning, great-value B&B in historical 17th-century building. 12 rooms. MC/VI

Sedlescombe
Brickwall Hotel (££) ◆◆◆
The Green
TN33 0QA
Tel: 01424 870253
Fax: 01424 870785
Overlooking the village green, this hotel retains its Tudor character yet incorporates modern bedroom facilities. Wood-paneled, oak-beamed restaurant offers traditional food. Well-trained staff provide attentive service. 23 rooms. AE/DI/MC/VI

HAMPSHIRE
Brockenhurst
Whitley Ridge Country House (££) ◆◆
Beaulieu Road, SO4 7QL
Tel: 01590 622354
Fax: 01590 622856
Delightful 18th-century hunting lodge; cozy atmosphere and good-quality food. 13 rooms. Restaurant. AE/DI/MC/VI

New Milton (New Forest)
Chewton Glen
(£££ including dinner) ◆◆◆
Christchurch Road
BH25 6QS
Tel: 01425 275341
Fax: 01425 272310
Glossy, state-of-the-art country house; superb leisure facilities, modern cooking. 52 rooms. Satellite TV. Restaurant. AE/DI/MC/VI

Winchester
Wykeham Arms (££–£££)
73 Kingsgate Street
SO23 9PE
Tel: 01962 853834
Fax: 01962 854411
Full of character, this 250-year-old pub is centrally located. Offers stylish bedrooms and imaginative bar food. 13 rooms. AE/DI/MC/VI

ISLE OF WIGHT
Seaview
Seaview (££) ◆◆◆
High Street, PO34 5EX
Tel: 01983 612711
Fax: 01983 613729
Family-oriented hotel with enjoyable bars and a good seafood restaurant. 16 rooms. AE/DI/MC/VI

KENT
Canterbury
Victoria Hotel (£) ◆◆
59 London Road
CT2 8JY
Tel: 01227 459333
Fax: 01227 781552
A short walk from the city center. Attractively decorated bedrooms vary but are well maintained with excellent facilities. Bustling bar with satellite TV. Country Carvery restaurant. Friendly, willing staff. 34 rooms. AE/DI/MC/VI

Dover
East Lee (£)
108 Maison Dieu Road
CT16 1RT
Tel: 01304 210176
Fax: 01304 210176
Attractive, well-presented house; modern bedrooms, all with en-suite facilities, TV and telephone. Traditional breakfast served in charming dining room; vegetarians catered to. 4 rooms. MC/VI

WEST SUSSEX
Chichester
Ship (££) ◆◆◆
North Street
PO19 1NH
Tel: 01243 778000
Fax: 01243 788000
Georgian-style hotel close to town center. Restaurant offers an interesting choice of dishes. 34 rooms. MC/VI

East Grinstead (Weald)
Gravetye Manor (£££) ◆◆◆
RH19 4LJ
Tel: 01342 810567
Fax: 01342 810080
Magnificent Elizabethan manor on delightful grounds; elaborate cuisine in formal restaurant. 18 rooms. MC/VI

Midhurst
Angel Hotel (££) ◆◆◆
North Street
GU29 9DN
Tel: 01730 812421
Fax: 01730 815928
Behind a Georgian facade the Angel conceals earlier Tudor origins. The lounge has a "country house" feel. Rustic bar and brasserie. Restaurant with daily changing menu. Efficient service. Individually decorated bedrooms combine style with comfort. 28 rooms. AE/DI/MC/VI

HOTELS

EASTERN ENGLAND

CAMBRIDGESHIRE
Cambridge
Garden House (£££) ♦♦♦♦
Granta Place
Mill Lane
CB2 1RT
Tel: 01223 259988
Fax: 01223 316605
Fashionable, modern riverside hotel, convenient to the city center. 117 rooms. Satellite TV. AE/DI/MC/VI

Old School (£)
9 Greenside
Waterbeach
CB5 9HW
Tel: 01223 861609
Fax: 01223 441683
Converted old school in a village just outside Cambridge. 8 rooms. AE/DI/MC/VI

ESSEX
Dedham (Stour Valley)
Maison Talbooth
(£££) ♦♦♦
Stratford Road
CO7 6HN
Tel: 01206 322367
Fax: 01206 322752
Stylish country-house hotel with restaurant, La Talbooth, serving uncomplicated English fare ½ mile down the road. 10 rooms. AE/DI/MC/VI

LINCOLNSHIRE
Lincoln
D'Isney Place (££)
Eastgate
LN2 4AA
Tel: 01522 538881
Fax: 01522 511321
Upscale city center B&B. Breakfast is served in bedrooms only. 17 rooms. AE/DI/MC/VI

Stamford
George of
Stamford (£££) ♦♦♦
St. Martins, PE9 2LB
Tel: 01780 755171
Fax: 01780 757070
Fascinating 16th-century coaching inn. 47 rooms. Satellite TV. Restaurant. AE/DI/MC/VI

NORFOLK
Grimston (nr. King's Lynn)
Congham Hall Country House (£££) ♦♦♦
Lynn Road, PE32 1AH
Tel: 01485 600250
Fax: 01485 601191
Georgian country house with lovely herb garden and gourmet 7-course dinners. 14 rooms. AE/DI/MC/VI

Norwich
Maid's Head (££) ♦♦♦
Tombland, NR3 1LB
Tel: 01603 209955
Fax: 01603 613688
Centuries-old inn with cozy, well-equipped accommodation reminiscent of the hotel's earlier days. 82 rooms. AE/DI/MC/VI

Titchwell (north coast)
Titchwell Manor (££) ♦♦
PE31 8BB
Tel: 01485 210221
Fax: 01485 210104
Unpretentious, laid-back, family-run hotel overlooking marshes and sea. 15 rooms. Restaurant. AE/DI/MC/VI

NOTTINGHAMSHIRE
Langar
Langar Hall (£££) ♦♦
NG13 9HG
Tel: 01949 860559
Fax: 01949 861045
Highly individual and elegant rural family home; good classic British food. 11 rooms. Restaurant. AE/DI/MC/VI

SUFFOLK
Lavenham (Stour Valley)
Angel (££) ♦♦
Market Place, CO10 9QZ
Tel: 01787 2473884
Fax: 01787 248344
A 15th-century inn; simple bedrooms, a good pub atmosphere and decent bar food. 8 rooms. AE/MC/VI

Southwold (Suffolk coast)
Crown at Southwold (£) ♦♦
90 High Street
IP18 6DP
Tel: 01502 722275
Fax: 01502 727263
Georgian inn with good choice of seafood and wine in the restaurant. 12 rooms. AE/DI/MC/VI

Stoke-by-Nayland (Stour Valley)
Angel Inn (£)
Polstead Street
CO6 4SA
Tel: 01206 263245
Fax: 01206 263373
A 16th-century inn serving some of the best bar meals in the country. 6 rooms. AE/DI/MC/VI

THE HEART OF ENGLAND

GLOUCESTERSHIRE
Cheltenham
Cleeve Hill (££)
Cleeve Hill, GL52 3PR
Tel: 01242 672052
Outstandingly solicitous, immaculate B&B just outside town. 10 rooms. AE/MC/VI

Cirencester
The Crown of Crucis (££)♦♦♦
Ampney Crucis, GL7 5RS
Tel: 01285 851806
Fax: 01285 851735
A 16th-century Cotswold

stone coaching inn. Modern
bedrooms and good food.
25 rooms. Restaurant.
AE/DI/MC/VI

Lower Slaughter
Lower Slaughter Manor
(£££ including dinner) ◆◆◆
GL54 2HP
Tel: 01451 820456
Fax: 01451 822150
*Elegant 17th-century manor;
modern French cuisine
served in restaurant.
15 rooms. AE/DI/MC/VI*

Stow-on-the-Wold
Wyck Hill House (££) ◆◆◆◆
Burford Road
GL54 1HY
Tel: 01451 831936
Fax: 01451 832243
*Magnificent country house
set in beautiful grounds;
elegant public areas.
Restaurant offers imagina-
tive, tempting dishes. 30
rooms. AE/DI/MC/VI*

OXFORDSHIRE
Burford
Andrews Hotel (££)
High Street, OX18 4QA
Tel: 01993 823151
Fax: 01993 823240
*B&B with splendid after-
noon teas and pretty
rooms in a timbered 15th-
century house. 7 rooms.
AE/MC/VI*

Great Milton (near Oxford)
Le Manoir aux Quat'
Saisons (£££) ◆◆◆◆
Church Road, OX44 7PD
Tel: 01844 278881
Fax: 01844 278847
*Raymond Blanc's dazzling
cooking – about the best in
Britain – is served in a
luxurious, but unintimidat-
ing, country house set in a
quiet village. 19 rooms.
Satellite TV. AE/DI/MC/VI*

Moulsford (Thames)
Beetle & Wedge (££) ◆◆
Ferry Lane, OX10 9JF
Tel: 01491 651381
Fax: 01491 651376
*Riverside hotel; both
excellent formal and
informal dining. 10 rooms.
Restaurant. AE/DI/MC/VI*

Oxford
Cotswold House (£)
363 Banbury Road, OX2 7PL
Tel: 01865 310558
Fax: 01865 310558
*First-rate, modern guest
house 2 miles from city
center. 7 rooms. No
credit cards.*

The Randolph (£££) ◆◆◆◆
Beaumont Street
OX1 2LN
Tel: 01865 247481
Fax: 01865 791678
*City hotel in grand Victorian
style – an Oxford institu-
tion. 109 rooms. Satellite
TV. AE/DI/MC/VI*

SHROPSHIRE
Shrewsbury
Albright Hussey (££) ◆◆◆
Ellesmere Road, SY4 3AF
Tel: 01939 290571
Fax: 01939 291143
*Moated 16th-century manor
with English, Italian and
French cuisine. 14 rooms.
Restaurant. AE/DI/MC/VI*

Lion & Pheasant Hotel
(£) ◆◆
49–50 Wyle Cop, SY1 1JX
Tel: 01743 236288
Fax: 01743 244475
*A 16th-century timbered
inn that has maintained many
original features.
Comfortable bar lounge
offers a range of meals;
full menu in beamed
restaurant. 19 rooms.
AE/DI/MC/VI*

WARWICKSHIRE
Leamington Spa
Lansdowne (££) ◆
87 Clarendon Street
CV32 4PF
Tel: 01926 450505
Fax: 01926 421313
*Pretty, centrally located
Georgian hotel. The excel-
lent menu offers Aberdeen
Angus beef as a specialty.
14 rooms. Restaurant.
MC/VI*

Stratford upon Avon
Welcombe Hotel and Golf
Course (£££) ◆◆◆◆
Warwick Road
CV37 0NR
Tel: 01789 295252
Fax: 01789 414666
*Jacobean manor house set
in 800 acres of parkland.
Friendly staff offer very pro-
fessional and caring service.
Interesting and accom-
plished selection of dishes
served in light airy dining
room. Bedrooms have
delightful views of gardens
and grounds. 67 rooms.
AE/DI/MC/VI*

Victoria Spa Lodge (£)
Bishopton Lane
CV37 9QY
Tel: 01789 267985
Fax: 01789 204728
*High-quality B&B in a
Victorian house along a
canal. 7 rooms. MC/VI*

WORCESTER
Broadway (Cotswolds)
Lygon Arms (£££) ◆◆◆◆
WR12 7DU
Tel: 01386 852255
Fax: 01386 858611
*Combination of a 16th-
century coaching inn and
the best in modern luxury.
Modern English country
cooking. 66 rooms. Satellite
TV. AE/DI/MC/VI*

WALES

CARMARTHENSHIRE
Brechfa
Ty Mawr Country (££) ◆◆
SA32 7RA
Tel: 01267 202332
Fax: 01267 202437
A truly cozy and off-the-beaten-track haven; fine home cooking and baking. 5 rooms. Restaurant. AE/MC/VI

CEREDIGION
**Eglwysfach
(near Machynlleth)**
Ynyshir Hall (£££) ◆◆◆
SY20 8TA
Tel: 01654 781209
Fax: 01654 781366
Small Georgian country house surrounded by a bird reserve. Imaginative food served in the restaurant. 8 rooms. AE/DI/MC/VI

CONWY
Llandudno (north coast)
Banham House Hotel & Restaurant (£) ◆◆
2 St Davids Road
LL30 2UL
Tel: 01492 875680
Fax: 01492 875680
A small, welcoming hotel in a quiet residential area. High standards throughout, impeccably maintained. Bedrooms equipped with modern facilities. Extensive range of food served with warm hospitality. 6 rooms. No credit cards.

DENBIGHSHIRE
St. Asaph
Plas Elwy Hotel & Restaurant (£–££) ◆◆
The Roe, LL17 0LT
Tel: 01745 582263
Fax: 01745 583864
Friendly hotel that dates partially to 1850, with much of its period character preserved. Bedrooms vary in size and style, all well equipped; smart public rooms comfortably furnished. Wide range of food in attractive restaurant. 13 rooms. AE/MC/VI

GWYNEDD
Penrhyndeudraeth
Hotel Portmeirion (££–£££) ◆◆◆
Portmeirion
LL48 6ET
Tel: 01766 770228
Fax: 01766 771331
Upscale, boldly designed hotel in this unusual Italianate village. 37 rooms. Restaurant. AE/DI/MC/VI

Pwllheli (Lleyn Peninsula)
Plas Bodegroes Restaurant (£££ including dinner) ◆◆
Nefyn Road
LL53 5TH
Tel: 01758 612363
Fax: 01758 701247
Romantic Georgian restaurant with rooms, serving some of Wales's best food. 11 rooms. AE/MC/VI

Tal-y-Llyn (Snowdonia)
Minffordd
(£££ including dinner) ◆◆
Minffordd
LL36 9AJ
Tel: 01654 761665
Fax: 01654 761517
A 17th-century inn with a welcoming cottage atmosphere. 6 rooms. Restaurant. MC/VI

ISLE OF ANGLESEY
Beaumaris
Ye Old Bull's Head Inn (££) ◆◆
Castle Street
LL58 8AP
Tel: 01248 810329
Fax: 01248 811294
Comfortable 15th-century inn with a lively bar and good restaurant. 15 rooms. AE/MC/VI

MONMOUTHSHIRE
Whitebrook (Wye Valley)
Crown at Whitebrook (££) ◆◆
NP5 4TX
Tel: 01600 860254
Fax: 01600 860607
Excellent French food and simple bedrooms in a remote restaurant with rooms. 12 rooms. AE/DI/MC/VI

POWYS
**Hay-on-Wye
(Brecon Beacons)**
Old Black Lion (£) ◆◆
26 Lion Street
HR3 5AD
Tel: 01497 820841
Simple and lively beamed pub; restaurant with hearty country cooking. 10 rooms. AE/MC/VI

**Llyswen
(Brecon Beacons)**
Llangoed Hall (£££) ◆◆◆◆
LD3 0YP
Tel: 01874 754525
Fax: 01874 754545
The grandest Edwardian country house imaginable, complete with butler. Exquisite modern British cooking. 23 rooms. AE/DI/MC/VI

PEMBROKESHIRE
Tenby
Penally Abbey (£££) ◆◆◆
Penally
SA70 7PY
Tel: 01834 843033
Fax: 01834 844714
Small country house with sea views and delightful historic features. 12 rooms. Restaurant. AE/MC/VI

THE NORTH

CHESHIRE
Chester
Chester Grosvenor
(£££) ◆◆◆◆
Eastgate Street
CH1 1LT
Tel: 01244 324024
Fax: 01244 313246
Very pricey, famous city center hotel; top-notch haute cuisine. 86 rooms. Satellite TV. AE/DI/MC/VI

Redland (££)
64 Hough Green
CH4 8JY
Tel: 01244 671024
Fax: 01244 681309
Grand Victorian time capsule a mile from the city center. B&B 13 rooms. AE/MC/VI

CUMBRIA
(all in the Lake District)
Ambleside
Drunken Duck (££)
Barngates, LA22 0NG
Tel: 015394 36347
Fax: 015394 36781
Hugely popular country inn with upscale bedrooms. 10 rooms. AE/MC/VI

Grasmere
White Moss House (£££) ◆
Rydal Water, LA22 9SE
Tel: 015394 35295
Fax: 015394 34612
A dreamy, tiny country house with Wordsworth connections; amazingly affordable vintage wines. 7 rooms. Satellite TV. Restaurant. MC/VI

Howtown
Sharrow Bay Country House (£££ including dinner) ◆◆◆
Sharrow Bay
CA10 2LZ
Tel: 017684 86301

Fax: 017684 86349
Britain's first and most famous country-house hotel, on the shores of Ullswater; even tea is an unforgettable experience here. 28 rooms. Restaurant. MC/VI

Wasdale Head
Wasdale Head Inn (££) ◆◆
CA20 1EX
Tel: 019467 26229
Fax: 019467 26334
Famous, extremely remote hiking and climbing base. Bars and restaurant serve good choice of food. 9 rooms. MC/VI

Windermere
Miller Howe (£££) ◆◆
Rayrigg Road
LA23 1EY
Tel: 015394 42536
Fax: 015394 45664
Theatrical, highly individual restaurant in an Edwardian country house. 12 rooms. AE/DI/MC/VI

DERBYSHIRE
Baslow
Cavendish (£££) ◆◆◆
DE45 1SP
Tel: 01246 582311
Fax: 01246 582312
Upscale, tasteful hotel, encompassing the original 18th-century inn on the edge of the Chatsworth Estate. 24 rooms. Satellite TV. Restaurant. AE/DI/MC/VI

Buxton
Hartington Hotel (£) ◆◆
18 Broad Walk
SK17 6JR
Tel: 01298 22638
Fax: 01298 22638
Family-run hotel with lake and garden views. Bedrooms have traditional comfort and attractive furnishings. Good, honest home cooking

served in an attractive dining room. 17 rooms. AE/MC/VI

Hathersage
Hathersage Inn Hotel & Restaurant (££) ◆◆
Main Road, S32 1BB
Tel: 01433 650259
Fax: 01433 651199
Early Victorian hotel located opposite the railway station. Sympathetically extended to provide good modern accommodation. Secure parking. 100 rooms. AE/DI/MC/VI

DURHAM
Durham
Three Tuns (£££) ◆◆◆
New Elvet, DH1 3AQ
Tel: 0191 386 4326
Fax: 0191 386 1406
Extensively refurbished, 16th-century inn – the most interesting of this city's limited accommodations. 47 rooms. Satellite TV. Restaurant. AE/DI/MC/VI

GREATER MANCHESTER
Manchester
Victoria & Albert Hotel (£££) ◆◆◆◆
Water Street, M60 9EA
Tel: 0161 832 1188
Fax: 0161 834 2484
Comfortable, modern hotel in an imaginative warehouse conversion opposite Granada Studios.156 rooms. Satellite TV. AE/DI/MC/VI

LANCASHIRE
Blackpool
Sunray (£)
42 Knowle Avenue
Queens Promenade
FY2 9TQ
Tel: 01253 351937
Fax: 01253 593307
Classic resort guest house with enthusiastic owners. Some thoughtful extras in rooms. 9 rooms. AE/MC/VI

NORTHUMBERLAND
Alnwick
Hotspur Hotel (££) ◆◆
Bondgate Without
NE66 1PR
Tel: 01665 510101
Fax: 01665 605033
Town center hotel recognized in summer by colourful window boxes. Smart bedrooms have been upgraded. Popular bar; restaurant serves enjoyable home-cooked meals. 23 rooms. MC/VI

Hexham
Middlemarch (£)
Hencotes, NE46 2EB
Tel: 01434 605003
Fax: 01434 605003
B&B in a lovely Georgian townhouse. 3 rooms. No credit cards.

NORTH YORKSHIRE
Grassington
(Yorkshire Dales)
Ashfield House (£)
BD23 5AE
Tel: 01756 75284
Fax: 01756 75284
Pretty, wood-beamed house; country cooking. 7 rooms. MC/VI

Ingleby Greenhow
(Yorkshire Moors)
Manor House
(££ including dinner)
TS9 6RB
Tel: 01642 722384
Rural, 18th-century farmhouse with exposed beams, full of character; home cooking. 3 rooms. DI/MC/VI

Pickering
(Yorkshire Moors)
White Swan (££) ◆◆
Market Place, YO18 7AA
Tel: 01751 472288
Fax: 01751 472288
Traditional old inn with quaint bedrooms, hearty dinners and an amazing wine selection. 12 rooms. AE/MC/VI

Reeth
(Yorkshire Dales)
Arkleside (£)
DL11 6SG
Tel: 01748 84200
Fax: 01748 84200
Rustic little hotel converted from 16th-century cottages. 9 rooms. MC/VI

York
Holmwood House (£)
112–114 Holgate Road
YO2 4BB
Tel: 01904 626183
Fax: 01904 670899
Attractive B&B in a Victorian terrace close to the city center. 12 rooms. AE/MC/VI

Middlethorpe
Hall (£££) ◆◆◆
Bishopthorpe Road
YO2 1QB
Tel: 01904 64124
Fax: 01904 620176
Sumptuous hotel in a country house surrounded by beautiful parkland. 30 rooms. Restaurant. AE/MC/VI

SCOTTISH LOWLANDS

BORDERS
Kelso
Sunlaws House (£££) ◆◆◆
Heiton
TD5 8JZ
Tel: 01573 450331
Fax: 01573 450611
Vast, historic baronial mansion on 200 acres of woodland. There is a golf course in the grounds. 22 rooms. Restaurant. AE/DI/MC/VI

Jedburgh
The Spinney (£)
Langlee, TD8 6PB
Tel: 01835 863525
Fax: 01835 864883
Dapper, modern B&B, on several acres of well-maintained grounds. 3 rooms. MC/VI

CITY OF EDINBURGH
Edinburgh
Channings (£££) ◆◆◆
South Learmonth Gardens
EH4 1EZ
Tel: 0131 315 2226
Fax: 0131 332 9631
Discreet, extremely comfortable hotel along an Edwardian terrace. 48 rooms. Restaurant. AE/DI/MC/VI

Drummond House (££)
17 Drummond Place
EH3 6PL
Tel: 0131 557 9189
Fax: 0131 557 9189
Elegant house in the city's New Town; socializing is part of the experience. 4 rooms. MC/VI

CITY OF GLASGOW
Glasgow
One Devonshire
Gardens (£££) ◆◆◆
1 Devonshire Gardens
G12 0UX
Tel: 0141 339 2001
Fax: 0141 337 1663
Breathtakingly opulent and dramatically furnished adjoining townhouses. Memorable Scottish dinners. 27 rooms. Satellite TV. Restaurant. AE/DI/MC/VI

DUMFRIES AND GALLOWAY
Portpatrick
Knockinaam
Lodge (£££) ◆◆
DG9 9AD
Tel: 01776 810471

Fax: 01776 810435
This small, exquisite country house enjoys utter waterside isolation; fine modern French cuisine. 10 rooms. Restaurant. AE/DI/MC/VI

Gretna
Solway Lodge Hotel (£) ♦♦
Annan Road, DG16 5DN
Tel: 01461 338266
Fax: 01461 337791
A family-run hotel offering a choice of accommodation; two honeymoon suites with four-poster beds and chalet block rooms ideal for overnight stops. Home-made meals offered in restaurant. 10 rooms. AE/DI/MC/VI

EAST LOTHIAN
Gullane
Greywalls (£££) ♦♦♦
Muirfield, EH31 2EG
Tel: 01620 842144
Fax: 01620 842241
Glorious country house next to famous Muirfield golf course. 22 rooms. Restaurant. AE/DI/MC/VI

FIFE
Aberdour
Hawkcraig House (£)
Hawkcraig Point
KY3 0TZ
Tel: 01383 860335
Good home cooking and great views in this simple waterside guest house. 2 rooms. No credit cards.

St. Andrews
Rufflets Country House (£££) ♦♦♦
Strathkinness Low Road
KY16 9TX
Tel: 01334 472594
Fax: 01334 478703
Laid-back Edwardian country house 1½ miles from St. Andrews. 25 rooms. Restaurant. AE/DI/MC/VI

STIRLING
Callander
Roman Camp (££–£££) ♦♦♦
FK17 8BG
Tel: 01877 330003
Fax: 01877 331533
Romantic hideaway country-house hotel in a 17th-century hunting lodge; remarkable period interiors. 14 rooms. Restaurant. AE/DI/MC/VI

SCOTTISH HIGHLANDS

ABERDEENSHIRE
Banchory
Banchory Lodge (££) ♦♦♦
AB31 3HS
Tel: 01330 822625
Fax: 01330 825019
Well-established old-fashioned Georgian country house; popular with anglers. 22 rooms. Restaurant. AE/DI/MC/VI

Bridge of Marnoch
Old Manse of Marnoch (££) ♦
AB54 7RS
Tel: 01466 780873
Fax: 01466 780873
A stylish country-house hotel in a lovely Georgian building; terrific breakfasts. 5 rooms. Restaurant. MC/VI

ARGYLL & BUTE
Arduaine
Loch Melfort (££) ♦♦♦
PA34 4XG
Tel: 01852 200233
Fax: 01852 200214
Relaxing Edwardian hotel with spectacular views. 27 rooms. Restaurant. MC/VI

Port Appin
Airds (£££) ♦♦♦
PA38 4DF
Tel: 01631 730236
Fax: 01631 730535

A plush ferry-inn conversion on the banks of Loch Linnhe. 12 rooms. Restaurant. AE/MC/VI

HIGHLAND
Fort William
Inverlochy
Castle (£££) ♦♦♦♦
PH33 6SN
Tel: 01397 702177
Fax: 01397 702953
Grandest of Scotland's mansions on 500 acres of parkland. A visit is unforgettable. 17 rooms. AE/MC/VI

Grantown-on-Spey
Culdearn House (££–£££ including dinner) ♦♦
Woodlands Terrace
PH26 3JU
Tel: 01479 872106
Fax: 01479 873641
Enthusiastically-run Victorian hotel offering over 50 varieties of malt whiskey; home-cooked food. 9 rooms. DI/MC/VI

Inverness
Dunain Park (£££) ♦♦
IV3 6JN
Tel: 01463 230512
Fax: 01463 224532
Classic, unstuffy Georgian country house in a wooded location. 12 rooms. Restaurant. AE/DI/MC/VI

Letterfinlay
Letterfinlay Lodge Hotel (£–££) ♦♦
PH34 4DZ
Tel: 01397 712622
Welcoming hotel with spectacular views. Relaxing lounges, a snug bar, attractive dining room. Bedrooms vary in size with both modern and traditional appointments. 13 rooms. AE/DI/MC/VI

Shieldaig
Tigh an Eilean (£££) ◆◆
IV54 8XN
Tel: 015205 755251
Fax: 015205 755321
Civilized yet remote little waterside hotel; charming hosts and excellent seafood. 11 rooms. MC/VI

Ullapool
Ceilidh Place (£££) ◆◆
West Argyle Street
IV26 2TY
Tel: 01854 612103
Fax: 01854 612886
All-in-one bookstore, coffee house, bar, restaurant, arts venue and comfy hotel. 13 rooms. AE/DI/MC/VI

PERTH & KINROSS
Blairgowrie
Angus Hotel (££) ◆◆
PH10 6NQ
Tel: 01250 872455
Fax: 01250 875615
Established hotel overlooking the town square. Most bedrooms have been smartly upgraded. Spacious bar with nonsmoking area. Restaurant. Leisure center available. 81 rooms. AE/MC/VI

SCOTTISH ISLANDS
North Uist, Western Isles
Lochmaddy Hotel (££) ◆◆
Lochmaddy, HS6 5AA
Tel: 01876 500331
Fax: 01876 500210
Close to ferry terminal; a welcoming hotel popular with visiting anglers offering enjoyable home-cooked fare. 15 rooms. AE/MC/VI

Mull
Druimard Country House (£££) ◆
Dervaig, PA75 6QW
Tel: 01688 400345
Fax: 01688 400345
Next to the local theater,
this modest country house serves Scottish cuisine. 6 rooms. Restaurant. MC/VI

Shetland
Busta House (££) ◆◆◆
Brae, ZE2 9QN
Tel: 01806 522506
Fax: 01806 522588
An 18th-century building with a popular bar and traditional restaurant. 20 rooms. AE/DI/MC/VI

Skye
Harlosh House (££) ◆
Harlosh, IV55 8ZG
Tel: 01470 521367
Fax: 01470 521367
Tiny hotel with magnificently isolated, peerless mountain views and serious food. 6 rooms. Restaurant. MC/VI

Hotel Eilean Iarmain (££) ◆◆
Isle Ornsay, IV43 8QR
Tel: 01471 833332
Fax: 01471 833275
Cozy waterside inn with distinctive Gaelic accents. 12 rooms. AE/MC/VI

NORTHERN IRELAND

ANTRIM
Belfast
Camera (£)
44 Wellington Park
BT9 6DP
Tel: 01232 660026
Fax: 01232 667856
Charming B&B in Victorian house near the university. 9 rooms. MC/VI

Renshaws Hotel (££) ◆◆
75 University Street
BT7 1HL
Tel: 01232 333366
Fax: 01232 333399
Popular rendezvous for students. Bedrooms offer
good standard amenities. Split-level bistro/bar; recently refurbished restaurant. 20 rooms. AE/DI/MC/VI

Carnlough
Londonderry Arms (££) ◆◆◆
BT44 0EU
Tel: 01574 885255
Fax: 01574 885263
Georgian coaching inn once owned by Sir Winston Churchill; hearty Irish food. 21 rooms. AE/DI/MC/VI

COUNTY DOWN
Hollywood
Culloden (£££) ◆◆◆◆
BT18 0EX
Tel: 01232 425223
Fax: 01232 426777
Elegant 19th-century baronial mansion – probably the province's best hotel. 87 rooms. Satellite TV. AE/DI/MC/VI

LONDONDERRY
Coleraine
Greenhill House (£)
24 Greenhill Road
Aghadowey, BT51 4EU
Tel: 01265 868241
Fax: 01265 868365
Secluded Georgian country guest house set in the Bann Valley; good home cooking. 6 rooms. MC/VI

TYRONE
Omagh
Royal Arms Hotel (£) ◆◆
51 High Street
BT78 1BA
Tel: 01662 243262
Fax: 01662 245011
Popular hotel in center of town. Good-value buffet; wine bar; restaurant provides good selection from the à-la-carte and fixed-price menus. 19 rooms. MC/VI

RESTAURANTS

"If you want to eat well in England, eat three breakfasts," Somerset Maugham once said. This is no longer the case. During the last 20 years or so, food in Britain has dramatically improved.

Traditional dishes – a "ploughman's lunch" (bread, cheese and pickle) in a pub, fish and chips from a takeout, roast beef and Yorkshire pudding for Sunday lunch – still form the backbone of eating out for many. At the same time, there are plenty of top restaurants offering what is loosely termed as "modern British" cooking (a very rough parallel could be made with California cuisine in the United States) – inventive fare borrowing a wealth of foreign influences.

There are Italian, French, Chinese and Indian restaurants throughout the country, along with an increasing number of Spanish, Japanese and Thai establishments. In London, you can eat any type of food under the sun.

Listed below are some of the best restaurants in Britain. Advance reservations are invariably necessary. Last orders refers to the latest time a meal can be ordered.

Each restaurant has been inspected by the Automobile Association. For a comprehensive guide, obtain a current copy of *Best Restaurants*, published by the Automobile Association.

AAA DIAMOND RATING
Diamond ratings are on a scale of one to five and range from simple, home-style cooking to superlative standards of cuisine. (See p.286 for more details.)

◆ **one diamond** denotes simple, carefully prepared food based on good-quality, fresh ingredients.

◆◆ **two diamonds** denote cooking that displays a high degree of competence. The menu should include some imaginative dishes, making use of high-quality raw ingredients, as well as some tried-and-tested favorites. Flavors should be well balanced.

◆◆◆ **three diamonds** denote imaginative menus with dishes that are accurately cooked and demonstrate well-developed technical skills and a high degree of flair in their composition. Most items will be made in the kitchen, such as breads, pastries, pasta and petits fours.

◆◆◆◆ **four diamond** cuisine should be innovative, daring, highly accomplished and achieve a noteworthy standard of consistency, accuracy and flair throughout all elements of the meal.

◆◆◆◆◆ **five diamonds** is the supreme accolade, made to chefs at the very top of their profession. Creativity, skill and attention to detail will produce dishes cooked to perfection, with intense, exciting flavors in harmonious combinations, and faultlessly presented. Expect to find luxury ingredients such as lobster, truffles and foie gras, often in unexpected combinations.

In this guide we have used the following abbreviations for the major credit cards:

AE = American Express
DI = Diners Club
MC = Mastercard
VI = Visa

The following price ranges apply for a meal for one, including service but not drinks:

(£)   under £15
(££) £15–30
(£££) over £30

LONDON

Bloomsbury
Museum Street Café (££) ♦♦
47 Museum Street, WC1
Tel: 0171 405 3211
Chic, tiny restaurant; grills and simple but effective dishes. Last orders 9:30 p.m. Closed Saturday, Sunday and public holidays. AE/DI/MC/VI

Chelsea
Daphne's Restaurant (£££) ♦♦♦
110–112 Draycott Avenue
SW3
Tel: 0171 589 4257
Popular Italian restaurant; good atmosphere and an attractive menu. Last orders 11:20 p.m. Closed December. AE/DI/MC/VI

La Tante Claire (£££) ♦♦♦♦♦
68 Royal Hospital Road
SW3
Tel: 0171 352 6045
Unique French cooking, created in a very popular, busy restaurant. Last orders 11 p.m. Closed Saturday, Sunday and public holidays. AE/DI/MC/VI

Covent Garden
Neal Street Restaurant (£££) ♦♦♦
26 Neal Street, WC2
Tel: 0171 836 8368
A bastion of Italian cooking; many dishes reflect the owner's passion for pasta and mushrooms. Last orders 11 p.m. Closed Sunday and public holidays. AE/DI/MC/VI

Knightsbridge/Kensington
Bibendum Restaurant (£££) ♦♦♦♦
Michelin House
81 Fulham Road, SW3
Tel: 0171 581 5817
Pioneer of modern bistro-style cooking. Simple dishes in an art-deco building. Last orders 11:30 p.m. Closed December 25. AE/MC/VI

Bombay Brasserie (££) ♦♦
Courtfield Close
Courtfield Road, SW7
Tel: 0171 370 4040
Grandiose setting for cosmopolitan cuisine. Last orders midnight. Closed December 25. AE/DI/MC/VI

Clarke's (£££) ♦♦♦
124 Kensington
Church Street, W8
Tel: 0171 221 9225
A popular restaurant with a reputation for quality. Last orders 10 p.m. Closed Saturday, Sunday, December 25 and summer break. MC/VI

Downstairs at 190 Queensgate (££) ♦♦
190 Queen's Gate, SW7
Tel: 0171 581 5666
This lively seafood restaurant offers accomplished cooking at reasonable prices. Last orders midnight (dinner only). Closed Sunday. AE/DI/MC/VI

Leith's (££) ♦♦♦
92 Kensington Park Road
W11
Tel: 0171 229 4481
Home-grown organic produce used in modern British cuisine. Last orders 11:30 p.m., Sunday 10 p.m. AE/DI/MC/VI

Turner's (£££) ♦♦♦
87–89 Walton Street, SW3
Tel: 0171 584 6711
Close to Harrods; offers carefully prepared, good-value French cuisine. Last orders 11 p.m., Sunday 8.30 p.m. Closed Saturday lunch. AE/DI/MC/VI

Marylebone/Regent's Park
Odette's (££) ♦♦♦
130 Regent's Park Road
NW1
Tel: 0171 586 5486
Uncomplicated, subtle cooking in a friendly neighborhood setting. Last orders 11 p.m., Sunday, 8:30 p.m. Closed Saturday lunch and Sunday evening, December 25 and public holidays. AE/DI/MC/VI

South Bank
Blue Print Café (££) ♦♦
The Design Museum
Shad Thames, SE1
Tel: 0171 378 7031
Bright, modern bistro-cum-brasserie with a vibrant atmosphere, serving fresh light fare in a superb riverside setting. Last orders 10:30 p.m. Closed Sunday dinner. AE/DI/MC/VI

Le Pont de la Tour (££) ♦♦
36d Shad Thames
SE1
Tel: 0171 403 8403
Popular riverside restaurant owned by Sir Terence Conran and specializing in seafood and classic dishes. Last orders midnight. Closed Saturday lunch. AE/DI/MC/VI

RSJ The Restaurant on the South Bank (££) ♦♦
13a Coin Street, SE1
Tel: 0171 928 4554
Unpretentious bistro/brasserie with pine-boarded floors, offering a good range of dishes. Last orders 11 p.m. Closed Saturday lunch, all day Sunday and public holidays. AE/MC/VI

West End
Alastair Little (£££) ◆◆◆
49 Frith Street, W1
Tel: 0171 734 5183
International dishes in a restaurant where the atmosphere is casual and the food serious. Last orders 11:30 p.m. Closed Saturday lunch and all day Sunday. AE/MC/VI

Atlantic (££) ◆◆
20 Glasshouse Street, W1
Tel: 0171 734 4888
Fax: 0171 734 3609
A brash, lively place with young crowds clustering round the American-style bar. Extensive menu with most dishes reflecting a modern European (or Continental) sensibility. Last orders midnight. Closed Saturday, Sunday and public holidays. AE/MC/VI

Bahn Thai (££) ◆◆
21a Frith Street, W1
Tel: 0171 437 8504
Informative menus, so Thai food novices have an excellent starting point. Last orders 11:15 p.m., Sunday, 10:30 p.m. Closed public holidays. AE/MC/VI

Café Fish (££) ◆
39 Panton Street
Haymarket, SW1
Tel: 0171 930 3999
A bustling, convivial French atmosphere prevails in this bistro-style fish restaurant, where the cooking style is complemented by good, fresh food. Last orders 11:30 p.m. Closed Saturday lunch, all day Sunday and public holidays. AE/DI/MC/VI

L'Escargot (££) ◆◆
24 Greek Street, W1
Tel: 0171 437 2679
A well-established Soho restaurant serving vibrant French cooking. Last orders 11:30 p.m. Closed Saturday lunch and all day Sunday. AE/DI/MC/VI

Le Gavroche (£££) ◆◆◆◆◆
43 Upper Brook Street, W1
Tel: 0171 408 0881
Award-winning restaurant; the very best in modern French cuisine. Last orders 11 p.m. Closed Saturday, Sunday and public holidays. AE/DI/MC/VI

The Greenhouse (££) ◆◆◆
27a Hay's Mews, W1
Tel: 0171 499 3331
Modern, traditional British dishes served in a lively atmosphere. Last orders 11:30 p.m. Closed Saturday lunch and public holidays. AE/DI/MC/VI

The Ivy (££–£££) ◆◆◆
1 West Street
Covent Garden, WC2
Tel: 0171 836 4751
In the theater district, this restaurant offers eclectic brasserie-style food. Last orders midnight. Closed December 25. AE/DI/MC/VI

Langan's (££) ◆◆
Stratton Street, W1
Tel: 0171 491 8822
Large, lively restaurant part owned by actor Michael Caine. Last orders 11:45 p.m. Closed Saturday lunch and all day Sunday. AE/DI/MC/VI

Mitsukoshi (££–£££) ◆◆
14–20 Regent Street, SW1
Tel: 0171 930 0317
Serene Japanese restaurant. Last orders 9:30 p.m. Closed Saturday and public holidays. AE/DI/MC/VI

Orso (££) ◆◆
27 Wellington Street, WC2
Tel: 0171 240 5269
Accomplished and well-established Italian restaurant. A place to be seen. Last orders midnight. Closed December 25. No credit cards.

Poons (£–££) ◆◆
Leicester Square, WC2
Tel: 0171 437 1528
A wide choice of excellent, good-value Cantonese dishes in a bustling, informal setting. Last orders 11:30 p.m. Closed December 25. AE/DI/MC/VI.

Westminster
Quaglino's (£££) ◆◆
16 Bury Street, SW1
Tel: 0171 930 6767
Brasserie food in an awesome setting based on the ballroom of an ocean liner. Last orders Monday to Thursday 11:30 p.m., Friday, Saturday 12:30 a.m., Sunday 10:30 p.m. AE/DI/MC/VI

THE WEST COUNTRY

AVON
Hunstrete
Hunstrete House (££)◆◆◆
Chelwood
Tel: 01761 490490
Modern English cooking served in an elegant 18th-century property on beautifully kept grounds with rural views. Last orders 9:30 p.m. AE/MC/VI

BRISTOL
Bristol
Harvey's (£££) ◆◆◆
12 Denmark Street
Tel: 0117 927 5034
British cooking served in the medieval vaults of famous

RESTAURANTS

former wine merchants. Last orders 10:45 p.m. Closed Saturday lunch, all day Sunday and public holidays. AE/DI/MC/VI

CORNWALL
Falmouth
Greenpublic Hotel (££) ◆
Harbourside
Tel: 01326 312440
Nightingales, the restaurant in what is reputedly Falmouth's first hotel, offers interesting and well-balanced dishes. Last orders 9:45 p.m. Closed December 25 to mid-January. AE/DI/MC/VI

Fowey
Food for Thought (££) ◆◆
The Quay
Tel: 01726 832221
Delightful little restaurant in a riverside setting. Imaginative seafood dishes. Last orders 9 p.m. (dinner only). Closed Sunday and December 25 to mid-March. AE/MC

Newquay
Whipsiderry Hotel (£) ◆
Trevelgue Road, Porth
Tel: 01637 874777
Idyllic pub-style hotel overlooking Porth Beach. Food is served in both the restaurant and bar. Last orders 8 p.m. MC/VI

St. Ives
Pig 'n' Fish (££) ◆◆
Norway Lane
Tel: 01736 794204
A wide array of beautifully cooked French and Italian fish and shellfish dishes in a simple oceanfront setting. Last orders 9:30 p.m. Closed Sunday, Monday and mid-December to March 1. MC/VI

DEVON
Barnstaple
Halmpstone Manor Hotel (££) ◆◆
Bishop's Tawton
Tel: 01271 830321
Relaxed, attentive service accompanies enjoyable food. Excellent use of fresh local produce. Last orders 9 p.m. (lunch available by arrangement only). Closed November 1 to January. AE/DI/MC/VI

Dartmouth
Carved Angel Restaurant (£££) ◆◆◆
2 South Empublicment
Tel: 01803 832465
Much-lauded Mediterranean cooking and treatment of fish in this decades-old restaurant. Last orders 9:30 p.m. Closed Sunday dinner, all day Monday and January 1 to mid-February. No credit cards.

Exeter
Ebford House Hotel (££) ◆◆
Ebmouth Road
Tel: 01392 877658
Sophisticated modern cuisine in the formal setting of a pleasant Georgian hotel near Topsham. Local produce used. Last orders 9:30 p.m. Closed Saturday lunch, all day Sunday and December 25. AE/DI/MC

DORSET
Bournemouth
Langtry Manor Hotel (££) ◆
26 Derby Road
East Cliff
Tel: 01202 553887
An Edwardian theme prevails at this hotel, once the love nest of Lillie Langtry and King Edward VIII. The dining room has a minstrel's gallery. Last orders 9 p.m. (dinner only). AE/DI/MC/VI

Dorchester
The Mock Turtle (££) ◆◆
34 High West Street
Tel: 01305 264011
Adventurous, friendly little restaurant. Good value. Last orders 9:30 p.m. Closed Saturday and Monday lunch and all day Sunday. MC/VI

Swanage
The Cauldron Bistro (££) ◆
5 High Street
Tel: 01929 422671
Good-value, enjoyable food prepared from fresh local ingredients. Last orders 9:30 p.m. Closed Monday, Tuesday lunch (summer), all day Tuesday (winter) and January. AE/DI/MC/VI

SOMERSET
Bath
Woods Restaurant (£–££) ◆◆
9–13 Alfred Street
Tel: 01225 314812
Eclectic fare in a Georgian building – both formal and informal dining. Well-prepared meals. Last orders 11 p.m. Closed Sunday dinner. MC/VI

Bruton
Truffles Restaurant (££) ◆◆
95 High Street
Tel: 01749 812255
This atmospheric cottage restaurant serves imaginative, predominantly French cuisine. Last orders 9 p.m. Closed Sunday dinner, all day Monday and last 2 weeks of January. MC/VI

Shepton Mallet
Shrubbery Hotel (£) ◆
Commercial Road

Tel: 01749 346671
A bright, comfortable, unpretentious hotel with a small, congenial restaurant. Menus feature English, French and Italian cuisine. Last orders 9 p.m. Closed Sunday dinner. MC/VI

Taunton
Castle Hotel (££) ◆◆◆◆
Castle Green
Tel: 01823 272671
Appetizing presentation of technically faultless cooking in the modern British style, served in an authentic castle. Last orders 9 p.m. AE/DI/MC/VI

WILTSHIRE
Bradford on Avon
Woolley Grange (££) ◆◆◆
Woolley Green
Tel: 01225 864705
Fine food is served at this restaurant in a Jacobean house set in beautiful grounds. Last orders 9:30 p.m. Closed Saturday lunch. AE/DI/MC/VI

Salisbury
Milford Hall Hotel (££) ◆
206 Castle Street
Tel: 01722 417411
This Georgian mansion features an interesting and ambitious menu. Last orders 9:30 p.m. AE/MC/VI

SOUTH AND SOUTHEAST ENGLAND

BERKSHIRE
Ascot
Jade Fountain (££) ◆
38 High Street
Sunninghill
Tel: 01344 27070
A smart Chinese restaurant with a loyal local following, offering a menu that sticks

to mostly the favorite Chinese dishes of Westerners. Last orders 10:15 p.m. Closed December 25. AE/DI/MC/VI*

Bray (close to Windsor)
Waterside Inn (£££) ◆◆◆◆
Ferry Road
Tel: 01628 620691
Outstanding French cooking in a riverside setting. Last orders 10 p.m. Closed Tuesday lunch, Sunday dinner, all day Monday, 3rd week in October, 2nd week in April and for 5 weeks beginning December 26. DI/MC/VI

Shinfield
L'Ortolan (£££) ◆◆◆◆◆
The Old Vicarage
Church Lane
Tel: 01734 9783883
L'Ortolan presents exquisitely prepared French cuisine in an elegant country-house setting. Last orders 9:30 p.m. Closed Sunday dinner and all day Monday. AE/DI/MC/VI

EAST SUSSEX
Brighton
Whytes (££–£££) ◆◆
33 Western Street
Tel: 01273 776618
Converted fisherman's cottage just off the waterfront. Charmingly hospitable. Fresh produce and locally caught fish. Last orders 9:30 p.m. (dinner only). Closed Sunday, Monday and last 2 weeks of February. AE/MC/VI

Hastings and St. Leonards
Rösers Restaurant
(££) ◆◆◆
64 Eversfield Place
Tel: 01424 712218
Classic French cuisine with

Mediterranean influences in an unlikely waterfront setting opposite the pier. Last orders 10 p.m. Closed Saturday, Sunday and Monday lunch, 2 weeks in January, and in June. AE/DI/MC/VI*

Jevington (near Eastbourne/South Downs)
Hungry Monk (££) ◆◆
Polegate
Tel: 01323 482178
Pretty beamed cottage restaurant of long standing serving imaginative French/English dishes. Last orders 10:15 p.m. (dinner only except Sunday, when open for lunch). Closed December 25 and public holidays. AE

HAMPSHIRE
Brockenhurst
Le Poussin (££) ◆◆◆
The Courtyard
Brookley Road
Tel: 01590 623063
Simple but tasteful restaurant; dishes cooked to order from daily fresh produce. Last orders 9 p.m. Closed Monday and Tuesday. MC/VI

Winchester
Hunters (£–££) ◆◆
5 Jewry Street
Tel: 01962 860006
Good-value modern cooking and tasty desserts served in a bistro-style setting. Last orders 10 p.m. Closed Sunday and December 25. AE/DI/MC/VI

KENT
Canterbury
Falstaff Hotel (££) ◆
St. Dunstans Street
Tel: 01227 462138
Beamed 15th-century inn

built to accommodate pilgrims. Last orders 9:45 p.m. AE/DI/MC/VI

Royal Tunbridge Wells
Thackeray's House Restaurant (££) ◆◆◆
85 London Road
Tel: 01892 511921
Very elegant, smart dining in William Makepeace Thackeray's former home. Last orders 10 p.m. Closed Sunday dinner and all day Monday. MC/VI/D

Sissinghurst
Rankins (££) ◆◆
The Street
Tel: 01580 713964
Between the post office and the general stores, this uncomplicated little restaurant has a good reputation for serious food. Last orders 9 p.m. Closed Sunday dinner, all day Monday, Tuesday and 1st week in September. MC/VI

SURREY
Bagshot
Pennyhill Park Hotel (££–£££) ◆◆◆
London Road
Tel: 01276 471774
An extensive range of quality dishes are elaborately presented in this elegant hotel restaurant. Last orders 10:30 p.m. AE/DI/MC/VI

Claygate
Le Petit Pierrot (££–£££) ◆◆
4 The Parade
Tel: 01372 465105
Small country-town restaurant; chef Jean-Pierre Brichot provides French cuisine with quality and flair. Last orders 7:15 p.m. Closed Saturday lunch and

all day Sunday, the week following December 25 and 1 week in summer. AE/MC/VI

Guildford
The Manor (££) ◆
Newlands Corner
Tel: 01483 222624
Conveniently located just outside town, this hotel is situated on 6 acres of mature parkland. Last orders 10 p.m. Opening times vary – call for details. AE/DI/MC/VI

WEST SUSSEX
Chichester
Little London (££) ◆
38–39 Little London
Tel: 01243 530735
Pleasant restaurant named after the part of town in which it is located. The ambitious chef emphasizes modern cooking. Last orders 10:30 p.m. Closed Sunday, December 26 and January 1. AE/DI/MC/VI

Midhurst
Angel Hotel (££) ◆◆◆
North Street
Tel: 01730 812421
A rich and imaginative choice of dishes is offered at this attractive 16th-century coaching inn. Convivial atmosphere. Last orders 10 p.m. AE/DI/MC/VI

Storrington
Manleys (££) ◆◆◆
Manleys Hill
Tel: 01903 742331
Excellent value for money from a family team who produce confident, classically-based cooking with individual flair in delightful surroundings. Last orders 9 p.m. Closed Monday and first 10 days of January. AE/DI/MC/VI

EASTERN ENGLAND

CAMBRIDGESHIRE
Cambridge
Midsummer House Restaurant (£££) ◆◆
Midsummer Common
Tel: 01223 369299
Eat exciting cooking in elegant, atmospheric surroundings. Last orders 10 p.m. Closed Saturday lunch, Sunday dinner, all day Monday and first week in January. AE/DI/MC/VI

Melbourn
Sheen Mill (££) ◆◆
Station Road
Tel: 01763 261393
A peaceful waterside restaurant serving enjoyable and uncomplicated modern cooking. Last orders 10 p.m. Closed Sunday dinner and public holidays. AE/MC/VI

ESSEX
Coggeshall
White Hart (££) ◆◆
Market End
Tel: 01376 561654
Heavy oak beams dominate the rooms of this historic inn, where the rich Italian cooking has refreshingly honest flavors. Last orders 9:45 p.m. Closed Sunday dinner. AE/DI/MC/VI

HERTFORDSHIRE
St. Albans
Sopwell House (££) ◆◆
Cottonmill Lane
Tel: 01727 864477
The Magnolia Conservatory Restaurant is the showpiece of this Georgian hotel; modern English cooking excites the palate. Last orders 10 p.m. Closed Saturday lunch and Sunday dinner. AE/DI/MC/VI

Tring
Rose & Crown Hotel (££) ◆
High Street
Tel: 01442 824071
Imposing Tudor-style hotel offering imaginatively cooked food served in the attractive, split-level Carriages Restaurant. Last orders 9:45 p.m. Closed Sunday dinner. AE/DI/MC/VI

LINCOLNSHIRE
Grantham
Harry's Place (£££) ◆◆◆
17 High Street
Great Gonerby
Tel: 01476 561780
Small, detached house, where perfectly cooked food is the aim. Last orders 9:30 p.m. Closed Sunday,.. Monday and December 25. MC/VI

Lincoln
Wig and Mitre (££) ◆
29 Steep Hill
Tel: 01522 535190
Aimiable 14th-century inn, full of character; restaurant and bar food. Last orders 11 p.m. Closed December 25. AE/MC/VI

NORFOLK
Norwich
Adlard's (£££) ◆◆◆
79 Upper St. Giles Street
Tel: 01603 633522
Smart, very welcoming Anglo/French restaurant. Last orders 10:45 p.m. Closed Sunday dinner, Monday lunch and the week following December 25. AE/MC/VI

Wells-next-the-Sea
Moorings Restaurant
(££) ◆◆
6 Freeman Street
Tel: 01328 710949
Highly imaginative food at

an informal local haunt. Last orders 8:30 p.m. Closed Tuesday, Wednesday and Thursday lunch. No credit cards.

NOTTINGHAMSHIRE
Langar
Langar Hall (££) ◆
Langar (behind the church)
Tel: 01949 860559
The imaginative short menu of classic British dishes reveals a hint of Mediterranean influences. This comfortable country hotel is surrounded by gardens. Last orders 9:45 p.m. Monday to Thursday, 10 p.m. Friday and Saturday. Closed Sunday. AE/DI/MC/VI

Nottingham
Sonny's (££) ◆◆
3 Carlton Street
Hockley
Tel: 0115 9473041
A popular café/brasserie style restaurant. The surroundings are simple, the atmosphere lively and the service friendly. Last orders 10:30 p.m. Closed public holidays. AE/MC/VI

SUFFOLK
Aldeburgh
Regatta Restaurant (££) ◆
171 High Street
Tel: 01728 452011
Good-value restaurant/wine bar serving excellent desserts. Last orders 10 p.m. Closed Monday and Tuesday during winter. AE/DI/MC/VI

Fressingfield
(inland from Southwold)
Fox & Goose Inn (££) ◆◆◆
Nr. Diss
Tel: 01379 586247
Creative cooking in an

authentic, friendly village pub . Last orders 9:30 p.m. Closed Monday, Tuesday, December 25 and January 1. MC/VI

THE HEART OF ENGLAND

GLOUCESTERSHIRE
Cheltenham
Greenway Hotel (££) ◆◆◆
Shurdington
Tel: 01242 862352
Delightful, ivy-clad Elizabethan house set among colorful gardens and surrounded by parkland. Last orders 9:15 p.m. Closed Saturday lunch. AE/DI/MC/VI

Le Champignon
Sauvage (££) ◆◆◆
14 Suffolk Road
Tel: 01242 573449
Authentic French country cooking and friendly service. Last orders 9:15 p.m. Closed Saturday lunch, all day Sunday, public holidays, December 25 to January 3 and 2 weeks in summer. AE/DI/MC/VI

HEREFORDSHIRE
Ledbury
Feathers Hotel (££) ◆
High Street
Tel: 01531 635266
Centuries-old timber-framed inn in the town center. Quills Restaurant is more formal, while the brasserie has a varied menu with modern overtones. Last orders 9.30 p.m. AE/DI/MC/VI

Leominster
The Marsh Country
Hotel (££) ◆◆
Eyton
Tel: 01568 613952

RESTAURANTS

Nestled in rural surroundings, this 14th-century timbered house offers honest British dishes based on high-quality, fresh ingredients. Last orders 8:30 p.m. Closed 3 weeks in January. AE/MC/VI/D

NORTHAMPTONSHIRE
Hellidon
Hellidon Lakes Hotel (££) ♦
Tel: 01327 262550
In the village of Daventry, this modern hotel has lovely views over the valley and golf course. The restaurant is known for generous portions. Last orders 9:30 p.m. AE/DI/MC/VI

OXFORDSHIRE
Great Milton (near Oxford)
Le Manoir aux Quat'Saisons (£££) ♦♦♦♦♦
Church Road
Tel: 01844 278881
Fine 15th-century manor house in a pretty village. This is the place to come for exquisite French cuisine prepared by Raymond Blanc, an undisputed master chef. Last orders 10:15 p.m. AE/MC/VI

Oxford
Le Petit Blanc (££) ♦♦
71-72 Walton Street
Tel: 01865 510999
Contemporary brasserie with a fun atmosphere. Flexible changing menu of modern dishes; special children's menu. Last orders 11 p.m. Closed December 25. AE/DI/MC/VI

Whites (£££) ♦♦
19 High Street, Woodstock
Tel: 01993 812872
Dishes to suit all tastes, as well as excellent wines. Last orders 10 p.m. Closed

Sunday dinner and all day Sunday during university vacations. AE/DI/MC/VI

RUTLAND
Oakham
Hambleton Hall (£££) ♦♦♦♦
Hambleton
Tel: 01572 756991
Accomplished cooking that compares with some of London's best restaurants, presented in a fine country house. Reservations are essential. Last orders 9:30 p.m. AE/DI/MC/VI

SHROPSHIRE
Bridgnorth
Haywain Restaurant (££) ♦♦
Hampton Loade
Tel: 01746 780404
This smart cottage-style restaurant, in a secluded rural location near the River Severn, is the delightful setting for an unusual eating experience. Last orders 9:30 p.m. Closed Sunday dinner and all day Monday. AE/DI/MC/VI

STAFFORDSHIRE
Burton-upon-Trent
Riverside Hotel (££) ♦
Riverside Drive, Branston
Tel: 01283 511234
Charming modernized inn standing on the riverbank; the popular restaurant has fine views. Good range of freshly prepared dishes. Last orders 10 p.m., Sunday 8:30 p.m. Closed Saturday lunch. AE/MC/VI

WARWICKSHIRE
Stratford-upon-Avon
The Boathouse (££) ♦♦
Swan's Nest Lane
Tel: 01789 297733
Riverside venue with gondola ferry service for

theater visits. Interesting decor. Rich, hearty flavors on the menu. Last orders 9:30 p.m. AE/DI/MC/VI

WEST MIDLANDS
Birmingham
Shimla Pinks (££) ♦
214 Broad Street
Tel: 0121 633 0366
Classic versions of popular Indian dishes are offered. Specialties include southern Indian garlic chili chicken. Last orders 11 p.m. Closed Saturday and Sunday lunch, December 25 and January 1. AE/DI/MC/VI

WORCESTER
Worcester
Brown's Restaurant (££) ♦♦
The Old Cornmill
South Quay
Tel: 01905 26263
Modern cooking served in a striking warehouse conversion beside the river. Last orders 9:45 p.m. Closed Saturday lunch and Sunday dinner. AE/MC/VI

WALES

BRIDGEND
Coed-y-Mwstwr (££) ♦
Coychurch
Tel: 01656 860621
Paneled, Victorian-style dining room serving such modern Welsh dishes as medallions of wild venison on a turnip and celeriac rösti with a rich cranberry, thyme and cinnamon sauce. Last orders 10 p.m. AE/DI/MC/VI

CARDIFF
Cardiff
Le Cassoulet (££) ♦♦
5 Romilly Crescent
Canton
Tel: 01222 221905

Charming little bistro serving provincial French food. Last orders 10 p.m. Closed Saturday lunch, all day Sunday and Monday, 2 weeks following December 25 and August. AE/DI/MC/VI

Chikako's Japanese Restaurant (££) ◆
10–11 Mill Lane
Tel: 01222 665279
An authentic Japanese restaurant producing delicious dishes, including a selection of seafood and vegetables in a soup. Last orders 11 p.m. AE/MC/VI

CEREDIGION
Aberystwyth
Conrah Hotel (££) ◆◆
Ffosrhydygaled
Chancery
Tel: 01970 617941
The secret behind the exceptional freshness of the food served here is the kitchen garden which yields a ready supply of herbs and vegetables. Last orders 9 p.m. Closed the week of December 25. AE/DI/MC/VI

CONWY
Conwy
The Old Rectory Country House (££) ◆◆◆
Llanrwst Road
Colwyn Bay
Tel: 01492 580611
With stunning views of Conwy Castle, this restaurant, set in a stylish Georgian hotel, has a daily changing menu in a relaxed atmosphere. Dinner only at 8 p.m. AE/DI/MC/VI

Llandudno
St. Tudno Hotel (££) ◆◆◆
The Promenade
Tel: 01492 874411
The restaurant in this

award-winning small hotel on the seafront serves quality modern British cooking with Welsh and classical French influences. Last orders 9:15 p.m., Sunday 9 p.m. AE/DI/MC/VI

DENBIGHSHIRE
Llangollen
Bryn Howel Hotel (££) ◆◆◆
Tel: 01978 860331
The hotel overlooks the Vale of Llangollen and the lawns lead down to the canal. The Cedar Tree Restaurant has a daily changing menu geared to fresh market produce. Last orders 9 p.m. AE/DI/MC/VI

Ruthin
Ye Olde Anchor Inn (£–££) ◆◆
Rhos Street
Tel: 01824 702813
This 18th-century hostelry in the town center provides good choice and variety, with dishes reflecting an Asian influence. Last orders 9 p.m. MC/VI

GWYNEDD
Llanberis
Y Bistro (££) ◆
Glandwr
43–45 Stryd Fawr
Tel: 01286 871278
In the heart of Snowdonia, this is a popular, attractive, long-running village restaurant serving Welsh food with French overtones. Last orders 9:45 p.m. Closed Sunday and public holidays. MC/VI

MONMOUTHSHIRE
Abergavenny
Llanwenarth Arms Hotel (£) ◆
Brecon Road

Tel: 01873 810550
International-style dishes using local game are served in this welcoming inn overlooking the River Usk. Last orders 9:45 p.m., Sunday 8:15 p.m. AE/DI/MC/VI

Llanddewi Skyrrid
The Walnut Tree Inn (££) ◆◆◆
Abergavenny
Tel: 01873 852797
Historic inn located in the Brecon Beacons, serving Italian fare. Last orders 10:15 p.m. Closed Sunday, Monday, the week of December 25 and 2 weeks in February. No credit cards.

PEMBROKESHIRE
Tenby
Penally Abbey Country House (££) ◆◆
Penally
Tel: 01834 843033
Overlooking Caldey Island and Carmarthen Bay, this seaside restaurant has a small but interesting menu making good use of fresh produce. Last orders 9 p.m. AE/MC/VI

SWANSEA
Reynoldston
Fairyhill Hotel (££) ◆◆◆
Tel: 01792 390139
At the heart of the Gower Peninsula, this 18th-century mansion is set on 24 acres of woodland and has its own trout stream. Seafood features prominently. Last orders 9:15 p.m. AE/MC/VI

Swansea
Windsor Lodge Hotel (££) ◆
Mount Pleasant
Tel: 01792 642158
High standards maintained in a delightful Georgian house.

The varied menu provides quality dishes, good textures and pleasant flavors. Last orders 9:30 p.m. Closed Sunday and December 25. AE/DI/MC/VI

THE NORTH

CHESHIRE
Chester
The Chester Grosvenor Hotel (£££) ◆◆◆
Eastgate Street
Tel: 01244 324024
The restaurant in this centrally located hotel has a reputation for turning out trendy dishes utilizing luxurious ingredients. Last orders 9:30 p.m. Closed Sunday dinner and Monday lunch. AE/DI/MC/VI

Nantwich
Churche's Mansion (££) ◆◆
Hospital Street
Tel: 01270 625993
An atmospheric 16th-century house. British modern cooking is served using hand-picked ingredients from the best local suppliers. Last orders 9:30 p.m. Closed Sunday dinner, all day Monday and 2 weeks in January. DI/MC/VI

CUMBRIA
Cartmel
Uplands Hotel (££) ◆◆
Haggs Lane
Tel: 015395 36248
Consistently classy and talented cooking is offered in this restaurant; a refreshing lack of pomposity. Fine country-side views and a warm welcome are added attractions. Last orders 8 p.m. Closed Monday and Tuesday, and Wednesday lunch. AE/MC/VI

Windermere
Fayrer Garden House (££) ◆
Lyth Valley Road
Tel: 015394 88195
A Victorian lakeside house, with a beautiful conservatory restaurant. Fixed-price menu changes daily to reflect market availability of seasonal produce. Last orders 8:15 p.m. AE/MC/VI

Rogers Restaurant (££) ◆◆
4 High Street
Tel: 015394 44954
A well-established, intimate restaurant on the edge of Windermere village, serving simply presented classical French cuisine. Last orders 9:30 p.m. Closed Sunday. AE/DI/MC/VI

DERBYSHIRE
Baslow
Fischer's (£££) ◆◆◆
Baslow Hall
Calver Road
Tel: 01246 583259
Classical French and modern European cuisine is served at this elegant country manor house; the good-value Café Max offers an alternative. Last orders 9:30 p.m. Closed Sunday dinner. Café Max closed Sunday dinner except for residents. AE/DI/MC/VI

Ridgeway
The Old Vicarage (£££) ◆◆◆
Ridgeway Moor
Tel: 01142 2475814
The ever-reliable food served in this 1840s village house marries the best of local and other British produce with an array of imaginative influences. A haven of civilized dining.

Last orders 10:30 p.m. Closed Saturday lunch, Sunday dinner, all day Monday and January 1–10. AE/MC/VI

DURHAM
Hartlepool
Krimo's Restaurant (£) ◆
8 The Front
Seaton Carew
Tel: 01429 90022
Good-value Mediterranean cuisine is offered at this popular waterfront restaurant. Last orders 9 p.m. Closed Saturday lunch, all day Sunday, Monday and last 2 weeks in August. MC/VI

GREATER MANCHESTER
Manchester
Market Restaurant (££) ◆◆
Edge Street/104 High Street
Tel: 0161 8343743
Unpretentious spot for truly eclectic cooking. Good beer is served as well as fine wine. Last orders 9:30 p.m. Closed Sunday, Monday, Tuesday, Christmas and Easter weeks and most of August. AE/DI/MC/VI

Victoria and Albert Hotel (££) ◆◆
Water Street
Tel: 0161 8321188
Converted from an early Victorian warehouse on the banks of the River Irwell, opposite Granada Studios. This modern, luxury hotel boasts a lively blend of French, Mediterranean and New World dishes cooked by an enthusiastic chef. Last orders 9:30 p.m. Closed Saturday lunch and Sunday dinner. AE/DI/MC/VI

Yang Sing (££) ◆◆
34 Princess Street
Tel: 0161 2362200
*This universally
acknowledged Cantonese
restaurant in the heart of
Manchester's Chinatown
offers a wide range of
authentic dishes. Last
orders 11 p.m. AE/MC/VI*

LANCASHIRE
Longridge
**Paul Heathcote's
Restaurant** (£££) ◆◆◆◆
104–106 Higher Road
Tel: 01772 784969
*Lancashire's foremost
restaurant, with top-quality
ingredients cooked with
consistent flair and attention
to detail. Last orders 9:30
p.m. Closed Monday.
AE/DI/MC/VI*

LINCOLNSHIRE
Winteringham
**Winteringham
Fields** (££–£££) ◆◆◆◆
Tel: 01724 733096
*A 16th-century country
house "restaurant with
rooms," in the village
center, serving a good
choice of Swiss and French
provincial cooking. Last
orders 9:30 p.m. Closed
Saturday lunch, Sunday,
Monday, 2 weeks following
December 25 and early
August. AE/MC/VI*

MERSEYSIDE
Birkenhead
Capitol (£) ◆
29 Argyle Street
Hamilton Square
Tel: 0151 647 9212
*This popular Chinese
restaurant is said to be
Birkenhead's oldest – the
meals confirm its reputation.
Last orders 11 p.m.
AE/MC/VI*

Southport
Royal Clifton Hotel (££) ◆
Promenade
Tel: 01704 533771
*Long-established hotel with
a prominent promenade
position. Modern, English
dishes are served in the
restaurant – guests can
choose from the daily set
menu or the popular
à la carte. Last orders
9:30 p.m. (dinner only).
AE/DI/MC/VI*

NORTHUMBERLAND
Berwick-upon-Tweed
Marshall Meadows Hotel
(££) ◆
Tel: 01289 331133
*An elegantly decorated
Georgian country house set
in wooded grounds flanked
by farmland. A daily menu
of chef's specialty
selections offers chargrilled
wild boar and fillet of
English ostrich. Last orders
9:30 p.m. MC/VI*

NORTH YORKSHIRE
Easington
Grinkle Park Hotel (££) ◆
Saltburn-by-the-Sea
Tel: 01287 640515
*High-quality, meticulously
presented English/French
cooking, based on local
produce, is served at this
elegant Victorian mansion
set in parkland. Last orders
9 p.m. AE/DI/MC/VI*

Harrogate
The Boar's Head (££) ◆◆
Ripley
Tel: 01423 771888
*Consistently high standards
in a comfortable and relaxed
setting. Many of the
furnishings and paintings are
from Ripley Castle. Last
orders 9:30 p.m.
AE/DI/MC/VI*

York
Knavesmire Manor Hotel
(££) ◆
302 Tadcaster Road
Tel: 01904 702941
*A late Georgian property
overlooking York
Racecourse where the
modern British cooking uses
local produce whenever
possible. Last orders 9 p.m.
(dinner only). AE/DI/MC/VI*

Melton's Restaurant
(££) ◆◆
7 Scarcroft Road
Tel: 01904 634341
*A solid, dependable
restaurant offering a wide
variety of dishes and cuisine
types. Last orders 10 p.m.
Closed Sunday dinner,
Monday lunch, December
25 to mid-January and in
late August. MC/VI*

SOUTH YORKSHIRE
Sheffield
Charnwood Hotel (£) ◆
10 Sharrow Lane
Tel: 0114 2589411
*Georgian hotel with a good
reputation for a plentiful and
elegant table. There are two
eating options – the lively
Brasserie Leo or the more
formal Henfrey's. Last
orders 9 p.m. (Leo's
11 p.m.). Closed Sunday
and the week of December
25. AE/DI/MC/VI*

TYNE AND WEAR
Boldon
Forsters Restaurant (££) ◆◆
2 St. Bedes, Station Road
Tel: 0191 5190929
*One of the northeast's
leading restaurants, serving
good-value, light modern
cooking. Last orders 10 p.m.
Closed Sunday, Monday and
2 weeks in June.
AE/DI/MC/VI*

RESTAURANTS

Newcastle-upon-Tyne
21 Queen Street (£££) ◆◆◆
Quayside
Tel: 0191 222 0755
Smart, modern atmosphere and classically based French cuisine. Last orders 10:30 p.m. Closed Sunday, Monday and public holidays. AE/DI/MC/VI

WEST YORKSHIRE
Bradford
Restaurant Nineteen (££) ◆◆◆
19 North Park Road, Heaton
Tel: 01274 492559
The large Victorian house standing next to Lister Park offers an appetizing choice of imaginative, modern British dishes. Last orders 9:30 p.m. Closed Sunday, Monday, 1 week in May and September, and 2 weeks in January. AE/MC/VI

Leeds
Brasserie Forty Four (££) ◆◆
42–44 The Calls
Tel: 0113 2343232
This hugely popular restaurant is a fun place to eat. It offers a good choice of modern menus with a strong Mediterranean influence. Last orders 10:30 p.m. Closed Sunday and public holidays. AE/DI/MC/VI

Haley's Hotel (££) ◆◆
Shire Oak Road, Headingley
Tel: 0113 278 4446
Located on the quiet outskirts of Leeds, this restored Victorian home serves modern English cooking in a refined atmosphere. Last orders 9:45 p.m. Closed Sunday dinner and December 25. AE/DI/MC/VI

SCOTTISH LOWLANDS

ARGYLL AND BUTE
Kilmartin
Cairn Restaurant (£) ◆
Lochgilphead
Tel: 01546 510254
Small, refreshingly unpretentious country bistro popular with locals and visitors. Its Victorian decor makes an attractive backdrop to the international and regional cuisine. Last orders 10 p.m. Closed Tuesday and in January. No credit cards.

BORDERS
Kelso
Sunlaws House (££) ◆◆
Heiton
Tel: 01573 450331
Fine baronial mansion, surrounded by acres of woodland and gardens on the banks of the River Tweed. The accomplished Scottish/ French cooking has a modern style. Last orders 9:30 p.m. AE/DI/MC/VI

Peebles
Cringletie House (££) ◆
Tel: 01721 730233
This beautiful red-sandstone Scottish Borders baronial home offers carefully prepared and imaginative dishes. Good use is made of the kitchen garden for fresh vegetables. Last orders 7:30 p.m. Closed January 1 to mid-March. AE/MC/VI

CITY OF EDINBURGH
Edinburgh
Atrium (££) ◆◆◆
Cambridge Street
Tel: 0131 228 8882
Avant-garde city center location for modern Scottish cooking with cosmopolitan influences. Last orders 10:30 p.m. (11 p.m. during Edinburgh Festival). Closed Saturday lunch, all day Sunday and December 25–January 1. AE/MC/VI

Malmaison (££) ◆
1 Tower Place, Leith
Tel: 0131 5556868
This modishly designed brasserie and hotel – once a seaman's mission – offers a good choice of Mediterranean-style food. Last orders 10:30 p.m. AE/DI/MC/VI

The Vintners Room (££) ◆◆
87 Giles Street, Leith
Tel: 0131 554 6767
Wine bar and candelit restaurant in a converted Georgian warehouse. Last orders 10:30 p.m. Closed Sunday and 2 weeks following December 25. AE/MC/VI

CITY OF GLASGOW
Glasgow
Buttery Restaurant (££) ◆◆
652 Argyle Street
Tel: 0141 221 8188
High-class Scottish and French cuisine in splendidly grand Victorian surroundings. Last orders 10:30 p.m. Closed Saturday lunch, all day Sunday, December 25 and January 1. AE/DI/MC/VI

DUMFRIES & GALLOWAY
Moffat
Beechwood Hotel (£) ◆
Harthorpe Place
Tel: 01683 220210
This Victorian country house overlooks the town. The imaginative 5-course, fixed-

priced menu offers a choice of mainly Scottish dishes at each course. Last orders 8:45 p.m. Closed January 1 to mid-February. AE/MC/VI.

Newton Stewart
Kirroughtree Hotel
(££) ♦♦♦
Minnigaff
Tel: 01671 402141
Fresh local produce brings acclaim to the Anglo/French cuisine offered in the restaurant at this 18th-century mansion which stands on peaceful grounds. Last orders 9 p.m. Closed January 1 to mid-February. MC/VI

Portpatrick
Knockinaam
Lodge (£££) ♦♦♦
Tel: 01776 810471
The setting for excellent traditional British cuisine is stunning; with panoramic views of cliffs, sea and beach. Last orders 9:30 p.m. AE/DI/MC/VI

FIFE
Cupar
Ostlers Close
Restaurant (££) ♦♦♦
Bonneygate
Tel: 01334 655574
Tucked away in an alley, this unpretentious, simply styled restaurant serves uncomplicated food to locals and visitors alike. Last orders 9:30 p.m. Closed Sunday, Monday and December 25–January 1. AE/MC/VI

St. Andrews
St. Andrews Old Course
Hotel (£££) ♦♦
Old Station Road
Tel: 01334 474371
Modern resort hotel with

splendid views over the old golf course to the sea beyond. The menu offers a good Taste of Scotland selection. Last orders 10:30 p.m. Closed December 25. AE/DI/MC/VI

SOUTH AYRSHIRE
Troon
Lochgreen House (££) ♦♦
Monktenhill Road
Southwood
Tel: 01292 313343
Seasonal Scottish produce is competently prepared and presented in modern style in a magnificent oak-paneled restaurant. Last orders 9 p.m. AE/MC/VI

STIRLINGSHIRE
Aberfoyle
Braeval (£££) ♦♦♦
Tel: 01877 382711
This converted old mill, with exposed stone walls and flag-stone floors, is a wonderful setting for the set menu, based on carefully prepared quality produce. Last orders 9:30 p.m. Closed Monday, Tuesday, February, June and November. MC/VI

Stirling
Stirling Highland
Hotel (££) ♦
Spittal Street
Tel: 01786 475444
High above the town and close to Stirling Castle, this imposing hotel has strong, modern Scottish flavors influenced by French cuisine. Last orders 9:30 p.m. Closed Sunday dinner. AE/DI/MC/VI

WEST LOTHIAN
Linlithgow
Champany Inn (££) ♦♦♦
Tel: 01506 834532
This plush, homely period

restaurant serves prime-quality chargrilled steaks and has an excellent wine list. Last orders 10 p.m. Closed Saturday lunch, all day Sunday, December 25 and January 1. AE/DI/MC/VI

SCOTTISH HIGHLANDS

ABERDEENSHIRE
Aberdeen
Ardoe Hotel (££) ♦♦
Blairs, South Deeside Road
Tel: 01224 867355
Baronial hall with turrets, heraldic inscriptions, high ornate ceilings and splendid wood paneling, reached by a tree-lined drive. Good use of fresh Scottish produce. including game, seafood and prime Aberdeen Angus. Last orders 9:45 p.m. AE/DI/MC/VI

Ballater
Darroch Learg
Hotel (££) ♦♦
Braemar Road
Tel: 013397 55443
Season game and salmon feature prominently in this Victorian-themed restaurant in a rural, riverside setting. Last orders 9 p.m. Closed December 25 and January 2–31. AE/DI/MC/VI

Inverurie
Thainstone House
(££) ♦♦
Tel: 01467 621643
Set in 40 acres of parkland. An elegant Georgian room is the setting for innovative, modern food. The finest raw ingredients are used to produce distinctive, wholesome flavors. Last orders 9:30 p.m. AE/DI/MC/VI

HIGHLAND
Fort William
Inverlochy Castle
Hotel (£££) ◆◆◆
Tel: 01397 702177
Set amid 500 acres of grounds with Ben Nevis and the Highlands as a backdrop, this solid-stone structured hotel has an interior of unabashed luxury, and the food lives up to expectations. Last orders 9:30 p.m. AE/MC/VI

Isle of Skye (Ardvasar)
Ardvasar Hotel (££) ◆
Tel: 01471 844223
This unpretentious hotel, in Ardvasar village, offers genuine hospitality, good food and a friendly atmosphere. Last orders 8:15 p.m. Closed November. MC/VI

Kingussie
The Cross (£££) ◆◆◆
Tweed Mill Brae
Ardroilach Road
Tel: 01540 661166
This delightful restaurant has an original beamed ceiling and exposed stone walls. Once an old tweed mill, it makes good use of local fish, meat and game. Last orders 9 p.m. Closed Tuesday, December, and part of January, and in February. MC/VI

PERTH AND KINROSS
Aberfeldy
Guinach House
Hotel (££) ◆◆
By the "Birks"
Urlar Road
Tel: 01887 820251
It is for the food that most seek out this secluded little hotel. The love of cooking in the kitchen is matched by a hospitable and friendly

atmosphere. Last orders 9:30 p.m. Closed December 25. MC/VI

Dunkeld
Kinnaird (£££) ◆◆◆
Kinnaird
Tel: 01796 482440
Grand country house dating from 1770 that has been recently renovated with great charm and good taste; set on an estate of around 9,000 acres. The food is of a high standard, as the prices suggest. Last orders 9:30 p.m. Closed Monday, Tuesday and Wednesday in January and February. AE/MC/VI

St. Fillans
Four Seasons (££) ◆◆
Crieff
Tel: 01764 685333
The surrounding scenery is spectacular, with uninterrupted views over Loch Earn. The daily changing menu offers Scottish cuisine with an international influence. Last orders 9:30 p.m. Closed December 25–January 31. AE/DI/MC/VI

NORTHERN IRELAND

ANTRIM
Portrush
(Causeway Coast)
Ramore (££) ◆◆
The Harbour
Tel: 01265 824313
A friendly welcome.is guaranteed at this upbeat restaurant overlooking the harbor. Fish from the quay is the main attraction on the menu. Last orders 10:30 p.m. Closed Sunday, Monday, December 25 and January 1. MC/VI

ARMAGH
Belfast
Roscoff (££) ◆◆◆
7 Lesley House
Shaftesbury Square
Tel: 01232 331532
The province's top restaurant. Bright modern dining room; international dishes. Last orders 10:30 p.m. Closed Saturday lunch, all day Sunday, Easter Monday and July 12. AE/DI/MC/VI

COUNTY DOWN
Holywood
Culloden Hotel (££) ◆
Tel: 01232 425223
Some fine French-style dishes are prepared for the hotel's Mitre Restaurant. The Cultra Inn on the grounds offers less formal dining. Last orders 9:45 p.m., Sunday 8:30 p.m. Closed Saturday lunch. AE/DI/MC/VI

Portaferry
Portaferry Hotel (££) ◆◆
10 The Strand
Tel: 012477 28231
A welcoming hotel on the shore of Strangford Lough. The dining room offers good views and a varied fixed-price menu. Last orders 9 p.m. Closed December 25. AE/DI/MC/VI

LONDONDERRY
Limavady
The Lime Tree (££) ◆
60 Catherine Street
Tel: 015047 64300
A simply appointed restaurant serving generous portions of good food. Fresh fish is a specialty alongside other delights such as rich beef, mushroom and Guinness pie. Last orders 9:30 p.m. Closed Monday and Tuesday. AE/MC/VI

INDEX

ACKNOWLEDGEMENTS

The following photographers and libraries assisted in the preparation of this book:

ZEFA PICTURES LTD 87

The remaining photographs are held in the Automobile Association's own photo library (AA PHOTO LIBRARY) with contributions from:

P AITHIE 159; A BAKER 1; 142/3; P BAKER 29, 60, 80/1, 109; J BEAZLEY 123, 165, 175, 211, 214/5, 225, 242/3; M BIRKITT 5a, 55, 110, 118; E A BOWNESS 169; I BURGUM 137, 141, 145, 155; J CARNIE 6, 240; D CORRANCE 191, 207; D CROUCHER 166/7; S DAY 5b, 177, 204/5, 222, 229, 233; E ELLINGTON 217, 221, 235; R ELLIOTT 194/5, 230/1; P ENTICKNAP 103; R FLETCHER 75; D FORSS 83, 84/5, 88, 93, 126/7; S GIBSON PHOTOGRAPHY 199; P KENWARD 36/7, 285; A LAWSON 51, 66/7, 146/7; C LEES 13, 183; S & O MATTHEWS 116/7, 120/1, 164; E MEACHER 56, 76/7; C MOLYNEUX 115, 156/7; J MORRISON 186; R MORT 15, 35; R MOSS 71; G MUNDAY 245, 249, 251, 254/5; D NOBLE 99, 100/1; C PARK 189; N RAY 72; P SHARP 202/3; B SMITH 16/7, 19, 40/1; T SOUTER 79, 105, 133; F STEPHENSON 134; R STRANGE 26, 30; M TAYLOR 213; T TEEGAN 59; M TRELAWNY 39, 42, 45; R VICTOR 16a, 46, 48; W VOYSEY 95, 96; R WEIR 226, 239; J WELSH 128, 149; L WHITWAM 119, 185; H WILLIAMS 68/9, 151; P WILSON 43, 257; T WOODCOCK 8/9, 33

CONTRIBUTORS

Copy editors: Donna Dailey, Chester Krone, Hilary Hughes
Researchers: Colin Follett, Neil Wilson
Indexer: Marie Lorimer